Bearing Witness to Change

Forensic Psychiatry and Psychology Practice

Bearing Witness to Change

Forensic Psychiatry and Psychology Practice

E D I T O R S

Ezra E. H. Griffith MD
Emeritus Yale School of Medicine,
New Haven, Connecticut, USA

Michael A. Norko MD, MAR
Yale University School of Medicine,
New Haven, Connecticut, USA

Alec Buchanan PhD, MD
Yale University School of Medicine,
New Haven, Connecticut, USA

Madelon V. Baranoski PhD
Yale University School of Medicine,
New Haven, Connecticut, USA

Howard V. Zonana MD
Yale University School of Medicine,
New Haven, Connecticut, USA

CRC Press
Taylor & Francis Group
Boca Raton London New York

CRC Press is an imprint of the
Taylor & Francis Group, an **informa** business

CRC Press
Taylor & Francis Group
6000 Broken Sound Parkway NW, Suite 300
Boca Raton, FL 33487-2742

Printed on acid-free paper
Version Date: 20160607

International Standard Book Number-13: 978-1-4987-5423-1 (Paperback)

Visit the Taylor & Francis Web site at
http://www.taylorandfrancis.com

and the CRC Press Web site at
http://www.crcpress.com

Contents

Editors and Contributors

Editors

Ezra E. H. Griffith, MD
Professor Emeritus of Psychiatry and African-American Studies
Senior Research Scientist in Psychiatry
Department of Psychiatry
Yale School of Medicine
New Haven, CT, USA

Michael A. Norko, MD, MAR
Associate Professor
Department of Psychiatry
Yale School of Medicine
New Haven, CT, USA
and
Director of Forensic Services
Connecticut Department of Mental Health and Addiction Services

Alec Buchanan, PhD, MD
Associate Professor
Department of Psychiatry
Yale School of Medicine
New Haven, CT, USA

Madelon V. Baranoski, PhD
Professor
Department of Psychiatry
Yale School of Medicine
New Haven, CT, USA
Vice Chair, Yale University Institutional Review Board

Howard V. Zonana, MD
Professor
Department of Psychiatry
Yale School of Medicine
Clinical Professor (Adjunct) of Law
Yale Law School
New Haven, CT, USA

Contributors

Gwen Adshead, MD
Consultant Forensic Psychiatrist and Psychotherapist
Fareham
Hants, UK

Paul Amble, MD
Clinician and Forensic Psychiatrist
Department of Psychiatry
Yale School of Medicine
New Haven, CT, USA
and
Chief Consulting Forensic Psychiatrist
Connecticut Department of Mental Health and Addiction Services

Daniel S. Barron, PhD
Medical Student
Yale School of Medicine
New Haven, CT, USA

Chyrell Bellamy, MSW, PhD
Assistant Professor
Department of Psychiatry
Yale School of Medicine
and
Director, Peer Services and Research
Program for Recovery and
Community Health
Department of Psychiatry and
Connecticut Mental Health Center
New Haven, CT, USA

Patricia Benedict, BA
Director, Citizens Project
Program for Recovery and
Community Health
Department of Psychiatry and
Connecticut Mental Health Center
New Haven, CT, USA

Dominique Bourget, MD
Associate Professor in Psychiatry
University of Ottawa
and
Staff Forensic Psychiatrist
The Royal Ottawa Hospital
Ottawa, Ontario, Canada

Philip J. Candilis, MD, DFAPA
Director, Forensic Psychiatry
Fellowship
St Elizabeth's Hospital/Department of
Behavioral Health
Washington DC, USA
and
Clinical Professor of Psychiatry
George Washington University School
of Medicine and Health Sciences
Howard University College of
Medicine
Adjunct Professor of Psychiatry
Uniformed Services University of
Health Sciences

Larry Davidson, PhD
Professor
Department of Psychiatry
Yale School of Medicine
and
Director, Program for Recovery and
Community Health
Department of Psychiatry and
Connecticut Mental Health Center
New Haven, CT, USA

Charles C. Dike, MD, MPH, FRCPsych
Assistant Professor
Department of Psychiatry
Yale School of Medicine
New Haven, CT, USA
and
Assistant Medical Director
Connecticut Department of Mental
Health and Addiction Services

Paul DiLeo, MS, FACHE
Chief Operating Officer
Connecticut Department of Mental
Health and Addiction Services
and
Lecturer
Department of Psychiatry
Yale School of Medicine
New Haven, CT, USA

Spencer Higgins, JD
Faculty
Cold Spring School
New Haven, CT, USA

Emily A. Keram, MD
Assistant Clinical Professor
Psychiatry and the Law Program
UCSF School of Medicine
San Francisco, CA, USA
and
Staff Psychiatrist
Santa Rosa VA Community Based
Outpatient Clinic
Santa Rosa, CA, USA

Reena Kapoor, MD
Associate Professor
Department of Psychiatry
Yale School of Medicine
New Haven, CT, USA
and
Chief of Forensic Psychiatry
Connecticut Valley Hospital, Whiting Forensic Division
Middletown, CT, USA

Bandy Lee, MD, MDiv
Assistant Clinical Professor
Department of Psychiatry
Yale School of Medicine
New Haven, CT, USA
and
Lecturer, Global Health Studies
Faculty of Arts and Sciences
Yale University

Richard Martinez, MD, MH
Director, Forensic Psychiatry Training Programs
and
Robert D. Miller Professor of Forensic Psychiatry
University of Colorado, Denver Medical School
Colorado Office of Behavioral Health
Denver, CO, USA

Daniel Papapietro, PsyD
Clinical Assistant Professor
Department of Psychiatry
Yale School of Medicine
New Haven, CT, USA
and
Forensic Psychologist
Director, Psychotherapy Service
Connecticut Valley Hospital, Whiting Forensic Division
Middletown, CT, USA

Debra A. Pinals, MD
Director of the Program in Law, Psychiatry, and Ethics
Clinical Professor of Psychiatry
Department of Psychiatry
University of Michigan Medical School
Ann Arbor, MI, USA
and
Director of Forensic Services
Massachusetts State Department of Mental Health Services
Boston, MA, USA

Maya Prabhu, MD, LLB
Assistant Professor
Department of Psychiatry
Yale School of Medicine
New Haven, CT, USA
and
Consulting Forensic Psychiatrist
Connecticut Department of Mental Health and Addiction Services

Michael Rowe, PhD
Associate Professor
Department of Psychiatry
Yale School of Medicine
and
Co-Director, Program for Recovery and Community Health
Department of Psychiatry and Connecticut Mental Health Center
New Haven, CT, USA

Tracey Sondik, PsyD
Director, Behavioral Intervention Service
Connecticut Valley Hospital
Middletown, CT, USA

Paul F. Thomas, JD
Lecturer
Department of Psychiatry
Yale School of Medicine
New Haven, CT, USA

Barry W. Wall, MD
Director of Forensic Services
Eleanor Slater Hospital
Cranston, RI, USA
and
Clinical Professor
Alpert Medical School of Brown University
Providence, RI, USA

Alexander Westphal, MD, PhD
Assistant Professor
Department of Psychiatry
Yale School of Medicine
New Haven, CT, USA
and
Consulting Forensic Psychiatrist
Connecticut Department of Mental Health and Addiction Services

John L. Young, MD, MTh
Clinical Professor
Department of Psychiatry
Yale School of Medicine
New Haven, CT, USA

Preface

We think it important that from time to time we pause and think about change in the exercise of our professional disciplines. We believe such reflection often bears fruit. It is in contemplating past events in the context of their development and evolution that we may find ways to modify our present activities and even design a pathway for the future. Change is influenced by a variety of events, people, political activity, fiscal considerations, scientific discoveries, legal decision-making, and other circumstances. It is in understanding their interaction and effect on our work that we can become better practitioners and more able theorists.

In this text, we reflect here on the changes that have appeared over the last several decades in forensic psychiatry and psychology. All of us editors have spent a good part of our professional lives mulling over problems we have encountered at the interface of psychiatry, psychology, and the law. But the contributions of forensic mental health professionals occur within a continuously changing landscape, shaped profoundly by all the elements we have already listed. Certainly, we have two subspecialties that first defined themselves in terms of applying our basic disciplines to answering legal questions. But now those specialties are critical leaders in setting standards of forensic treatment, addressing ethics, and managing the murky boundaries between our disciplines and the law.

We have asked colleagues practicing in different arenas, carrying out scholarship, managing forensic institutions, utilizing the law as an agent of change, engaging in fiscal and policy management, and training forensic psychiatrists and psychologists to help us contemplate these matters and formulate something we can say about the path to the future. We hope this collective reflection on change will help our disciplines discard arbitrariness and rigidity, while embracing opportunities to theorize about past accomplishments and contributions and hopefully construct a clearer pathway to modernized practice within our disciplines.

So we wish to document and contextualize some of the changes that have occurred. In the Introduction, we introduce the reader to an historical perspective on change in forensic psychiatry and psychology. In the first section, covering the first five chapters of the text, we discuss major external influences that have impacted the practice of forensic psychiatry and psychology over time. But their collective impact has been significant and lasting. Examples of such influential elements are: the law; consumer movements (such as those related to the widely-discussed Recovery Movement and the more recent and evolving notion of Peer Counselors); dynamic, global, social upheavals (such as war) that dislocate people and produce refugees and immigrants who then seek forensic psychiatry and psychology services so as to achieve resettlement and citizenship; technological and scientific advances (spearheaded by leaders in genetics, brain imaging, media technology, and neuroscience) that have progressively influenced the thinking of forensic psychiatrists and psychologists; and political and fiscal contexts, particularly at the local level, that especially impact the creative approaches of the forensic professional seeking to improve care of forensic patients in both institutions and the community.

In the second section, entitled "Forensic Psychiatry and Psychology as Their Own Change-Agents," and covering the next three chapters, we consider the subspecialty disciplines as change-agents that have contributed to shaping the professionalism of its own practitioners in a number of distinctive ways. Recent literature has demonstrated convincingly that forensic psychiatrists and psychologists have been reflecting seriously on the ethics principles that should be used as guideposts for the moral basis of work in the disciplines. Such reflection has been buttressed and amplified by technical mechanisms such as the use of narrative and performative elements in the written and oral activities of the forensic specialist. In addition to a host of other developments in the field, emphasis on ethics, professionalism, and performative techniques have strengthened the professional identity of the forensic specialist, and enhanced efforts to improve the education and formation of the disciplines' own trainees.

The third section is focused on "Changes in the Traditional Evaluative and Consultative Roles of the Forensic Psychiatrist and Psychologist" and spans five chapters. Chapter 9 reminds us of the traditional activities of the forensic specialist who performed evaluations of individuals for criminal and civil courts. In this role, the expert consulted to the courts and utilized psychological expertise to answer questions raised by the legal system. This traditional role has been influenced by developments in the knowledge base of the expert. Changes have been wrought by advances in diagnosis, pathology, imaging, and the unexpected explosion in technology and even social media.

Other chapters in this third section also demonstrate unequivocally that other constituencies have decided to make use of the forensic expert's knowledge base. Thus we dedicate a chapter to consideration of how Veterans' Courts and the general military system are utilizing forensic expertise. Indeed, the military has dedicated millions of dollars to understanding how post-traumatic stress disorder has impacted the military's justice system. Thus, it is safe to say that the forensic specialist's work has expanded in consultation to legal and other organized administrative systems. Other potent examples of this expansion are covered in the chapters on legislative consultation and work with Catholic Annulment Courts and general church entities pursuing activities such as the evaluation of clergy who have participated in problematic sexual behavior.

We must also understand other changes or evolutions of forensic roles, as in the management of forensic systems. Forensic psychiatrists and psychologists are asked to provide thoughtful and useful advice to individuals and systems demanding this expertise. Forensic psychiatrists and psychologists serve as directors of forensic services; directors and medical directors of prison units; medical directors of forensic hospitals; directors of court diversion services; and directors of court clinics. In all of these roles, they face new challenges requiring professional expertise and novel collaborations. These types of administrative positions bear witness to the need for forensic professionals to provide advice to clinical teams about the evaluation and management of risk; to state and county governments asking for consultations concerning the development of their statutes focused on one forensic matter or another; and to hospital managers who have the responsibility for the health care of forensic patients.

In the fourth section (entitled "Forensic Practice in the Treatment and Care of Patients," and encompassing seven chapters) we focus on change that is related to the management and treatment of individuals who have had involvement with law enforcement systems. This activity was not particularly heralded by some, in the early days of the subspecialties, as worthy of intensive consideration by the forensic specialist, at least in the United States. In England, it is often said that this clinical forensic work developed much more quickly. Recent developments have made the differences less pronounced. In this section we will highlight the roles of U.S. forensic specialists in applying, adapting, and developing treatments and management strategies for patients in several systemic loci: jails and prisons; forensic treatment facilities; jail diversion units; and some longer-term psychiatric inpatient services that house patients who present significant violence.

These patients generally require management and treatment that attend seriously to matters of risk and to the complex problems of reintegrating the patients into their home communities. Hence, the influence of this change is causing the forensic professional to recognize the importance of caring better, and in a highly specialized interdisciplinary context, for these "forensic patients" who deserve more than just the usual forensic evaluation and later assignment to traditional care. One chapter will focus attention on treatment techniques usually employed in the clinical setting, while another will contemplate the resurgent emphasis on violence risk, which is a profound concern of all those dealing with the psychiatric patient who has been in contact with the law enforcement system. While it is acknowledged that some of the clinical techniques discussed in these chapters have been utilized for decades, we emphasize that the urgent and recent emphasis on returning all hospitalized patients to their home communities has pulled the forensic professional more powerfully into the work and forced adaptation of the work to the transitional bridge between hospital and community. Other chapters tackle the task of channeling these patients away from jail on the one hand, and on the other hand smoothing the community re-entry of those who have been incarcerated or hospitalized. The first of the two final chapters closes this section with a discussion of the interplay of science, therapeutics, politics, and public opinion in the management of patients with problem sexual behaviors. The final chapter addresses matters related to the clinical systems of correction agencies.

The Conclusion ("Summarizing Change in Forensic Psychiatry and Psychology Practice") encourages forensic professionals and others to think deeply about the nature of change in forensic work and to grasp where that change may take the field in the future. As we all engage more earnestly in this change-based discourse, we will see more clearly how the field has progressed and developed in many directions. It has evolved from its founding focus on the courtroom, offering practitioners a wider choice of activities to embrace, and providing the field with a guide to future paths for development. We may appreciate how our work has been influenced by other interests that emerge primarily from outside the formal traditions of medicine and psychology and that expand the work of physicians and psychologists. Here the chapter also makes the point that although the future seems bright, all is not settled in the discipline. There are still areas that provide ample room for debate and questioning, and that harbor challenges for the future. But we look forward to distinction and promise for the subspecialties of forensic psychiatry and psychology.

In this text, we emphasize that there is a demand for renewed consideration of the parameters that define the activities of the modern forensic mental health professional. It is time to think differently about the structures within which we do our work, about the form and meaning of our activities, and about their range. We conclude from this that the modern forensic specialists are being influenced to develop new identities. They are being asked to view, in refashioned terms, the knowledge base, the practice standards, and the expanding arenas of work. All this must inevitably impact the evolution of the specialties.

We hope that training programs, as well as junior and senior forensic practitioners of all mental health disciplines, will find the text useful. It should also be valuable to those leading forensic services in departments of mental health across the country, and to legislators, other administrators, and lawyers seeking to advance their understanding of what the forensic specialist can contribute to interdisciplinary policy discussions.

Ezra E. H. Griffith, MD
Michael A. Norko, MD, MAR
Alec Buchanan, PhD, MD
Madelon V. Baranoski, PhD
Howard V. Zonana, MD

INTRODUCTION

Legacy of Change for Mental Health Professionals

Howard V. Zonana

From the outset, medical jurisprudence of insanity was one of the important topics at the first scientific meeting of the Association of Medical Superintendents of American Institutions for the Insane (which later became the American Psychiatric Association) in 1844. Isaac Ray had published the *Medical Jurisprudence of Insanity*, the first of six editions in 1838 (Ray 1838). The first volume of the *American Journal of Insanity* published a paper by D.C. Coventry MD, Professor of Medical Jurisprudence, outlining "the forms in which insanity becomes the subject of legal investigation" as follows (Coventry 1844–5, 134–5):

1. the plea of insanity as a bar to punishment in criminal prosecution;
2. the propriety of confinement when danger to the individual himself or to others is apprehended;
3. the capacity and right of an insane person, or one supposed to be insane, of managing his own affairs; and
4. the state of mind necessary to constitute a valid will.

These themes have continued to provoke debate and proposals for changes in the law that have altered over time but remain contentious. It was not until the 1970s that an increasing number of psychiatrists began to devote substantial portions of their practice to forensic work and cases. This was enhanced by the formation of a forensic subspecialty association and the introduction of board certification.

The practice of forensic psychiatry and the roles of its practitioners are determined by a combination of factors. These include the current scientific understanding of the nature of mental illness, availability of treatment systems, and the legal requirements for the use of mental conditions in the resolution of legal disputes. Medical professional organizations have developed criteria for the creation of subspecialties based on perceived need for quality control, treatment needs of special populations, and the need for additional education and training above that provided in basic training. Forensic psychiatry and the legal system have changed their practices and guidelines in concert and independently over the past fifty years. I will try to review some of the significant changes during this period by selecting examples that have affected the practice of both general psychiatry as well as forensic psychiatry, such as:

1. substantive and procedural civil rights for persons with mental illness being involuntarily hospitalized or medicated;
2. decisions by the U.S. Supreme Court such as (a) the death penalty and competency to be executed, and (b) the use of involuntary medication for restoration of competence to stand trial;
3. the transformation of state mental hospitals into forensic facilities;
4. sex offender civil commitment;
5. mental health treatment in jails and prisons and the recognition of a constitutional right to treatment in correctional settings; and
6. ethical guidelines and expert witness testimony.

THE CIVIL RIGHTS OF PATIENTS

The ideas that prompted patient rights to refuse treatment and the legal challenges to civil commitment arose in the 1960s in the midst of a wide array of advocacy for civil rights in many arenas. Several attorneys and civil rights groups began a crusade to abolish civil commitment. Connecticut's commitment law at that time required a judge to find that the person was mentally ill and a fit subject for treatment in a mental hospital. Being mentally ill was loosely defined as having a mental or emotional condition which "has substantial adverse effects on his or her ability to function" and which "requires care and treatment" (Conn. Gen. Stat. 17-176 and 17-178; *Mayock* 1968). This was the legislature's way of allowing physicians broad discretion to determine who needed to be confined in mental hospitals.

Thomas Szasz (Szasz 1960, 1974), beginning in 1960, provided a theoretical rationale for attorneys to oppose civil commitment. He attacked the legitimacy of the concept of mental illness, and explicitly denied that mental illness exists in any scientific sense but instead merely as arbitrarily defined categories of behavior. He also argued that most patients were competent to refuse medication.

In 1971 Alberta Lessard was involuntarily committed for being mentally ill after she was found "running up and down the apartment aisle on the second floor banging on doors and shouting that the communists were taking over the country that night ... and that we should do something right away." One of the police officers stated, "She kept talking about burning some evidence in a sink, evidence of her as a bubble dancer ... some caricature or picture depicting her as a bubble dancer. She said she had burned this along with other evidence, something to do with a secret invention." She was also alleged to have jumped from her second-story window and said she "no longer had the will to live in that she might, if returned to the apartment, jump again" (*Lessard* 1972; Torrey 2008, 225). She retained counsel through the Milwaukee Legal Services which, rather than defend only Ms. Lessard, decided to file a class-action suit on behalf of "all persons 18 years of age or older who are being held involuntarily pursuant to any emergency temporary or permanent commitment provision of the Wisconsin involuntary commitment statute" (Torrey 2008, 77).

In October 1972, a three-judge panel of the U.S. District Court declared Wisconsin's existing civil commitment statute unconstitutional (*Lessard* 1972). It held that proof of mental illness and dangerousness must be proven "beyond a reasonable doubt," a much more rigorous legal standard than the existing clear and convincing evidence standard. They also held that involuntary hospitalization should be used "only as a last resort" when there are not less drastic means for achieving the same basic goal. The argument made was that confinement in a mental hospital was equivalent to being confined in jail and patients, like criminal defendants, deserve the same legal protections. In 1979, the U.S. Supreme Court ultimately resolved this question, when it decided *Addington v. Texas* (*Addington* 1979), holding that involuntary commitment to a hospital was significantly different than being confined in a prison and that "clear and convincing evidence" was the minimum standard required for hospitalization. The decision noted that it was difficult to prove future dangerousness beyond a reasonable doubt.

The notion that hospitalized patients might be entitled to treatment arose during the same period (Birnbaum 1960; *Donaldson* 1974, 519–21). A few courts recognized such a right as based on state law or on the U.S. Constitution. Confinement without treatment became a ripe target for litigation. However, in 1975 when the *O'Connor v. Donaldson* case reached the Supreme Court, Mr. Donaldson's attorneys altered their strategy (concerned that treatment could enhance the ability to civilly commit patients) and dropped the argument for a constitutional right to treatment. Although initially filed as a right to treatment case, Mr. Donaldson had been confined in a Florida state hospital for fifteen years after being hospitalized by his parents because he expressed paranoid fears that he was being poisoned. He thereafter actively refused any treatment and continued to deny that he was mentally ill. His physician urged him to take medication but did not release him, even though there were offers from friends to support him in the community. Numerous probate court reviews of his status supported continued confinement. Eventually, when transferred to a new physician, he was released. The key holding in the decision was that mental illness alone cannot justify a state locking a person up and keeping him indefinitely in simple custodial confinement. "In short, a State cannot constitutionally confine, without more, a nondangerous individual who is capable of surviving safely in freedom by himself or with the help of willing and responsible family members or friends" (*O'Connor* 1975, 576). In a concurring opinion, Justice Burger noted that he opposed any constitutional right to treatment, as confinement of the mentally ill had a long history prior to any known treatments (*O'Connor* 1975, 568).

The American Civil Liberties Union (ACLU) interpreted this decision to mean that it was unconstitutional to commit an individual for treatment who is not dangerous. They maintained the individual must be considered capable of surviving safely if his life is not in imminent danger. Even if that interpretation was not correct, most states incorporated "dangerousness" as an important or sole criterion of civil commitment. A number of states added "grave disability" as a criterion in addition to mental illness.

Civil commitment allows detention and treatment of individuals who may be dangerous or gravely disabled by physicians with judicial oversight. This is based on the combination of police and *parens patriae* powers of the state (Pinals and Mossman 2012). It permits the override of an individual's wishes at times and thus creates tensions about the appropriate boundaries which can only be resolved in a legal framework involving the Constitution, federal and state laws, case law, and regulations and professional ethics. These issues have been and will continue to be controversial as the more recent debates about outpatient commitment illustrate.

One result of the tightening of commitment standards was that a significant number of people who were seriously ill but not dangerous were unable to be involuntarily hospitalized and were released back into the community from emergency rooms. Many continued to be ill and disruptive in the community so that the police had no alternative but to arrest them and bring them into the criminal justice system when complaints were filed. Many were then found incompetent to stand trial for minor charges, and hospitalized for restoration of their competence. Their underlying mental illness was often treated in the process. Once the criterion of dangerousness was introduced, psychiatrists had to document evidence of current dangerousness and make predictions about the likelihood of future dangerous behavior.

Determinations of dangerousness, or more accurately risk, by psychiatrists are now sought in a variety of clinical as well as legal settings:

1. Emergency room decisions of the need for emergency certification by a physician.
2. Full civil commitment hearings.
3. Decisions about Tarasoff disclosures when civil commitment is not possible or not sufficient to avert the risk.
4. Non-capital cases where judges and probation officers are looking at sentencing decisions and trying to predict antisocial risk.
5. Capital sentencing in states where future dangerousness is a criterion to be considered by the jury.
6. Evaluation of risk in sexual predator hearings in the twenty states that have adopted such statutes.
7. Disability evaluations where return to duty involves the use of weapons after some injury or inappropriate use.

Dangerousness and risk assessments have evolved considerably since the 1974 statement by the American Psychiatric Association (APA) saying, "Psychiatric expertise in the prediction of 'dangerousness' is not established" (APA Task Force 1974, 33). In 1983, going against the recommendations of the American Psychiatric Association and American Psychological Association in amicus briefs, and in spite of reports that two out of three long-term predictions were wrong, the Supreme Court concluded, in *Barefoot v. Estelle* (*Barefoot* 1983) that prediction testimony from mental health professionals in death penalty hearings was, nonetheless, admissible. The majority opinion by Justice White argued that excluding such testimony would be like asking the court to "disinvent the wheel," (*Barefoot* 1983, 896) given the long history of permitting such testimony by lay as well as expert witnesses. Justice White also felt the adversarial process would be able to deal with unreliable evidence. The dissent by Justice Blackmun expressed concern that expert opinion by professionals would have undue weight on jurors' opinions.

Until the 1980s, expert testimony on the topic was primarily based on clinical experience. Dr. James Grigson, a frequent prosecution witness, testified in a number of death penalty cases, two of which reached the U.S. Supreme Court. He predicted with 100% certainty that the defendant was going to be dangerous in the future, based on his experience of having seen thousands of defendants in criminal cases. In one case, in 1973, he reached that conclusion after a one-hour evaluation for competency to stand trial (*Estelle* 1981). In another case, in 1978, he made similar predictions with no personal interview, responding only to a hypothetical description of the crime and history (*Barefoot* 1983). Had he been a little more humble about the degree of accuracy he might have escaped the sanctions ultimately imposed on him for this testimony by the APA. No such certainty was supported in the scientific literature.

Since then, prediction techniques have evolved to include more structured actuarial approaches. Instruments designed for predictions of violence and sexual offending have been developed. These instruments can predict imperfectly but with better error rates than chance alone. In addition, there are *adjusted actuarial assessments* that take into account individualized factors not used by the instrument alone. *Structured professional judgments* take into account a number of factors that have been associated with risk but do not rate the risk by using numbers. All of these methods rely on comparisons to the conduct of other individuals and have significant false positive and false negative results. Attempts to develop actuarial instruments that use both static factors as well as dynamic ones have skyrocketed. Tests using static or unchanging factors are of limited use in clinical settings where release issues need to be assessed frequently (Buchanan et al. 2012). The courts have excluded some testimony using risk instruments if they have not been sufficiently validated.

While these instruments may be valuable in civil and criminal settings where there is time to perform adequate evaluations, they have not reached a state where their use in emergency rooms for purposes of civil commitment or certification would be feasible. Emergency situations generally involve conditions where a person has made actual attacks or threats towards others or themselves and the collection of such information is usually checked with collateral sources. The decision for hospitalization has usually been made and the actuarial factors play more of a role at the time of discharge. Individuals providing expert testimony, however, need to be aware of the use of these instruments and the groups for whom they have been validated.

These instruments are currently used most frequently by Departments of Correction and for screening and follow-up of sexually violent predators.

U.S. SUPREME COURT DECISIONS ON THE DEATH PENALTY AND MENTAL HEALTH ISSUES

During the last fifty years the Supreme Court began to take an interest in mental health related questions and has issued at least sixty-six opinions affecting persons with mental illness in civil and criminal settings. These opinions have included such areas as confidentiality and privilege, death penalty, insanity defense, competence to stand trial, civil commitment, sex offenders, right to refuse treatment, juveniles, and expert witness testimony standards (AAPL 2014a).

Forensic psychiatry is largely a derivative practice, in the sense that it relies primarily on legal standards, procedures, and definitions in performing evaluations for the courts or attorneys. Thus, evolving legal case law and federal and state statutory changes have a direct effect on how forensic evaluations are conducted and reports prepared. They also have raised ethical conflicts for practitioners.

A noteworthy example involves competency and the death penalty, an area where the U.S. Supreme Court has been particularly active. A significant case in point, which raised major concerns for mental health professionals, was *Ford v. Wainwright* in 1986 (*Ford* 1986). In that case, the court held that the common law as well as the Eighth Amendment barred the execution of the "insane." Although the majority did not reach a definition for the threshold criteria for impairment, Justice Powell suggested that the Eighth Amendment forbids the execution only of those who are "unaware of the punishment they are about to suffer and why they are to suffer it" (*Ford* 1986, 422). This became the working standard until 2007, when the court clarified that the awareness of the state's announced reason or the fact of an imminent execution is not sufficient. "A prisoner's awareness of the State's rationale for an execution is not the same as a rational understanding of it. *Ford* does not foreclose inquiry into the latter" (*Panetti* 2007, 2862).

The *Ford* decision raised several ethical questions for forensic psychiatrists:

1. Was it ethical to evaluate and testify in death penalty cases?
2. Was it ethical to make the final determination of competence (the *Ford v. Wainwright* majority thought that a panel of psychiatrists could adjudicate the question)?
3. Was it ethical to treat an inmate on death row to restore his competence to be executed?

When such questions arise, individual psychiatrists may answer them for themselves, but professional organizations such as the American Psychiatric

Association or the American Academy of Psychiatry and the Law (AAPL) and the American Medical Association (AMA) generally attempt to develop guidelines for the profession. In this circumstance the APA's Council on Psychiatry and the Law collaborated with the AMA's Council on Ethical and Judicial affairs (CEJA) to develop an ethical guideline, which answered the above questions in a nuanced fashion. That policy, passed in 1995, has remained in effect (AMA 1995). The ethics code, while permitting psychiatrists to perform "competency to be executed" evaluations in these cases, does not support physicians, in lieu of judges, being the final adjudicator of legal competence. It also states that the use of medication solely for the purpose of restoration, so that execution can proceed, is not ethical. It does allow for the use of medication if someone is deemed to be in a state of severe distress and suffering—but only until the person can express an informed judgment about whether or not he wishes to continue the medications. The guidelines also state that physicians who are opposed to the death penalty, and do not wish to participate in these cases, should not be forced to do so.

In addition to the competency issue, the Supreme Court has also addressed the appropriateness of the death penalty for specific groups such as cognitively impaired and adolescent offenders. Again, the APA and AAPL expressed the views of the profession as to what science can contribute to the discussion by the submission of amicus briefs to the courts and the development of policy statements. In this situation the American Bar Association, the American Psychological Association and the National Alliance on Mental Illness (NAMI) have joined the American Psychiatric Association in endorsing a policy recommending that severe mental illness should be a bar to execution (American Bar Association 2005).

INVOLUNTARY MEDICATION

Although it may seem esoteric to have a separate standard for competency to be executed, it reflects changes in thinking by the mental health professions and the law, moving from the idea that persons with mental illness must be globally incompetent if they met the criteria for civil commitment to a more nuanced approach. Up until the late 1960s or early 1970s, it was not unusual for states to permit the use of involuntary medication without further review for patients who were involuntarily certified or committed to a mental hospital. In 1975, a class action case in Massachusetts, *Rogers v. Okin*, challenged the forcible use of medication in patients in all circumstances short of an emergency, without a specific judicial finding of incompetence (*Rogers* 1979). At the same time, the requirements for informed consent for all medical patients were being refined, making the patient a more active partner in the decision-making process. For psychiatric patients, this led to more substantial legal proceedings for most involuntary treatment, except in an emergency. The profession also had to develop guidelines for the criteria required to allow a patient to be a voluntary patient, following a case where someone was voluntarily admitted to a hospital when he believed he was "in Heaven" (*Zinermon* 1990). Competence is now assessed by defined task-specific criteria, which are codified in statute or case law. For example, there are many competency criteria for determining capacity to: give informed consent for medications or treatment, volunteer for research, be a voluntary patient, consent to release of records, parent a child, write a will, make business contracts, and carry a weapon.

This right to refuse medication has also been problematic for the criminal justice system when defendants refuse treatment after having been found incompetent to stand trial. Since 1972, there are limitations on the time that defendants can be held if they remain incompetent. *Jackson v. Indiana* held that indefinite commitment of a man, who was deaf and mute and charged with stealing a purse, was unconstitutional (*Jackson* 1972). States were given discretion to set the maximum period of confinement before a civil commitment hearing had to be held to justify continued confinement. Jurisdictions have varied considerably in setting limits, e.g. Connecticut has a maximum of eighteen months, while Rhode Island can hold someone up to two thirds of the possible sentence for the crime, or up to thirty years for a possible life sentence. This has led to several problems, including the extended hospitalization of those charged with misdemeanors who deny they are ill and reject medication, yet remain incompetent. They often require extended hospitalizations to see if they could improve without medications. Another problem is that the use of medication becomes part of a legal negotiation. In the Russell Weston Jr. case (*Weston* 2000) the defense argued that they would not object to the use of appropriate medications to treat delusions if the Government took the death penalty off the table. The defense team also argued that since Mr. Weston was in isolation and had guards at his door, he was not dangerous. He had killed two guards at the U.S. Capitol building and had an elaborate delusional system. The Government said they would not take the death penalty off the table until he was competent and they could conduct their own evaluation, resulting in a standoff. This kept him in isolation and untreated for over two years. States developed algorithms for determining when medication could be forced solely for the purpose of competency restoration. These included such factors as the severity of the crime, appropriateness of the medication, likelihood of successful restoration etc. (e.g., *State v. Garcia*

1995). In the Wanda Barzee case (*State of Utah* 2007) following the abduction of Elizabeth Smart, the Chief Justice of the Utah Supreme Court opined that, in order to treat Ms. Barzee solely to restore competence to stand trial, "'the substantially likely' standard requires that the chance for restoration to competency be great. To the extent that such a likelihood can be quantified, it should reflect a probability of more than seventy percent." Medication for her was approved but not for her co-defendant, Brian David Mitchell.

In 2002, the U.S. Supreme Court heard the *Sell* case (*Sell* 2003) to decide if the Constitution permits the federal government to forcibly administer antipsychotics to a criminal defendant who was mentally ill, but not dangerous, for the sole purpose of making him competent to stand trial for serious but nonviolent crimes. The Court announced a complicated chain of factors that criminal courts should consider.

First, "a court must find that *important* governmental interests are at stake. The Government's interest in bringing to trial an individual accused of a serious crime is important. Special circumstances may lessen the importance of that interest. The defendant's failure to take drugs voluntarily, for example, may mean lengthy confinement in an institution for the mentally ill—and that would diminish the risks that ordinarily attach to freeing, without punishment, one who has committed a serious crime" (*Sell* 2003, 180).

Second, it must find that administration of the drugs is substantially likely to render the defendant competent to stand trial. "At the same time, it must find that administration of the drugs is substantially unlikely to have side effects that will interfere significantly with the defendant's ability to assist counsel in conducting a trial defense, thereby rendering the trial unfair" (*Sell* 2003, 181).

"Third, the court must conclude that involuntary medication is *necessary* to further those interests. The court must find that any alternative, less intrusive treatments are unlikely to achieve substantially the same results. And the court must consider less intrusive means for administering the drugs, e.g. a court order to the defendant backed by the contempt power, before considering more intrusive methods" (*Sell* 2003, 181).

"Fourth … the court must conclude that administration of the drugs is *medically appropriate*, i.e., in the patient's best medical interest in light of his medical condition" (*Sell* 2003, 182).

The Court also offered an alternate route:

"Courts typically address involuntary medical treatment as a civil matter, and justify it on these alternative, [civil commitment] grounds. Every state provides avenues through which, for example, a doctor or institution can seek appointment of a guardian with the power to make a decision authorizing medication—when in the best interests of a patient who lacks the mental competence to make such a decision" (*Sell* 2003, 182). "If a court authorizes medication on these alternative grounds, the need to consider authorization on only trial competence grounds will likely disappear" (*Sell* 2003, 183).

Thus the court permitted hospitals to use civil courts and civil criteria with less strict criteria to permit forced medication on those grounds. They reasoned that allowing this bypass of the criminal court would decrease the frequency of requests to medicate solely to restore competence. In response to *Sell*, for example, the Connecticut General Assembly enacted procedures for involuntary medication to restore competence to stand trial that were parallel to the civil procedures (Connecticut General Statutes 17a-543a).

TRANSFORMATION OF STATE MENTAL HOSPITALS INTO FORENSIC FACILITIES

During the nineteenth century, the local community as well as the state shared the hospital costs for treatment of persons with mental illness. The first half of the nineteenth century saw the opening of several private and public mental hospitals. By 1844, there were twenty-two public and corporate hospitals and three private institutions (Hamilton 1944). From 1840 to 1870, 45–50% of patients at the Worcester State Hospital had been hospitalized for less than a year and only 13% had been in the hospital for more than five years (Grob 1992). By the turn of the century states assumed all of the costs for such hospitalizations. Senility began to be defined as a mental disorder and chronic patients were transferred from almshouses to state mental hospitals. In the first half of the twentieth century the type of patients hospitalized in state mental hospitals changed to a significantly older population that needed long-term custodial care. By 1930 nearly 80% of psychiatric hospital beds in Massachusetts were occupied by chronic patients. Various forms of senility and paresis accounted for about half of all first admissions in 1946. As late as 1958 nearly a third of all resident state hospital patients were over age 65 (Grob 1992, 11).

The experiences of the World War II period seemed to show the efficacy of community and outpatient treatments. In addition, the idea that early intervention in the community might be more efficacious was taking hold. Social activists emphasized that total institutions like large mental hospitals could never be other than repressive and dehumanizing. Thorazine, a new psychotropic medication, had been introduced in 1954 in the United States. This was the first drug that seemed to have a significant positive impact on debilitating symptoms in psychotic patients in a way that permitted individuals to live safely in the community.

Thus began the emptying of the state hospitals and their closures, first as a trickle and then as a flood, in a movement that has become known as deinstitutionalization. The number of psychiatric patients in public hospital facilities peaked in 1960, with estimates from 535,000 to 560,000 patients. The total U.S. population at the time was 180 million. This represented a hospitalization rate of 297.6 per 100,000. By 1980 the hospitalized population had dropped to 235,934, with the hospitalization rate dropping to 36.9 per 100,000. By 2010 the total number of patients in public facilities had dropped to 43,318, with a hospitalization rate of 14.0 per 100,000. The total U.S. population reached 308 million (Census.gov 2011).

In the first decade from 1956 to 1965, only 16% of those who would be ultimately discharged were released from the hospital. Between 1966 and 1975, 54% of the patients were deinstitutionalized and between 1976 and 1984 18% more were released. Thus, three quarters of the patients who were being deinstitutionalized left the hospital between 1966 and 1984. Following the passage of Medicare and Medicaid in 1965, many of the elderly and senile patients were transferred to nursing homes. At least forty state psychiatric hospitals were closed during this period. Many patients were discharged into communities that did not have adequate resources to provide necessary services such as intensive treatment, housing, and job rehabilitation programs. The Community Mental Health Centers Act introduced by President Kennedy was short-lived, following President Reagan's program to replace it with block grants to the states (Goldman and Grob 2015).

Of course, there were some groups of patients for whom the state remained responsible, who required treatment in inpatient settings. These included defendants found incompetent to stand trial and insanity acquittees. Some states also permit courts to refer patients to mental health facilities for pre-sentence evaluations if they require inpatient levels of care during the evaluation. These "forensic patients" have become core populations for many state facilities and thus have transformed many state hospitals into predominantly forensic facilities, which require increased levels of security. Many state facilities now have maximum-security units as well as step-down or medium security units. These patients generally require periodic re-evaluations and testimony before criminal courts or administrative bodies to review the justifications for their confinement. Between 1988 and 2008, the proportion of Vermont State Hospital admissions accounted for by forensic patients increased 50%; in Massachusetts, 281%; in New York, 309%; and in Pennsylvania, 379% (Fisher, Geller and Pandiani 2009, 680).

SEX OFFENDER CIVIL COMMITMENT

Another significant impact on state mental health facilities and the appropriate boundaries of civil commitment has been the problem of sex offenders. There have been two eras where half of the states passed statutes confining such offenders in state hospital or correctional facilities. The first wave occurred between the late 1930s to the early 1960s and can be grouped as "sexual psychopath" legislation. Approximately thirty states and the District of Columbia enacted versions of sexual psychopath statutes in response to a sex crime panic that swept the nation after a wave of media publicity about violent sexual crimes committed against children. In 1937 alone, the *New York Times* published 143 articles on sex crimes and created a new category of articles to be catalogued. Also in 1937, J. Edgar Hoover called for a "war on the sex criminal," emphasizing that "the sex fiend, most loathsome of all the vast army of crime, has become a sinister threat to the safety of American childhood and womanhood" (Hoover 1937). In 1947 Hoover claimed the most rapidly increasing type of crimes were perpetrated by degenerate sex offenders (Hoover 1947). At a time when both the medical profession and the public often equated homosexuality with pedophilia it is not surprising that the sexual psychopath laws contain clear homophobic elements (see also Chapter 11).

Between 1935 and 1965, city, state, and federal officials established commissions to investigate sexual crimes and passed statutes to transfer authority over sex offenders from courts to psychiatrists and funded specialized institutions for the treatment of sex offenders. As a result, in most states a man accused of rape, sodomy, child molestation, indecent exposure, or corrupting the morals of a minor—if diagnosed as a sexual psychopath—could receive an indeterminate sentence to a psychiatric rather than a penal institution until he was deemed no longer dangerous. While definitions varied, in most states the laws defined the sexual psychopath as someone whose "utter lack of power to control his sexual impulses" made him "likely to attack … the objects of his uncontrolled and uncontrollable desires" (Denno 1998, 1352).

When it first appeared in Europe in the late nineteenth century, the diagnosis of psychopathy did not refer exclusively either to sexual abnormality or to men; akin to the concept of moral insanity, it was applied to habitual criminals who were normal mentally but exhibited abnormal social behavior. Kraepelin use the term "psychotic psychopathic personality" in his 1904 textbook to refer primarily to criminals with unstable personalities, vagabonds, liars, and beggars, although he also listed prostitutes and homosexuals (Freedman 1987). In 1905, Adolf Meyer introduced the concept of the psychopath into the United States, where sexual crime remained synonymous with female immorality (Freedman, 1987). Despite psychiatric ambivalence, proposed legislation incorporated the psychopathic diagnosis into the law in most states.

Michigan passed the nation's first sexual psychopath law in 1935 (Mich. Pub. Acts, 1935; *People v. Chapman*, 1942; *People v. Frontczak* 1938). The statute ordered a judge to conduct a thorough review before sentencing anyone who had been convicted of indecent exposure or gross indecency if he appeared "feeble-minded, epileptic … to be psychopathic, or a sex degenerate or a sex pervert, with tendencies dangerous to public safety …" (*Frontczak* 1938, 535). In making this determination a judge or jury had to call two or more reputable physicians, including one psychiatrist. If this evidence proved "to the satisfaction" of the judge or jury that the defendant was a sexual psychopath that caused him to be a "menace to the public safety," the court was instructed to order him to a state hospital institution until the defendant had "ceased to be a menace to the public safety because of said mental condition" (*Frontczak* 1938, 535). In that event he would either be released or ordered to complete his custodial sentence. In *Pearson v. Probate Court* (*Pearson* 1940), the United States Supreme Court held that states have the right under their police powers to single out sexually dangerous persons for special treatment out of the larger class of sex offenders. The court held that sexual psychopaths or sexually dangerous persons constituted a dangerous element that the state legislature had the right to control. The Equal Protection Clause required that for some people to be treated differently than the larger group, their classification must be reasonably related to the objectives of the legislation.

The sexual psychopath statutes took three basic forms. Seventeen states required that a person be convicted of some crime before he could be committed for treatment. Although some of the states required the *conviction* be for a sex offense, others did not. Seven states required that the individual only *be charged* with a crime (Florida, Illinois, Indiana, Iowa, Michigan, Missouri, Washington). Of these, only Washington required that the charge be sex-related. Four states (Minnesota, Massachusetts, New Hampshire, and Wisconsin) and the District of Columbia *did not require charges or a conviction*; instead, commitment could occur upon cause that the person was a sexual psychopath.

Paul Tappan studied the first cases committed under the New Jersey law. He found that among those committed were twenty-nine charged with open lewdness, twelve with rape, seven with sodomy, two with indecent exposure, one with possessing obscene pictures, three with exhibitionism, and two with fellatio (Tappan 1950, 13–14).

The discussions of sexual deviancy were significantly affected by the surveys done by Alfred Kinsey (Kinsey, Pomeroy, and Martin 1948; Pomeroy et al. 1953). His studies of male and female sex practices seemed to spur the most wide-ranging debate on sexuality. They forced Americans to confront the gap between actual behavior and what people believed to be deviant behavior (Jones 1997, xi). The books challenged long-held sexual beliefs. Among males, for example, Kinsey found that masturbation was nearly universal, that one-half of married men had engaged in extramarital intercourse, and that 95% had broken the law in some way at least once to achieve an orgasm. Among females, Kinsey discovered that 90% had petted premaritally, one-half had experienced premarital intercourse, and that 25% of the married women had been involved in extramarital intercourse.

Kinsey's statistics on homosexuality were among his most widely publicized results. Among males, 50% had reacted erotically to other males, while 37% had at least one postadolescent homosexual experience involving orgasm. The findings for females were substantially lower; 28% had responded erotically to other females, while 13% had achieved orgasm with another woman.

In an effort to quell the sex crime panic, many states hastily enacted sexual psychopath statutes. Several states established commissions to study sex offenses and sexual psychopath legislation to better understand the issue prior to crafting a law, but public pressure to address the problem led several of the legislatures to pass sexual psychopath laws even before the commission reports were received. This rush to pass statutes often resulted in laws that the commissions later opposed. For example, Massachusetts established a commission in April 1947 and enacted a sexual psychopath law three months later (Sutherland 1950, 145). The report the commission issued in April 1948 recommended amending the law that committed aggressive sexual deviants to the Department of Correction on the basis that sexual psychopaths required a therapeutic institution that is neither a prison nor a hospital but somewhere between these two types (Sutherland 1950). Similarly, New Jersey created a commission on March 10, 1949, enacted a sexual psychopath law on April 11, 1949 and received the commission report denouncing the statute on February 1, 1950. Five states (California, Illinois, Michigan, Minnesota, and Oregon) established commissions several years after passing legislation.

In analyzing the problem of forcible sexual assaults, seven of the nine commissions ended up questioning the reasonableness of including consensual homosexual sodomy within the purview of sexual psychopathy. In almost all states consensual sodomy was a felony, subject to the same penalties as forcible sodomy. Those sentences could be extreme, even resulting in life imprisonment; other states had a five-year minimum sentence. These severe sentences indicated the extent to which American society opposed any sexual acts that deviated from the perceived norm. Kinsey was a vocal opponent of both consensual sodomy laws and sexual psychopath statutes. He denounced both as "completely out of accord with the realities of human behavior" and argued that the "capricious enforcement which these laws now receive offers the opportunity for maladministration of police and political graft and for blackmail which is regularly imposed both by underworld groups and by the police themselves" (Pomeroy et al. 1953, 20). Seven of the nine commissions recommended removing consensual sodomy from the purview of the sexual psychopath laws, but only three states did so. Manfred Guttmacher, a forensic psychiatrist, chaired the Forensic Committee of the Group for the Advancement of Psychiatry (GAP). Their 1949 report, "The Psychiatrically Deviated Offender," warned against going with the tide of the sexual psychopath laws and they further revised their report after reviewing Kinsey's 1948 study (Committee on Forensic Psychiatry of GAP 1950).

Freedman has described the status of these laws in the 1950s:

> By the early 1950s, California criminal courts sentenced only 35% of convicted sex offenders to mental institutions as psychopaths; 54% went to prisons and 11% to the youth authority. Prior to 1953 annual commitments of psychopaths averaged thirty-seven in each state with a special law. Revised laws and new facilities in the 1950s increased commitments in several states; Michigan and Maryland for example each averaged 100 per year. Few of those committed, however, were the homicidal sex maniacs on whom the sex crime panic had originally focused. They tended to be white men, often professionals or skilled workers, who were overrepresented among those convicted of sexual relations with children and minor sexual offenses. Black men, who continued to be overrepresented among those convicted of rape, were more likely be imprisoned or executed than to be treated in mental institutions (Freedman 1987, 97).

Kinsey's work also had a profound influence on the American Law Institute's (ALI) decision to exclude consensual sodomy from the Model Penal Code (MPC) that they were developing. A group of prominent judges, lawyers, and law professors had founded the ALI in 1923 with the purpose of simplifying and clarifying American law as well as adapting legal codes to meet changing social needs (Hazard 1994, 3; Goodrich and Wolkin 1961, 5–7). In 1950 the ALI turned to the criminal law and its administration. They decided to create a model statutory code that would be a source to state legislatures to update their penal laws and assist them in their efforts.

The committee went back and forth over the decision to add or exclude the consensual sodomy provision, not so much because of disagreement on the policy but because of fears that the public feeling in the country was so strong that a code that did not punish this kind of behavior might be discredited. Judge Learned Hand made an impassioned plea at the time of the final decision, which ultimately helped the vote to eliminate the consensual sodomy provision from the Model Penal Code. Until 1980 almost all sodomy law repeals were the result of states rewriting their entire penal codes, and the Model Penal Code influenced all of them (George 2015, 250–60). Gradually, between 1970 and 1990 these laws were either repealed or not utilized.

The sexually violent predator (SVP) statutes beginning in 1990 became the second major effort to confine sexual offenders in psychiatric hospitals in the U.S. In 1989, after completing a ten-year sentence for sexual assault, a man raped and emasculated a seven-year-old boy. This led the State of Washington to pass a statute in 1990 that permitted the indefinite civil commitment of sex offenders to civil mental hospitals at the end of their full prison sentence. The only requirement for a concomitant mental illness was a "mental abnormality" that was very loosely defined. Nothing excluded antisocial personality disorder as a sufficient criterion, thus confounding the distinction between criminal behavior and behavior that had a significant mental illness contribution. Several other states and the federal government quickly adopted similar statutes. By 2008, twenty states and the District of Columbia passed similar statutes. These "sexual predator" statutes faced a number of constitutional challenges, involving due process, ex-post facto and double jeopardy arguments. The Supreme Court, however, has upheld the constitutionality of these statutes three times (*Kansas v. Crane*, 2002; *Kansas v. Hendricks*, 1977; *U.S. v. Comstock* 2010). The APA published a Task Force Report opposing these statutes in 1999, opining, "legislators have used psychiatric commitment to effect non-medical societal ends that cannot be openly avowed … this represents a misuse of psychiatry" (APA 1999, 174). There are currently 4,500–4,700 offenders held under these statutes. Only 10% have been released or discharged from these programs.

Minnesota has committed 714 individuals since 1994 and has discharged none from the program. In July 2015, a federal court concluded that Minnesota's civil commitment statutory scheme is unconstitutional both on its face and as applied (*Karsjens* 2015). The court concluded that the statutory scheme is not narrowly tailored and results in a punitive effect and application contrary to the purpose of civil commitment and that the Minnesota Sex Offender Program (MSOP), implementing the statute, systematically continues to confine individuals in violation of constitutional principles. The court was concerned that (1) the state does not conduct periodic independent risk assessments or otherwise evaluate whether an individual continues to meet the initial commitment criteria or the discharge criteria if an individual does not file a petition; (2) those risk assessments that have been performed have not been performed in a constitutional manner; (3) individuals have remained confined at the MSOP even though they have completed treatment or sufficiently reduced their risk; (4) discharge procedures are not working properly at the MSOP; (5) although the statute allows the referral of committed individuals to less restrictive alternatives, this is not occurring in practice because there are insufficient less restrictive alternatives available for transfer and no less restrictive alternatives available for initial commitment; and (6) that although treatment has been made available, the treatment program structure has been an institutional failure as there is no meaningful relationship between the treatment program and an end to indefinite detention.

Treatment programs are not consistent between states, with some states requiring a minimum fourteen months to complete the program and others requiring six years as a minimum. Outside consultants reviewing the programs are concerned about the high false positive rate and the low level of recidivism for this population. At one point, Florida offered a group of 140 offenders who had just been committed an opportunity to be under strict probation and live in the community. If they got into any trouble, then the SVP commitment would be reactivated. Over a one to ten-year period only five offenders (3.6%) were convicted of a sexual felony offense (Carr, Schlank, and Parker 2013). These were individuals who had been deemed dangerous enough to have been committed at the end of their sentence but in fact did not represent an actual risk that required an inpatient level of care.

As before, major problems are beginning to surface in the implementation of these statutes.

MENTAL HEALTH TREATMENT IN JAILS AND PRISONS

As noted above, the tightening of civil commitment criteria coupled with deinstitutionalization resulted in larger numbers of individuals with mental illness ending up in jails and prisons. Prisons had previously dealt with inmates with mental illness by transferring them to state mental hospitals but these beds became less available as many state hospitals closed. The lack of adequate treatment in correctional facilities became a focus of many individual and class action lawsuits. In 1976, the U.S. Supreme Court held, in *Estelle v. Gamble* (*Estelle* 1976, 104), that a state could not be deliberately indifferent to the health care needs of a prisoner—effectively a right to treatment.

> We therefore conclude that deliberate indifference to serious medical needs of prisoners constitutes the "unnecessary and wanton infliction of pain," proscribed by the Eighth Amendment. This is true whether the indifference is manifested by prison doctors in their response to the prisoner's needs, or by prison guards in intentionally denying or delaying access to medical care or intentionally interfering with the treatment once prescribed. Regardless of how evidenced, deliberate indifference to a prisoner's serious illness or injury states a cause of action under §1983 (*Estelle* 1976, 104–5).

Thus, under this ruling, if prison officials do not perform mental health screening for suicidality or mental illness they can be found deliberately indifferent to providing adequate health care.

Prisons have generally been understaffed for mental health treatment and overcrowded as the prison and jail populations have expanded from 200,000 in 1975 to over 1.6 million in 2009 (1,574,700 in 2013) in state and federal facilities (Carson 2014). In 1990, a case was filed in California, alleging that prisoners with serious mental illness do not receive minimal, adequate care (*Coleman* 1995, 1293). At that time the prisons were designed for a population of 80,000 but the population was almost double that. The district court ruled against the state and a Special Master was appointed to oversee remedial efforts by the state, but twelve years later he reported that the level of mental health care was deteriorating. A receiver was then appointed and reported three years later that a remedy was not possible without reducing overcrowding. The Supreme Court (*Brown* 2011) agreed with the three-judge court that overcrowding was a major factor. In addition there were high vacancy rates for medical and mental health staff (54% for psychiatrists); but even if the positions were filled, there was no space for them. The court supported the lower court ruling that the prison population should be capped at 137.5% of design capacity and provided a two-year deadline for compliance.

Correctional psychiatry facilities are not subject to the usual controls of hospital accreditation standards. Special correctional guidelines have been developed but many facilities have not applied for accreditation. Forensic psychiatrists have played a role in monitoring settlements from lawsuits that have shown inadequate assessment and treatment programs. The American Psychiatric Association has also issued Task Force Reports on Guidelines on Psychiatric Services in Correctional Facilities (APA 2015).

ETHICAL GUIDELINES AND EXPERT WITNESS TESTIMONY

Psychiatrists and other physicians had been testifying in courts for many years before the American Board of Medical Specialties (ABMS) recognized forensic psychiatry as a subspecialty in 1992. Expert testimony in general, and by psychiatrists and other mental health professionals in particular, has been a focus of concern by the profession as well as a target of criticism from many sources. In his 1933 American Psychiatric Association presidential address, Dr. James V. May called for a qualifying board to be established to certify specialists in psychiatry and neurology, stressing the urgent need of such certification as a means of eliminating the inadequately trained pseudo-expert who did much to discredit expert testimony. The public has remained skeptical of both the insanity defense and expert witness testimony. They consistently overestimate its use and interpret the defense as "getting off" in spite of the fact that acquittees often spend longer in the hospital post acquittal than they would have spent in prison if convicted. This was epitomized in 1995, when a proposed New Mexico statute setting out licensing requirements for psychiatrists and psychologists reportedly passed both houses of the New Mexico legislature before the governor vetoed it. The statute provided that a mental health professional who testifies in a criminal case "shall wear a cone shaped hat that is not less than 2 feet tall. The surface of the hat shall be imprinted with stars and lightning bolts." Additionally, the legislation required that the expert "shall be required to don a white beard that is not less than 18 inches in length and shall punctuate crucial elements of his testimony by stabbing the air with a wand" (Olsen 2012). (There are different versions of what actually happened. Senator Scott Duncan, who introduced the bill, told a blogger the clause was removed before the bill reached the House floor.)

Beginning in the early 1980s several academics have also made strong statements questioning whether psychiatric experts have much that is useful to say to the legal system. Alan Stone argued that there were no ethical guidelines of substance for forensic work and that experts had nothing relevant to say regarding issues of criminal responsibility (Stone 1984a, 1984b). Additional criticisms by Stephen Morse (2006), David Faigman (1989), David Faust and Jay Ziskin (Ziskin and Faust 1988) asked for further exclusion of much expert testimony in criminal responsibility cases. After the Hinckley case in 1982, four states (Utah, Montana, Idaho, and Kansas) abolished their insanity defense.

The courts have also struggled with expert testimony. In the seminal *Daubert* (1993) case, the Supreme Court granted certiorari to decide whether the so-called *Frye* (or general acceptance) test, which was used by some federal courts in determining the admissibility of scientific evidence, had been superseded by the enactment of the Federal Rules of Evidence. The court held unanimously that the *Frye* test had not survived. Six justices on the Supreme Court joined Justice Blackmun in setting forth a new test for admissibility. The majority opinion announced that the trial judge is the "gatekeeper" who must screen proffered expertise, and the objective of the screening is to ensure that what is admitted "is not only relevant, but reliable" (*Daubert* 1993, 589). There was nothing particularly novel about a trial judge having the power to make admissibility determinations, but the majority opinion stated that the trial court has not only the power but the obligation to act as gatekeeper. In order to determine whether proffered scientific testimony or evidence satisfies the standard of evidentiary reliability, a judge must ascertain whether it is "grounded in the methods and procedures of science" (*Daubert* 1993, 590). Although general acceptance of the methodology within the scientific community is no longer dispositive, it remained a factor to be considered.

In 1998 the Supreme Court, in *Kumho Tire Company v. Carmichael*, granted certiorari on a case to decide if the trial judges' gatekeeping obligation under *Daubert* applies only to scientific evidence or if it extends to proffers of "technical or other specialized knowledge," and other categories of expertise specified in Federal Rule of Evidence 702 (*Kumho* 1999, 141). A split had developed in the circuit courts on this issue. In addition there was uncertainty about whether disciplines like economics, psychology and other "soft" sciences counted as science. In an opinion by Justice Breyer, the court held that the trial court's gatekeeping obligation extends to all expert testimony and rejected the 11th Circuit's split between experts who rely on the application of scientific principles and the expert who relies on skill or experience-based observation. The court opined that "no clear line" can be drawn between the different kinds of knowledge, and "no one denies that an expert might draw a conclusion from a set of observations based on extensive and specialized experience" (*Kumho* 1999, 156). The opinion adopts a flexible approach, stressing the importance of identifying "the particular circumstances of the particular case at issue" (*Kumho* 1999, 150). The court must then make sure that the proffered expert will observe the same standard of intellectual rigor in testifying as he or she would employ when dealing with similar matters outside the courtroom. Justice Breyer also rejected the notion that the *Daubert* principles were always relevant. "The conclusion in our view is that we can neither rule out, nor rule in, for all cases and for all time the applicability of the factors mentioned in *Daubert*, nor can we now do so for subsets of cases categorized by category of expert or by kind of evidence. Too much depends on the particular circumstances of the particular case at issue" (*Kumho* 1999, 150).

Although scientific validity is important, it is not the only thing. Another principle is a litigant's fundamental interest in having his or her full, individualized story told to the court and the second is the general interest in a fair process. This is illustrated in the 1987 U.S. Supreme Court decision *Rock v. Arkansas* (*Rock* 1987). In that case the court had to determine whether an Arkansas statute barring testimony by a defendant who had been subject to hypnosis was a permissible restriction on that right. Acknowledging that memories induced through hypnosis can be fabricated, the majority asserted that a *per se* rule such as Arkansas's was unconstitutional. The statute did not permit the trial court to take into account the reasons for undergoing hypnosis, the circumstances under which it took place or any independent verification of the information it produced. It also did not recognize that cross-examination, expert testimony, and cautionary instructions could counteract some of the inadequacies of posthypnotic testimony. Thus they argued that a case-by-case approach is mandated unless the court can show that "hypnotically enhanced testimony is always so untrustworthy and so immune to the traditional means of evaluating credibility that it should disable a defendant from presenting her version of the events for which she is on trial" (*Rock* 1987, 61).

The courts are still struggling with the aftermath of *Daubert* and the exclusion of psychiatric testimony (Slobogin 2007). Some testimony has been excluded but it is usually based on the expert having relied on a test that had not been sufficiently validated rather than experts having relied on clinical experience.

Another approach to improving the quality of psychiatric testimony is to provide increased training, education and board certification. This turned out to be a highly political process that took over twenty years to accomplish. In the time from 1970 to 1975 the American Psychiatric Association's Committee on Psychiatry and the Law urged the establishment of a forensic psychiatry certification board but the APA Board of Trustees declined to do so, citing the Federal Trade Commission's heightened scrutiny of professional organizations as the main reason. Invitations to the American Board of Medical Specialties (ABMS) and the American Board of Psychiatry and Neurology (ABPN) were also fruitless. The real impetus came from the Law Enforcement Assistance Administration (LEAA). The LEAA was a federal agency within the U.S. Department of Justice. It administered federal funding to state planning agencies and local law enforcement agencies and funded educational programs, and research, and research related to local crime initiatives. The LEAA was interested in improving the quality of expert testimony and began offering grants for certification and planning in a number of areas including forensic psychiatry. In response to this, the Forensic Sciences

Foundation (a nonprofit organization created by the American Academy of Forensic Sciences (AAFS) to receive research grants) developed a constitution and bylaws for the American Board of Forensic Psychiatry (ABFP). These were recorded in the District of Columbia on June 15, 1976. AAPL and AAFS were co-sponsors; the APA declined. In 1986, the American Board of Psychiatry and Neurology (ABPN) again declined to recognize additional subspecialties in psychiatry. But in July 1991, the APA Board of Trustees accepted the APA Commission on Subspecialty Requests to approve forensic psychiatry. The American Board of Medical Specialties (ABMS) then approved the ABPN's request in 1992. An examination committee was developed and the first exams were offered in 1994. After an initial five-year period when experience qualified for sitting for the exam, a one-year full-time residency program was required to obtain specialty certification. By 2010 there were forty-two ACGME-accredited forensic psychiatry programs. Close to 90% of the graduates sought subspecialty certification. From 1976 to 1993, 260 psychiatrists were certified in forensic psychiatry by the ABFP. From 1994 to 2014, the ABPN awarded 2,125 certificates in forensic psychiatry.

AAPL and the APA have worked to enhance written ethical guidelines for forensic work. Committees and individuals have provided ethical consultation and the development of principles to guide the work. Individuals such as Jonas Rappeport, Paul Applebaum, Philip Candilis, Richard Martinez, Michael Norko, Robert Weinstock, Ezra Griffith, Alec Buchanan, Tom Gutheil, and Larry Strasburger have all made important contributions to the ethical dimensions of that work. The APA's Council on Psychiatry and the Law has developed position statements on many topics, including one condemning the use of psychiatrists in interrogation of prisoners (APA 2014). AAPL has developed practice guidelines for a variety of forensic evaluations such as criminal responsibility (AAPL 2007, 2014b), competence to stand trial (AAPL 2007), and disability evaluations (AAPL 2008).

Professional organizations are playing an increasingly active role in the political process, both in legislative and case law initiatives (see also Chapter 11). The APA's Committee (formerly Commission) on Judicial Action has written or signed onto over 100 amicus briefs on cases going to the Supreme Court or other appellate courts. The APA Council on Psychiatry and Law has drafted position statements, resource documents, and task force reports, and reviewed the scientific literature, providing positions that the organization adopted or forming the basis for the amicus positions submitted to the courts. The Division of Government Relations provides commentary on proposed legislation and regulations. They also are more attentive to professional ethics and practice guidelines

In the criminal justice system, the role of psychiatry is dependent upon the degree of individualization that is felt to be important by the courts. Over the past fifteen years there has been a substantial upswing in the number of cases where defense attorneys are looking for psychiatric evaluations, both before and immediately after an indictment. These requests have not necessarily been for the usual competency to stand trial or criminal responsibility evaluations. Rather the attorneys are looking for a good narrative of the person's life so that the current charges can be put into some perspective. These evaluations are then used to negotiate with the prosecutor to see if some acceptable outcome can be achieved early in the criminal process. This may affect the charges with which the person is ultimately charged or to which the person may plead.

CONCLUSION

The last half-century has been an active period in the boundaries between psychiatry and the law. Forensic Psychiatry training programs have developed into a recognized subspecialty of psychiatry and have been dedicated to educating and training psychiatrists so that experts provide higher quality testimony that is more scientifically grounded, and that strives for objectivity in the face of the adversarial pressures of the legal system. The special patient populations in penal and maximum-security treatment settings frequently require more knowledge of legal proceedings and the ability to testify about changes in status in courts or administrative bodies. Ethical questions frequently arise about the limits of confidentiality and dual agency when treating individuals with concomitant criminal charges or where information may be released to parole boards or other bodies not directly related to treatment. As long as the death penalty remains viable the appropriate role of providing treatment or forensic assessments remains ethically challenging. The field continues to evolve and often represents the public face of psychiatry.

BIBLIOGRAPHY

AAPL. 2007. "Practice Guideline for the Forensic Psychiatric Evaluation of Competency to Stand Trial." *Journal of the American Academy of Psychiatry and the Law* 35: S3–S72.

———. 2008. "Practice Guideline for the Forensic Evaluation of Psychiatric Disability." *Journal of the American Academy of Psychiatry and the Law* 36: S3–S50.

———. 2014a. "Landmark Cases." Accessed November 30, 2015. www.aapl.org/landmark_list.htm.

———. 2014b. "Practice Guideline for Forensic Psychiatric Evaluation of Defendants

Raising the Insanity Defense." *Journal of the American Academy of Psychiatry and the Law* 42: S3–S76.

Addington v. Texas, 441 U.S. 418 (1979).

American Bar Association. 2005. "Recommendations of the American Bar Association Section of Individual Rights and Responsibilities Task Force on Mental Disability and the Death Penalty." *Catholic University Law Review* 54: 1115.

American Medical Association. 1995. Council on Judicial and Ethical Affairs (CEJA). *Code of Medical Ethics 2012–2013: Current Opinions with Annotations*. AMA Press. Opinion 2.06 Capital Punishment.

American Psychiatric Association Task Force. 1974. *Clinical Aspects of the Violent Individual*. APA Press.

American Psychiatric Association. 1999. *Dangerous Sex Offenders*. APA Press.

———. 2014. "Position Statement on Psychiatric Participation in Interrogation of Detainees." Approved by the Board of Trustees May 2006; reaffirmed December 2014.

———. 2015. *Psychiatric Services in Correctional Facilities, Third Edition*. APA Press.

Barefoot v. Estelle, 463 U.S. 880 (1983).

Birnbaum, M. 1960. "The Right to Treatment." *American Bar Association Journal* 46: 499–504.

Brown v. Plata, 134 S. CT 436 (2011).

Buchanan, A., R. Binder, M. Norko, and M. Swartz. 2012. "Resource Document on Psychiatric Violence Risk Assessment." *American Journal of Psychiatry* 169 (3): 340.

Carr, C., A. Schlank, and K.C. Parker. 2013. Review of Florida's Sexually Violent Predator Program Office. Available at http://media.cmgdigital.com/shared/news/documents/2013/09/23/09.23_SVPP_Report.pdf. Accessed April 19, 2016.

Carson, E.A. 2014. "Prisoners in 2013." *Bureau of Justice Statistics*, September, NCJ 247282.

Census.gov. 2011. Accessed November 28, 2015. http://quickfacts.census.gov/qfd/states/00000.html.

Coleman v. Wilson, 912 F.Supp. 1282 (1995).

Committee on Forensic Psychiatry of GAP. 1950. "Psychiatrically Deviated Sex Offenders" Report #9 May 1949, Revised February 1950, 1–12.

Conn. Gen Stat. 17a-543a.

Conn. Gen Stat. 17-176 and 17-178.

Coventry, C.B. 1844–45. "Medical Jurisprudence of Insanity." *American Journal of Insanity* 1: 134–14.

Daubert v. Merrell Dow Pharmaceuticals, Inc. 509 U.S. 579 (1993).

Denno, D. 1998. "Life before the Modern Sex Offender Statutes." *Northwestern University Law Review* 92: 1317.

Donaldson v. O'Connor, 493 F.2d 507 (1974).

Estelle v. Gamble, 429 U.S. 97 (1976).

Estelle v. Smith, 451 U.S. 454 (1981).

Faigman, D. 1989. "To Have and Have Not: Assessing the Value of Social Science to the Law as Science and Policy." *Emory Law Journal* 38: 1005–95.

Fisher, W.H., J. Geller, and J. Pandiani. 2009. "The Changing Role of the State Psychiatric Hospital." *Health Affairs* 28 (3): 676–84.

Ford v. Wainwright, 477 U.S. 399 (1986).

Freedman, E.B. 1987. "Uncontrolled Desires: The Response to the Sexual Psychopath." *The Journal of American History* 74: 83–106.

George, M.A. 2015. "The Harmless Psychopath: Legal Debates Promoting the Decriminalization of Sodomy in the United States." *Journal of the History of Sexuality* 24: 225–61.

Goldman, H. and G. Grob, 2015. "Defining Mental Illness in Mental Health Policy." *Health Affairs* 34: 737.

Goodrich, H.F. and P.A. Wolkin. 1961. *The Story of the American Law Institute, 1923–1961.* St. Paul, MN: American Law Institute Publishers.

Grob, G.N. 1992. "Mental Health Policy in America: Myths and Realities." *Health Affairs* 11 (3): 7–22.

Hamilton, S. 1944. "History of American Mental Hospitals." In *One Hundred Years of American Psychiatry*, edited by Joan K. Hall, Gregory Zilboorg, and Henry A. Bunker. pp. 73–166. New York: Columbia University Press.

Hazard, G.C. Jr. 1994. *The American Law Institute: What It Is and What It Does.* Rome: Centro di Studi e Richerche di Diritto Comparato e Straniero.

Hoover, J.E. 1937. "War on the Sex Criminal." *New York Herald Tribune*. This Week Magazine Section. Sept. 26, at 2.

———. 1947. "How Safe Is Your Daughter?" 144 *American Magazine* July, at 32.

Jackson v. Indiana, 406 U.S. 715 (1972).

Jones, J.H. 1997. *Kinsey: A Public/Private Life*. New York: W.W. Norton.

Kansas v. Crane, 534 U.S. 407 (2002).

Kansas v. Hendricks, 521 U.S. 346 (1977).

Karsjens, K.S. et al. v. Jesson L., et al. 2015 WL 4478972 (2015).

Kinsey, A.C., W. Pomeroy, and C.E. Martin. 1948. *Sexual Behavior in the Human Male.* Philadelphia: W.B. Saunders.

Kumho Tire Co. v. Carmichael, 526 U.S. 137 (1999).

Lessard v. Schmidt, 349 Fed.Supp. 1078 (1972).

Lessard v. Schmidt. 1972. Stipulation of Facts, Civil Action Case No. 71–C–602, Appendix 1, Testimony of Officer James D. Mejchar, March 30.

Mayock v. Martin, 245 A2d 574 (1968).

Michigan Public Acts 1935, page 141, No. 88, enacted May 27, 1935.

Morse, S. 2006. "Brain Overclaim Syndrome and Criminal Responsibility: A Diagnostic Note." *Ohio State Journal Criminal Law* 3: 397–412.

O'Connor v. Donaldson, 422 U.S. 563 (1975).

Olsen, W. 2012. "Dressing psychiatrists like wizards on the witness stand." *Overlawyered*. Accessed on November 30, 2015. http://overlawyered.com/2012/01/dressing-psychiatrists-like-wizards-on-the-witness-stand/.

Panetti v. Quarterman, 127 S.Ct. 2842 (2007).

Pearson v. Probate Court, 60 S. Ct. 523 (1940).

People v. Chapman, 4 N.W.2d 18 (Mich. 1942).

People v. Frontczak, 281 NW 534 (1938).

Pinals, D. and D. Mossman. 2012. *Best Practices in Forensic Mental Health Assessment: Evaluation for Civil Commitment*. New York: Oxford University Press.

Pomeroy, W.B., P.H. Gebhard, C.E. Martin, and A.C. Kinsey. 1953. *Sexual Behavior in the Human Female*. Philadelphia: W.B. Saunders.

Ray, I. 1838. *A Treatise on the Medical Jurisprudence of Insanity*. Boston: Little Brown & Co.

Rock v. Arkansas, 483 U.S. 44 (1987).

Rogers v. Okin, 478 F.Supp. 1342 (1979).

Sell v. U.S., 539 U.S. 166 (2003).

Slobogin, C. 2007. *Proving the Unprovable: the Role of Law, Science, and Speculation in Adjudicating Culpability and Dangerousness*. American Psychology-Law Society Series. Oxford University Press.

State of Utah v. Barzee, 177 P.3d 48 (2007).

State v. Garcia, 658 A.2d 947 (Conn 1995).

Stone, A.A. 1984a. "The Ethical Boundaries of Forensic Psychiatry: a View from the Ivory Tower." *Bulletin of the American Academy of Psychiatry and the Law* 12: 209–19.

———. 1984b. "The Ethics of Forensic Psychiatry: a View from the Ivory Tower." In *Law, Psychiatry and Morality*. Washington DC: American Psychiatric Press, 57–75.

Sutherland, E.H. 1950. "The Diffusion of Sexual Psychopath Laws." *American Journal of Sociology* 56: 142–8.

Szasz, T.S., 1960. "The Myth of Mental Illness." *The American Psychologist* 15 (2): 113–18.

———. 1974. *The Myth of Mental Illness: Foundations of a Theory of Personal Conduct*. New York: Harper & Row.

Tappan, P.W. 1950. *New Jersey Commission on The Habitual Sex Offender: Report and Recommendations of the Commission on the Habitual Sex Offender*. Trenton Press.

Torrey, E.F. 2008. *The Insanity Offense*. New York: W.W. Norton.

U.S. v. Comstock, 560 U.S. 126 (2010).

Weston v. U.S., 206 F.3d 9 (2000).

Zinermon v. Burch, 494 U.S. 113 (1990).

Ziskin, J. and D. Faust. 1988. *Coping with Psychiatric and Psychological Testimony*. Vols 1 to 3. Venice, CA: Law and Psychology Press.

SECTION 1

Major External Influences on Change in Forensic Psychiatry and Psychology

CHAPTER 1

The Law's Influence on Change in the Evidentiary Rules and in the Realm of Sentencing Mitigation

Paul F. Thomas

INTRODUCTION

As discussed in the introductory chapter, recent decades have marked significant evolution of substantive and procedural law, through landmark litigation, legislation, and regulation that has broadened the range of legal issues that may allow for the expertise of mental health professionals, especially forensic psychiatrists, in achieving resolution. From its notable focus on the insanity defense and a defendant's competency to participate in criminal proceedings, psychiatric expertise has been relied upon in other phases of the criminal justice process (e.g. compelled treatment to restore competency; post-conviction treatment; sentencing; post-conviction habeas proceedings). And, increasingly, forensic psychiatrists have been called upon for their expertise in civil cases claiming emotional injuries and trauma, in family and probate court, and in administrative adjudications involving claims for benefits from agencies such as the Veterans Administration and the Social Security Administration, and claims for relief from deportation. In all of these realms, the opportunity for forensic psychiatric participation has been guided, if not controlled, by rules of evidence governing the admissibility of expert testimony generally, and particularly by the liberalization of the rules to recognize the value of properly qualified experts in the adversarial process.

This chapter will discuss the rules of evidence that shape the role of forensic psychiatry in judicial proceedings, and will explore one area of significant expansion of psychiatric testimony: sentencing mitigation.

THE FEDERAL RULES OF EVIDENCE: DOOR OPENER AND GATE KEEPER

The expanded opportunities for forensic psychiatrists to be heard in judicial proceedings has resulted not just from the judicial and legislative recognition of substantive and procedural rights of individuals with mental health problems. While that evolution is the essential context within which psychiatry *may* play a role, the necessary prerequisite for forensic psychiatrists to indeed participate is the recognition that expert witnesses *should* be heard in the adversary legal process. Adjudication requires the presentation of evidence to support claims and defenses, be the issues criminal or civil or administrative, and attorneys are utilitarian: they seek *persuasive and admissible* evidence wherever it may be found. Beyond the traditional direct and circumstantial evidence, testimonial and documentary, expert testimony has become a critical element of proof in many cases.

The Federal Rules of Evidence, in force since 1975 and influential also in the enactment of many parallel state evidence codes, have made courts generally receptive to the participation of expert witnesses: "Expert testimony is liberally admissible under the Federal Rules of Evidence" (Weinstein 2008). These rules, federal and state, have opened the door to forensic psychiatric experts and defined the expertise that must be derived from experience, education, and training. Rule 702 of the Federal Rules of Evidence simply states:

> A witness who is qualified by knowledge, skill, expertise, training or education, may testify in the form of an opinion or otherwise if,
> (a) the expert's scientific, technical, or other specialized knowledge will help the trier of fact to understand the evidence or to determine a fact in issue;
> (b) the testimony is based on sufficient facts or data;
> (c) the testimony is the product of reliable principles and methods; and
> (d) the expert has reliably applied the principles and methods to the facts of the case.

The Advisory Committee Notes to the 1972 Proposed Rules (enacted in 1975) recognized the guiding principle that "[a]n intelligent evaluation of facts is often difficult or impossible without the application of some scientific, technical, or other specialized knowledge." Similarly, Connecticut Code of Evidence, §7-1 states:

> A witness qualified as an expert by knowledge, skill, experience, training, education or otherwise may testify in the form of an opinion or otherwise concerning scientific, technical or other specialized knowledge, if the testimony will assist the trier of fact in understanding the evidence or in determining a fact in issue.

The Rule embodies a judicial "gatekeeper" role in response to a pair of Supreme Court cases that addressed the need for courts to exclude unreliable expert testimony: *Daubert v. Merrell Dow Pharmaceuticals, Inc.* (*Daubert* 1993) and *Kumho Tire Co. v. Carmichael* (*Kumho* 1999). The Advisory Committee Notes explain that Rule 702 was amended in 2000, in response to those cases, "to affirm the trial court's role as gatekeeper and provide some general standards that the trial court must use to assess the reliability and helpfulness of the proffered expert testimony." The Rules Committee noted the following non-exclusive set of factors that have been considered by trial courts in determining reliability:

1. Whether experts are "proposing to testify about matters growing naturally and directly out of research they have conducted independent of the litigation or whether they have developed their opinions expressly for purposes of testifying."
2. Whether the expert has unjustifiably extrapolated from an accepted premise to an unfounded conclusion.
3. Whether the expert has adequately accounted for obvious alternative explanations.
4. Whether the expert "is being as careful as he would be in his regular professional work outside his paid litigation consulting."
5. Whether the field of expertise claimed by the expert is known to reach reliable results for the type of opinion the expert would give.

Advisory Committee Notes to 2000 Amendments

Rule 702 has standardized the foundational requirements for the admissibility of expert witnesses generally and has clarified for attorneys and judges when experts may be presented and the nature and scope of permissible expert testimony. The Advisory Committee Notes to the rule comment that even after the Supreme Court in *Daubert* (*Daubert* 1993) defined the judicial "gatekeeper" role, "rejection of expert testimony is the exception rather than the rule." Moreover, the Committee cited *Daubert* (*Daubert* 1993) for the basic premise that "[v]igorous cross-examination, presentation of contrary evidence, and careful instruction on the burden of proof are the traditional and appropriate means of attacking shaky but admissible evidence."

In the various realms identified in the introductory chapter where mental health issues may arise or be central in judicial proceedings, Rule 702 can be read by attorneys, ethically bound to zealously represent clients, as an invitation to offer psychiatric testimony whenever, in the language of Rule 702(a), the psychiatrist's "specialized knowledge will help the trier of fact to understand the evidence or to determine a fact in issue." Moreover, the Rule standardizes the inquiry that attorneys, courts, and psychiatrists should undertake in assessing whether forensic psychiatric evidence should be offered. This assessment is necessarily contextual, i.e. focused in the issues presented in a particular case in light of the procedural and substantive law governing the issues. By way of example, in a criminal case where a defendant was charged with assisting in the filing of false tax returns, where the government claimed the defendant knew returns were false that showed zeros on all lines, could psychiatric testimony assist the trier of fact (and the defense) by explaining how the defendant's narcissistic personality disorder could cause him to believe to be true something that was false? In 2007 the Ninth Circuit Court of Appeals reversed a conviction after a trial where this proffered evidence was excluded (*Cohen* 2007, 1123–5). The proposed but excluded testimony satisfied the liberal rule favoring admissibility. Although Federal Rule of Evidence 704(b) precludes expert testimony that provides "an opinion or inference as to whether the defendant did or did not have the mental state or condition constituting an element of the crime charged," the *Cohen* court reasoned that the psychiatrist could nonetheless have offered—with limitations set by the court to avoid violating Rule 704(b)—that the defendant suffered from a personality disorder that the jury could consider in the mix of evidence to decide if the defendant had the ability to form the required intent to evade the tax laws.

The prerequisites for admissibility do not predict persuasiveness, but they do provide a basic template for effective expert testimony. First, for forensic psychiatrists, foundational knowledge derived from experience, training, and education that is the core of specialty training. Second, the evidentiary basis for an opinion essential and sufficient to reach a sound conclusion. Third, the reliable application of reliable principles and methods to the data, including an adequate consideration of obvious alternative explanations. Fourth, whether the psychiatrist has approached the forensic evaluation with the same care he/she would outside the realm of serving as a paid expert. These are the requirements identified in Rule 702, they are what attorneys consider in retaining experts, and, most importantly, they are what fact-finders assess in weighing the expert testimony. While the focus of forensic psychiatric testimony will vary and derive from the specifics of the case and the procedural posture and substantive legal issues raised, the nature and scope of the testimony, and to a large extent the form of the testimony, will be defined by Rule 702.

The Expanding Role of Forensic Psychiatry in Criminal Sentencing

As notorious as they may be, insanity defense cases are rare. What is far more common, more so than competency questions, is the issue of sentencing mitigation based on diminished mental capacity or the presence and history of mental health problems. Nationally, in both federal and state courts, only a small percentage of criminal cases go to trial. The vast majority are resolved by plea negotiation and agreements. While many of those resolutions produce a fixed and binding sentence, that is not always the case, and it is rarely so in federal court. Rather, the parties agree upon the charge to which the defendant will plead guilty, possibly with an agreed minimum or maximum sentence, and leave to the court the responsibility for determining where on the spectrum defined either by the parties or by statute, which sets any minimum and maximum authorized punishment, the sentence should lie. In this realm, the litigation of an appropriate sentence, forensic psychiatry has a growing presence.

The federal criminal justice system best exemplifies the highly structured approach to sentencing that, even in less formalistic state systems, has made psychiatric evidence, testimonial, or documentary a common element of the mix of relevant information upon which judges rely in fashioning appropriate sentences. As noted, federal sentencing rarely follows a plea agreement that prescribes a specific sentence. Thus, judges are left with the task of determining the sentence. Until the mid-1980s, federal judges were largely left to their discretion in deciding where in the range of punishment established by statute, e.g. minimum or no imprisonment to a maximum of twenty years, to set the sentence. This practice was criticized for the unwarranted disparity of sentences that might be imposed on similar offenders, often with a racial disparity, and in 1984 Congress radically reformed federal sentencing with the enactment of the Sentencing Reform Act (18 USC § 3551). The Sentencing Reform Act prescribed specific factors that judges must consider in reaching their decisions, and, more controversially, it established the United States Sentencing Commission with a mandate to design a set of guidelines with standards and procedures that would eliminate unwarranted sentencing disparity. While the factors identified by statute are relevant, indeed mandatory for consideration, generally conformed to established practice, they were overridden by the mandate to adhere to the guidelines absent exceptional circumstances. To understand the emergence of forensic psychiatric expertise in this process the Sentencing Reform Act and the guidelines must be explained in some detail.

Under the Sentencing Reform Act (18 USC § 3553(a)):

> The court shall impose a sentence sufficient, but not greater than necessary, to comply with the purposes set forth in paragraph (2) of this subsection. The court, in determining the particular sentence to be imposed, shall consider—
>
> (1) the nature and circumstances of the offense *and the history and characteristics of the defendant*;
>
> (2) the need for the sentence imposed—
>
> (A) to reflect the seriousness of the offense, to promote respect for the law, and to provide just punishment for the offense;
>
> (B) to afford adequate deterrence to criminal conduct;
>
> (C) to protect the public from further crimes of the defendant; and
>
> (D) to provide the defendant with needed educational, or vocational training, medical care, or other correctional treatment in the most effective manner.

These considerations and needs would seemingly permit the exercise of broad judicial discretion in fulfilling the statutory mandate of "determining the particular sentence" that is "sufficient but not greater than necessary." That discretion, fully exercised, would have permitted the very disparities the Sentencing Reform Act was intended to eliminate and it added a critical provision that limited sentencing courts by requiring them to confine their sentences within the limits set by applicable guideline ranges:

> the court shall impose a sentence of the kind and within the range, referred to in subsection (a)(4), unless the court finds that there exists an aggravating or mitigating circumstance of a kind, or to a degree, not adequately taken into consideration by the Sentencing Commission in formulating the guidelines that should result in a sentence different from that described (18 USC § 3553(b)(1)).

Pursuant to the Sentencing Reform Act, the United States Sentencing Commission was established and it promulgated a complex and detailed set of mandatory sentencing regulations, modified periodically, that are known as the Sentencing Guidelines (USSC 2015a). These guidelines required sentencing courts to determine, at the conclusion of a process that entailed consideration of a pre-sentence report prepared by the U.S. Probation Office and sentencing memoranda submitted by the parties and a sentencing hearing, the applicable guidelines sentencing range and whether or not to sentence below, within or above the applicable range. The applicable range was to be determined from a dual-axis grid that used Guidelines measures of criminal history and seriousness of the offense to lead the court to the intersection that set a permissible range in months of imprisonment. The guidelines assigned predetermined measures of seriousness to criminal histories and to specific offenses and characteristics of those offenses, and sentencing courts were compelled to engage in an oft-times challenging task of determining what provisions and corresponding points applied and then, except as permitted by the Sentencing Guidelines themselves or the exception noted above, to sentence within the range.

The progressive legislative intentions that gave rise to the Sentencing Guidelines did not meet with favorable responses from the defense bar and many judges, who opposed the formulaic and largely impersonal calculation of sentences and the substantial increase of sentence length for most defendants under the new Guidelines. They responded by trying to shift focus to provisions in the Guidelines that allowed for mitigation, referred to as "departures" from the offense level and criminal history category-driven sentences, or the broader statutory provision allowing for a sentence outside the range if the court found "a mitigating circumstance of a kind, or to a degree, not adequately taken into consideration by the Sentencing Commission in formulating the guidelines" (18 USC § 3553(b)(1)). In 2005 the legal obstacles to more flexible sentencing, particularly consideration of mitigating factors, were ameliorated when the Supreme Court held the Guidelines unconstitutional insofar as they were mandatory and, instead, they were salvaged by treating them as advisory (*Booker* 2005). They still must be calculated in all cases and the applicable range must be weighed as an important sentencing factor, indeed as a benchmark, but sentencing judges have greater leeway in sentencing outside the range to achieve the fundamental statutory purposes of sentencing as tailored to the individual and the specific offense.

This rather mystical sounding and complex legal sentencing context radically changed sentencing practices and led defense attorneys to recognize the value of forensic psychiatric expertise in the service of sentencing mitigation. Even when mandatory, the Guidelines contained provisions that opened this door. The 1986 Sentencing Reform Act mandated that sentencing courts consider "the history and characteristics of the defendant," (18 USC § 3553(a)(1)) and the Sentencing Guidelines addressed this, to some extent, in a section entitled "Specific Offender Characteristics." This section identified various basic characteristics and it classified them, variously, as not relevant or not ordinarily relevant or relevant in deciding if departure from the otherwise applicable sentencing range may be warranted. Two of these provisions expressly related to an offender's mental health: one addressing diminished capacity and the other, more broadly, mental and emotional conditions.

The Sentencing Commission authorized sentencing courts to depart downward for diminished capacity, but it defined the concept narrowly and limited its scope in a way that rendered it generally unavailing, even with a finding that the defendant had diminished capacity at the time of the offense. The rule stated:

> A downward departure may be warranted if (1) the defendant committed the offense while suffering from a significantly reduced mental capacity; and (2) the significantly reduced mental capacity contributed significantly to the commission of offense. Similarly, if a departure is warranted under this policy statement, the extent of the departure should reflect the extent to which the reduced mental capacity contributed to the commission of the offense. (USSC 2015a, §5K2.13)

The Guidelines defined "significantly reduced mental capacity" as "a significantly impaired ability to (A) understand the wrongfulness of the behavior comprising the offense or to exercise the power of reason; or (B) control behavior that the defendant knows if wrongful" (USSC 2015a, §5K2.13). The utility of this basis for mitigation for offenders with diminished mental capacity, even if well established by credible forensic expert testimony, was reduced by the second prong of the policy statement:

> However, the court may not depart below the applicable guideline range if (1) the significantly reduced mental capacity was caused by the voluntary use of drugs or other intoxicants; (2) the facts and circumstances of the defendant's offense indicate a need to protect the public because the offense involved actual violence or serious threat of violence; (3) the defendant's criminal history indicates a need to incarcerate the defendant to protect the public; or (4) the defendant has been convicted of [specified sex offenses]. (USSC 2015a, §5K2.13)

The possible presence and applicability of the disqualifying factors might well weigh against raising diminished capacity as a basis for sentencing mitigation, but the question of mental capacity—even if excluded under the Guidelines—is one that was raised under the mandatory guidelines and is raised under the now-advisory guidelines as an important element of a defendant's "history and characteristics." To do so persuasively, attorneys routinely rely on the expertise of forensic psychiatrists who can both develop the essential background developmental and psychiatric history and present the type of thorough, detailed and neutral report and opinion that courts will credit.

A less restrictive guideline specific offense characteristic addresses mental and emotional conditions more generally:

> Mental and emotional conditions may be relevant in determining whether a departure is warranted, if such conditions, individually or in combination with other characteristics, are present to an unusual degree and distinguish the case from the typical cases covered by the guidelines …
>
> In certain cases a downward departure may be appropriate to accomplish a specific treatment purpose … (USSC 2015a. § 5H1.3)

This policy statement lacks any requirement of a causal nexus with the offense and has no disqualifying limitations. As such, it is the focus for most mental health-oriented sentencing mitigation. Indeed, one of the foremost issues explored by defense counsel, where guilt has been established by plea or trial, is whether the defendant suffered from mental health problems that could mitigate against a guideline driven sentence and, if so, would they be best developed and presented by a forensic psychiatrist.

The magnitude of the possible role for forensic psychiatry in the criminal sentencing process, particularly the open guilty plea practice in federal court that leaves judges to impose specific sentences based on the statutory factors and advisory guidelines discussed above, can be seen from statistics and data reported by the United States Sentencing Commission. On a quarterly and annual basis the Commission publishes reports detailing criminal dispositions, broken down by district, appellate region and national, and, of particular interest for mitigation purposes, the numbers and percentages of below-guidelines sentences. While the data does not reflect the extent of mental health oriented departures, it demonstrates, with regional variation, the general willingness of sentencing courts to find grounds for sentencing below calculated ranges. In fiscal year 2014 the Commission analyzed 75,836 sentences imposed by federal judges, 4,192 from the Second Circuit, and 355 from the District of Connecticut (USSC 2015b). Nationally, only 46% of sentences were within the guideline range and a mere 0.5% were above the range. In the Second Circuit, which covers New York, Vermont, and Connecticut, the numbers were more favorable for defendants: 30.1% of the sentences were within the guideline range and 0.3% were above the range. In Connecticut, even fewer sentences were within the guideline range. There, only 26.5% of sentences fell within the guideline range and all but 0.3% of the departures were below range. Although the frequency of below-range sentences is less in other parts of the country, the national average is above half for such sentences, reflecting a significant receptivity to mitigating factors.

The implication of this data in the realm of federal sentencing for forensic psychiatry is that criminal defense counsel will look to psychiatrists to develop and present reports and testimony documenting the nature and extent of defendants' mental health problems, the relationship of those problems to defendants' criminal histories and immediate offenses, and the opportunities to effectively manage and reduce the risk of reoffending through treatment. The considerations are built into the sentencing statute, are not excluded by the Sentencing Guidelines, are frequently relied upon by defense counsel, and can be instrumental and persuasive in sentence mitigation. The well-developed expert evidence provided by forensic psychiatrists can be the essential neutral evidence that sentencing courts may accept as valid in the otherwise adversarial process.

REFERENCES

Booker v. United States, 543 U.S. 220 (2005).

Daubert v. Merrell Dow Pharmaceuticals, Inc., 509 U.S. 579 (1993).

Kumho Tire Co. v. Carmichael, 526 U.S. 137 (1999).

18 United States Code (USC) § 3551 et seq.

18 United States Code (USC) §§ 3553(a)(1) and (b)(1).

United States Sentencing Commission (USSC). 2015a. Guidelines Manual.

———. 2015b. Statistical Information Packet Second Circuit Fiscal Year 2014.

United States v. Cohen, 510 F. 3rd 1114 (9th Cir. 2007).

Weinstein, J.B. 2008. *Weinstein's Federal Evidence, Second Edition.* 702.02[1].

CHAPTER 2

Contribution of Peer (Consumer) Providers to Change in Forensic Practice

Michael Rowe, Chyrell Bellamy,
Patricia Benedict, and Larry Davidson

INTRODUCTION

Peer-provided services for people with mental illnesses have grown exponentially over the past fifteen years. Deployment of persons with histories of mental illness as mental health providers has been described as vital for transformation of mental health care systems to a recovery orientation in the U.S., most notably in the 2003 President's New Freedom Commission report (USDHHS 2003). Since 1999, many states have secured Medicaid reimbursement for peer services (CMS 2005), and the Veterans Administration has mandated that all its facilities hire peer specialists (Chinman, Shoai, and Cohen 2010). Between 2002 and 2006, the Centers for Medicare & Medicaid Services granted over $125 million in systems change efforts emphasizing peer-based services, most of these for persons with serious mental illnesses (Davidson 2013; Chinman et al. 2014).

The inclusion of peer-provided services in mental health care, which is outside the context of mutual support groups, dates from the early 1990s, with people in recovery from mental illness being hired and trained to provide a variety of supports, often as assistants to case managers. In the past decade, however, use of peer staff in mental health care has shifted toward the unique role and skills of peers who self-disclose as being in recovery from mental illness and who provide services distinct from traditional case management. Peer services oriented toward the needs of persons with forensic histories, however, are comparatively new, and little research has been published on their effectiveness (Davidson et al. 2006). Provision of forensic peer services for persons with criminal charges and current or recent incarceration involves special challenges, including entry into prisons for peers with previous criminal charges, the potential for tension between peer-based services and the culture and legalities of forensic mental health care, and the related question of how to deliver recovery-oriented care under conditions of constraint, with strong psychiatric and sometimes lay supervision through forensic review boards.

In this chapter we begin by reviewing the nature of peer support in mental health care and our own and others' research on peer services. We then discuss forensic peer support and our research and training in this area, including forensic peer specialist outreach and support as an alternative to outpatient commitment, and peers as a core component of citizenship-based interventions for persons with previous criminal charges. We follow with a brief review of citizenship-informed forensic peer training for work in and outside of prisons. Finally, we turn to a discussion of key themes, challenges, and responses in regard to the deployment of peers as staff in forensic settings.

"GENERIC" PEER SERVICES IN CLINICAL CARE AND RELEVANT RESEARCH

While people in recovery can provide conventional services, peer support *per se* involves, and is thought to derive its benefits from, individuals' self-disclosure of their disability and recovery and their willingness to draw on their experience in their work with clients. Unlike peer to peer support as practiced in Alcoholics Anonymous (AA), Narcotics Anonymous (NA), and behavioral health advocacy groups, peer services in conventional mental health care involve unidirectional relationships in which peer mentors or specialists provide supports intended to help their clients, not themselves.

Key elements of peer support are: The *instillation of hope through positive self-disclosure*, demonstrating to clients that they can gain some control over their illness; *role modeling*, including self-care and use of "street smarts" to negotiate day-to-day life and service systems in the context of poverty, stigma, and discrimination; *the unique relationship of peer providers and recipients*, characterized by trust and acceptance, understanding and empathy; and the peer provider's credibility for having "been there" (Mead, Hilton, and Curtis 2001; Solomon 2004; Davidson et al. 2006).

Peer support in contemporary mental health care occurs in the overarching context and framework of personal and social recovery for people with mental illnesses and in the related context of efforts to transform mental health care and systems to recovery perspectives and practices. Recursively, peer support in mental health care provides concrete illustrations of recovery in practice. Peer staff embody the capabilities of people with mental illness, including severe and persistent mental illness, to work at high levels in mentoring and providing emotional and practical supports to people with the life challenges of mental illness and the associated and complicating challenges of stigma and discrimination, trauma, poverty, and lack of valued roles in society.

Peer support, while not constituting clinical care, both points out some of the limitations of clinical care and challenges clinical care to link itself with supports that nourish the whole person. Regarding the latter, peer staff, as above, convey to clients a shared experience of having "been there." They also convey to clients in their actions, words, and "presence," that mental illness is only a part of one's life and that the hope for positive change is not an idle one. These aspects of peer support are not unique—clinicians and case managers may talk with clients about their own life challenges. They also understand that their clients face difficulties of poverty and lack of mainstream opportunities. They, too, can communicate hope to their clients and demonstrate hope and belief in them as individuals. Yet research (as discussed below) has shown that there is "something special" and different about peer staff's ability to provide these benefits.

Peer support integrated into clinical care contributes to the transformation of systems of mental health care to a recovery orientation and foundation in principle and practice. While peer support is not treatment, its inclusion on clinical teams testifies to its relevance to clinical care and of expanding care to include attention to the lived experience of clients in their everyday lives outside clinical treatment. This is not to say that clinical staff lack such knowledge. Given that their training often focuses on narrower individual and intrapsychic issues, however, and that care provided in institutions in which charting and licensing requirements may privilege risk and safety concerns over "having a full life," peer staff may provide needed reminders and support for inclusion of these issues as part of well-rounded clinical care. One current model for this process is that of linking psychosocial services and supports to clinical care.

Integration of peer staff into clinical care is not without its difficulties and tensions. In our own practice and research over the past two decades, the following three are examples of issues and concerns that may arise at clinician-clinical team and administrative-system levels. For each concern, we suggest potential responses to it, and a brief assessment of its validity:

- *Mental health care is stressful work.* "People with mental illness may be too fragile to engage in such difficult work, which may exacerbate their own illness or cause it to recur after remission." *Response*: Work of all sorts can be stressful. Living in poverty, often accompanied by a lack of meaningful and valued activities, is stressful too. Living in such conditions may have a negative impact on one's self-image and view of one's prospects. Per the Americans with Disabilities Act of 1990 (http://www.ada.gov/), however, some peer staff may at times require "reasonable accommodations" for periods of mental health difficulties. Such accommodations may have an impact on the workload of clinical teams, but significant accommodations are often made for non-disabled people as well, during times of personal or family crisis or other concerns. In any case, the ADA is the law.
- *Lack of training.* "Non-professionals, especially those with their own mental health difficulties, are not equipped to work with people with serious mental illnesses. This is just too much to expect of them." *Response*: Peer staff provide support and role modeling not clinical care. Research has suggested the particular effectiveness of peer staff support for people with serious and persistent mental illnesses. That said, peer staff, like other staff, require support and supervision in what can often be difficult and stressful work.
- *Boundary issues.* "Maintaining proper boundaries is a core principle of clinical care. The difficulty of doing so increases for peer staff, who may identify more closely with their clients than do clinical staff, may know and have had friendly contacts with their clients in the past as clients in the same care institution, and may be more likely to have been or be neighbors, fellow students, friends, etc. with clients in the local community." *Response*: Boundaries vary by the nature of the work. As peer staff are not providing clinical care, it follows that the boundaries they should maintain with clients need not mirror those of clinical staff. Still, boundaries do exist for peer staff. Peer support in mental health care is not mutual—from one peer to another—but unidirectional—from the peer staff person to the client. Thus while peer staff may have somewhat more casual and friendly relationships with clients due to the nature of the work they do, boundary issues still arise. These problems are a proper concern in supervision for peer staff, as they are for clinical staff. Previous connections of friendship or shared experiences may in some cases, but rarely in our experience, lead to decisions not to assign a peer staff member to a given client, or to

reassign the client to another peer staff member. Such decisions, however, may well occur with regard to clinical staff with their clients.

Research on "peers who disclose" as providers of care has not kept pace with their growing presence in mental health programs. Our own research has demonstrated that: (a) peer-run groups may be able to decrease recidivism related to social isolation, demoralization, and lack of self-efficacy among persons with mental illness and increase outpatient service use (Davidson et al. 2000); (b) peer-run groups can generate benefits such as increased social functioning, reductions in problems associated with alcohol and money spent on alcohol, and increased benefit from skills training (Wexler et al. 2008); (c) peers can facilitate person-centered care planning, increase people's sense of ability to change their lives and manage their illness, decrease their psychotic symptoms, and increase community integration (Tondora et al. 2010); and (d) peer support may decrease re-hospitalizations among people with histories of frequent hospitalizations (Bellack 2006; Davidson et al. 2005; Davidson and Roe 2007; Sledge et al. 2011). In summary, by facilitating a person-centered care planning process, peer staff can enhance the responsiveness of mental health care and help clients gain greater sense of control and ability to make positive changes in their lives.

FORENSIC PEER SERVICES AND SUPPORT

Forensic peer support involves trained peer specialists with histories of mental illness and criminal charges helping those with similar histories, with an emphasis on understanding the impact of the culture of incarceration on their behavior and recognition of trauma and post-traumatic stress disorder that are prevalent among this population (Davidson and Rowe 2007). As with "generic" peer support, forensic peer specialists' most important functions may be to instill hope and serve as credible models of personal recovery and of retrieval of a participating and valued life in society. Forensic peer specialists also help justice-involved persons re-entering their home communities to engage in treatment and support services and to anticipate and address the psychological, social, and financial challenges of re-entry. They may help returning individuals adhere to conditions of supervision, such as probation and parole, while serving as community guides, coaches, and advocates who link their clients to housing, jobs or vocational and educational services, and behavioral health treatment. They may model useful skills, and help to reduce the risk for relapse and other crises through one-to-one support. Forensic peer specialists may also provide additional supports such as sharing their experiences as returning offenders and modeling their own recoveries, encouraging clients to let go of attitudes and behaviors learned as survival mechanisms in criminal justice settings that are maladaptive outside of them, providing clients with information on rights and responsibilities of discharged offenders and on satisfying criminal justice system requirements and conditions, accompanying clients to initial probation meetings or treatment appointments, and encouraging them to engage in mental health and substance abuse treatment and attend abstinence-based mutual support groups.

Forensic-peer research and training. Two of our studies suggest that peer staff develop working alliances with "difficult-to-engage" patients more quickly than non-peers and that among people with co-occurring substance use disorders, peer support appears to contribute to decreased alcohol and other substance use. We note that the first of these two studies—the Peer Engagement Specialist Project—stretches the definition of forensic peer supports in that, while many participants had previous justice system involvement, this was not a requirement of participation. We discuss the study here because of its relevance to our theme and because participants who did not have previous criminal charges were, in most cases, at risk of it. We also briefly discuss our combined peer and forensic peer specialist training program.

The Peer Engagement Specialist Project. In 2000, the Connecticut Legislature was considering passage of an outpatient commitment statute for persons with mental illness who are unengaged in, or who refuse, treatment and who have histories of violence or the threat of violence against self or others. Under the proposed legislation, a judge presented with evidence that the person met the target criteria could mandate treatment, including forced medication, for the individual. Some mental health experts were in favor of the statute, which appeared likely to pass. Advocacy groups in the state, however, approached key legislators and proposed the alternative of hiring and deploying peer staff on several community-based treatment teams that worked with members of the target group, with an evaluation to determine their effectiveness in persuading the target group to enter treatment. The Connecticut Legislature agreed and funded the program and the Yale Institution for Policy Studies funded the research.

Eight full-time equivalent Peer Engagement Specialists, two in each of four community-based treatment teams across the state, were hired, and received broad-based didactic, experiential, and practical training in applying their personal experiences to work effectively with clients. At all sites, peer providers carried an average caseload of ten to twelve clients and received guidance from clinical supervisors. Traditional providers who participated in the project worked in tandem with peer providers and typically carried twice the peer provider caseload. Peer staff were hired and trained specifically to draw on their personal histories of mental illness as a means of enhancing their credibility with the target population and as a vehicle for increasing hope, modeling self-care, and demonstrating the benefits of participation in treatment. In addition to attending to their clients' basic needs, they aimed to enhance clients' access to social and leisure activities and valued social roles.

In a randomized controlled trial of the project, we compared the quality of treatment relationships and engagement in peer-based and regular case management. We also assessed the value of positive relationship qualities in predicting motivation for and use of community-based services and support groups. One hundred and thirty-seven adults with serious and persistent mental illnesses who met the target criteria were enrolled and participated in a prospective randomized clinical trial with two levels of intervention—peer specialist and case management (peer), and case management alone (regular), with baseline and six- and twelve-month follow-up interviews assessing treatment relationships, motivation, and service use, along with clinician ratings of participants' initial engagement and monthly attendance in treatment.

Results showed that participants perceived higher positive regard, understanding, and acceptance from peer providers rather than from regular providers at six-month follow-up, with initially unengaged clients showing more contacts with case managers in the peer condition and decreasing contacts in the regular condition. Six-month positive regard and understanding positively predicted twelve-month treatment motivation for psychiatric, alcohol, and drug use problems and attendance at Alcoholics and Narcotics Anonymous meetings. In addition, regression analysis showed an association at six months between improved quality of life and fewer obstacles to recovery and the experience of *invalidation*, that is, critical comments regarding their behavior, from peer staff. These statistically significant findings at six months, as with those regarding higher positive regard, understanding, and acceptance, were not found at twelve-month follow-up. While further research would be required to understand fully the reasons for this difference, hypotheses to be tested in such research, partly through qualitative methods, might be that that the novelty of peer support may diminish for clients over time as they begin to see peers as providers of services much like others, or that non-peer staff "catch up" with peer staff with regard to conveying acceptance of and regard for their clients (possibly influenced by the example of peer staff).

The Peer Engagement Specialist study provided the first indication that peer providers possess distinctive skills in communicating positive regard, understanding, and acceptance to clients and a facility for increasing treatment participation among the most disengaged clients, leading to greater motivation for further treatment and use of peer-based community services. Thus peer providers may serve a valued role in quickly forging therapeutic connections with persons typically considered to be among the most alienated from the health care service system. The findings also suggest that peer providers may be effective in fostering clients' progress by challenging attitudes, values, and behaviors that may undermine their recovery (Jewell, Davidson, and Rowe 2006; Sells et al. 2006; Sells et al. 2008).

The Citizenship Intervention. The Citizenship Intervention (CI) is an ongoing non-clinical individual- and group-level social intervention based on an applied theoretical framework of citizenship as a means of supporting the social inclusion of people with mental illnesses. We have defined citizenship as a strong connection to the "five Rs" of *rights*, *responsibilities*, *roles*, and *resources* that society offers to people through public and social institutions, and *relationships* involving associational life in one's community. Citizenship complements individual recovery by focusing on the social elements required to achieve full membership in a democratic society (Rowe et al. 2001). The citizenship framework is derived from research on outreach to persons who are homeless (Rowe 1999) and the clinical practice of jail diversion (Rowe and Baranoski 2000), as well as from social science theories emphasizing civic participation as a measure of one's involvement in society (Durkheim 1933; Bellah et al. 1996). We use the past tense below to describe the CI, as evaluated, from the ongoing CI project. The initial, evaluated intervention has been modified somewhat over time, including extending the intervention from four to six months.

The CI consisted of three integrated components: individual peer mentor support, an eight-week citizenship class, and an eight-week valued role component, followed by a graduation ceremony. *Peer mentor support* involved matching individual CI participants with a peer mentor to help them identify goals and set priorities for achieving them, to share coping strategies and lessons learned as people working on their own recoveries, and to advocate for participants' access to social services, employment, education, and housing. This component spanned the citizenship classes and valued role projects.

The citizenship class enhanced participants' (students') problem-solving and other life skills for daily living, their ability to establish social networks based on mutual trust and shared interests, and their knowledge of available community resources. A (non-clinician) director facilitated twice-weekly two-hour classes of six to ten participants over an eight-week period. Classes were led by the project director, a peer mentor, or individuals from the community or service system (e.g. a staff person from the local housing authority, a business owner talking about the qualities he looks for in an employee etc.).

Class topics included "negotiating" the criminal justice system, assertiveness training and self-advocacy, problem-solving and time management, relationship building, self-help groups, housing in the local community, vocational and educational resources, social integration, public speaking, and others. Class content consisted of didactic presentations, group discussions, class exercises, and assignments.

Following completion of the class component, students drew on their life experiences and class learning to design and participate in an eight-week valued role project that involved "giving back" to the community while teaching community members that people with mental illnesses and criminal histories can fulfill valued roles in society. Students chose to conduct either group or individual valued role projects. In one valued role project, students conducted a training for cadets at a local police academy on how to approach people who are homeless, and may have mental illnesses, on the street. A student who chose an individual, rather than a group, valued role project cooked Thanksgiving dinner for her family, a part of her community in which she had been seen as someone who could only receive, not give. In taking on this valued role, she proved otherwise to her family and herself (Rowe 2015).

Our study of the CI assessed its effectiveness in reducing psychiatric symptoms, alcohol and drug use, and increasing quality of life for persons with serious mental illness and criminal charges within two years previous to enrollment. One hundred and fourteen adults participated in a randomized controlled trial of the four-month citizenship intervention versus usual services. Linear mixed model analyses were used to assess the intervention's impact on quality of life, symptoms, and substance use. After controlling for baseline covariates, participants in the experimental (citizenship) condition reported significantly increased quality of life, greater satisfaction with and amount of activity, higher satisfaction with work, and reduced alcohol and drug use over time. However, participants in the citizenship condition also reported increased anxiety/depression and agitation at six months (but not twelve months) and significantly increased negative symptoms at twelve months (Clayton et al. 2013; Rowe 2015). Our findings suggest that community-oriented citizenship interventions for persons with serious mental illness and criminal histories may facilitate improved clinical and community outcomes in some domains, with some negative clinical findings suggesting the need for post intervention peer mentor support for intervention participants. While our study design did not enable us to distinguish the separate impact of each of the three program components, our findings are suggestive of the positive impact of forensic peer specialists on the progress that the CI fostered in participants' lives.

Forensic Peer Training. In 2013, we designed and provided what we believe to be the most extensive, if not the first ever, training in forensic peer specialist work for Peerstar, Inc., a for-profit organization that provides citizenship-informed peer counseling and support for persons with mental illness both prior to and following discharge from jails and prisons in six Pennsylvania counties. The training combined both "generic" and forensic peer components.

Generic peer training draws on elements of both Intentional Peer Support (Mead, Hilton, and Curtis 2001) and person-centered planning (Kincaid et al. 2005). Key topic areas and themes include "listening differently," "connection vs. disconnection," "having hope," "making choices," "starting over again and again," "having the same rights as others," "doing everyday things," "staying clean from my drug of choice," "looking forward to life," and "being looked at as a whole person." A feature of both the generic and forensic portions of the training is that of attending to the skills and approaches required of peer specialists, *and* of counseling peer trainees on ways to keep in touch with and address their own personal responses to the work, as persons in recovery who may still struggle with some of the same issues regarding which they counsel and support their clients. Self-care and self-awareness, with good supervision and support, are emphasized throughout.

The second half of the training involves working with people with current or past incarcerations. Key topics and themes are reconnecting with family and friends; working through emotions; post-release issues while still incarcerated; working with probation or parole; outpatient and residential mandated programs; seeking employment with a criminal record; addressing gaps in work history; interactions with police; and race, culture, sex, and gender issues. For brevity's sake, we review here key points of discussion and counseling with clients in regard to only two of these topics—"reconnecting with family members" and "issues while incarcerated."

Reconnecting with family members includes talking with clients about the current status of their relationships with family members and asking them if they have legal restrictions regarding contact with them. Forensic Peer Specialists (Peers) are counseled to help clients identify possible positive and negative results of reuniting with family members. If some negative results are likely, Peers should talk with clients about how to make contact with the least amount of negative impact, through sending letters or cards or making phone calls, as examples, before making face-to-face meetings. If clients are prohibited from visiting their children, they may be able to send a letter or card. Finally, family members may expect returning persons to be changed or fully recovered from past behavior and problems. Peers talk to their clients about how to prepare themselves and respond to such expectations.

Issues while incarcerated involve both instrumental and expressive elements, and sometimes both at once. Instrumental issues include beginning to help the client address, while still incarcerated, basic needs of housing, obtaining standard means of identification (i.e. not only a Corrections I.D., which may not be accepted for many purposes and in any case is highly stigmatizing); seeking employment or applying or reapplying for disability entitlement income, connecting or reconnecting with health and behavioral health care including medications; and understanding and meeting probation and parole stipulations including child support, attendance at mandated programs, restitution, protective orders, and more. Expressive issues include reconnecting with family and friends as above and feelings of powerlessness and anger over (mis)treatment from correction officers, other inmates, and family and friends while incarcerated. Feelings of powerlessness and anger may be mixed and complicated with guilt over clients' roles in difficult situations, even if the client was coerced, was acting in self-defense, or acting in other ways that are normative in prison settings but unacceptable outside them.

Peers are encouraged to share their re-entry experiences, if acceptable in the working relationship. Peers should listen and empathize, validating their client's feelings and perceptions even if they have not shared the experience that prompted them. They should explore re-entry plans with their clients, gathering resource information from the communities to which they will be released. Peers should also explore with clients their plans for taking up and maintaining healthy and positive behaviors upon community re-entry. Perhaps as importantly as showing empathy toward their clients and providing them with practical information, Peers must encourage their patience with, and realistic expectations of, themselves and family and others during community re-entry. Peers may also discuss with their clients the process of obtaining a pardon, even if the official pardon itself is five or more years down the road. Finally, Peers should remind and encourage their clients to follow the rules of their prison or jail facility to the letter as they plan for their release and community re-entry.

FORENSIC PEER SUPPORT MEETS FORENSIC PSYCHIATRIC TREATMENT

The practice of forensic peer specialist work, based in recovery and citizenship frameworks, has points of tension with forensic psychiatry treatment, given that the latter must respond to the public safety agendas of judges and other key figures, and of the public at large. The consequences for persons with mental illness who have been remanded to incarceration or to forensic psychiatric hospitalization, which are by no means the same thing but that we consider together for this discussion, include but are not limited to delays in discharge from inpatient forensic care, and post-discharge supervision and other constraints as for other offenders but with the added stigma and discrimination associated with mental illness. It is critical to note that these "points of tension" occur in professional-theoretical and legal, institutional, and socio-structural and cultural contexts that affect both peer and psychiatric practices, albeit with major differences in power and privileges for each. We briefly discuss each of these contexts, in turn.

Professional-theoretical and legal contexts. Forensic peer specialists (Peers) and psychiatrists (or other mental health professionals) both have concerns for the well-being of persons with mental illness and forensic involvement. Forensic peers provide practical and emotional support and advocacy for forensic clients, or patients, in the contexts of recovery and/or citizenship frameworks aimed at empowering them to take charge of their lives and achieve full and valued membership in society. Forensic health care professionals provide mental health treatment while, at the same time, having legal responsibilities and the power to weigh their patients' needs in the context of public safety, regardless of the fact that public fears about violence among persons with mental illness are highly exaggerated. Individual forensic psychiatrists' and psychologists' assessment of their patients' recovery prospects vary from more to less aligned with those of forensic peers. Our own experience is that there is a gradual, if slow, shift in favor of peers' abilities to act as mentors, role models, and trusted counselors of forensic-involved persons. Among forensic professionals with whom we are in contact, this shift is sometimes linked with a favorable view of recovery-related frameworks, and sometimes more practically oriented toward the skills of peer staff themselves. In either case, the shift also appears to be related to a gradual shift in the public mental health field in general toward hiring and deploying peer staff in care settings and teams. While forensic care lags behind other domains of mental health care (which themselves have far to go to achieve maximal deployment of peer staff), this general shift toward acceptance, along with Medicaid reimbursement for peer work in most states, may have a positive impact on forensic practice. Such shifts will not be merely attitudinal but will draw on what we anticipate will be a growing evidence-base for forensic peer services and supports. Forensic peers, on the other hand, are learning that (as is the case for work with people who have representative payees and other constraints) recovery, citizenship, and empowerment are, if anything, more needed by persons with mental illness and forensic involvement *because of* the multiple constraints under which they live.

Institutional contexts. Institutional issues for the deployment of peers in forensic hospital and prison settings include entry, acceptance, and boundaries around their work within those settings. Peers with incarceration histories may be barred from entering prisons to work with inmates, and may be more informally barred from working in forensic inpatient units. Administrative support and shifts in local, regional, and state authority support for innovation can help to pave the way for entry of peers in these settings. Concerns about the impact of peer deployment on staff employment may slow the effective entry of peers in these settings. Our own experience is that administrative support, previous innovations, focused deployment, and an overarching philosophy or institutional plan and direction can support the success of forensic peer initiatives. In a state psychiatric hospital in Connecticut, for example, the CEO has led collaborative community efforts among staff and patients to reduce violence in all hospital units, with positive results. This effort helped to create an environment in which forensic peer work in the context of developing a citizenship project for forensic patients who are transitioning, gradually, to community re-entry has, at this early date, been favorably received.

Socio-structural and cultural contexts. Persons with mental illness and forensic involvement face positive and negative social and cultural realities. On one hand, a shift toward reducing incarceration and focusing on community re-entry supports has occurred in public and policy domains in the U.S. On the other, well-publicized tragedies of killings committed by, or suspected to have been committed by, persons with mental illnesses undermine the impact of such positive trends. These current conditions have their own long historical foundations, and change will come slowly. In our own experience, we see some positive trends as well as significant barriers. We see forensic trainees who are more interested in and attentive to the impact of social conditions of poverty and social and health care inequities on the psychiatric problems and overall well-being of persons with mental illnesses than was the case only a few years ago. We also see, and are involved with acting on, a growing, if still tentative, use of peers in prison and forensic inpatient settings. We also live and conduct services research in the state in which the Sandy Hook tragedy occurred and continues to have an impact on public attitudes. Overall, however, it appears to us that interest in, or consideration of, the potential contribution of peer staff in forensic settings is on a gradual upward slope.

CONCLUSION

Forensic Peer Specialists embody the potential for recovery for people who confront the dual stigmas associated with serious mental illnesses and criminal justice system involvement. Forensic Peer Specialists are able to provide critical aid to persons in the early stages of re-entry, in much the same way that peer specialists who support peers with mental illness "alone" have been able to engage into treatment persons with serious mental illnesses (Solomon 2004; Sledge et al. 2011). We anticipate that continuing practice and research will provide better answers regarding the effectiveness of peer and forensic peer support beyond the engagement phase, and are encouraged by initial findings on forensic peer services and supports delivered within recovery- and citizenship-based applied frameworks.

There are considerable challenges to the integration of forensic peers into clinical forensic practice. A question put to us recently by a highly experienced forensic psychiatrist who is sympathetic to the inclusion of peers, while related to themes discussed above, merits brief discussion here in closing out this chapter. His question was, "Can clinicians and teams be confident that forensic peers will report evidence of risk of harm to self or others that patients confide to them?" This question was prefaced by the expert's comment that some colleagues believed, or had been told, that forensic peer-patient discussions were confidential, even from the rest of the clinical team. We suggest that the question and the assumption behind it raise two main issues: first, the developmental stages of peer integration into clinical care, including understanding the nature of peer-patient interactions, and second, a debate within the peer support community itself.

The process of integrating peer staff into clinical care is characterized by an understandable clinician lack of knowledge of just what it is that peer staff do and how this is manifested in peer staff-peer-patient interactions. Peer staff reach out, as "people who have been there" and as people in a recovery process that includes one's "whole" life—goals and dreams, relationships, work, and community and society. This is by no means to say that non-peer clinicians share no such interests or discussions with their patients, but that these are central concerns of peer staff and at the core of their unique ability to engage with their peers. (We should also note, again, that our research shows that peer staff have a unique ability to engage "unengaged" people *into* treatment and self-help groups.) Peer staff, while they are not trained and, we argue, do not need to conduct risk assessments (that's what clinicians do), never minimize what they see as extreme or volatile behavior of peer-patients. Their approach, however, is to explore with these clients ways to address their current situation including, at times, persuading them to seek help from their clinicians. We note that such dilemmas occur frequently even in such innovative practice as mental health outreach to people who are homeless, which host tensions between non-clinical staff who may "err" on the side of client autonomy in their reluctance to call in the team psychiatrist to assess a client's possible need for commitment to inpatient care, and clinicians who may "err" on the side of coercion in the same situation. These differences are discussed and debated, and lead to best-judgment decisions, after avenues of persuasion and collaboration with the client have been fully explored (Rowe et al. 2002).

And yet there is a debate, and there are differences of opinion, in the peer community on the question as to whether peers should contribute their unique talents to clinical care, possibly ending up as traditional mental health technicians in all but name, or should, instead, work outside traditional systems of care, offering peer-to-peer support and not being beholden to mental health teams with primarily clinical concerns, including risk assessment. It will have to suffice, here, to say that peers can and do take stands on both sides of these issues; that peers who work in clinical care including forensic clinical care take their work and responsibilities seriously, wishing to maintain their unique approaches but recognizing their co-responsibility to their teams; and that, in the early stages of this innovation in forensic practice, much further discussion needs to occur between peer staff and clinicians in regard to such important questions.

REFERENCES

Bellack, A.S. 2006. "Scientific and Consumer Models of Recovery in Schizophrenia: Concordance, Contrasts, and Implications." *Schizophrenia Bulletin* 32 (3): 432–42.

Bellah, R.N., R. Madsen, W.M. Sullivan, A. Swidler, and S.M. Tipton. 1996. *Habits of the Heart: Individualism and Commitment in American Life*. Berkeley: University of California Press.

Centers for Medicare & Medicaid Services (CMS). 2005. U.S. Department on Health and Human Services (DHHS). http://www.cms.hhs.gov/systemschange/compendium01-02.pdf. Baltimore, MD.

Chinman, M., P. George, R.H. Dougherty, A.S. Daniels, S.S. Ghose, A. Swift, and M.E. Delphin-Rittmon. 2014. "Peer Support Services for Individuals with Serious Mental Illnesses: Assessing the Evidence." *Psychiatric Services* 65 (4): 429–41.

Chinman M., R. Shoai, and A. Cohen. 2010. "Using Organizational Change Strategies to Guide Peer Support Technician Implementation in the Veterans Administration." *Psychiatric Rehabilitation Journal* 33 (4): 269–77.

Clayton, A., M.J. O'Connell, C. Bellamy, P. Benedict, and M. Rowe. 2013. "The Citizenship Project, Part II: Impact of a Citizenship Intervention on Clinical and Community Outcomes for Persons with Mental Illness and Criminal Justice Charges. *American Journal of Community Psychology* 51: 114–22.

Davidson, L. 2013. "Peer Support: Coming of Age or Miles to Go Before We Sleep?" *The Journal of Behavioral Health Services & Research* 42: 96–9.

Davidson, L., M. Chinman, D. Sells, and M. Rowe. 2006. "Peer Support Among Adults with Serious Mental Illness: A Report from the Field." *Schizophrenia Bulletin* 32: 443–50.

Davidson, L., M. O'Connell, J. Tondora, M.R. Staeheli, and A.C. Evans. 2005. "Recovery in Serious Mental Illness: A New Wine or Just a New Bottle?" *Professional Psychology: Research and Practice* 36 (5): 480–7.

Davidson, L. and D. Roe. 2007. "Recovery From Versus Recovery In Serious Mental Illness: One Strategy for Lessening Confusion Plaguing Recovery." *Journal of Mental Health* 16 (4): 1–12.

Davidson, L. and M. Rowe. 2007. *Peer Support within Criminal Justice Settings: The Role of Forensic Peer Specialists*. Delmar, NY: National GAINS Center.

Davidson, L., D.A. Stayner, M.J. Chinman, S. Lambert, and W.H. Sledge. 2000. "Preventing Relapse and Readmission in Psychosis: Using Patients' Subjective Experience in Designing Clinical Interventions." In *Outcome Studies in Psychological Treatments of Psychotic Condition*, edited by Brian Martindale, pp. 134–56. London: Gaskell Publishers.

Durkheim, E. 1933. *Division of Labor in Society*. Translated by George Simpson. New York: Free Press. London: Collier Macmillan.

Information and technical assistance on the Americans with Disabilities Act. http://www.ada.gov/index.html.

Jewell, C., L. Davidson, and M. Rowe. 2006. "The Paradox of Engagement: How Political, Organizational and Evaluative Demands Can Hinder Innovation in Community Mental Health Services." *Social Service Review* 8: 3–26.

Kincaid, D., J.T. Knab, and H.B. Clark. 2005. "Person-Centered Planning." *Mental Health Law & Policy Faculty Publications Paper No. 702*, http://scholarcommons.usf.edu/mhlp_facpub/702.

Mead, S., D. Hilton, and L. Curtis. 2001. "Peer Support: A Theoretical Perspective." *Psychiatric Rehabilitation Journal* 25: 134–41.

Rowe, Michael. 1999. *Crossing the Border: Encounters Between Homeless People and Outreach Workers*. Berkeley: University of California Press.

———. 2015. *Citizenship and Mental Health*. 2015. New York: Oxford University Press.

Rowe, M., J. Frey, M. Bailey, D. Fisk, and L. Davidson. 2002. "Clinical Responsibility and Client Autonomy: Dilemmas in Mental Health Work at the Margins." *American Journal of Orthopsychiatry* 71: 400–7.

Rowe, M., B. Kloos, M. Chinman, L. Davidson, and A.B. Cross. 2001. "Homelessness, Mental Illness, and Citizenship." *Social Policy and Administration* 35: 14–31.

Rowe, M. and M. Baranoski. 2000. "Mental Illness, Criminality, and Citizenship." *Journal of the American Academy of Psychiatry and the Law* 28: 262–4.

Sells, D., L. Davidson, C. Jewell, P. Falzer, and M. Rowe. 2006. "The Treatment Relationship in Peer-Based and Regular Case Management Services for Clients with Severe Mental Illness." *Psychiatric Services* 57 (8): 1179–84.

Sells, D., R. Black, L. Davidson, and M. Rowe. 2008. "Beyond Generic Support: The

Incidence and Impact of Invalidation Within Peer-Based and Traditional Treatment for Clients with Severe Mental Illness." *Psychiatric Services* 59 (11): 1322–7.

Sledge, W., M. Lawless, D. Sells, M. Wieland, M.J. O'Connell, and L. Davidson. 2011. "Effectiveness of Peer Support in Reducing Readmissions of Persons with Multiple Psychiatric Hospitalizations." *Psychiatric Services* 62 (5): 541–4.

Solomon, P. 2004. "Peer Support/Peer Provided Services: Underlying Processes, Benefits, and Critical Ingredients." *Psychiatric Rehabilitation Journal* 27 (4): 392–401.

Tondora, J., M. O'Connell, T. Dinzeo, R. Miller, C. Bellamy, R. Andres-Hyman, and L. Davidson. 2010. "A Clinical Trial of Peer-Based Culturally Responsive Person-Centered Care for Psychosis for African Americans and Latinos." *Clinical Trials* 7: 368–79.

U.S. Department of Health and Human Services (DHHS). 2003. *Achieving the Promise: Transforming Mental Health Care in America. President's New Freedom Commission on Mental Health. Final Report.* DHHS Pub. No. SMA-03-3832. Rockville, MD: U.S. Department of Health and Human Services.

Wexler, B., L. Davidson, T. Styron, and J.S. Strauss. 2008. "Severe and Persistent Mental Illness." In *40 Years of Academic Public Psychiatry*, edited by Selby C. Jacobs and Ezra E.H. Griffith, pp. 1–20. London: Wiley.

CHAPTER 3

Global Developments and Forensic Practice

Maya Prabhu and Bandy Lee

INTRODUCTION

Few images from 2015 have been so indelible as those of the exodus of migrants and refugees from Africa and the Middle East trying to make their way into Europe, by boat, by train, or by arduous trek. For some observers, the scenes of men, women, and children being met with barbed wire fences, armed police officers, or trains to "reception camps" painfully recollect the reason for the creation of the international framework put into place after World War II to help similarly displaced persons (Lyman 2015). When the United Nations High Commission on Refugees (UNHCR) was founded in 1951, its mandate was envisioned to be needed for only three years (UNHCR 2000). Sixty-five years later, the need for a global system to register, house, resettle, or repatriate millions is more critical than ever. On June 20, 2015, World Refugee Day, UNHCR reported that the increase in persons of concern in 2014 was the largest leap ever seen in one year, with an average of 42,500 people having left their home countries every day; in total over sixty million people are under UNHCR's auspices (UNHCR 2015a). The UN High Commissioner for Refugees described 2015 as a "moment of truth," calling on the world's wealthiest countries not to abandon the historical principle of sheltering refugees (UNHCR 2015b).

While there is ongoing debate as to whether individual countries have responded to these events as generously as they might have, many civil organizations and individual persons have stepped forward to assist. In particular, legal organizations and attorneys have built on existing models of pro bono engagement and advocacy (Johnson and Perez 1998) to develop an increasingly global model of immigration clinic (Hurwitz 2003). Most often involving close collaboration with law school programs, these clinics have had remarkable success in assisting persons seeking asylum, not just locally but abroad. These clinics have also created opportunities for a new forensic psychiatry service entity. Immigration legal teams often require forensic psychiatric expertise in a variety of ways, from referrals for forensic assessments of mental illness in order to establish asylum claims; to requests for guidance for treatment; to more personal consultation for the legal team members (Meffert et al. 2010; De Jesús-Rentas, Boehnlein, and Sparr 2010). This chapter describes one such model of psychiatric and legal collaboration to illustrate the dynamic interactive partnership of psychiatrists and lawyers, with a special focus on asylum seekers' cases. It also considers the impact of ethics and culture in this unique area of forensic practice.

LEGAL BACKGROUND

While asylum seekers and refugees are often portrayed as successfully negotiating resettlement through persistence or importunity alone, permanent legal resettlement is, in fact, a complex legal process, circumscribed by UNHCR's and receiving countries' specific immigration procedures. As defined by UNHCR, resettlement is the formal transfer of refugees from one asylum country to another state which has agreed to admit them. According to UNHCR, less than 1% of refugees are put forth for resettlement, which is the option of last resort after repatriation or integration into a country of refuge has been deemed unviable (UNHCR 2015c).

In the United States, the relevant legal framework is the Refugee Act of 1980, which incorporated the definition of refugees and asylees found in the 1951 international treaty, the Convention Relating to the Status of Refugees (U.S. Refugee Act 1980; UN General Assembly, 1951, 1967). Although the terms "refugee" and "asylum seekers" are colloquially used interchangeably, and the grounds for receiving asylum status and refugee status are similar under the Immigration and Nationality Act (1982), the procedural steps for each group are quite different. Both refugee and asylum seekers bear the burden of showing they cannot live in their home country due a reasonable fear or proof that they have suffered past prosecution or have a well-founded fear of persecution on account of race, religion, nationality, membership in a particular social group, or political opinion. However, refugees must secure their status while they are outside of the United States (see Table 3.2).

TABLE 3.1 Other Important Terms as Defined by UNHCR*

Migrant	There is no universally accepted definition. It is usually understood to cover cases where the decision to migrate is taken not because of a direct threat of persecution or death, but mainly to improve lives by finding work, or in some cases for education, family reunion, or other reasons.
Asylum seeker	An individual who is seeking international protection. In countries with individualized procedures, an asylum-seeker is someone whose claim has not yet been finally decided on by the country in which the claim is submitted. Not every asylum-seeker will ultimately be recognized as a refugee, but every refugee was initially an asylum-seeker.
Convention refugee	A person who is outside his or her former country of origin owing to well-founded fear of persecution for reasons of race, religion, nationality, membership of a particular social group or political opinion, who is unable or unwilling to avail himself or herself of the protection of that country, or to return to it for reasons of fear of persecution, and who is not otherwise excluded from the refugee definition.
Internally displaced persons (IDPs)	An individual who has been forced or obliged to flee from his home or place of habitual residence ... in particular as a result of or in order to avoid the effects of armed conflicts, situations of generalized violence, violations of human rights or natural or human-made disasters, and who have not crossed an internationally recognized state border."
Persons of concern	A person whose protection and assistance needs are of interest to UNHCR. This includes refugees, asylum-seekers, stateless people, internally displaced people and returnees.
Stateless person	An individual who is not considered as a national by any state under the operation of its law, including a person whose nationality is not established.

* UNHCR 2016 and UNHCR 2015d

U.S. immigration laws do not limit the number of people who can be awarded asylum in the United States each year. By contrast, each year, the President in consultation with Congress sets a "refugee admissions ceiling," which establishes the number and groups who are of special humanitarian concern and who will be eligible for admission. At the end of 2015, only twenty-eight countries in the world participate in UNHCR's resettlement program, with the United States being the largest receiving country by number of refugees, followed by Australia and Canada (UNHCR 2015c). For both refugees and asylum seekers, multiple government agencies handle different aspects of the review of claims. For both groups, adjudicators are responsible for ascertaining and evaluating relevant facts in order to rule on claims.

In practice, the burden falls on applicants to develop and present their claims (Ardalan 2015, 1013). Not surprisingly, hurdles including language barriers, legal illiteracy, trauma histories, and fear of government agents impede the applicants' ability to meet their burden of proof. Under U.S. and

TABLE 3.2 Some Distinctions Between Asylum Seekers and Refugees Under U.S. Law

Asylum Seekers	Refugees
Refugee status or asylum may be granted to people who have been persecuted or fear they will be persecuted on account of race, religion, nationality, and/or membership in a particular social group or political opinion.	
Must already be in the U.S.	Must still be outside of the U.S.
May be seeking admission at a port of entry	Must be of special humanitarian concern to the U.S.
May apply for regardless of country of origin or current immigration status.	Does not include anyone who ordered, incited, assisted, or otherwise participated in the persecution of any person on account of race, religion, nationality, membership in a particular social group, or political opinion.

international law, an asylum applicant's testimony must be given the "benefit of the doubt" (Ardalan 2015, 1014) but, in recent years, adjudicators have increasingly required extensive proof and corroboration for fear of fraud and concerns for security. The Transactional Records Access Clearinghouse, a research center at Syracuse University, which reviewed data obtained from the Executive Office for Immigration Review (EOIR), reported that the asylum denial rate rose to 47.2% in 2013 and reached 50.2% during 2014 (TRAC 2014).

Competent legal representation has been shown to be helpful for winning an asylum claim. Studies published since 2008 indicate there is a clear benefit to having representation by counsel during immigration proceedings (Ramji-Nogales, Schoenholtz, and Schrag 2007; GAO 2008). Although immigrants have a right to counsel in deportation proceedings, asylum seekers and refugees do not have a right to government-appointed representation in any immigration proceedings and many face the process either unrepresented or pay for legal services on their own.

ROLES FOR FORENSIC PSYCHIATRISTS IN ASYLUM AND REFUGEE CASES

Because professional legal services for asylum seekers and refugees are so limited, law student clinics have become a crucial part of providing representation. These clinics, in which students supervised by attorneys assist individuals in making their claims, have been in existence in North America since the 1960s for the dual purposes of advancing social justice causes as well as creating opportunities for practical training (Giddings et al. 2011). Through the clinics, attorneys are increasingly requesting mental health professionals to give their input into the legal process not only to make a diagnosis, but also to decipher the different contributing factors of their clients' circumstances, and in some cases to function as a mediator. Since success of the application hinges on the credibility of the narrative and testimony, the role for the forensic psychiatrist is critical, not only in providing written expert reports, but also in helping attorneys understand and address difficulties in working with clients: Is a certain presentation due to psychopathology or personality? Or is it due to situation or culture? What accounts for the difficulty in communicating, or the seeming discrepancy in their story?

Because the conditions that lead to the necessity of asylum are often the very conditions that impair applicants' ability to present their story credibly or to work with their attorney, the answers to these questions perhaps weigh more heavily than in most other legal cases. Psychiatric evaluations and psychological testing that provide organized life histories coupled with diagnostic evaluations of the effects of past trauma are relevant to the criteria needed for refugee status (Zonana 2010.)

Several forensic training programs have set up consultation agreements with legal clinics (Zonana 2010). During the past fifteen years, for example, faculty and forensic psychiatry fellows from the Yale Law and Psychiatry Program have worked with the Jerome Frank Law Center's Immigration Clinic at Yale Law School (Prabhu and Baranoski 2012). The relationship begins with joint attendance at didactic seminars and lectures in which an overview of immigration law is presented and cases are reviewed. As the legal teams progress with formulating a legal approach with their clients, the forensic physicians take on a variety of roles, including:

1. consultant, regarding questions of effective interview techniques, building client rapport, potential for retraumatization in the interviews for clients with PTSD;
2. educator, especially about manifestations of psychiatric illness, barriers to memory, and evidence of malingering;
3. evaluator and testifier, providing written and testimonial expertise in support of the legal opinion.

While legal teams often query the presence of post-traumatic stress disorder, a wide variety of conditions, like mood disorders and even psychotic illnesses, may be present and have an impact on clients' capacity to articulate their case in the lucid and organized fashion that is expected. For psychiatry fellows and faculty, it is helpful to be familiar with guidelines and recommendations published by Physicians for Human Rights (PHR 2012), which along with forty organizations, especially the Human Rights Foundation of Turkey, coordinated the publication of the Istanbul Protocol (UN 2004), the first internationally recognized protocol on how to recognize and document symptoms of torture for judicial findings. Psychiatrists are also likely to be asked to opine upon the possibility of malingering or exaggeration. Because a credible account is the core of an asylum case, the lack of malingering may bolster the argument for credibility (Prabhu and Baranoski 2012).

But far beyond this technical skill-set, we would suggest that the psychiatrist is also of benefit when they are able to maintain and model for the legal team's "emotional competence" (Pope and Brown 1996), which calls for self-knowledge, self-acceptance, and self-monitoring. Asylum seekers and refugees have often survived extraordinary experiences and the examiner must be able to listen carefully to accounts of these experiences and to assess their effects. Legal teams often find themselves deeply challenged by these descriptions and the psychiatric consultant may be called upon to help manage the emotional impact of these details and on occasion to identify mental health supports for both the client and the legal representation.

CULTURAL COMPETENCE

Cultural competence is also an essential skill for the forensic psychiatrist evaluating cases of asylum. Culture has been defined as "a set of guidelines (both explicit and implicit) which individuals inherit as members of a particular society, and which tells them how to *view* the world, how to experience it *emotionally*, and how to *behave* in it in relation to other people ..." (Helman 2014, 2–3). Cultural competence is so integral to the human make-up that anthropologist Clifford Geertz went as far as to say that culture is not something added on to a finished animal but was *centrally ingredient* in the production of human beings themselves (Geertz 1973, 46–7). Being so integral, it is also likely to be the least examined or questioned, especially when one is surrounded by individuals and institutions of the same culture.

In major psychiatric disorders, culture is found not only to shape the individual meaning and significance of those disorders but to influence their causes, manifestations, and final course (Kirmayer 2001, 2003; Kleinman 1988; Leff, 1988). For this reason, the cross-cultural validity of the *Diagnostic and Statistical Manual of Mental Disorders* (DSM) categories and screening tools has been called into question (Kleinman 1987; Lee et al. 2008; van Ommeren, Saxena, and Saraceno 2005).

Cultural competence, therefore, begins with an awareness of the self as a cultural being with implicit beliefs and assumptions, and the ability to step outside of them in an intercultural encounter. This complexity is the reason why anthropological research makes use of both *emic* (insider) and *etic* (outsider) observations in studying any culture. Striving for cultural competency, forensic psychiatrists must recognize the possibility that their own discipline and the law may be too culture-bound, in their favoring of individual-centered analyses over social and cultural context, to give proper due to the diverse cultures that one might potentially come across in asylum situations. Thus cultural competence involves adopting an attitude of flexibility, openness, and respect, and may consist of the following components:

1. Building an awareness of one's own culture.
2. Expanding one's cultural imagination.
3. Becoming informed of various cultural beliefs and practices.
4. Developing intercultural skills of observation and communication.
5. Incorporating cultural interpretation into reports and testimonies.

Cultural competence, while an important requirement in any comprehensive forensic psychiatric evaluation, becomes especially critical and complex in properly assessing refugees and asylum applicants. Few other forensic encounters require, to the same degree, that the consultant conceive of psychiatric and legal notions as tacit cultural knowledge (Geertz 1983) so as to communicate effectively with the client.

For example, it may be necessary to explain the very notion of legal representation, ensuring that the client does not see the attorney as being on the same side as the government, given our peculiar advocacy system. When diagnosing a psychiatric illness, implications of blame or stigma are important considerations, as is taking into account the client's own units of organization; a diagnosis of post-traumatic stress disorder, for instance, may be seen as offensive in cultures that view trauma as a social disorder (Pupavac 2004; Young 1997).

Communication of concepts may need to go far beyond literal translations, and a professional language translator can sometimes also play the role of a cultural translator (Hudelson 2005); for remote cultures, additional research or a cultural consult may be required. Clients may find it particularly hard to give accounts of painful experiences because of feelings of shame, even when the events are not their fault; some cultures may sanction against the very expression of negative emotion. A broad knowledge base of common cultural beliefs and practices can be useful, while at the same time keeping in mind that the culture does not determine the individual. Significant individual variability exists even within small cultural units, especially where cultures are shifting and meeting. In all situations, the key skill is openness to the client's narrative, so that one can hear the story—no matter how remote in culture or in range of experience.

Using this approach, mental health professionals can make important contributions to asylum claims by:

1. Providing a culturally-appropriate diagnostic formulation.
2. Explaining how culture and psychiatric symptoms might contribute to any perceived deficits in credibility.
3. Recommending culturally-sensitive treatments or estimating potential mental health effects of repatriation.
4. Accounting for unexpected presentations or difficulties in communication.
5. Assuming a supportive role to both the client and the attorney as they face re-traumatization and vicarious traumatization through the recounting of an applicant's difficult story.

Asylum and refugee cases are complicated by many factors. Culture is the filter through which legal assistance, psychiatric assessments, and all communication must pass. The task of reaching common language and meaning is at the center of effective assessments and treatment. The following cases illustrate some of the critical interactions between the client and the psychiatrist and attorney. These examples are composites of many different cases representing different countries and cultures. No actual clients are presented in the vignettes.

Case Vignette 1 (Lee 2013)

Mr. M., a 59-year-old East African man, was referred for a competency to stand trial evaluation after being charged with assault on a correctional officer while in the county jail on minor charges. He had been brought to the U.S. as part of a humanitarian relief program from a refugee camp in Tanzania. Originally, however, he was from an isolated rural region in another country, where a civil war had ravaged his village. Although in the U.S. for several years, he still did not speak any English and required a Swahili interpreter. During the interview, he revealed that he believed he was being taken for execution when placed in a red jumpsuit (the standard garment for punitive segregation) and taken by the correctional officer out of his cell. He had witnessed others led to their death in the same manner when he had been imprisoned during the war in his country. That day in the American jail, in "the struggle for my life," he bit the correctional officer. Whereas he was originally incarcerated for a much more minor charge and had no history of violence, things started to escalate with the stress of imprisonment, and he now faced a felony charge.

In terms of competency, he had difficulty conceiving an objective judicial system, and kept asking when all the involved parties were going to assemble to discuss the resolution, as it would have been done in the restorative justice model that is common in East African villages. He had no formal education and previously worked as a farmer and a herdsman. In Swahili, words for many legal concepts are lacking. The court ordered inpatient restoration, but after eighteen months, he still had difficulty appreciating the essential concepts, and education at the pace of a few hours per week (as per the availability of interpreters, who were rare) was inadequate to do what only an immersion in the new culture could produce.

Case Vignette 2 (Lee 2014)

Mrs. S. was a 72-year-old South Korean widow and mother of two children, referred for an evaluation of her psychiatric symptoms prior to her asylum interview. Her chief complaint was that she had been feeling "heaviness and fire in my chest" after an argument with her son before leaving her country. She had gathered her savings to buy a ticket to the U.S., where her nephew lived, but upon visiting him decided that she could not stay with him and quietly left to live with another woman of similar age to whom she was introduced in church. To her attorneys, she explained that fifteen years ago, when their son was unable to find a job, Mrs. S.'s husband gave him their entire savings, which the son invested unsuccessfully in a business. The couple survived on governmental assistance until the son was finally employed, at which time the assistance stopped, and the couple was forced to move in with him. Since that time, arguments became frequent, with the son kicking and punching the father, who later died from a stroke. The son turned his violence toward his mother, and Mrs. S. decided she had to leave her country.

In Korea, Mrs. S. found herself caught between the rejection by her own son and a social system that still relied on the principle of *hyo* (filial piety, the Confucian social contract that was the bedrock of Korean culture for centuries). How could she explain that she suffered far more than the physical abuse, that she faced total abandonment and humiliation? Her legal team initially viewed the case through American culture and saw domestic violence. With help from a cultural interpreter and through additional research, the forensic psychiatrist was able to provide the attorney on the case with a culturally-specific diagnosis as well as a detailed description of the hardship that would befall Mrs. S. should she return to South Korea. In the absence of governmental persecution, it is necessary to show that the government is incapable of protecting or ensuring the survival of an asylum applicant, as is often the case in successful domestic violence claims. On this basis, Mrs. S. was granted asylum.

EXPANDING INTO REFUGEE WORK

In recent years, the Yale Law and Psychiatry Program expanded its work to include the Iraqi Refugee Assistance Project (now the International Refugee Assistance Project, or IRAP), a clinic founded by Yale Law students to assist Iraqi refugees. The project has now extended its legal services to represent emerging high-risk refugee populations in the Middle East and North Africa with a special focus on female survivors, children with medical emergencies, and lesbian, gay, bisexual, transgender/transsexual, and intersexed (LGBTI) individuals. An original impetus for IRAP's work was to assist Iraqis and Afghans who had worked as interpreters for the U.S. military and then faced persecution after the withdrawal of American forces.

Unlike asylum seekers who are in a place of relative physical safety, having made their way to the U.S., refugees abroad continue to find themselves in precarious situations. In addition to traumas they had experienced in their country of origin, after flight they often are in "countries of first refuge" or refugee camps with limited access to work, education for children or health care. As a result, refugees may present to their lawyers with more acute and pervasive psychiatric distress. Because of complex licensing issues which vary by country, forensic psychiatry assistance to legal teams who work abroad largely takes the form of education around issues of the management of distressed applicants. A major role for forensic psychiatrists is consultation about the establishment of alliance with clients who are most often only in sporadic contact or through unreliable phone, Skype or other electronic means. Support for the legal teams who, unlike those working with asylum seekers, are now experiencing their clients' crises "in real time" but at great distance is imperative.

CONCLUSIONS AND FUTURE DIRECTIONS

There are many avenues through which forensic psychiatry has come to participate in global developments, and many more potential ways in which it could contribute. Over the past decade, for example, "No Health Without Mental Health" has been a tenet for a global mental health campaign and a new generation of health advocates. Launched in the *Lancet* in 2007, this movement has drawn attention to the lack of mental health resources worldwide (Prince, Patel, and Saxena 2007; Patel et al. 2011). Global mental health initiatives have also changed the medical education landscape, leading to both increased coursework and international experiences (Marienfeld and Rohrbaugh 2013). Psychiatry training programs are just beginning to develop global mental health (GMH) education and training opportunities in response to growing demands by globally attuned and human rights-minded young physicians to be involved with communities outside their own culture.

Forensic psychiatry in the field of asylum seekers and refugees is one way to further address this interest in global health. While the human tragedy that lies behind these cases cannot be minimized, such legal-forensic collaborations are rewarding opportunities for trainees and physicians to become exposed to and join a network of advocates working on international causes; to consider ethical dilemmas which come along with working with vulnerable populations and to observe cultural differences through the lenses of multiple systems—legal and medical.

ACKNOWLEDGMENT

The authors would like to gratefully acknowledge Grace Lee for her valuable input on the cultural knowledge base of this chapter.

REFERENCES

Ardalan, S. 2014–15. “Access to Justice for Asylum Seekers: Developing an Effective Model of Holistic Asylum Representation.” *University of Michigan Journal of Law Reform* 48 (4): 1001–38.

Convention Relating to the Status of Refugees. 1951. 189 UNTS 150.

De Jesús-Rentas, G., J. Boehnlein, and L. Sparr. 2010. “Central American Victims of Gang Violence as Asylum Seekers: The Role of the Forensic Expert.” *Journal of the American Academy of Psychiatry and the Law* 38 (4): 490–8.

GAO. 2008. *U.S. Asylum System: Significant Variation Existed in Asylum Outcomes across Immigration Courts and Judges*. Washington: GAO.

Geertz, C. 1973. *The Interpretation of Cultures: Selected Essays*. New York: Basic Books.

———. 1983. *Local Knowledge*. New York: Basic Books.

Giddings, J., R. Burridge, S.A.M. Gavigan, and C.F. Klein. 2011. “The First Wave of Modern Clinical Legal Education.” In *The Global Clinical Movement: Educating Lawyers for Social Justice*, edited by Frank S. Bloch. Boston: Oxford University Press.

Helman, C.G. 2014. *Culture, Health and Illness: An Introduction for Health Professionals*. Oxford: Butterworth-Heinemann.

Hudelson, P. 2005. "Improving Patient-provider Communication: Insights from Interpreters." *Family Practice* 22: 311–16.

Hurwitz, D.R. 2003. "Lawyering for Justice and the Inevitability of International Human Rights Clinics." *Yale Journal of International Law* 28 (2): 505–50.

Immigration and Nationality Act. 1982. Pub. L. U.S. No. 82-414.

Johnson, K.R. and A. Perez. 1997–1998. "Clinical Legal Education and the U.C. Davis Immigration Law Clinic: Putting Theory into Practice and Practice into Theory." *SMU Law Review* 51 (5): 1423–60.

Kirmayer, L.J. 2001. "Cultural Variations in the Clinical Presentation of Depression and Anxiety: Implications for Diagnosis and Treatment." *Journal of Clinical Psychiatry* 62: 22–30.

———. 2003. "Failures of Imagination: The Refugee's Narrative in Psychiatry." *Anthropology & Medicine* 10 (2): 167–85.

Kleinman, A. 1987. "Anthropology and Psychiatry. The Role of Culture in Cross-cultural Research on Illness." *British Journal of Psychiatry* 151 (4): 447–54.

———. 1988. *Rethinking Psychiatry: From Cultural Category to Personal Experience.* New York: Free Press.

Lee, B., S.F. Kaaya, J.K. Mbwambo, M.C. Smith-Fawzi, and M.T. Leshabari. 2008. "Detecting Depressive Disorder with the Hopkins Symptom Checklist-25 in Tanzania." *International Journal of Social Psychiatry* 54 (1): 7–20.

Lee, B.X. 2013. Teaching and lecture notes (unpublished).

———. 2014. Teaching and lecture notes (unpublished).

Leff, J. 1988. *Psychiatry Around the Globe: A Transcultural View.* London: Gaskell/Royal College of Psychiatrists.

Lyman, R. 2015. Treatment of Migrants Evokes Memories of Europe's Darkest Hour. *New York Times*, September 4. Accessed December 1, 2015. http://www.nytimes.com/2015/09/05/world/treatment-of-migrants-evokes-memories-of-europes-darkest-hour.html?_r=0.

Marienfeld, C. and R.M. Rohrbaugh. 2013. "Impact of a Global Mental Health Program on a Residency Training Program." *Academic Psychiatry* 37 (4): 276.

Meffert, S., K. Musalo, D.E. McNiel, and R.L. Binder. 2010. "The Role of Mental Health Professionals in Political Asylum Processing." *Journal of the American Academy of Psychiatry and the Law* 38 (4): 479–89.

Patel, V., N. Boyce, P.Y. Collins, S. Sazena, and R. Horton. 2011. "A Renewed Agenda for Global Mental Health." *Lancet* Published online: 17 October 2011.

Physicians for Human Rights (PHR). 2012. *Examining Asylum Seekers: A Clinician's Guide to Physical and Psychological Evaluations of Torture and Ill-Treatment.* New York: PHR. Accessed December 2, 2015. http://physiciansforhumanrights.org/library/reports/examining-asylum-seekers-manual-2012.html#sthash.T3j94VVF.dpuf.

Pope, K.S. and L.S. Brown. 1996. *Recovered Memories of Abuse: Assessment, Therapy, Forensics.* Washington, DC: American Psychological Association.

Prabhu, M. and M. Baranoski. 2012. "Forensic Mental Health Professionals in the Immigration Process." *Psychiatric Clinics of North America.* 35 4: 929–53.

Prince, M., V. Patel, and S. Saxena. 2007. "No Health without Mental Health." *Lancet.* Published online Sept 4. DOI:10.1016/S0140-6736(07)61238-0.

Pupavac, V. 2004. "Psychosocial Interventions and the Demoralization of Humanitarianism." *Journal of Biosocial Science* 36 (4): 491–504.

Ramji-Nogales, J., A.I. Schoenholtz, P.G. Schrag. 2007. "Refugee Roulette: Disparities in Asylum Adjudication." *Stamford Law Review* 60: 295–412.

TRAC Immigration. 2014. "Rise Seen in Asylum Denial Rates." Accessed December 1, 2015. http://trac.syr.edu/immigration/reports/361/.

UN General Assembly. 1951. "Convention Relating to the Status of Refugees." *United Nations, Treaty Series* 189: 137. Accessed December 3, 2015. http://www.refworld.org/docid/3be01b964.html.

———. 1967. "Protocol Relating to the Status of Refugees." *United Nations, Treaty Series* 606: 267. Accessed September 1, 2015. http://www.unhcr.org/refworld/docid/3ae6b3ae4.html

UN Istanbul Protocol. 2004. *Manual on the Effective Investigation and Documentation of Torture and Other Cruel, Inhuman or Degrading Treatment or Punishment*. New York and Geneva: UN.

UNHCR. 2000. *The State of the World's Refugees. Fifty Years of Humanitarian Action.* New York: UNHCR.

———. 2015a. "Worldwide Displacement Hits All-time High as War and Persecution Increase." Accessed December 1, 2015. http://www.unhcr.org/558193896.html.

———. 2015b. *Statement by António Guterres on World Refugee Day 2015*. Available at: http://www.unhcr.org/558016eb6.html.

———. 2015c. "Resettlement." Accessed December 1, 2015. http://www.unhcr.org/pages/4a16b1676.html.

———. 2015d. "UNHCR viewpoint: 'Refugee' or 'migrant'—Which is right?." Accessed April 8, 2016. http://www.unhcr.org/55df0e556.html.

———. 2016. "Global Appeal 2016–2017." Accessed April 8, 2016. http://www.unhcr.org/ga16/index.xml

United States Refugee Act of 1980. Pub. Law 96-212. 94 Stat. 102.

van Ommeren, M., S. Saxena, and B. Saraceno. 2005. "Mental and Social Health during and after Acute Emergencies: Emerging Consensus?" *Bulletin of the World Health Organization* 83 (1): 71–5.

Young, A. 1997. *The Harmony of Illusions: Inventing Post-Traumatic Stress Disorder.* Princeton, NJ: Princeton University Press.

Zonana, H. 2010. "Commentary: The Role of Forensic Psychiatry in the Asylum Process." *American Journal of Psychiatry Law* 38 (4): 499–501.

CHAPTER 4

Brain in the Balance: Neuroimaging in the Courtroom

Daniel S. Barron, Spencer Higgins, and Alexander Westphal

> … I'll ne'er believe a madman till I see his brains*.
>
> *Feste,* Twelfth Night, *Shakespeare (Act 4, Scene 2, Line 2133)*

In this chapter, we discuss the use of neuroscience in the courtroom with particular attention to brain imaging, or neuroimaging. Because neuroimaging measures brain structure and function, it has been applied as legal evidence in assessing criminal behavior and moral responsibility. After briefly discussing some of these applications, we discuss the legal, philosophical, and scientific admissibility of neuroimaging: in *Legal Admissibility* we review relevant rules of evidence and case law; in *Philosophical Admissibility* we explain how the court's view of free will may be unhelpful in assessing criminal behavior and moral responsibility, arguing for an approach based on cognitive neuroscience; in *Scientific Admissibility* we review neuroimaging's theoretical headwaters, as much to showcase its strengths as its limitations. Our overarching goal is to present a pathology-based framework rooted in neuroscience that could help guide legal deliberations.

* While there are many essential functions produced by the cerebellum, midbrain, brainstem, etc., throughout this paper, we will define "brain" as the cerebral cortex and, therefore, "brain function" as functions produced by the cerebral cortex.

LEGAL APPLICATIONS OF NEUROIMAGING

A variety of structural and functional neuroimaging modalities have been used in legal proceedings. Structural neuroimaging, including magnetic resonance imaging (MRI) and computerized tomography (CT) scans, can detect structural brain abnormalities such as tumors, damage from trauma, and congenital anomalies. Functional neuroimaging, including positron emission tomography (PET) and functional MRI (fMRI), can detect changes in the brain's activity.

Many forms of structural brain pathology have clear-cut functional implications. For example, a large brain bleed identified on a structural scan can be tied to a loss of motor function in an area served by that part of the brain. However, in some cases, the functional correlates of structural abnormalities are unclear or simply unknown. This is particularly true of the complex brain processes (e.g. moral reasoning, sexual behavior, psychiatric illness), in which a variety of brain systems may be involved, that are most often associated with legal proceedings. Furthermore, abnormal functional imaging results, in the absence of any structural correlate, are also complicated to interpret.

There are a number of legal contexts in which neuroimaging has been introduced as evidence. The Hinckley trial is frequently described as the first use of modern neuroimaging techniques in the courtroom. In 1981, John Hinckley Jr. shot and seriously injured Ronald Reagan's press secretary James Brady during an attempt to assassinate Reagan. He also injured Reagan and two people assigned to Reagan's security detail. He used an insanity defense during the trial, and introduced the results of a CT scan indicating that he had brain atrophy, something that is found in groups of people with schizophrenia, to support the defense. He was ultimately found not guilty by reason of insanity.

The first well-publicized use of fMRI occurred during the sentencing phase of Brian Dugan's 2009 trial. Dugan had committed a series of rapes and murders, and was eligible for the death penalty. He underwent an fMRI scan that included tasks that allowed comparisons to a group of people with psychopathy. While Dugan's scans were not ultimately shown to the jury, an expert testified to their content and implications. Dugan's lawyers used the testimony to argue that he was a psychopath and, therefore, had an impaired ability to control his behavior. Dugan ultimately did receive the death penalty (Hughes 2010).

Neuroimaging has been applied to a variety of other legal situations. For example, lie detection is a very controversial application. Currently, there are multiple commercial companies that specialize in using fMRI to detect lies. But while there is a developed literature on the neural correlates of deception, there are concerns about whether it is meaningful to compare cued deception in an experimental setting to *in vivo* deception (Spence 2010; Davatzikos et al. 2005).

Another application is to validate claims of physical injury. For example, tort law and personal injury cases often hinge on whether a person suffers debilitating pain. In these cases, the question of malingering can be central: is the person feigning pain, hoping to get a large settlement? Finally, neuroimaging has been used as a way to detect activity within the brain's pain centers as evidence of the validity of a pain claim (Greely 2015).

LEGAL ADMISSIBILITY

The law of evidence defines what may and may not be entered as evidence in a court of law. The federal courts and the individual state courts each set their own rules of evidence, and while there is variation between what is allowed in each state, most states conform substantially with the template set by the Federal Rules of Evidence. In addition to the collected rules of evidence, courts also decide questions of admissibility by looking to tests created in case law. To introduce neuroimaging results as evidence, the party hoping to present the evidence must put an expert witness on the stand who can testify to the scientific underpinnings of the evidence and explain its relevance to that particular case.

Federal Rules of Evidence

Determining the admissibility in a trial of neuroimaging results requires consideration of the Federal Rules of Evidence 104, 401, 402, 403, 702, 801, 802, 803, and 901. This list is not exhaustive but provides a framework for discussion.

Ultimately, the trial judge is the arbiter as to whether an expert witness and any accompanying neuroimaging results will be able to be presented as evidence. Federal Rule of Evidence 104 sets forth that as a preliminary matter, the judge "must decide whether a witness is qualified … or evidence is admissible" (Fed. R. Evid. 104(a)). Prior to determining admissibility, the judge must also determine whether the proffered evidence is relevant (Fed. R. Evid. 104(b)). To determine whether neuroimaging results are relevant in a specific case, the judge must be able to ascertain whether the specific application of neuroimaging is based on sound science.

Dependent on the type of legal claim, every court case has a framework of legal questions that must be answered by reference to the facts presented at trial. The facts that may be considered are only those which make a particular factual answer to a legal question either more or less likely (Fed. R. Evid. 401). Accordingly, neuroimaging need only perform a Bayesian function, making a factual claim more or less likely to be true, not serving as an empirical demonstration that a claim is or is not true, absolutely (see Fed. R. Evid. 402). And the court must weigh the probative value of evidence against the prejudicial effect it may have (Fed. R. Evid. 403). This final factor is particularly important in the situation of neuroimaging, where highly technical, even beautiful, images may unduly impress juries, but may in fact be minimally relevant.

Even when a piece of evidence is relevant, there may also be other legal hurdles which would prevent its admission at trial. For instance, it is conceivable that neuroimaging results may invoke hearsay rules contained in Federal Rules of Evidence 801, 802, and 803 which prohibit testimony in many instances of assertions, both written and verbal, made out of court. Additionally, there is a potential issue with authentication in Federal Rules of Evidence 901. Anyone hoping to enter neuroimaging evidence at trial must produce proof that the neuroimaging results are what they claim to be, i.e. they are the results of the relevant patient and test at the correct time (Fed. R. Evid. 901(a)). This is all to say that anyone hoping to enter any evidence, let alone neuroimaging, must be very careful in preparing the presentation.

Finally, the party hoping to offer neuroimaging evidence must also meet the requirements set forth in Federal Rules of Evidence 702, which states that a witness may offer expert testimony if:

(a) the expert's scientific, technical, or other specialized knowledge will help the trier of fact to understand the evidence or to determine a fact in issue;
(b) the testimony is based on sufficient facts or data;
(c) the testimony is the product of reliable principles and methods; and
(d) the expert has reliably applied the principles and methods to the facts of the case.

Rule 702 was rewritten in 2000 in response to a case law change in *Daubert v. Merrell Dow Pharmaceuticals, Inc.*, 509 U.S. 579 (1993) (Fed. R. Evid. 702 advisory committee's note). Rule 702 applies directly only in federal court, and state courts often follow a different standard of admissibility based in case law. For this reason, an overview of the history of the case law is useful to understanding what legal tests might govern what expert testimony is admissible.

Case Law Traditions

In addition to the Federal Rules of Evidence, the question of whether expert scientific testimony and the results of scientific tests are admissible depends on an application of case law. As stated above, prior to determining admissibility a court is asked to assess the reliability of expert scientific testimony as part of the analysis required by Fed R. Evid. 104 and 401. There are two main case law traditions in this area: *Frye v. United States*, 293 Fed. 1013 (D.C. Cir. 1923) and *Daubert v. Merrell Dow Pharmaceuticals, Inc.*, 509 U.S. 579 (1993). In the older of the two cases, *Frye v. United States*, the D.C. Circuit Court of Appeals held that expert testimony is admissible if the knowledge underlying the opinion is "sufficiently established to have gained *general acceptance in the particular field which it belongs*" (*Frye* at 1014 (emphasis added)).

The second case law tradition is known as the *Daubert* trilogy. It is composed of three cases from the U.S. Supreme Court: *Daubert v. Merrell Dow Pharmaceuticals, Inc.*, 509 U.S. 579 (1993); *General Electric Co. v. Joiner*, 522 U.S. 136 (1997); and *Kumho Tire Company v. Carmichael*, 526 U.S. 137 (1999). In *Daubert v. Merrell Dow*, the U.S. Supreme Court held that the *Frye* "general acceptance" test had been superseded by the promulgation of the Federal Rules of Evidence 702 (*Daubert* at 587). The opinion went on to set forth a test for the admissibility of expert testimony (*Daubert* at 593–4). This test was later adopted in the most recent iteration of Federal Rule of Evidence 702 cited above (Fed. R. Evid. 702 advisory committee's note).

While federal courts are governed by the *Daubert* test in the Federal Rules of Evidence, the states are somewhat more fragmented. As of 2012, the *Frye* "general acceptance" test is still followed in nine states (Fisher 2012; Cheng and Yoon 2005). The *Daubert* legal test for the admissibility of expert scientific testimony is followed in twenty-two states (see Fisher 2012, 807). Together the differing legal tests for admissibility set forth in *Daubert* and *Frye* are followed by thirty-one states. The other nineteen states have their own nonconforming legal traditions, which typically involve elements of both *Daubert* or *Frye* or applications of each tradition to different types of cases or evidence (807). In navigating the legal issues surrounding admissibility of expert testimony regarding neuroimaging results, both legal traditions may have to be considered.

PHILOSOPHICAL ADMISSIBILITY

In this section, we look more closely at the question of free will and argue that the courts would do well to transition from this framework towards a more evaluative approach of mental capacity that is rooted in cognitive neuroscience.

The legal basis of criminal responsibility is generally *not* taken as the knowledge of the accused persons that their behavior is criminal or even unlawful. To reach a conviction would require the accused to have a demonstrable, complete knowledge of the criminal law. A common legal maxim is that *ignorantia non excusat*. However, this applies only to the criminal law, and it has been disputed (Yochum 1999), and there are naturally exceptions (*R. v. Crosswell*, 2007 ONCJ 25). In addition to the "external" requirement of *actus reus*, the fact that the action occurred, there is the "internal" requirement of *mens rea*, the intention to commit a legally forbidden act, which requires only *scienter*, the knowledge that the action is wrong. Neither *mens rea* nor *actus reus* explicitly requires or denies free will. Instead, the very formulation of *mens rea* suggests that the brain produces certain mental capacities which, when present, supply the capacity for moral deliberation, as discussed further below.

Nevertheless, philosophical intrigues regarding the existence of free will or its deterministic denial are, after centuries of stalemate, still hotly debated in the legal literature, especially in the United States (Ayer 1946). This debate centers as much on free will's existence as it does the legal system's presupposition of its existence.

The Supreme Court itself has opined on the relevance of free will to the law as a whole. In *Morisette v. United States* (1952), the court declared that a "universal" foundation stone in the U.S. legal system's approach to punishment, sentencing, and incarceration was the "belief in freedom of the human will and a consequent ability and duty of the normal individual to choose between good and evil." Notwithstanding the strong, romantic affirmation of free will, such a belief might of course prove *false*, and it is a pity that the court declared only the *belief in* and not the *fact of* or at least *evidence of*, to be the "universal" element in the law. While such language affirmed free will, it did not explicitly deny determinism.

As if to resolve any ambiguity, in *U.S. v. Grayson* (438 U.S. 41, 1978) the court flatly declared that "a deterministic view of human conduct … is inconsistent with the underlying precepts of our criminal justice system." This ruled simultaneously against the philosophical view known as "compatibilism" (the view that free will and determinism are compatible). The court's view is one that may chafe at the empirical sensibilities of scientists and other nonlawyers, including philosophers.

Free will, according to the court's definition, is inconsistent with the underlying precepts of neuroscience. A defining (or "universal" foundation, to apply the court's language) tenet of neuroscience is that behavior is the end-product of brain function. The brain, in turn, is an organ whose function is based on biochemical processes. This biochemistry is determined by an interplay of genetic and environmental factors. So any behavior produced by the brain is also determined. So no human action is free.

This neuroscientific instantiation of determinism is part of a much larger philosophical debate between free will and determinism in explaining moral behavior. This debate spans centuries and it is extremely unlikely that a qualitative account of moral behavior that appeals to all parties will be formulated any time soon. *Pace* the court, it therefore would be prudent for those working in forensic psychiatry and concerned with the role of new and developing technologies in the assessment of criminal liability to try to reach a view that either uses a separate theoretical framework or a different behavioral approach. For example, rather than claiming that determinism is inconsistent with the law (as the court did in *Grayson*), we suggest the possibility that it is *irrelevant* to the law.

Our claim that determinism is irrelevant to the law has been stated in a slightly different fashion by H.L.A. Hart (Hart 1961) and, subsequently, by Stephen Morse. Their framework showcases:

> The importance of excusing conditions in criminal responsibility is derivative, and it derives from the more fundamental requirement that for criminal responsibility there must be "moral culpability," which would not exist where the excusing conditions are present (Hart 1961, 101).

Such excusing conditions make someone less criminally culpable, as if a baseline "culpability" existed from which blame could be subtracted as defects in moral deliberation are detected. We do not disagree with this framework; however, our framework stems from a fundamentally different ontology.

Our framework is better expressed from evolutionary neuroscience, wherein we would not claim a dog has "moral culpability" or "moral capacity" simply because the dog does not have the neural systems necessary for that behavior, namely neocortical areas that process and output information necessary for judgment, moral reasoning, and accountability. It is perfectly reasonable to assume, as we would, that if a phylogenically lower mammal lacks these specific neural systems and, therefore is not morally responsible, an individual *Homo sapiens* may (through some genetic or developmental defect) possess these neural systems either in part or in a dysfunctional form. Such partial possession would thus prohibit the full expression of judgment, moral reasoning, and accountability in that individual. Whether or not these neural systems are determined or free is irrelevant, but whether or not an individual possesses requisite neural systems and whether or not they are functioning properly is of great importance in determining moral capacity.

Whether the brain is free or determined is the wrong question to ask when evaluating someone's criminal responsibility. Rather, we argue that criminal responsibility is based on the individual's mental capacity, meaning if they pass "the moral capacity test." According to Vincent, in *Neuroscience and Legal Responsibility*:

> … responsible [liable] people are those who have the right mental capacities in the right degree—that is, the mental capacities required for moral agency. What justifies holding some people responsible for what they do is that their actions issue from mechanisms that bestow upon them mental capacities like the ability to perceive the world without delusion, to think clearly, to guide their actions by the light of their judgments, and to resist acting on mere impulse. (Vincent 2013)

These "cognitive" qualities are specific mental and behavioral phenomena that can be measured through cognitive tests. Their presence and the presence of other mental characteristics like them is what is required to establish the basis of responsibility, and the precise mechanism of their genesis or non-genesis in the brain is irrelevant. Whether or not the brain is itself free or determined is irrelevant to the existence of moral responsibility, and may even introduce an element of incoherence. For it is very far from clear what it would mean for someone whose criminal liability is under assessment to possess or not possess a "free brain."

As far as the law is concerned, it is persons and not brains who are criminally liable. Furthermore, it is hard to see the relevance of the brain's ultimate freedom or determinism in cases, e.g. of rape, murder, or theft. Rather, it is much more clear how to evaluate what mental capacities the accused had at the time of the crime and why they were so.

It is, we think, a separate question whether there is to be found a neurophysiological explanation for a failure of mental capacity. The fact that a cyst in the brain *interferes* with brain function and actually produces aberrant behavior (see below) does not suggest that, in the *absence* of a cyst, the brain is either free or determined. What we do know is that the presence of a cyst in a given brain region interferes with the brain in a predictable manner, resulting in diminished mental capacity. Whether the brain is free or determined with or without the presence of a cyst is irrelevant. Instead it is relevant to define and restore the failed mental capacity (i.e. by removing the cyst).

Our view is that forensic psychiatry's role in criminal liability cases will increasingly hinge on the refinement of the mental taxonomy, the description of such mental capacities, and the discovery of empirically-driven tests that may aid in the assessment of criminal responsibility. Here neuroimaging is promising.

SCIENTIFIC ADMISSIBILITY, GENERAL

The scientific endeavor of associating specific behaviors with specific brain structures and functions is known as function-location mapping; the goal of which is to form a *map* of which functions occur where in the brain. This endeavor is not new. Recent technologies such as magnetic resonance imaging (MRI) and positron emission tomography (PET) trace their theoretical foundations to millennia-old clinical observations that damage to specific brain areas produced predictable behavioral abnormalities. Instead of a methodological exposition (which can be found elsewhere (Vallabhajosula 2015)), we provide an historical overview of the development of function-location mapping. The goal of this historical overview is to give the reader a keen sense of the types of experiments and observations that led to the rise of modern neuroimaging. Understanding where these ideas come from conveys a sense of neuroimaging's purpose and limitations.

Theoretical Headwaters

Many historical overviews of forensic neuroimaging begin with the account of Phineas Gage, a nineteenth-century man who suffered a brain injury that caused significant changes in his personality (Macmillan 2008). But its roots are far older. Galen of Pergamon (129–200CE), a Roman physician, made some of the first function-location maps. Galen systematically defined different types of head trauma and introduced terms like apoplexy, hemiplegia, and contra coup. Based on methodical clinical observations, he localized sensory and motor function to ventricles in the anterior (cerebrum) and posterior (cerebellum) brain, respectively (Finger 1994).

From these earliest function-location maps, the overall goal did not change much: behavioral functions were associated with specific brain regions. As theory progressed and experimental methods improved, the maps became more specific and more accurate. The precise location of the brain's functional activity has changed greatly.

For example, Nemesius of Emesa, a fourth-century Christian bishop, associated specific mental functions to the brain's multiple ventricles, which he called cells (Clarke and Jacyna 1987). This functional division into cells became known as the Cell Doctrine, of which there are many examples in both Western and Eastern Medieval medical texts (Clarke and Dewhurst 1972). Although this association of activity with the ventricles was incorrect, it persisted for centuries.

One of the first to move away from localizing behavior to the ventricles was Rene Descartes (1596–1650). Descartes described the pineal gland as the governing center of the body (Descartes 2001). In line with his view that all animals are merely machines, Descartes also outlined the first neural circuit, pairing afferent visual inputs with efferent behavioral motor responses, thus forming the foundation of modern concepts of integrated neural systems. Descartes also developed a method for representing three-dimensional objects within a coordinate system, which proved extremely useful in the development of modern function-location mapping, further discussed below.

Franz Gall (1758–1828) proposed the first real attempt to tease brain function into specific mental processes localized to the brain's cortex. He subdivided the cortex into twenty-seven discrete organs, each with a separate mental and moral function that could be measured indirectly via the contours of the overlying cranium (Finger 1994; Clarke and Jacyna 1987). Gall's revolutionary "crainoscopy," though widely criticized and eventually discredited (in part because it gave birth to "phrenology" (Clarke and Jacyna 1987)), provided the conceptual foundation for subsequent functional subdivisions of the cortex. Paul Broca, discussed below, proclaimed Gall's "great principle of cerebral localization … [was] … the starting point for every discovery in cerebral physiology in our century" (Schiller 1979).

Aphasia and Electrophysiology Energize Localization

In the 1820s a French doctor, Jean Baptiste Bouillaud (1796–1881), reported that the anterior cerebral lobes coordinated speech. So convinced was he that damage to the anterior cerebral lobe *causes* a deficit in speech production that, after presenting sixty-four supporting lesion-deficit cases during a conference, Bouillaud offered "500 francs to anyone who will provide me with an example of a deep lesion of the anterior lobules of the brain without a lesion of speech"(Bouillard 1825; Stookey 1963). The prize remains unclaimed.

Later, in 1861, the esteemed French physician Paul Broca (1824–1880) reported the case of Tan, a 21-year-old patient with focal, progressive loss of articulate speech. Post-mortem dissection of Tan's brain showed a lesion precisely where Bouillaud predicted. A combination of Bouillard's case studies paired with Broca's final demonstration cemented the concept that brain lesions could be paired with specific behavioral deficit, reviving the impetus to create a function-location map of the brain.

Not long after Broca's observation, Emil du Bois-Reymond (1818–1896) showed that nerves function by the conduction of electrical activity and Richard Caton (1842–1926) showed that visual stimuli produced notable changes in the posterior brain's electrical signal. These discoveries led to the development of electrophysiology.

Electrophysiology studies aimed either to elicit a particular behavior, e.g. leg movement, by stimulating a particular brain region or to detect a change in the brain's recorded electrical signal associated with a behavior. By recording where in the brain specific behaviors were elicited, David Ferrier produced the first empirically validated function-location maps of the orangutan brain which he then applied to the human brain (Ferrier 1876).

Ferrier's electrical function-location mapping had almost immediate application to neurosurgery. Wilder Penfield (1891–1976), a neurosurgeon, and Herbert Jasper (1906–1999), an electroencephalographer, used a combination of EEG and intraoperative electrical stimulation to guide the neurosurgical treatment of epilepsy (Penfield and Jasper 1954). By observing abnormal brain activity during a seizure, they could discover what and where dysfunctional brain tissue was *causing* the seizure. The standard of treatment then (and now) was to cut out the dysfunctional piece of brain, thus curing the seizures. Penfield was careful to map brain regions responsible for, e.g. leg movement, so as not to damage them during the epilepsy surgery.

To create these maps, he would stimulate the cortex and observe a behavioral response. By keeping fastidious notes of which cortical regions evoked which behaviors across hundreds of patients, Penfield mapped regions responsible for motor and sensory function. Penfield's work substantially enriched function-location mapping, yielding the sensory and motor homunculus, which are found in every individual's brain (Jasper and Penfield 1949).

Cartesian Stereotaxic Systems: Averaging in the Third Dimension

Demonstrations that function-location mapping was not only *possible*, but *useful* greatly promoted the science. However, the level of spatial precision required to describe each functional area was soon greater than that offered by standard neuroanatomical nomenclature. For example, when Victor Horsley (1857–1916) and Charles Beevor (1854–1908) discovered a brain area responsible for the thumb muscles, they found that describing the "thumb area" in anatomical terms (on the motor strip, anterior-superior to the intersection of the intraparietal sulcus and fissure of Rolando) was not only too general, but confusing (Beevor and Horsley 1890). They devised a system for dividing the brain's surface into small, uniform squares and reporting function-location pairs at a particular square. This was a great achievement; however, mapping sub-cortical regions (e.g. the thalamus) added a new dimension to the problem: a third dimension.

In 1908, Horsley and R.H. Clarke, a fellow neurosurgeon, published a technique for 3D function-location mapping: stereotaxy (Horsley and Clarke 1908). By placing thirty-two rhesus monkey brains into a fixed 3D coordinate space, Horsley and Clarke produced a probabilistic map that showed, *on average*, where anatomical landmarks and behavioral functions were most commonly represented within this coordinate space. Stereotaxic techniques provided a means of guiding experimental protocols (DSB used it as an undergraduate to record rat VTA neurons) and a language for precise cross-disciplinary communication.

In 1967, Jean Talairach (1911–2007) published the first human stereotactic atlas with a fundamental improvement to Horsley and Clarke's method (Talairach et al. 1967). To overcome individual differences in brain size, Talairach developed a "proportional orthogonal space" wherein brains were oriented to anatomical landmarks (the anterior commissure) and scaled to a grid system (Talairach and Tournoux 1988). To demonstrate that his system could be used to describe brain structure *and* function, Talairach used his grid system to plot function-location associations of many of his patients. He showed that while individual variance existed, useful function-location information could be gained across many individuals by referencing his "proportional orthogonal space." Talairach later updated his 1967 atlas as a guide for digital neuroimaging (Talairach and Tournoux 1988).

This history—presented all too quickly—demonstrates a series of points: First, that brain structure and function are causally related. Two corollaries of this point are that injury to a brain region causes loss of the function produced by that region and that activation (or use) of a particular brain function *causes* activity within its corresponding brain area. Second, behavioral functions can be localized either by stimulating a brain structure that produces that function or by recording brain activity while a subject is performing a particular behavior and observing which brain regions are active. Third, while individual function-location maps vary, on average, function and structure have common associations across individuals.

SCIENTIFIC ADMISSIBILITY OF DIGITAL NEUROIMAGING

Function-location mapping was confined to the neurosurgical suite or the morgue because it required direct contact with brain tissue. While the theoretical foundation was present, the methods to further pursue function-location mapping were not, until the second half of the twentieth century.

The rise of nuclear physics, computing power, and mathematical modeling produced novel techniques to investigate the brain *in vivo* and *en masse* without the necessity of direct contact with the brain. Computed tomography (CT), positron emission tomography (PET) and magnetic resonance imaging (MRI) each produce a 3-D, digital image that captures different aspects of the brain. The specifics of these different methods are expertly reviewed elsewhere (consider McRobbie et al. 2007). To create useful representations of the brain's structure and function, many technical obstacles had to be overcome, of which individual-to-group mapping was of central importance.

Individual-to-group Mapping

As can be imagined, each individual's 3-D brain image is of slightly different shape (heads come in different shapes and sizes). To allow a group of individuals' brains to be statistically compared in a meaningful way, the neuroimaging community has developed spatial registration methods that transform an individual's digital brain image from its natural size and shape into a standardized coordinate-based form as defined by a reference brain image. The most common reference brain used today is based on the Talairach atlas (Talairach 1967, 1988; Lancaster et al. 2000).

Registration of these digital images to a coordinate space (e.g. Talairach's space) allows robust, noninvasive function-location mapping in both individual and group studies (Fox et al. 1988; Raichle 2006). By reporting their results within the same coordinate space, separate laboratories using different imaging modalities can precisely communicate and synthesize their efforts. Furthermore, by referencing the same coordinate space, knowledge of the human brain can be continuously updated and clarified with subsequent experiments and methods (Fox 1995; Evans et al. 2012). Such information can clarify what brain regions are responsible for what behaviors at the level of the brain's tissue, gyrus, lobe, and hemisphere.

Such endeavors, however, are typically limited to group analyses wherein data from multiple individuals is grouped. Groups can then be compared to one another based on task (e.g. one group tapping their finger, the other resting quietly) or patient population (e.g. persons with depression are compared to persons without). The application of such results to the individual is problematic because the statistics used in the original analysis were not intended for applicability to the individual. This is commonly known as the group-to-individual problem.

The group-to-individual problem is not intended to suggest that group studies are *not* applicable to individuals—for in theory they could be. It simply means that results gained from a group study must first be tested and validated in individuals, often with different, more appropriate statistical methods. The direct application of results from group studies to the individual without explicit testing in and across individuals is an improper and inadmissible application of neuroimaging.

Individual Differences

The claim that neuroimaging can detect individual differences in brain structure and function is undeniably true: No two brains have identical structural or functional organization. What this means in terms of behavior is unclear. Excepting very large differences, we do not have an accurate model that correlates behavior to brain structure and function on the group level and certainly not on the individual level. Indeed, given the individual differences in structure and function, a pan-explanatory model may not be possible. Notwithstanding this explanatory gap, there are specific, legally relevant observations of brain structure and function.

FRAMEWORK FOR FUTURE APPLICATIONS: AN APPEAL TO PATHOLOGY

The role of neuroimaging in legal proceedings remains, to some degree, *terra incognita*. While function-location mapping has a long historical precedent and enjoys scientific admissibility, the way in which brain function ties to individual brain regions in the context of higher-level cognitive capabilities remains unclear. Furthermore, where and how the brain dysfunctions, resulting in impaired mental capacities, is still a subject of research. As is the case in any organ, the removal of previously present capacities through dysfunction represents the realm of pathology.

Pathology is "the study of structural, biochemical, and functional changes in cells, tissues, and organs that underlie disease … pathology attempts to explain the whys and wherefores of the signs and symptoms manifested by patients while providing a rational basis for clinical care and therapy" (Kumar et al. 2010, 4). This definition is largely unchanged since Virchow, the father of modern pathology, who in the 1800s encouraged his students to "think microscopically." There is little controversy regarding some pathology: you diagnose cirrhosis directly via microscope and indirectly via certain parameters of liver function.

Pathology of the brain's structure and function are less decisive. Why? Because normal, microscopically healthy brain tissue can produce a very large number of functions. As in all organs, however, there is a general, average structure for brain tissue. But there are also healthy variants of normal structure that allow for the healthy, normal variants in brain function. Such variety fuels the engine of evolution and allows the diversity that defines humanity's greatest minds and achievements.

Determining what brain function is healthy and what is pathological is not impossible. To do so, we recommend applying standard rules of pathology:

Are the cells, tissues, and organs damaged? Are the structural, biochemical, and functional makeup of the brain malfunctioning? Is the function of the brain risking damage to other organs? These are not simply questions of social norm or value judgments regarding what is acceptable or expected.

Structural brain pathology is readily detectable on the individual level. Tumors, the aftermath of strokes, infections, and autoimmune destruction can be detected with neuroimaging with relative ease. This is because it is clear what is being looked for. A stroke in the amygdala causes Klüver–Bucy syndrome, the effects of which are unlikely to diminish with time.

Functional brain pathology is more difficult to detect at the group and individual level because we are still trying to sort out how the healthy brain is functionally organized and what this means in terms of behavior. The most likely way for functional brain abnormalities to be both studied and detected is by the development of quantitative biomarkers.

Biomarkers of brain disease take advantage of the implicit organization of the brain. Neurons, the brain's smallest processing unit, are organized into local neural centers that are organized into brain-wide neural systems. Neural centers form larger neural systems that are responsible for brain functions such as vision, language, judgment, motor behavior, etc. (Smith et al. 2009). Psychiatric disorders such as PTSD, major depression, and dementia have marked effects on brain-wide neural systems (Lee, Smyser, and Shimony 2012; Greicius et al. 2004). Importantly, these psychiatric disorders also present clear behavioral consequences to the patient across any society: they interfere with the patient's ability to hold a job, to interact with their friends and family, and to attend to the activities of daily life. Biomarkers are being developed to assist in the diagnosis and treatment of these patients.

It is important to note that differences in political views (Knutson et al. 2006), religious belief (Kapogiannis et al. 2009), sexual orientation (Hu et al. 2008), and many other brain processes have been correlated to differences in brain function. However, these effects are limited to specific neural centers—typically those involved in a particular behavior—not to brain-wide neural systems. They result from normal variation and are sculpted by an individual's genetic and environmental makeup. Given this information, biomarkers should classify pathology of brain function as affecting brain-wide neural systems, not neural centers.

Brain biomarkers promise to play a role in the search for value-free psychiatric diagnoses. Biomarkers that aim to diagnose brain diseases based on the effect a disease has on a neural system (as opposed to neural center) could help avoid value-laden diagnoses and refine the medical professional's efforts to focus on brain pathology instead of brain persecution.

CONCLUSION

In this chapter, we have discussed some legal applications of neuroimaging and considered the legal, philosophical, and scientific admissibility of neuroimaging. We have argued that criminal responsibility may be more meaningfully understood in terms of mental capacities, which may be measured by psychological tests and, perhaps one day, by functional neuroimaging tests as a form of function-location mapping. To demonstrate some of the strengths and limitations of function-location mapping, we discussed its origins. Finally, we proposed a biomarker-driven, pathology-based framework rooted in function of neural systems that could help guide legal deliberations.

ACKNOWLEDGMENTS

The authors thank Kristin Budde (editing, brainstorming) and Genny Higgins (brainstorming) for their help in preparing this manuscript.

BIBLIOGRAPHY

Ayer, A. J. 1946. "Freedom and Necessity", reprinted in: AJ Ayer. *Philosophical Essays.* London: Macmillian Press.

Beevor, C.E., and V. Horsley. 1890. "A Record of the Results Obtained by Electrical Excitation of the So-Called Motor Cortex and Internal Capsule in an Orang-Outang (Simia Satyrus)." *Philosophical Transactions of the Royal Society of London. B* 181: 129–58.

Bouillard, J.B. 1825. "Recherches Cliniques Propres À Démontrer Que La Perte De La Parole Correspond À La Lésion Des Lobules Antérieurs Du Cerveau, Et À Confirmer L'Opinion De M. Gall. Sur Le Siège De L'Organe Du Langage Articulé." *Archives Générales De Médecine* 1 (8): 25–45.

Cheng, E.K. and A.H. Yoon. 2005. "Does Frye or Daubert Matter? A Study of Scientific Admissibility Standards." *Virginia Law Review* 22.

Clarke, E. and K. Dewhurst. 1972. *An Illustrated History of Brain Function*. Berkeley, CA: University of California Press.

Clarke, E. and L.S. Jacyna. 1987. *Nineteenth-Century Origins of Neuroscientific Concepts.* Berkeley: University of California Press.

Davatzikos, C., K. Ruparel, Y. Fan, D.G. Shen, M. Acharyya, J.W. Loughead, R.C. Gur, and D.D. Langleben. 2005. "Classifying Spatial Patterns of Brain Activity with Machine Learning Methods: Application to Lie Detection." *NeuroImage* 28 (3): 663–8. doi:10.1016/j.neuroimage.2005.08.009.

Descartes, R. 2001. *Discourse on Method, Optics, Geometry, and Meterology*. Translated by P.J. Olscamp. Indianapolis: Hackett Publishing.

Evans, A.C., A.L. Janke, D.L. Collins, and S. Baillet. 2012. "Brain Templates and Atlases." *NeuroImage* 62 (2): 911–22.

Ferrier, D. 1876. *The Functions of the Brain*. London: Smith, Elder, & Co.

Finger, S. 1994. *Origins of Neuroscience: A History of Explorations Into Brain Function*. New York: Oxford University Press.

Fisher, G. 2012. *Evidence*. 3rd ed. Foundation Press.

Fox, P.T., M.A. Mintun, E.M. Reiman, and M.E. Raichle. 1988. "Enhanced Detection of Focal Brain Responses Using Intersubject Averaging and Change-Distribution Analysis of Subtracted PET Images." *Journal of Cerebral Blood Flow & Metabolism* 8 (5): 642–53.

Fox, P.T. 1995. "Spatial Normalization Origins: Objectives, Applications, and Alternatives." *Human Brain Mapping* 3 (3): 161–4.

Greely, H.T. 2015. "Neuroscience, Mindreading, and the Courts: the Example of Pain." *Journal of Health Care Law and Policy*. doi:10.3389/neuro.09.031.2009/full.

Greicius, M.D., G. Srivastava, A.L. Reiss, and V. Menon. 2004. "Default-Mode Network Activity Distinguishes Alzheimer's Disease From Healthy Aging: Evidence From Functional MRI." *Proceedings of the National Academy of Sciences* 101 (13): 4637–42.

Hart, H. L. A. 1961. "Legal Responsibility and Excuses". In *Determinism and Freedom in Age of Modern Science*, edited by S. Hook. New York, NY: New York University Press.

Horsley, V. and R.H. Clarke. 1908. "The Structure and Functions of the Cerebellum Examined by a New Method." *Brain* 31 (1): 45–124.

Hu, S.H., N. Wei, Q.D. Wang, L.Q. Yan, E.Q. Wei, M.M. Zhang, J.B. Hu, M.I. Huang, W.H. Zhou, and Y. Xu. 2008. "Patterns of Brain Activation During Visually Evoked Sexual Arousal Differ Between Homosexual and Heterosexual Men." *American Journal of Neuroradiology* 29 (10): 1890–96. doi:10.3174/ajnr.A1260.

Hughes, V. 2010. "Science in Court: Head Case." *Nature March* 18. doi:10.1038/464340a.

Jasper, H. and W. Penfield. 1949. "Electrocorticograms in Man: Effect of Voluntary Movement Upon the Electrical Activity of the Precentral Gyrus." *Archiv Für Psychiatrie Und Nervenkrankheiten* 183(1–2). Springer-Verlag: 163–74. doi:10.1007/BF01062488.

Kapogiannis, D., A.K. Barbey, M. Su, G. Zamboni, F. Krueger, and J. Grafman. 2009. "Cognitive and Neural Foundations of Religious Belief." *Proceedings of the National Academy of Sciences* 106 (12): 4876–81.

Knutson, K.M., J.N. Wood, M.V. Spampinato, and J. Grafman. 2006. "Politics on the Brain: an fMRI Investigation." *Social Neuroscience* 1 (1): 25–40. doi:10.1080/17470910600670603.

Kumar, V., A.K. Abbas, N. Fausto, and J.C. Aster. 2010. *Robbins and Cotran Pathologic Basis of Disease*. 8th ed. New York: Elsevier.

Lancaster, J. L., Woldorff, M. G., Parsons, L. M., Liotti, M., Freitas, C. S., Rainey, L., et al. (2000). "Automated Talairach Atlas Labels for Functional Brain Mapping." *Human Brain Mapping*, 10(3), 120–131.

Lee, M.H., C.D. Smyser, and J.S. Shimony. 2012. "Resting-State fMRI: a Review of Methods and Clinical Applications." *American Journal of Neuroradiology* August. doi:10.3174/ajnr.A3263.

Macmillan, M. 2008. "Phineas Gage—Unravelling the Myth." *The Psychologist* 21 (9).

McRobbie, D.W., E.A. Moore, M.J. Graves, and M.R. Prince. 2007. *MRI From Picture to Proton*. Cambridge: Cambridge University Press.

Penfield, W. and H. Jasper. 1954. *Epilepsy and the Functional Anatomy of the Human Brain*. Boston: Little, Brown and Company.

Raichle, M.E. 2006. "The Brain's Dark Energy." *Science* 314: 1248–9.

Schiller, F. 1979. *Paul Broca*. Berkeley: University of California Press.

Smith, S.M., P.T. Fox, K.L. Miller, D.C. Glahn, P.M. Fox, C.E. Mackay, N. Filippini, K.E. Watkins, R. Toro, and A.R. Laird. 2009. "Correspondence of the Brain's Functional Architecture During Activation and Rest." *Proceedings of the National Academy of Sciences* 106 (31): 13040–5.

Spence, S.A. 2010. "Playing Devil's Advocate: the Case Against fMRI Lie Detection." *Legal and Criminological Psychology* 13 (1): 11–25. doi:10.1348/135532507X251597.

Stookey, B. 1963. "Jean-Baptiste Bouillaud and Ernest Auburtin: Early Studies on Cerebral Localization and the Speech Center." *JAMA: the Journal of the American Medical Association* 184 (13): 1024. doi:10.1001/jama.1963.73700260007011.

Talairach, J., G. Szikla, P. Tournoux, A. Prossalentis, M. Bordas-Ferrer, L. Covello, M. Jacob, and E. Mempel. 1967. *Atlas D'anatomie Stéréotaxique Du Télencéphale: Études Anatomo-Radiologiques*. Paris: Masson & C, Editeurs.

Talairach, J. and P. Tournoux. 1988. *Co-Planar Stereotaxic Atlas of the Human Brain. 3-Dimensional Proportional System: An Approach to Cerebral Imaging*. New York: Thieme Medical Publishers.

Vallabhajosula, B. 2015. *Murder in the Courtroom*. Oxford: Oxford University Press.

Vincent, N.A. 2013. "Law and Neuroscience." In *Neuroscience and Legal Responsibility*, edited by Nicole A. Vincent, pp. 1–24. Historical Context. Oxford: Oxford University Press.

Yochum, M.D. 1999. "The Death of a Maxim: Ignorance of Law Is No Excuse (Killed by Money, Guns and a Little Sex)." *The Journal of Civil Rights and Economic Development* 13 (November): 1–41.

CHAPTER 5

Politics and Money as Change-Agents in Forensic Systems

Paul DiLeo and Larry Davidson

Recent changes in the ways in which behavioral health care for the general public is funded, delivered, and evaluated in the U.S. are increasingly influencing care for forensic populations as well. These changes, as evidenced in other chapters in this volume, primarily involve shifting the locus of care from the hospital or other institutional settings to the community, shifting the focus of care from symptom reduction and maintenance to recovery and social inclusion, and shifting the costs of care from state general funds, augmented by federal block grants, to Medicaid as it expands significantly under the Affordable Care Act. This chapter deals with the roles political agendas and funding streams play in these shifts, especially in relation to the forensic systems that are being developed in local communities to offer persons with behavioral health conditions the opportunities, resources, and supports they need in order to take advantage of the "second chance" our society is beginning to offer them to reclaim their citizenship.

The federal Second Chance Act of 2008 and Connecticut's more recently passed House Bill 7104 (June 2015 Special Session, PA 15-2), which implemented the Governor's "Second Chance Society" initiative, are just two examples of these kinds of changes in how forensic services are framed within the context of public policy. With increasing recognition of the failures, and exorbitant costs, of the mass incarceration—especially of youth of color—that began with Reagan's expansion of the "war on drugs" in the early 1980s, forensic psychiatry is being swept up in a current of related reform efforts. These efforts span the continuum from diversion and alternatives to incarceration for first time, nonviolent offenders to the community re-entry of previously violent inmates and insanity acquittees. With these reforms come significant changes to the roles of forensic psychiatrists, from providing forensic evaluations, expert opinions, and care for persons in institutional settings to advocating for, developing, and staffing new community-based rehabilitation programs (Pinals 2014).

For forensic professionals to lead, influence, or at least inform—rather than follow unwittingly behind—these changes, it will be important for them to consider how policy and funding decisions are made in the "real world" as opposed to how they might be made ideally (i.e. based on available evidence) (Corrigan and Watson 2003). This chapter uses examples from recent initiatives in the State of Connecticut to illustrate a set of principles for guiding advocacy and legislative efforts to reform forensic psychiatric practice from the inside. We offer these principles in the hopes that such reforms can be more thoughtful and more effective over the longer term than the kinds of reforms that historically have been made hastily in response to externally imposed forces, such as the judicial intervention or oversight brought about by concerns related to civil rights violations or class action law suits (e.g. Hoge et al. 2002).

PRINCIPLES FOR USING POLITICS AND MONEY AS CHANGE-AGENTS

1. *Recognize that no one wants to pay for behavioral health services for forensic populations.* Policy makers find it regrettable enough that tax dollars have to be used to pay for jails and correctional institutions; they are hard-pressed to consider the provision of behavioral health care within these settings to be a budget priority. Funds for correctional institutions, and the judicial system as a whole, are justified primarily by concerns over public safety, by the need to get offenders off the streets and out of voters' neighborhoods. When proposals are made to cut correctional facility budgets, unions protest that it is only the correctional staff who stand between the community and the violent offenders whom they guard. Fear mongering of this type obviously cannot be used to promote the behavioral health or community re-entry of forensic patients.

Arguments to fund behavioral health care and to divert people from, or move them along and out of, the correctional system thus have to rely on other approaches. Current concerns over prison overcrowding and the mass incarceration of persons with substance-related arrests provide a somewhat effective foil for this purpose, but they alone stop well short of advocating for funding for behavioral health care. For this purpose, additional strategies are required and can, and should, be based on what we know about the forensic population.

Figure 5.1 offers an approximation of the penetration rates of serious mental illnesses and substance abuse or dependence within, and outside of, the jail and prison population. In the United States roughly 16% of persons in jails and prisons have a serious mental illness and roughly 65% of persons in jails and prisons have a substance use disorder (Osher et al. 2012). Among the 16% of persons with serious mental illnesses, over half of them will have a co-occurring substance use disorder, resulting in three subpopulations of interest (labeled in the figure). Among persons currently in jails and prisons, the smallest group (A) is comprised of those with serious mental illnesses, followed by a larger group (B) of persons with both a serious mental illness and a substance use disorder, and with the largest group (C) comprised of persons with substance use disorders only. Even under current legislation, the vast majority of these persons will eventually be released to the community, with that number approximating ten million persons per year nationwide (Osher et al. 2012).

These are the facts as best we know them. What they mean for policy makers is that at least one half of the people returning from jails and prisons to their communities each year will be struggling with a serious mental illness, a substance use disorder, or a combination of both. At the same time, recidivism rates for re-arrests among the overall prison population hover between

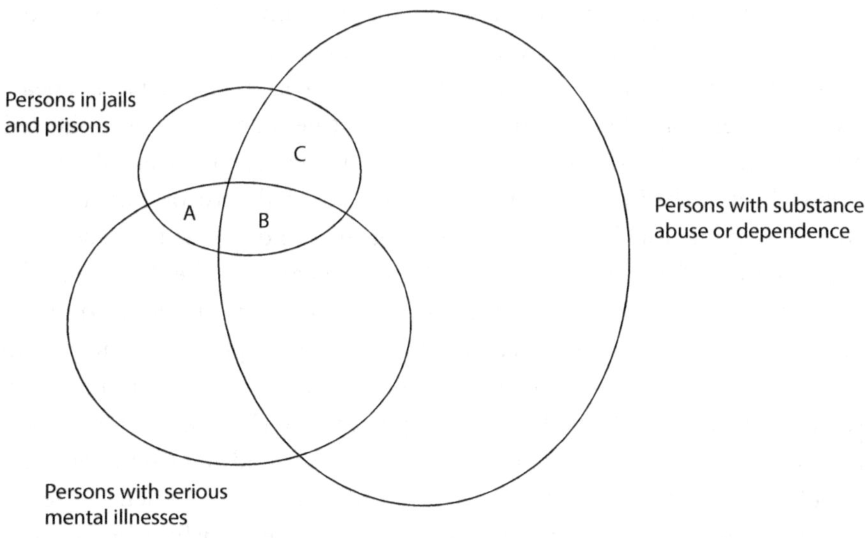

FIGURE 5.1 Overlapping Issues.

60% and 75% for the three to five years following release (National Institute of Justice 2015). If we are not to continue to see the criminal justice system as an expensive "revolving door," we will need to make targeted efforts to prevent reoffending and re-incarceration among those already in the criminal justice system. Given that untreated mental illnesses and active addictions pose major barriers to successful community re-entry, these targeted efforts will need to address these risk factors in a more effective and sustained way than has been tried in the past. This provides a more appealing basis upon which to argue for the funding of behavioral health care for the forensic population, especially when it can be shown to be a cost-effective strategy in reducing recidivism, as we discuss next.

2. Invest in strategies that can be shown to pay for themselves over time. Given that there is little new funding on the horizon for forensic services for the foreseeable future, a primary strategy for shifting the locus of care from institutions to the community is to find ways to reallocate existing funds. A key consideration in finding areas in which it is possible to do so is to target and reduce the use of costly acute care services that have been shown to effect little positive impact. For persons with substance use conditions, such an opportunity is afforded by those who have repeated detox admissions but who do not get connected to a lower level of care as a result. In the case of mental illnesses, similar opportunities can be found with persons who have repeated emergency room and/or acute psychiatric inpatient admissions. Ordinarily, such persons are viewed as placing undue burdens on a system rather than as presenting opportunities for reform. Moving from one perception to the other, though, unleashes both creativity and resources.

How does this work? Historically, persons who use costly services repeatedly have been considered "refractory" to treatment and have been labeled with a variety of derogatory terms such as "retreads," "frequent fliers," or "high utilizers." The implicit assumption underlying the use of these phrases is that it is somehow the person's own fault that he or she is using services "inappropriately"; that the problem lies with the person rather than with the system of care. Rather than viewing these persons as *the* problem, adoption of a recovery orientation suggests that we invite these persons to help us to redefine the problem in their own terms and that we look at the services being provided through the lens of their own perspective (Davidson et al. 2006). When asked, for example, they have described detox and acute inpatient care as not being very responsive to their needs and as not having much to offer in the way of initiating or sustaining changes in their everyday lives in the community (e.g. Davidson et al. 1997; Rowe et al. 2002). They have identified such issues as housing, poverty, unemployment, and discrimination as equally, if not more, pressing as their substance use or mental illness (Davidson et al. 1995; Rowe 1999), and often feel that there is little, if anything, that they can do to change their situation or improve any aspect of their health (Davidson et al. 1997; Schmutte et al. 2009).

Within this context, their repeated use of the emergency room or detox program begins to make more sense and to point to different types of interventions. From a systems point of view, it also begins to make sense to suggest that if a person has not yet connected to outpatient substance use treatment after thirty-eight detox admissions, he or she is unlikely to do so after admission numbers thirty-nine or forty—unless, that is, something else is to change as well. It is then in this realm of the "something else" that creativity can be brought to bear to make a better use of existing resources. Through a combination of care management and assertive outreach and case management—some of which has been provided by peer staff—the State of Connecticut's system of care has been able to generate a cycle of reinvestment by reducing acute service use among this population by an average of around 60%, freeing up millions of dollars to be reallocated to lower-cost outpatient and rehabilitative services and an array of community-based "recovery supports" (Davidson et al. 2010; Kelley and White 2011; Kirk 2011). These supports include supported housing, child care, transportation, supported employment, and flexible funds to meet other basic needs; addressing, in this way, the social determinants of health suggested by persons with mental illnesses and/or substance use as being the major barriers to their making productive use of treatment.

3. *Proactively address each point along the Sequential Intercept Model* (Munetz and Griffin 2006). The Sequential Intercept Model outlined over a decade ago by Munetz and Griffin provides a useful map of the territory traversed by persons with serious mental illnesses who come into contact, at various points, with the criminal justice system. It can now be enhanced by inclusion of junctures or interventions more specific to persons who are only struggling with substance use conditions (e.g. drug courts, mandated treatment). Taken together, this model highlights the numerous points at which persons with behavioral health conditions could be "intercepted" from the criminal justice system and offered diversion from, and alternatives to, incarceration, as well as draws attention to efforts to promote community inclusion as a way of preventing re-arrest. Research has shown both that punishment and deterrence-based approaches have little to no impact on offending behavior (Osher et al. 2012) and that providing behavioral health care in the

community is more cost-effective and has more of an impact on recidivism than treatment provided in incarcerated settings (Henrichson and Delaney 2012). As a result, proactive, strength-based, and community-focused care is likely to save criminal justice costs as well as behavioral health costs (Ettner et al. 2006); a saving which the State of Connecticut began to witness when it first instituted a jail diversion program over twenty years ago.

There are at least two major challenges involved in shifting in this way to a proactive approach to promoting community inclusion and preventing recidivism. First, there is the philosophical challenge involved in reconceptualizing forensic services to be recovery- and citizenship-oriented as opposed to, or at least in complementarity to, the traditional focus on containment and control in the service of public safety. Shifting orientation to recovery and the restoration of citizenship does not require giving up on the public safety agenda at the heart of forensic work. Rather, it in fact enhances this agenda by persuading patients and practitioners alike that reoffending and recidivism are more likely to be decreased to the degree to which the person regains a sense of meaning and purpose, occupies a valued social role, and has his or her basic needs met rather than to the degree to which he or she has become adjusted to life within an institution—whether that be a criminal justice or behavioral health setting.

The second challenge is more of a policy and fiscal matter than one of beliefs and attitudes. It has to do with who pays for what for whom under which circumstances. Traditionally, the criminal justice system has paid for the costs of incarceration and community-based supervision, as well as for the behavioral health care provided within correctional settings. The behavioral health system has paid for behavioral health services provided outside of correctional settings, and these funding streams have been siloed, even when the source of both streams may have been state budgets. Shifting to a predominantly community-based system first requires the two systems to collaborate and coordinate their efforts on behalf of people being served in both systems to make maximal use of state dollars. An argument may need to be made, for example, that state funds used to supply non-clinical resources such as housing, employment, and education be seen as investments in the person being served that will save the state money down the road in reduced criminal justice costs. With annual, or even bi-annual, state budget cycles, such an argument may be difficult to make prospectively, as the costs to be recouped may be projected to come from a future budget cycle. This is where having previous or current experience with successful care and case management initiatives such as those described above can be invaluable tools for making the case with legislators and governors that, in essence, enhanced care and community-based support are more effective and less costly than prolonged incarceration and control. A second strategy for shifting to community-based care is described as the next principle.

4. Make creative and maximal use of Medicaid dollars to enhance services. Implementation of the Affordable Care Act is resulting not only in more people having health care coverage, but also—and for our present purposes, especially—in more health care coverage being paid for by Medicaid through a combination of federal and state dollars. This includes the expansion of Medicaid to pay for a range of mental health and substance use services that previously were not covered. To the degree to which forensic services can be paid for by Medicaid, they will no longer represent as much of a drain on state general funds, whether these be allocated to the criminal justice or behavioral health systems. For states that participate in the Medicaid expansion enabled by the Affordable Care Act, these new dollars for new purposes offer a new source of funding for forensic services. In order to make this shift, however, a number of issues need to be addressed. We mention a few of these below.

First, under current legislation, Medicaid coverage is terminated upon a person's entry into a correctional setting and then needs to be reinstituted following discharge. This not only results in discontinuities in the person's own care (as he or she has to reapply once back in the community) but also in care being provided by two separate provider systems. Some states are considering suspending rather than terminating Medicaid eligibility during the period of incarceration as one way of reducing this discontinuity, as well as reducing the administrative demand placed on overworked state staff (Bainbridge 2012; Pinals 2014). Although a step in the right direction, this change will do little to coordinate care between the two systems, however. And with Medicaid being expanded to include at least 30%, and up to 80%, of persons coming into contact with the criminal justice system (Bainbridge 2012), there will only be an increased, rather than decreased, need for such coordination. As a white paper produced by the Bureau of Justice Assistance of the U.S. Department of Justice points out, the Affordable Care Act is likely to "result in individuals increasingly entering the criminal justice system with treatment and medication plans already established … [placing an] implied level of responsibility … on these criminal justice systems to maintain such established levels of care" (Bainbridge 2012, 15).

Second, Medicaid, as a health care plan, has been constrained by requirements of "medical necessity" in determining which services will be covered for which individuals with what health conditions. The purview of forensic psychiatry, on the other hand, is tasked with concerns with public safety, containment, and the evaluation and reduction of criminogenic risk. While potentially overlapping, these constructs are certainly not the same and allow for there to be some tension, at best, in the design and implementation of community-based forensic services. To the degree to which behavioral health conditions can be framed either as posing safety risks in and of themselves, as in those found not guilty by reason of mental disease or defect (NGRI) and substance-related cases, or as reducing a person's responsiveness to correctional interventions and thus posing risks for recidivism (Osher et al. 2012), these potentially competing paradigms can be viewed rather as complementary.

Where the two paradigms may remain more at odds is in relation to the issue of funding priorities. The allocation of limited criminal justice funds will be determined primarily by concerns about public safety and risk, while the allocation of limited behavioral health funds will be determined primarily by concerns with medical necessity. Cross-system collaborations can emerge where and when these priorities intersect (Pinals 2014), with the understanding that there are limits to what either system can manage on its own. For example, the criminal justice system may retain sole responsibility for those persons who have committed the most serious crimes and/or who pose the greatest risks. While for those persons who have less serious offenses and who pose less serious risks, but whose behavioral health needs are the greatest, the behavioral health system is increasingly in the position of being able to shoulder more of the burden for their care. For all of those persons who fall somewhere in between these two extremes, the Justice Center of the Council of State Governments has produced a very useful Criminogenic Risk and Behavioral Health Needs Framework to guide the development of different forms of collaboration between the criminal justice and behavioral health systems (Osher et al. 2012, 32–6). Use of this shared framework across systems promises to result in the cost-effective use of limited resources by identifying "the right people for the right interventions" based on an assessment both of the degree of risk posed and of the severity of the behavioral health needs presented, matching level of intensity of intervention with level of this combination of risk and need.

5. *Develop a shared language and understanding within the context of a public health model.* Our fifth and last principle for transforming forensic practice is to foster partnerships across state agencies and stakeholder groups. Often, this can be the surprising result of simply issuing an invitation for dialogue, as we witnessed in the State of Connecticut in the late 1990s. In this case, separate state agencies for mental health and addiction services had been

merged administratively into one state agency while, in effect, much else remained unchanged. As an initial, if important, step in realizing the effects of this merger in practice, the then commissioner of the merged state agency invited the leaders of the two recovery advocacy communities, one mental health and one addiction, to join together to create a shared vision for the system they would like to see. After a several month process of dialogue and negotiation, the two communities produced a common vision for a person and family-driven system of recovery-oriented care that still guides system reform efforts almost two decades later (Davidson et al. 2007). As a result, more progress has been made in Connecticut since then in bringing the two recovery advocacy communities together than in bridging the two provider communities, which remain to this day somewhat distinct.

More thoughtful and cost-effective decisions about the use of limited state dollars can be made when similar collaborations are developed across the criminal justice and behavioral health fields. In order to facilitate such collaborations, both fields can adopt a public health model that goes beyond a narrow focus on the individual offender/patient to a broader consideration of the social, economic, and political determinants of health and behavior. In addition to enabling the merging of funding streams and collaboration across professions, the adoption of a public health model places significantly more emphasis on prevention and health promotion efforts that are community-focused as well as community-based. If we have any hope of no longer being marked as that society which incarcerates the largest percentage of its population on earth, however, such proactive and community-focused interventions are inevitable (Power 2009).

CONCLUSION

Forensic psychiatrists interested in leading change may be challenged to adopt new models and learn new languages that will enable them to collaborate fluidly across state agencies, systems, and professions. In addition to being content experts, authoritative evaluators of risk and competency, and skilled clinicians, they will need to familiarize themselves with the differing priorities and agendas of elected officials, policy makers, funders, and other community-based practitioners. With respect to community practitioners in particular, there may be a fundamental difference in perspective on the role of "the community" in promoting recovery. Recovery-oriented practitioners strive to view the community as a welcoming and untapped reservoir of hospitality and as being the primary context in which recovery occurs. In fact, the 2003 President's New Freedom Commission on Mental Health Final Report defined recovery as "a life in the community" (DHHS 2003). In contrast, forensic practitioners have tended to view "the community" as a space that needs to be preserved and protected from the deleterious effects of crimes and criminals or as a space in which lacunae of hospitality must be created and nurtured. For the shift from correctional institutions to community-based forensic services to be successful, a more complex and nuanced understanding of the community is required that honors the validity of both perspectives. In the future, forensic psychiatry is likely to be judged as effective not only based on its successful rehabilitation of individual offenders but also on its role in creating more just and inclusive societies by addressing the social, economic, and political determinants of health and well-being along with pathology and criminogenic risk.

REFERENCES

Bainbridge, A.A. 2012. *The Affordable Care Act and Criminal Justice: Intersections and Implications.* Washington, DC: Bureau of Justice Assistance, U.S. Department of Justice.

Corrigan, P. and A.C. Watson. 2003. "Factors that explain how policy makers distribute resources to mental health services." *Psychiatric Services* 54: 501–7.

Davidson, L., E. Flanagan, D. Roe, and T. Styron. 2006. "Leading a Horse to Water: An Action Perspective on Mental Health Policy." *Journal of Clinical Psychology* 62: 1141–55.

Davidson, L., M. Hoge, M.E. Merrill, J. Rakfeldt, and E.E.H. Griffith. 1995. "The Experiences of Long-Stay Inpatients Returning to the Community." *Psychiatry: Interpersonal and Biological Processes* 58: 122–32.

Davidson, L., T. Kirk, P. Rockholz, J. Tondora, M. O'Connell, and A. Evans. 2007. "Creating a Recovery-Oriented System of Behavioral Health Care: Moving From Concept to Reality." *Psychiatric Rehabilitation Journal* 31: 23–31.

Davidson, L., D. Stayner, S. Lambert, P. Smith, and W.H. Sledge. 1997. "Phenomenological and Participatory Research on Schizophrenia: Recovering the Person in Theory and Practice." *Journal of Social Issues* 53: 767–84.

Davidson, L., W. White, D. Sells, T. Schmutte, M. O'Connell, C. Bellamy, and M. Rowe. 2010. "Enabling or Engaging? The Role of Recovery Support Services in Addiction Recovery." *Alcoholism Treatment Quarterly* 28: 391–416.

Department of Health and Human Services (DHHS). 2003. *Achieving the Promise: Transforming Mental Health Care in America.* Rockville: Substance Abuse and Mental Health Services Administration.

Ettner, S., D. Huang, E. Evans, D.R. Ash, M. Hardy, M. Jourabchi, and Y.-I. Hser. 2006. "Benefit-cost in the California Treatment Outcome Project: Does Substance Abuse Treatment 'Pay for Itself'?" *Health Services Research* 41: 192–213.

Henrichson, C. and R. Delaney. 2012. *The Price of Prisons: What Incarceration Costs Taxpayers.* New York: Vera Institute of Justice.

Hoge, M., J. Tebes, L. Davidson, and E.E.H. Griffith. 2002. "The Roles of Behavioral Health Professionals in Class Action Litigation." *Journal of the American Academy of Psychiatry and the Law* 30: 40–58.

Kelley, J. and W. White (eds). 2011. *Addiction Recovery Management: Theory, Research, and Practice*. New York: Humana Press.

Kirk, T. 2011. "Connecticut's Journey to a Statewide Recovery-Oriented Health-Care System: Strategies, Successes, and Challenges." In *Addiction Recovery Management: Theory, Research, and Practice*, edited by J. Kelley and W. White. pp. 209–34. New York: Humana Press.

Munetz, M. and P. Griffin. 2006. "Use of the Sequential Intercept Model as an Approach to Decriminalization of People with Serious Mental Illness." *Psychiatric Services* 57: 544–9.

National Institute of Justice. 2015. http://www.nij.gov/topics/corrections/recidivism/pages/welcome.aspx. Accessed August 15, 2015.

Osher, F., D.A. D'Amora, M. Plotkin, N. Jarrett, and A. Eggleston. 2012. *Adults with Behavioral Health Needs under Correctional Supervision: A Shared Framework for Reducing Recidivism and Promoting Recovery*. Washington, DC: Council of State Governments Justice Center.

Pinals, D. 2014. "Forensic Services, Public Mental Health Policy, and Financing: Charting the Course Ahead." *Journal of the American Academy of Psychiatry and the Law* 42: 7–19.

Power, A.K. 2009. "Focus on Transformation: A Public Health Model of Mental Health for the 21st Century." *Psychiatric Services* 60: 580–4.

Rowe, M. 1999. *Crossing the Border: Encounters Between Homeless People and Outreach Workers*. Berkeley: University of California Press.

Rowe, M., J. Frey, D. Fisk, and L. Davidson. 2002. "Engaging Persons with Substance Use Disorders: Applying Lessons From Mental Health Outreach to Homeless Persons." *Administration and Policy in Mental Health* 29: 263–73.

Schmutte, T., E. Flanagan, L. Bedregal, P. Ridgway, D. Sells, T. Styron, and L. Davidson. 2009. "Self-efficacy and Self-care: Missing Ingredients in Health and Healthcare Among Adults with Serious Mental Illnesses." *Psychiatric Quarterly* 80: 1–8.

SECTION 2

Forensic Psychiatry and Psychology as Their Own Change-Agents

CHAPTER 6

Recent Developments in Forensic Psychiatry Ethics

Philip J. Candilis and Richard Martinez

This chapter frames the progression of ethics from clinical practice to forensic work on individuals, families, community, and society. Forensic psychiatry works at the interface of law and medicine, involves unique problems of boundaries and dual agency in the professional–client relationship, and presents uncertainties and conflicting opinions about its accountability to society. Consequently, legal issues, the range of stakeholders, and the impact of psychiatric medicine on individual autonomy and public safety pose complex challenges for forensic professionals. These require alertness to boundaries and a more robust and dynamic professional ethics. This chapter tracks the recent developments of ethics in forensic psychiatry, from the emphasis on truth-telling and respect for persons to compassion and dignity, to the cultural formulation and context of forensic evaluations. It offers a unifying concept of professionalism and professional identity.

INTRODUCTION

Lying as it does at the intersection of law and psychiatry, forensic psychiatry falls under the influence of two disparate fields. Historically and philosophically, the law is a product of post-Enlightenment assumptions about human nature, often in direct conflict with developing scientific and psychologic understanding of human behavior. The law presumes the existence of free will; human beings are thought to be innately rational and to make voluntary decisions. Therefore, in the legal encounter, people are presumed sane, competent, and accountable. In medicine and psychiatry, such presumptions are appreciated as nuanced and complex. While the law forces the insanity defense, for example, to compartmentalize defendants into one of two categories, forensic practitioners appreciate the manner in which mental illness impairs rationality, voluntary choice, judgment, and decision-making along a continuum, not in absolutes. The law must be definitive in assigning blame or defining resolutions, while psychiatry interprets and infers, building on hypotheses and revising theories. Such contrasting approaches create tensions that are sometimes unresolvable.

Forensic psychiatry and psychology sit in the midst of such tensions, so they cannot be defined by the exclusive use of ethical traditions from either law or medicine. Forensic mental health therefore requires a synthesis of traditions, an integration where historical values of both professions join with modern developments in professionalism and ethics to lead toward a unique set of values and guidelines that can serve forensic clinicians.

At the clinical and practical level, these tensions are resolved in those common areas where psychiatrists are responsive to society's regulatory framework. Psychiatrists use legal mechanisms to commit patients when they are dangerous; they breach confidentiality to report child and elder abuse; they treat patients in uniquely regulated correctional and military settings; they evaluate and provide opinions on sanity and competency to stand trial; and they answer to the hospitals and licensing boards that privilege them. It may be clear that duties to the individual, community, society, and profession combine to create a unique professional ethic for forensic psychiatry.

Where disagreement arises is in the source and priority of forensic psychiatry's ethical principles, and the nature of the forensic practitioner's professionalism. Controversies persist in prioritizing the security of correctional settings over the confidentiality of inmate disclosures; in supporting military interrogations over the rights of the interviewee; in upholding Constitutional protections to bear arms over assessments of those who own weapons; and in advocating cultural sensitivity in a society still rife with prejudice, racism, and other forms of injustice. These are arenas where multiple obligations compete for the allegiance of the forensic professional.

It has been tempting merely to balance competing duties and loyalties in favor of the greater number or the most immediate perceived threat. "The greatest good for the greatest number" has been a bulwark of public policy since Bentham and Mill first articulated it a century and a half ago. And society's penchant for responding to threats by restricting personal freedom has a stout history—from the fledgling days of the Republic (i.e. the 1798 Alien and Sedition Acts) to the days following 9/11 (i.e. the 2001 Patriot Act). It is likewise tempting to assume the obligations of one's employer in deciding the priorities of a specific situation. Deciding one's ethics by the requirements of the job is an easy way to frame the moral requirements of a situation and absolve professionals from a more penetrating analysis. But, as will become clear, these approaches do little to provide consistent moral guidance for the wide-ranging experiences and situations of forensic practice.

EARLY ETHICAL APPROACHES TO FORENSIC PRACTICE

In general, theorists in forensic ethics have struggled with the central question of whether the forensic practitioner, in the role of expert evaluator, is primarily obligated to the goals and purposes of medicine, the values and goals of law, or some hybrid of the two. Before forensic psychiatry developed as a subspecialty with fellowship training and board certification, most early practitioners were general psychiatrists who evolved into forensic specialists. The initial challenge for many practitioners trained as clinicians involved questions of whether forensic practice involved a patient–physician relationship, and if not, what obligations were appropriate. Because most forensic experts were contracted by one side or the other in an adversarial proceeding, practitioners struggled with the questions of how to manage boundaries, competing roles, and conflicts of interests.

Indeed, in early examples of these approaches, articulations of forensic ethics prioritized either the legal frame or the medical. A founder of the American Academy of Psychiatry and the Law (AAPL), Seymour Pollack, distinguished forensic psychiatry from its clinical cousin, community psychiatry, by directing forensic evaluations primarily to the legal issues involving the patient (Pollack 1974). "Consultation is concerned," he wrote, "primarily with the ends of the legal system, justice, rather than the therapeutic objectives of the medical system." Pollack suggested that forensic specialists work outside their usual clinical roles and defer their ethics to those of the legal system.

Pollack's California colleague Bernard Diamond disagreed. He advocated that forensic psychiatry should participate in the reform of the legal system. Maintaining one's clinical and humanitarian mission was critical to the practice of psychiatry even when it worked with the law (Diamond 1959, 1992). Diamond famously wrote, "The psychiatrist is no mere technician to be used by the law as the law sees fit ..."

Robert Weinstock is a more recent proponent of this approach. He surveyed forensic psychiatrists in the 1980s (Weinstock 1986, 1988, 1989), and found that many considered themselves to be physicians bound by the ethics of medical practice. Weinstock acknowledged the ethics most professionals brought with them to their forensic practice. Balancing clinical and forensic values depending on the requirements of the case would become an important part of his later approach to weighing competing principles (Weinstock 2015).

These commentators recognized the tension between clinical and legal objectives. They were clear in their writings that moral values influence societal settings. The courtroom and consultation room were not immune to these concerns; even scientific data can have subjective influences—whether on the significance of a research finding or the difference of one clinical presentation from another. As legal definitions and culture differ between jurisdictions, so can psychiatric interpretations of similar data.

Thomas Gutheil recognized the unique ethical aspects of forensic practice. In describing decision analysis in malpractice cases, Gutheil et al. (1991) highlighted the difference between specific legal answers to courtroom questions and the more nuanced, probabilistic answers of clinical medicine. It was clear to these authors that there were many ethical tensions: one a tension of values in the balancing of community safety and patient liberty (e.g. as in civil commitment or correctional decisions). There was a similar tension of professions between judges and medical experts who applied their own risk analysis to cases (e.g. as when releasing sexual offenders), and a tension of strategies between those who weighed actuarial and clinical factors differently (e.g. as when assessing an individual's future risk of violence). These writers recognized that forensic practitioners would have to recognize tensions that arose from individuals, their institutions, and society at large—not just from psychiatry and the law.

Systems theorists like Richard Ciccone and Colleen Clements agreed (Ciccone and Clements 1984, 2001). Rather than generating conflicts between individuals and society by accepting historical models of competing principles, they recognized general human values of negotiation and brokering between systems of law and medicine. A more cooperative ethic of science and law gave professionals freedom to draw models of right action from both systems. Family and cultural values could even be used to resolve ethical dilemmas, and multiple levels of meaning could be found in forensic interactions.

Developing a mode of professionalism for forensic psychiatry would clearly require a more comprehensive theoretical approach than was previously available. Moreover, there would have to be a practical process for applying it every day. It was not enough to adopt the legal system's ethics or simply to define forensic practice by the ethical traditions of medicine and psychiatry. The legal system did not easily recognize the harms it could exact from its constituents—as when it pursued mandatory sentencing or overcharged defendants from non-dominant communities—nor did it recognize the challenges of examining participants who were diagnosed with a mental illness. Individuals diagnosed with mental illness may not recognize their best interests nor resist impulses that can harm them in the legal setting. For its part, the medical system did not easily recognize the deleterious effect of clinical advocacy (as when physicians testified directly for their patients) on a judicial system built on objectivity and fairness. Theoretical and practical unity would have to arise from a more clear-eyed view of the multifaceted intersection of law and psychiatry.

The effort to craft a comprehensive theory of forensic professionalism took a significant turn in 1997 when Paul Appelbaum articulated an approach to forensic work that clearly differentiated it from clinical practice (Appelbaum 1997). Appelbaum made clear that forensic psychiatry could not be guided solely by clinical and humanitarian purposes. Indeed, without the possibility of harming the individual evaluee, forensic psychiatry would be useless to the law. Appelbaum consequently cast his theory squarely into Pollack's camp.

In grounding forensic psychiatry in fundamental principles like justice, beneficence, and respect for persons, Appelbaum appealed to recognizable tenets of biomedical ethics—but with a twist. He elevated principles of justice and truth-telling into primary positions rather than balancing them in the classic *prima facie* equation favored by medical ethicists (i.e. Beauchamp and Childress 2001). For most ethics commentators to this point, balancing principles meant taking into account their equal weight: principles were equivalent "on their face," or "at first look." It was only after weighing the variables in each case that one principle outweighed another.

For Appelbaum, it was a hierarchical structure of principles that justified forensic psychiatry. Truth-telling (derived from beneficence) and justice were the primary values of clinical experts advising the courts. The truth encompassed the subjective truth of the professional's opinion and the objective truth of the forensic literature so there was room for personal and professional values, but there remained a clear judicial focus. As in clinical research, the rules in forensic psychiatry were different from clinical medicine, and as long as this difference was clear, the work was ethically justifiable.

Respect for persons, the basis for much human rights advocacy in the years to come, was relegated to a protective position. Respect for the evaluee assured that the psychiatrist could not conduct an unbridled search for truth: civil and constitutional rights remained in force, as when assessments could not occur before access to counsel. Moreover, there were still obligations of confidentiality and accurate representation, as when practitioners did not divulge irrelevant or provocative information. And if the evaluee collapsed, clinical ethics required the psychiatrist to perform emergency maneuvers. But these obligations were separate from the forensic role, a role clearly positioned in the judicial firmament.

Appelbaum's approach became the dominant model for a generation of forensic practitioners. It provided justification and guidance when professionals trained in the care and advocacy of patients found themselves engaging in actions that were not necessarily beneficial to evaluees. It was a theory that prioritized ethical principles in forensic practice, but did not fully develop a theory of professionalism for all forensic practitioners. The difficulty was that while Appelbaum's contribution addressed forensic practitioners engaged in expert evaluations and testimony, it did not address the myriad of other activities that involve forensic expertise. The practice of forensic psychiatry is a far broader enterprise, and cannot be guided by a singular ethical approach that emphasizes obligations to the law. While many practitioners may be involved in expert evaluations and testimony, many forensic practitioners are not. Indeed they may be engaged in additional activities that require broader guidance.

NEW DEVELOPMENTS IN FORENSIC ETHICS

In the last twenty years, forensic psychiatry has developed as a subspecialty, enlarged its scope of practice, and incorporated new developments in science, neuropsychiatry, the humanities, and social sciences. This has required new theory and reflection on the question of what it means to be a forensic practitioner.

Ezra Griffith addressed the limitations of an ethical foundation that elevated idealized principles of justice and truth without addressing the existing inequities of the legal system. In the U.S., for example, defendants from non-dominant cultural groups are disproportionately represented in the criminal justice system. Defendants who can afford better legal representation experience better outcomes. Consequently, the demographic realities of our judicial and correctional systems expose flaws that raise important questions about forensic psychiatry's loyalty to the current system. When participating in the system as it exists, one is co-opted to some degree by its failure to achieve goals of fairness and equality. These inequities are not accounted for by theories of forensic professionalism that work only at the level of prioritizing principles.

Griffith urged sensitivity to the differential impact of the legal system on persons of color, and identified a tool for assessing the true nature of the forensic encounter (Griffith 1998). This tool, the cultural formulation, could finally account for the influence of dominant cultural and political forces on non-dominant individuals, and address the dynamics of social control on vulnerable communities. Cultural sensitivity, cross-cultural practice, and narrative were consequently methods for addressing inherent bias while educating a system based in justice and fairness.

Themes of judicial inequity influence forensic professionals in their professional lives as well (Griffith 2005). As Griffith made clear in his later writings, there were personal, cultural, and community influences on the narratives of forensic experts themselves. They may experience challenges to their affinity for a system that is insensitive to cultural narratives, to a profession that ignores their unique developmental needs, and to their own personal sense of how to represent their community authentically. In fact, these issues raise difficulties for forensic professionals from all cultural groups—dominant and non-dominant—as they struggle to conduct forensic work with attention to the needs of an imperfect system, of vulnerable defendants, and imperfect procedures for addressing inequality. The specific influence of race and ethnicity on forensic practice, the moral foundations of practicing in a system with insufficient tools to address social vulnerability, and the importance of cultural formulation and self-reflection moved the theoretical discussion in a far more practical and realistic direction.

THE NEED FOR A MODEL OF PROFESSIONAL IDENTITY

Integrating principles and narrative into a unified view of forensic professionalism would be a critical next step for the evolution of forensic psychiatry ethics. In a series of articles, we proposed an approach that joined traditional principles of medical ethics with the narrative context of forensic encounters. Our goal was to define a unique professional ethics for forensic practitioners. In his 1997 treatise, Appelbaum had written: "For forensic psychiatrists, the primary value of their work is to advance the interests of justice." We could not disagree more. Rather, we offered a model of professional integrity that ties together core personal, community, and professional values to guide practitioners through the inevitable ethical discomfort of imperfect systems (Candilis and Martinez 2006; Candilis, Martinez, and Dording 2001; Martinez and Candilis 2005).

Principles work at the level of theory to ground ethical behavior, while narrative operates at the level of individual cases to flesh out the details. Context and culture consequently find their way into forensic opinions as a matter of course. We coined the term "robust professionalism" in an effort to broaden professional identity for forensic practitioners, and acknowledge that practitioners retain duties as physicians. Because forensic professionals often engage in working relationships that cannot be defined as traditional patient–physician relationships, practitioners cannot be guided chiefly by the prioritizing or balancing of classic principles of medical ethics.

Central to this unification of differing approaches was the rejection of narrow views of forensic role. Role theory, or conceptualizing the practitioner as meeting one's obligations by meeting the obligations of a role, is insufficient in guiding forensic practice. We often face multiple obligations to individuals, community, and profession. Professional roles and responsibilities defined narrowly ignore the complexity of the many obligations and the sources of those obligations. In fact, clean and pure divisions tend to obscure the hidden moral dangers, rather than clarify and make transparent the forensic practitioner's duties.

Adhering strictly to the requirements of a correctional system, of a military manual, or an organizational structure hid abuses that were amply exposed in the investigations surrounding correctional research, clinician-monitored military interrogations, and prosecutorial practices over the decades. Ignoring the humanity inherent to forensic practice led to unacceptable outcomes.

Along with Griffith's recognition of vulnerable individuals within the judicial system, we incorporated work by Matthew Wynia and his colleagues at the American Medical Association (Wynia et al. 1999, 2014) and Cruess and Cruess at McGill (1997, 2008). Wynia et al. (1999), for example, defined professionalism according to moral relationships. He wrote that the function of professionalism in society is to provide a "structurally stabilizing, morally protective force" that protects vulnerable persons and values. Here finally was an approach that offered a unified concept of professionalism—a view that cut across settings, theories, and cultures.

The power of this integration came from its recognition of multiple stakeholders and values. The individual evaluee, the court, the community, the profession, and society as a whole had a claim on the expert's work. The values of one's upbringing, education, and life experience could be recognized and unpacked. There were no influences that required veiling behind a role, a majority view, or an employer's pressure. Transparency and openness take the expert beyond common dual agency equations that only balanced one's responsibility to the court with the responsibility to the defendant, or responsibility to one's employer with responsibility to the profession. This is a "robust professionalism" that demands more of forensic practitioners and goes beyond the models of the time. Most importantly, we too have stressed that forensic practitioners are engaged in moral relationships. While these relationships may be multifaceted and complicated, our concept of professionalism accounts for the critical vulnerabilities of persons involved in forensic work. In this sense, we have tried to offer a professional identity model that embraces the variety of forensic practice, the complexity of loyalties involved, and the residual values of medicine.

The American Academy of Psychiatry and the Law states that forensic psychiatry is a "medical subspecialty that includes research and clinical practice in the many areas in which psychiatry is applied to legal issues." Integrity, transparency, cultural awareness, and self-reflection are but a few of the necessary elements for finding professionalism in this wide-ranging definition (Candilis 2009). We agree with Wynia and others that professional identity is an evolving process throughout one's life work—one that requires the proper habits of practice for an ethical, reliable, and credible practitioner. We were encouraged by AAPL's adoption of the ethical goal of "striving for objectivity" because objective truth is not possible given the conscious and unconscious biases or subjectivities of the work. Recognizing the subjectivity of loyalties and influences in forensic practice is very much part of a self-reflective and robust professional model.

HUMANITY, COMPASSION, AND RESPECT FOR DIGNITY

Some forensic psychiatrists have added further considerations to the development of a model of professional ethics for forensic psychiatry. Michael Norko, for example, found the foundational ethical tenets of forensic work in compassion for one's fellow man (Norko 2005). Drawing on secular and religious themes that crossed traditions and cultures, Norko placed the complexities of forensic professionalism squarely in the "larger context of human endeavor and struggle." Respect for persons in the forensic setting was an outgrowth of the commonality of human experience and compassion for others, not simply a curb on unfettered quests for truth. The obligations of the forensic encounter could now be extended not simply to clinical ethics but to the fundamental concern of one human being for another.

Alec Buchanan (2014, 2015) likewise called on respect for the dignity of individuals to take its place among the primary guiding principles of forensic psychiatry. Buchanan was clear that respect for persons, and their inherent dignity or worth, could not be relegated to a secondary position as Appelbaum had done. It is primary. That aspect of the person that deserved unconditional respect was dignity, a core element of medical and psychiatric ethics. Here again was a broader conceptualization of forensic ethics and professionalism than was available in narrow views of role or context.

Both Norko and Buchanan imply a new direction: that intrinsic to forensic practice is the witnessing and narrating of human tragedy and suffering. We believe that cultivation of such ethical practices are found in the listening, recording, writing, and speaking that are essential to forensic professionalism (Martinez 2014).

This appeal to the humanity of forensic professionals and their clients finds strong support in forensic psychology as well. Human rights and mental health advocates Tony Ward and Alfred Allan, for example, write powerfully of the obligations to basic human rights and the moral relationships established in professional encounters. Ward, for example, proposed a procedural approach that takes into account the narratives of each stakeholder while seeking unifying themes among them (Ward 2014). Proper decisions are those that can be justified by norms shared among participants. In a world of many values (what Ward calls "value pluralism"), this was a stalwart defense against the mere "defaulting" to one set of norms or another. This view resonated strongly with a robust professionalism that rejected the mere balancing of individual against society or professional against employer.

Allan, too, called for the balancing of ethical systems to take into account human rights when weighing individual, professional, legal, and public norms (Allan 2013). Historically, the dignity inherent to each person cut across communities and cultures in ways that few other ethical constructs did. It deserved special stature in the development of forensic professional ethics.

GOALS OF FORENSIC PSYCHIATRY

Since the development of forensic psychiatry as a subspecialty within psychiatry, a rich and thoughtful discourse has developed in the quest for a unified approach to forensic practice. While some writers have furthered our understanding of ethical problem-solving and theory to address ethical dilemmas such as dual roles and conflicts of interest, others have furthered discussion of an evolving professional identity that is unique to the forensic practitioner. Forensic practitioners are in need of a unified and inclusive statement of the goals of their relatively new subspecialty such as has recently been provided for medicine as a whole (Hanson and Callahan 1999). Those goals should move beyond narrow roles and exclusive loyalties to the justice system and recognize obligations to transform inequities and unfair practices. We believe that such a statement should recognize that forensic practitioners are given legitimacy because of their medical education and clinical expertise, and acknowledge that the practice is engaged in moral relationships with vulnerable individuals.

REFERENCES

Allan, A. 2013. "Ethics in Correctional and Forensic Psychology: Getting the Balance Right." *Australian Psychologist* 48 (1): 47–56.

Appelbaum, P.S. 1997. "A Theory of Ethics for Forensic Psychiatry." *Journal of the American Academy of Psychiatry and the Law* 25: 233–47.

Beauchamp, T.L. and J.F. Childress 2001. *Principles of Biomedical Ethics*. 5th ed. New York: Oxford University Press.

Buchanan, A. 2014. "Respect of Dignity as an Ethical Principle in Forensic Psychiatry." *Legal and Criminological Psychology* 19: 30–2.

———. 2015. "Respect for Dignity and Forensic Psychiatry." *International Journal of Law and Psychiatry* 41: 12–17.

Candilis, P.J. 2009. "The Revolution in Forensic Ethics: Narrative, Compassion, and a Robust Professionalism." *Psychiatric Clinics of North America* 32 (2): 423–35.

Candilis, P.J. and, R. Martinez. 2006. "Commentary: The Higher Standards of Aspirational Ethics." *Journal of the American Academy of Psychiatry and the Law* 34: 242–4.

Candilis, P.J., R. Martinez, and C. Dording. 2001. "Principles and Narrative in Forensic Psychiatry: Toward a Robust View of Professional Role." *Journal of the American Academy of Psychiatry and the Law* 29: 167–73.

Ciccone, R. and C. Clements. 1984. "The Ethical Practice of Forensic Psychiatry." *Bulletin of the American Academy of Psychiatry and the Law* 12 (3): 263–77.

———. 2001. "Commentary: Forensic Psychiatry and Ethics—the Voyage Continues." *Journal of the American Academy of Psychiatry and the Law* 29: 174–79.

Cruess, S.R. and R.L. Cruess. 1997. "Professionalism Must be Taught." *British Medical Journal* 315: 1674–7.

———. 2008. "Understanding Medical Professionalism: A Plea for an Inclusive and Integrated Approach." *Medical Education* 42 (8): 755–7.

Diamond, B.L. 1959. "The Fallacy of the Impartial Expert." *Archives of Criminal Psychodynamics* 3: 221–36.

———. 1992. "The Forensic Psychiatrist: Consultant vs. Activist in Legal Doctrine." *Bulletin of the American Academy of Psychiatry and the Law* 20: 119–32.

Griffith, E.E.H. 1998. "Ethics in Forensic Psychiatry: A Response to Stone and Appelbaum." *Journal of the American Academy of Psychiatry and the Law* 26: 171–84.

———. 2005. "Personal Narrative and an African-American Perspective on Medical Ethics." *Journal of the American Academy of Psychiatry and the Law* 33: 371–81.

Gutheil, T.G., H.J. Burstajn, A. Brodsky, and V. Alexander. 1991. *Decision-making in Psychiatry and the Law*. Baltimore: Williams and Wilkins.

Hanson, M.J. and D. Callahan (eds). 1999. *The Goals of Medicine: The Forgotten Issues in Health Care Reform*. Washington DC: Georgetown University Press.

Martinez, R. 2014. Professional Ethics in Forensic Psychiatry. Presented at the American Academy of Psychiatry and the Law annual meetings, October 2014, San Diego, California.

Martinez, R. and P. Candilis. 2005. "Commentary: Toward a Unified Theory of Personal and Professional Ethics." *Journal of the American Academy of Psychiatry and the Law* 33: 382–5.

Norko, M. 2005. "Commentary: Compassion at the Core of Forensic Ethics." *Journal of the American Academy of Psychiatry and the Law*. 33 (3): 386–9.

Pollack, S. 1974. *Forensic Psychiatry in Criminal Law*. Los Angeles: University of Southern California Press.

Ward, T. 2014. "The Dual Relationship Problem in Forensic and Correctional Practice: Community Protection or Offender Welfare?" *Legal and Criminological Psychology* 19: 35–9.

Weinstock, R. 1986. "Ethical Concerns Expressed by Forensic Psychiatrists." *Journal of Forensic Sciences* 31: 596–602.

———. 1988. "Controversial Ethical Issues in Forensic Psychiatry: A Survey." *Journal of Forensic Sciences* 33: 176–86.

———. 1989. "Perceptions of Ethical Problems by Forensic Psychiatrists." *Journal of the American Academy of Psychiatry and the Law* 17: 189–202.

———. 2015. "Dialectical Principlism: An Approach to Finding the Most Ethical Action." *Journal of the American Academy of Psychiatry and the Law* 43: 10–20.

Wynia, M.K., S.R. Latham, A.C. Kao, J. Berg, and L. Emanuel. 1999. "Medical Professionalism in Society." *New England Journal of Medicine* 341: 1612–16.

Wynia, M.K., M.S. Papadakis, W.M. Sullivan, and F.W. Hafferty. 2014. "More than a List of Values and Desired Behaviors: A Foundational Understanding of Medical Professionalism." *Academic Medicine* 89 (5): 712–14.

CHAPTER 7

Narrative and Performance in Forensic Psychiatry and Psychology Practice

Ezra E.H. Griffith

A NINETEENTH-CENTURY TALE

On December 16, 1897, at a meeting of the Boston Medico-Psychological Society, Dr. Walter Channing read a paper on the subject of medical expert testimony that was published the following year (Channing 1898). Born into a family of distinguished physicians, Channing founded the Channing Sanitorium in Wellesley, Massachusetts and was an expert witness in the trial of Charles Guiteau, who assassinated President James Garfield. Channing went on to become Professor of Mental Diseases at Tufts Medical College and died in 1921 at age seventy-two (Stedman, Blumer, and Howard 1922).

In his presentation, Channing referred to his "alienist" colleagues who testified as experts in court trials and noted that there was often cause for criticism of the way their testimony was presented and utilized (Channing 1898, 385). However, he decided, with apparent satisfaction, to demonstrate the correct method of introducing medical expert testimony in a court trial, where the experts' opinions were "received with respect and consideration ... determining the final issue of the case" (Channing 1898, 385). The matter concerned a New Hampshire murder that had been committed in April 1897 during a bank robbery. In Channing's early account, we see a psychiatrist engaged in a single-case study of his own work and that of his colleagues, as they evaluated a defendant and provided medical expert testimony in court.

As the narrative unfolds, we learn that a young Joseph Kelley was arrested in Montreal three days after the incident, and he apparently confessed fully. With sensitivity to the cultural context and a recognition of the audience's presence, the narrator included comments about the seventy-year-old victim who was the cashier of the bank and a somewhat feeble old man. This victim was "respected and esteemed by those who knew him, and his brutal murder aroused the indignation of the community and a strong feeling of hostility toward the murderer" (Channing 1898, 386).

Channing was actually one of the three experts selected by the state to examine the defendant, and defense counsel chose three other experts. Channing (1898) recounted some astute observations about how he and his colleagues had carried out the evaluation. For example, he questioned the wisdom of the state experts' examining the defendant together as opposed to doing so singly. He noted, too, that defense counsel generally accompanied his experts to their examination. In his published narrative, Channing weighed the advantage of having an examiner's potential bias diminished by the presence of a third party against the disadvantage of having multiple people present during an examination. He worried that the presence of multiple individuals could dilute the "accuracy and exactness" of an examination that resulted from a "close and continuous" interrogatory (Channing 1898, 386).

Experts at the trial provided descriptions that showed how they carried out their work. For example, they were attentive to: the need for a thorough physical and psychological examination of the defendant; the defendant's extensive account of the bank robbery; his social and "moral history" that included the defendant's immoral relations with women and his having contracted syphilis; his history of abusing alcohol; his interactive friendliness with others; and a careful mental status examination. In the evaluation of Kelley, obvious attention was paid to factors that could clarify whether he was telling the truth or attempting to dissimulate and curry favor.

Channing made it quite clear that the accused admitted guilt in a forthright manner and was given every opportunity to describe his delusions and hallucinations. The experts also looked at poetry and letters written by Kelley in their search for additional evidence to support findings from their direct observations of him. They paid attention to his lack of remorse. From these details, we see emerge the early structure of how the forensic work was done, and how the forensic specialists formulated and buttressed their opinions.

We learn from the narrative that in the end, Channing concluded Kelley "was not the subject of any form of insanity"; he lacked "maturity of judgment" and was "a degenerate with congenital or acquired criminal instincts" (Channing 1898, 400). But Channing did not reach a conclusion at the end of the examination about the ultimate question of whether the accused was responsible for his crime. I note here that every modern forensic specialist, even those in training, is aware of this vexing debate of whether courts should allow us to make pronouncements on the ultimate question in a criminal trial of whether the defendant had a mental state related to an element of the crime or the defense to the crime (Buchanan 2006).

Unrelated to the Kelley case and relatively recently, modern-day forensic specialists have written about matters that came up in the evaluation of Joseph Kelley. As examples, Channing recognized the potential bias of forensic examiners (see Large and Neilssen 2008; Wills 2008) and the problem of their partisanship (see Weiss 2015); he took note of the effect of local culture on the way community and court audiences might consider a case (see Carter and Forsyth 2009; Boehnlein, Schaefer, and Bloom 2005); he attended to the need for accuracy, exactness, and completeness in the examination (see Kaufmann 2013); and he mentioned the factor of potential dissimulation in forensic evaluations (see Drob, Meehan, and Waxman 2009). He also contended with the problem of diagnosing an evaluee in the context of a forensic examination (see Wills and Gold 2014).

However, this enumeration of details lacked what we might call today a certain punch and a coherent tying-together until Channing eventually turned, with surprising attentiveness, to the opening statement made by the defendant's lawyer. It is at that point we see Channing expand the focus of the story. It seems that he was forced to do so by the nature of the narrative weaved by the defense attorney in court. The lawyer noted that at age four years, Kelley had had a fall that left him in a coma for two or three days. During the period of further confinement to bed, young Kelley suffered from convulsions.

The lawyer described other developments that occurred during Kelley's adolescence. For example, witnesses heard Kelley speak of seeing the devil; he was sent to a reformatory because of uncontrolled stealing; he exhibited bizarre behavior, such as offering to a friend an expensive watch in exchange for a mere newspaper. On one occasion, he inexplicably took out a revolver and fired at a man he did not know who was standing in a field. It was not made clear in the narrative whether Channing and colleagues had missed this information during their examination of the defendant in the jail or the lawyer had strategically reserved it for himself. However, Channing (at page 405) did state that the defense counsel's words "had considerable weight as corroborative evidence of Kelley's peculiar mental condition … and made it more possible to understand his boy-man make-up and his stunted moral nature."

Still, we could say that at this juncture in the Channing narrative, a new picture of the defendant appeared, which led the experts of both sides to confer together and to decide that Kelley was not fully responsible for the crime. It was a remarkable development. Counsel for both sides agreed that Kelley should plead guilty. That done, the jury was dismissed, and all six experts presented their findings to the judge. Their essential point was that the defendant was deficient mentally, and this resulted in his having limited responsibility for the crime. The judge found Kelley guilty of murder in the second degree, and he was sentenced to thirty years' imprisonment, in sharp contrast to the death penalty that he was originally facing. The experts' arguments for limited or diminished responsibility were based on their view of the defendant's impaired brain development or degeneracy. The trial was over.

At least in Channing's account of things, there is a noticeable turn in the story. There is a pause in the enumeration of examination data, and the story takes on a new urgency, new meaning, and greater clarity. Consequently, I could reframe this nineteenth-century tale, by borrowing language and a framework from Langellier (1999), an authority on narrative and performance studies. I could say that the attorney reworked his client's narrative or perhaps created a fresh version and gave it new meaning. This counsel for the defense gave voice to his client; erased the silence created by his client's incapacities; and attached meaning to the accounts of the accused's life. The attorney placed the audience squarely in the midst of his client's life and evoked the image of his client as the member of a marginalized group with experiences commonly ignored by the broader society. The narrative was redone in a more personalized fashion. In this more pronounced meaning-making, the narrative became performative, which is to say the story took on a particular orientation. It gained in importance; the audience could understand better its seriousness; and they could appreciate why they should be interested in it. I recognize that now I am anticipating the fuller discussion of narrative and performance that will come later. But I think it important to attend to this turn in Channing's story.

It is precisely the subject of this chapter. Peterson and Langellier (2006) help us to understand that while Channing and his forensic colleagues were making or creating a narrative with details about Kelley's deeds, the defense attorney intervened to flesh out and perform the narrative, to do it. In his doing of the narrative, he gave it meaning, non-neutralized it, introduced salience, and connected the audience to Kelley's life.

This nineteenth-century review of the way alienists/psychiatrists conducted the forensic evaluation and presented their findings in court sets the stage for a focused examination of the influence that narrative and performance now play in the work of the present-day forensic specialist. In this chapter, I make the claim that the basic forensic work of yesteryear's psychiatrist and psychologist has been significantly influenced, particularly in the last fifteen to twenty years, by a better understanding of the theorizing carried out by colleagues in narrative and performance studies and other disciplines like anthropology, law, and social psychology. I apply this theorizing to conceptualization of the forensic psychology and psychiatry evaluation as performative narrative; and then I apply the notion of performative narrative to oral and written forensic work. I argue that it is time we forensic specialists appreciate more fully the connection of narrative and performance to specific domains of our work. It is my view that this strengthened connection enhances the quality of our practice.

CONCEPTUALIZING THE FORENSIC PSYCHIATRY AND PSYCHOLOGY EVALUATION AS PERFORMATIVE NARRATIVE

When I first started participating in forensic psychiatry in the late 1970s, I held the simplistic notion that I was required to reflect on a few basic ideas, recently captured aptly by Zemishlany and Melamed (2006). These authors saw forensic psychiatry (and by my extension, forensic psychology) as a bridge between two disciplines (psychiatry and the law) that simply had difficulty from time to time carrying on a meaningful dialogue. Psychiatry was a medical discipline preoccupied with providing therapeutic interventions in the least restrictive arena of care. The law was focused on principles such as freedom and rights of the individual and of the public; questions related to criminal responsibility; different types of legal competencies; and so on. Thus, in my scheme of the forensic work, I expected that the psychiatric or psychological evaluation would always be linked to a legal question and context. I believed that the traditions of evaluation and assessment learned in medical school and sharpened during specialized psychiatry training were sufficient for the forensic task.

Applying these principles retrospectively to the nineteenth-century Kelley case, I could easily see a number of legal themes emerging. They were related to the facts of the robbery-murder; the question of the defendant's capacity to plan the event; and certainly the difference between diminished and complete criminal responsibility. The nineteenth-century narrator raised his own concerns about the most fruitful and effective way to carry out the examination and to address the inherent problem of evaluator bias. He also took note of the cultural implications for the accused of causing the death of a feeble seventy-year-old man who was respected and esteemed by those who knew him. The narrator recognized the turn that the experts' story-telling had taken when the defense attorney got to his feet and made the story of the accused come to life by accentuating some important data about the accused's early development.

Portraiture

As I gradually developed an interest in telling stories about people, an interest that flourished with my teaching involvement in a university's Department of African-American Studies, I was dissatisfied with the reports I was preparing for my forensic psychiatry cases. Then one day in a conversation with a Yale professor of African-American Studies, he referred me to a text by Lawrence-Lightfoot and Davis (1997) on portraiture. It is in coming to grips with this text that I became familiar with expressions and ideas such as painting with words, studying life, capturing the texture and nuance of human experience, and viewing human experience as potentially framed and shaped by context.

These authors also illuminated the difference between empirical description and aesthetic expression; between listening to a story and listening for a story. They emphasized the role of the portraitist, the crucial influence of his predisposition and perspective. Then there was the declaration of blending "the curiosity of the biographer, the literary aesthetic of a novelist, and the systematic scrutiny of a researcher" (Lawrence-Lightfoot and Davis 1997, 15). Finally, these authors highlighted for me the concept of "voice," which has been so persistently present in my own work since then: voice as witness, voice as interpretation, and voice as preoccupation. All of these notions struck me again forcefully as I viewed Pablo Picasso's portraits of men and women during a recent visit to the refurbished Picasso Museum in Paris. The experience also highlighted the difficulty of digesting these ideas in light of Picasso's varied approaches to portraiture and applying them to our forensic tasks.

Incursion of Narrative

Of course, since my encounter with the ideas of Lawrence-Lightfoot and Davis, I have become more familiar with the work of scholars interested in narrative, particularly in anthropology, social psychology, law, and narrative and performance studies. I eventually concluded that carrying out a psychiatric/psychological evaluation with eyes fixed on the relevant legal parameters is not enough. It is not satisfactory for the expert just to enumerate and organize the findings of the evaluation that have been gleaned from a thorough clinical examination of the evaluee, from interviews of collateral witnesses and carrying out laboratory and psychological tests, and from reviewing documents—all of which would be reworked into a coherent narrative to be used for some legal purpose (Griffith, Stankovic, and Baranoski 2010, 33).

I began to understand, through numerous discussions with colleagues, that the forensic specialist must now approach the work with conceptual ideas in mind. He must expect that he will deliver the findings of his evaluation orally or in written form, and in a "forum that anticipates critical analysis, disagreement, and even verbal confrontation or cross-examination" (Griffith, Stankovic, and Baranoski 2010, 32).

The development of the forensic report has progressed over time, showing in its content steadily increasing organization, clarity, and specificity. Readers who have an interest in this development would find it useful to review the early presentations by Channing (1898) and by Porteous and Robinson (1915); then the work by Hoffman (1986) and Silva, Weinstock, and Leong (2003). These authors have provided a structure of both written and oral forensic reporting that permits systematic examination of the contents of such reports. A thorough and disciplined review of the forensic psychiatry report has recently been produced in a text edited by Buchanan and Norko (2011). But it is more the overall conceptualization of both oral and written reports as a form of narrative that has captured my interest. What ideas do the examiners bring to the evaluation process? What do they think they are doing and what are they intending to contribute to the search for justice? How do they approach the task of persuading the audience receiving their oral and written reporting?

I have found the work by Martinez particularly instructive. Martinez (2002) approached narrative through his interest in clinical work. As he reflected on human suffering, he argued that the efforts led by psychiatry and psychology to alleviate suffering of the sick were fortified through increased emphasis on medical humanities and narrative knowledge and methods (Martinez 2002, 129). Martinez justified the emphasis on narrative by pointing out that eliciting a checklist of information about the psychiatric patient, and by my extension the forensic evaluee, was not enough. The forensic specialist should encourage the evaluee to present a complete story of involvement with the legal system, and the evaluator should then begin the work utilizing a narrative perspective.

Martinez (2002, 132) focused on the case study of a single patient to demonstrate the advantages of the narrative approach in clinical work that came through encouraging the patient: to tell a complete story, with a developing understanding that the patient is seen as a person with unique difficulties; to develop and strengthen his own voice, which in turn positively impacts the partnership between evaluator and patient; to maintain voice in this context which helps the patient to retain dignity during the evaluative process, as the evaluator has the chance to evaluate the findings in a context of empathic connections. Thus, the process created through this narrative approach facilitates the evaluator's efforts to carry out the meaning-making in a balanced way, which is to say that the patient has the opportunity to author his own story, even if it is laced with efforts to malinger and mislead. Finally, Martinez (2002, 136) hailed the method for the opportunity it gave the evaluator to do his work on a foundation of humility and compassion. Needless to say, adjustments must be made as the evaluator moves from a context of clinical care to one of forensic evaluation.

Brooks (2006, 2) stated it more succinctly in raising the question about whether the law needs a narratology. He suggested we could see narrative as a way of presenting a story about some event in our world. In narrative, we are generally concerned about how the story's parts combine in a plot; about how we understand the beginning and end of an action; and about how the story moves through a state of disequilibrium to a state of reestablished order. Brooks also was clearly concerned about perspectives of story-telling: who saw what and was telling, and the relation of storyteller to the story. Brooks was focused on narrative and the law. I am interested here in narrative and our forensic work. I posit that Brooks' questions make sense and are relevant to my considerations, particularly when he notes that thinking about narrative facilitates answering a simple question: how and when do we know that our story, in which we report that an event has taken place, does not make sense?

Performance

Gutheil (2000, 140) framed things for us, indicating that the forensic specialist should understand court proceedings as theater, and should match the drama of his oral presentation to the language level of the audience. Gutheil emphasized in his own way the use of concepts and imagery to improve the clarity of one's oral and written explanations. Indeed, he began to frame his own view of performativity by stating that the presenter's dress, demeanor, and body language were all part of the performance task. He also recognized the interaction of the expert witness and the jury-audience, taking note of how factors such as logic and emotion could influence a jury. In this communication from 2000, Gutheil began to frame in a more structured fashion the interplay of the expert witness with audience and the formulation of elements that can potentially impact the message.

The following year, Bank (2001) made a clearer statement, presenting what he called the "courtroom communications model." Bank stated his model was influenced by social psychology, and its framework was built on three elements: speaker (expert), message (court testimony), and audience (judge/jury). It was important for the expert to have credibility (influenced by his expertise manifested by credentials and experience), trustworthiness (characterized by integrity in his use of data from the evaluation, for example), and presentational style. The message should represent an effective combination of logic and emotion. Members of the audience should be receptive to the testimony they are hearing, which would depend on the language used by the expert, his eye contact with the audience, and the use of his voice.

My reading of a 1975 article by Bauman (1975) was eye-opening. His work obviously predated the later contributions of Gutheil, Martinez, and others. But Bauman demonstrated how we in forensic work needed to integrate principles of narrative and performance. He highlighted the use of "performance" in talking about it as an organizing principle for verbal art applied to folklore. He shifted the thinking from "folklore as materials to folklore as communication" (Bauman 1975, 290).

As I tried to make the same change in reflecting on forensic reporting, I became convinced that the idea helped advance my own theorizing about my discipline. I could understand that creating the oral and written reports carried with it a "dual sense of artistic action," in Bauman's terminology, involving the doing/creating of the report on the one hand and the artistic event on the other hand. Furthermore, the creating of the forensic report involved the writer-speaker performer, the art form of narrative speaking-writing, and an audience (after all, forensic reporters don't speak or write to themselves).

Bauman helped me anticipate the reactions of some of my forensic colleagues to the notion that narrative and performance could be useful in our forensic work. My colleagues, in their resistance and objections, made two central points. First, they insisted that performance suggested distortion, obfuscation, exaggeration, or even joking and non-serious language. Their second point was that performance could be seen as a blatant disregard of ethics principles that our discipline was struggling so hard to develop. (Indeed, Martinez and Candilis (2011) emphatically underlined the point that the written forensic report must be conceptualized with an eye carefully focused on ethics principles. I agree enthusiastically with this point.) But I have always believed that my colleagues, unfamiliar with the concept of performance and unaware of the wide range of disciplines that have contributed to its development, have sought refuge by simply shunning the concept. In addition, I am persuaded that they have failed to recognize the essential task of communicating through their reports and have steadfastly ignored Bauman's notion (1975, 293) that "performance thus calls forth special attention to and heightened awareness of the act of expression." I believe my colleagues wanted to avoid this central point. It is that in our professional practice, we are engaged in a particularized form of communication about happenings in a sociopolitical and legal arena.

There are other points that merit emphasis here. Some colleagues ignore the notion that in the case of forensic reporting, I have never advocated that just anyone could tell stories in our disciplines of forensic psychiatry and psychology. Quite the opposite. Performing as a forensic specialist requires talent and sustained practice. There are ground rules and rituals specific to the contexts in which we operate. Furthermore, I argue that performance must be a cornerstone of forensic training that focuses on what Bauman (1975, 302) calls the display of competence, the focusing of attention on oneself as performer, and the enhancement of experience. Bauman (1975, 305) also noted that "It is part of the essence of performance that it offers to the participants a special enhancement of experience, bringing with it a heightened intensity of communicative interaction which binds the audience to the performer in a way that is specific to performance as a mode of communication."

APPLYING PERFORMATIVE NARRATIVE TO FORENSIC ORAL AND WRITTEN WORK

I eventually understood that, as Labov (1997, 395) put it, narrative was basically the choice of a "specific linguistic technique to report past events." It also often represented the narrator's effort to report on very important experiences in people's lives, and to understand what language and social life were all about. Labov (1997) emphasized the notion that the reactions of audiences to experiencing a narrative were part of a profoundly interactive phenomenon. I must confess that even this limited dimension of the work, that is to say the interrelatability of narrator and audience, had initially escaped me in forensic work. And yet in the Kelley story, the narrator informed us early on that the victim was a highly respected community member, and the defense attorney implicitly saw the significance of the victim's early experience with brain trauma. The story gradually took on meaning, and the audience was expected to appreciate better how the unfolding events of the robbery-murder were related to the defendant's life experiences. It was as though the narrator-physician and the narrator-lawyer were both working on a story and asking their audiences to try the story on, to see how it felt to them.

Structuring the Narrative

Of course, Labov (1997) has presented us a more structured framework for thinking about the narratives we create. He has introduced us to notions of evaluation, reportability, credibility, causality, the assignment of praise and blame, objectivity, and viewpoint. These techniques, once understood, help us to understand the work we do and also render our activity more conscious to us.

As an example, narrators participate in evaluating their narratives when they use language to emphasize certain events in the story. They use comparatives as they focus on particular events. They insert negatives in their descriptions. With reportability, the narrator decides, consciously or not, that the narrative will have a significant level of interest for the audience and not be banal or ordinary. Once the narrative has special interest for the audience, the listeners can no longer say, "So what?" Here Labov (1997) discussed the significance of setting up a hierarchy of reportable events so that the narrator eventually makes a choice of what constitutes the most reportable event so as to direct the audience's attention to the best among competing narratives. In the context of the Kelley story, it seems clear that the defendant's experience with brain injury and coma were essential features of a story that could hold the audience's attention and direct it to contemplating mental deficiency and its link to the notion of diminished responsibility.

The credibility of the narrative refers to the extent to which the audience believes that the narrator's events actually occurred. Labov cautions us that as reportability increases, credibility may decrease. The narrator, for a number of different reasons, may be taken with the idea of rendering an event reportable. He may repeat the telling of the event, embed it in jokes and other less serious techniques, and thus diminish its credibility. In order to heighten the credibility of a story, the narrator must pursue a theory of causality and try to answer a fundamental question of "How did that happen?" This is certainly an idea that must be considered, as expert and audience think about the relationship of mental disorder to a given crime (Buchanan and Zonana 2009).

Labov (1997) pointed out that as the narrator develops a theory of causality, he inevitably engages in assigning praise and blame to actors in his stories. He does this through a variety of different mechanisms, such as omitting events that detract from a reportable event he seeks to emphasize, utilizing a vocabulary that is evidently evaluative, and even assigning protagonists to categories that are transparently social types—such as categorizing a perpetrator of violence as a 250-pound, violent and drunken man.

Labov's comments on objectivity will interest forensic psychiatrists and psychologists to a considerable degree. First, he noted that narrators' observations can be influenced by their internal states. Hence reports of objective events (stating lucidly what someone said or did) tend to be seen as more credible than reports of subjective events (where we are told what someone felt emotionally). Reports of third-person witnesses are often considered more credible than statements from the main actors. These ideas of objectivity and credibility are of course part of the platform on which the modern forensic specialist builds the forensic narrative.

A final vital element in Labov's framework is his notion of viewpoint. Explicating this element in its most fundamental form, Labov noted that in literary narrative, events may be seen through the eyes of different participants in the story's telling, such as occurs in the use of flashbacks. This contrasts with oral narratives of personal experience where the narrator is bent on communicating the events as seen through his own eyes. The importance of understanding this vocabulary lies in the fact that the forensic narrator will be tempted to use different techniques in the forensic narrative in order to be persuasive. Thus every narrator must keep an eye on not stepping over the ethics line.

I have focused deliberately on presenting Labov's framework so as to enrich earlier conceptualizations of forensic narrative that colleagues and I have articulated (Griffith and Baranoski 2007; Griffith, Stankovic, and Baranoski 2010). Labov's contributions to the understanding of narrative rely on a structured approach that helps clarify what many forensic specialists do by rote or mechanically. His methodology also facilitates the task of teaching about how we do our work on a daily basis and present our findings in oral and written forms.

It has been commonly mentioned that the use and study of narrative has grown substantially over the last several decades. A casual perusal of the academic literature turns up narratives about minority groups, children, many different professional and vocational groups, conflict, politeness, the acquisition of identity, the loss of identity, groups with particular illnesses, resilience and adversity, life change, immigration, atrocities, incest, death, and so on. The breadth is vast, so much so that I was struck by the obvious political implications of narrative. In other words, while the formalistic, structural understanding of narrative is useful and necessary, analyzing the emotional content of stories has its own obvious import. It has its own political dimensions, the intent to make a specific argument and to do so persuasively.

Performance in Narrative

As Langellier (1999, 127) stated it, "… performance emphasizes the way telling intervenes between the experience and the story, the pragmatics of putting narrative into practice, and the functions of narrative for participants." Langellier (1999, 128) argued, too, that narratives generally have a political function (at least in the effort to constitute an audience and to be persuasive). Applying this to our work, the forensic narrator takes what he learns from reports by others and makes it the experience of those attending to the story. The narrator accomplishes this through a variety of performance features: for example, narrative detail, giving voice to actors, appeals to the audience, gestures and so on.

Not surprisingly then, scholars like Johnson (2005) have made us aware that many narratives are implicitly or explicitly narratives of identity and focus on matters of race, class, sexuality and with the purpose of evoking empathy or even provoking wrath and anger. Johnson (2005, 37) discussed efforts to "construct privileged identities in a favorable light while excluding alternative narratives from marginalized identity groups." This warning takes us back to our nineteenth-century Kelley story. It's evident that the defendant's lawyer recognized that his audience might likely be unfamiliar with stories of impaired brain development or degeneracy. The immediate task was to put his audience in the midst of his client's life and cultivate the audience's empathy. But there was also another mission at hand. The defendant, by his brain impairment and life experience, might very well have been in a subordinate group within the broader society. Consequently, it is this position of relative subordination that worries Johnson when it comes to the recounting of a life story about individuals like Kelley. Johnson seemed concerned that in this sort of context, the sociocultural difference between Kelley and the audience may lead to foreclosure of feelings of empathy from the audience. If that occurs, the audience may very well not overcome its prejudice and misconceptions about the defendant, as empathy is embargoed.

Throughout my excursions into narrative and portraiture, it has been an intriguing exercise to focus on a matter raised by Bamberg (1997), particularly as I have decided that the matter concerns forensic experts and their work. We forensic specialists are required to engage in the "act of telling—or 'representing' at a particular occasion in the form of a particular story—to intervene so to speak, between the actual experience and the story" (Bamberg 1997, 335). Assuming I grasp Bamberg's point correctly and his preferred focus on a pragmatic, performance-based approach to narrative instead of being unduly preoccupied with a structural approach, I proceed then to his emphasis on narrative positioning. (Others, like Langellier (1999, 126) talk of this distinction between traditional, structural approaches to narrative and pragmatic, performance-based narrative.) I first ask how we forensic specialists position our characters in relation to one another within the stories we tell.

Positioning in Performative Narrative

In discussions with colleagues, I have regularly argued that once finishing the introduction to my forensic report, I usually describe first (in a criminal case) the defendant's account of what transpired in the event, the most reportable event. I do so regardless of who has hired me for the forensic task. Victims follow, and then other collateral witnesses. I suggest that we should give our characters voice and even allow them to interact with each other. So a collateral police officer is allowed to speak freely and may contradict the version of the events recounted by the defendant, relatives, and others. At this stage, the narrator's voice is relatively muted. The act of giving voice means we allow the characters to define agency for themselves and discuss other factors impinging on their independence.

There are two other questions related to this process of narrative positioning (Bamberg 1997, 337). How does the narrator position himself to the audience and how does the narrator position himself to himself? I believe the narrator may use a number of different techniques to establish this connection to the audience. In court, it may take place through use of a particular vocal tone, a choice of specialized vocabulary or alternatively simple, lucid language. It may even take place through a mechanism of credentialing, where the narrator first explains his education and technical background, or talks about a particular form of life experience that justifies the narrator's engaging in this specialized type of narrative. Similarly, in thinking about the narrator's positioning of himself to himself, Bamberg suggested it comes down to how he defines himself, at least in relation to the task of narrating, and by extension to the overall forensic work. The question of "Who am I?" as I prepare for reporting orally or in writing on my forensic narrative highlights my own identity and helps me formulate internal personal views of my connection to the voices of the personages in the story. Indeed, I have repeatedly suggested that my understanding of positioning myself to myself helps me appreciate more substantively the roles of empathy and dignity in my work. (For a thorough discussion of this point, see Buchanan 2015.)

Langellier's (1999, 132) discussion of performative narrative is helpful to forensic psychiatrists and psychologists as they reflect on their work. Forensic narrators do not leave their daily lives behind when they participate in formulating forensic stories. Forensic narratives are a fundamental part of praxis. They also reflect culture and provide possibilities for us to rearrange relationships among our characters. "Personal narrative is a performance strategy with particular significance for socially marginal, disparaged, or ignored groups or for individuals with 'spoiled identities'" (Langellier 1999, 134). Therein lies the real relevancy of performative narrative to our forensic work. Plaintiffs in the civil context and defendants in the criminal context often have their identities spoiled, and they need support to have their stories articulated fairly and audibly.

CONCLUSION

It would be misleading to give the impression that narrative accounts pose no potential problems and that we in forensic psychiatry and psychology may therefore proceed to employ narrativity with no circumspection at all. Brooks (2006, 13) has cautioned us about this, stating that, "Narratives do not simply recount happenings; they give them shape, give them a point, argue their import, proclaim their results. And to do so they necessarily espouse some sort of 'point of view' or perspective, however hidden it may be, even from narrators themselves." Brooks (25) reemphasized his point: "We are always summoned to consider the possible omissions, distortions, rearrangements, moralizations, rationalizations that belong to any recounting." Brooks (25) finally put the icing on the cake with a thunderous conclusion, one that must remain in the minds of all those who engage in discussing narrative with trainees: "The more we study modalities of narrative presentation, the more we may be made aware of how narrative is never innocent but always presentational and perspectival, a way of working on story events that is also a way of working on the listener or reader."

Adshead (2014) has addressed this point directly in addressing the subject of stories and histories in forensic psychiatry. She referred specifically to what she called "spin" to describe a "process whereby different stories can be created, depending on which aspects of a factual truth are either exaggerated or diminished … humans tell stories that are the truth as they see it" (Adshead 2014, 437). I have already made the point carefully, in referring to the work of Martinez and Candilis (2011), that the use of performative narrative in psychiatry and psychology must be rooted consciously in a solid ethics base.

Nevertheless, I agree that there is no way we can escape the cautions noted above as we contemplate the use of narrative and performance in our forensic work. As closure to this point, I like how Brooks (2006, 18) teased us with a wonderful example of the potential treachery inherent to dabbling in narrative. He challenged his readers to focus on narrative relevance, asking whether discussion of the trauma of the victim's relatives was relevant to the guilt of the defendant. The tease continued in his reference to something being "over-relevant" (Brooks 2006, 22). He pointed out that in some cases, the story of past crimes must be excluded by courts, not because of their being irrelevant. Instead, it is because of the tendency for some of us to over-weigh the past events and thus deny to someone with a bad general record the chance to defend against a particular charge. So yes, narrative may be rich and filled with persuasive power, but we must be careful with it. I take Brooks's point here not as advocating deliberate omissions in forensic narratives. I assume that Brooks would agree that in doing so, the forensic narrator would create in certain cases significant ethics problems. Rather, I take his point as a warning that narrative is in practice a two-edged sword. It is a tool that we must employ with caution and reverence, always alert to potential problems of ethics, empathy, and dignity. Brooks (2006, 4) stated it elegantly and briefly, pointing out that narrative has the power to mislead. Thus there can be no unquestioned and absolute goodness of performative narrative.

We must all acknowledge that "stories may manipulate us" (Brooks 2006, 26). They may also provide to us forensic specialists "analytic instruments" for our toolkits and make us more aware of the "storied nature of our thinking" (Brooks 2006, 26). It is time we recognize more clearly that performative narrative has added a distinctive dimension to the work of forensic psychiatry and psychology specialists, providing us a way to make sense of the world and life around us. Narrative and performance in forensic work represent a way to see narrative in action (Gergen and Gergen 2006) and should therefore provoke more formalized reflection on how we use these techniques. With our present-day techniques of performance and narrative in hand, I hope that Channing would agree he might have made more of a to-do of Kelley's story.

REFERENCES

Adshead, G.M.J. 2014. "Commentary: Stories and Histories in Forensic Psychiatry." *Journal of the American Academy of Psychiatry and the Law* 42: 437–42.

Bamberg, M.G.W. 1997. "Positioning Between Structure and Performance." *Journal of Narrative and Life History* 7: 335–42.

Bank, S.C. 2001. "From Mental Health Professional to Expert Witness: Testifying in Court." *New Directions for Mental Health Services* 91: 57–66.

Bauman, R. 1975. "Verbal Art as Performance." *American Anthropologist* 77: 290–311.

Boehnlein, J.K., M.N. Schaefer, and J.D. Bloom. 2005. "Cultural Considerations in the Criminal Law: The Sentencing Process." *Journal of the American Academy of Psychiatry and the Law* 33: 335–41.

Brooks, P. 2006. "Narrative Transactions—Does the Law Need a Narratology?" *Yale Journal of Law & the Humanities* 18 (1): 1–28.

Buchanan, A. 2006. "Psychiatric Evidence on the Ultimate Issue." *Journal of the American Academy of Psychiatry and the Law* 34: 14–21.

———. 2015. "Respect for Dignity and Forensic Psychiatry." *International Journal of Law and Psychiatry.* Accessed June 4, 2015. http://dx.doi.org/j.ijlp.2015.03.002.

Buchanan, A. and H. Zonana. 2009. "Mental Disorder as the Cause of a Crime." *International Journal of Law and Psychiatry* 32: 142–6.

Buchanan, A. and M.A. Norko (eds). 2011. *The Psychiatric Report: Principles and Practice of Forensic Writing.* Cambridge: Cambridge University Press.

Carter, R.T. and J.M. Forsyth. 2009. "A Guide to the Forensic Assessment of Race-Based

Traumatic Stress Reactions." *Journal of the American Academy of Psychiatry and the Law* 37: 28–40.

Channing, W. 1898. "Medical Expert Testimony in the Kelley Murder Trial." *American Journal of Insanity* 54: 385–417.

Drob, S.L., K.B. Meehan, and S.E. Waxman. 2009. "Clinical and Conceptual Problems in the Attribution of Malingering in Forensic Evaluations." *Journal of the American Academy of Psychiatry and the Law* 37: 98–106.

Gergen, M.M. and K.J. Gergen. 2006. "Narratives in Action." *Narrative Inquiry* 16: 112–21.

Griffith, E.E.H. and M. Baranoski. 2007. "Commentary: The Place of Performative Writing in Forensic Psychiatry." *Journal of the American Academy of Psychiatry and the Law* 35: 27–31.

Griffith, E.E.H., A. Stankovic, and M. Baranoski. 2010. "Conceptualizing the Forensic Psychiatry Report as Performative Narrative." *Journal of the American Academy of Psychiatry and the Law* 38: 32–42.

Gutheil, T.G. 2000. "The Presentation of Forensic Psychiatric Evidence in Court." *Israeli Journal of Psychiatry and Related Sciences* 37: 137–44.

Hoffman, B.F. 1986. "How to Write a Psychiatric Report for Litigation Following a Personal Injury." *American Journal of Psychiatry* 143: 164–9.

Johnson, C. 2005. "Narratives of Identity: Denying Empathy in Conservative Discourses on Race, Class, and Sexuality." *Theory and Society* 34: 37–61.

Kaufmann, P.M. 2013. "Neuropsychologist Experts and Neurolaw: Cases, Controversies, and Admissibility Challenges." *Behavioral Sciences and the Law* 31: 739–55.

Labov, W. 1997. "Some Further Steps in Narrative Analysis." *The Journal of Narrative and Life History* 7: 395–415.

Langellier, K.M. 1999. "Personal Narrative, Performance, Performativity: Two or Three Things I Know For Sure." *Text and Performance Quarterly* 19: 124–44.

Large, M.M. and O. Nielssen. 2008. "Factors Associated With Agreement Between Experts in Evidence About Psychiatric Injury." *Journal of the American Academy of Psychiatry and the Law* 36: 515–21.

Lawrence-Lightfoot, S. and J. Hoffmann Davis. 1997. *The Art and Science of Portraiture.* San Francisco, Jossey-Bass Inc.

Martinez, R. 2002. "Narrative Understanding and Methods in Psychiatry and Behavioral Health." In *Stories Matter: The Role of Narrative in Medical Ethics*, edited by Rita Charon and Martha Montello, pp. 126–37. New York: Routledge.

Martinez, R. and P.J. Candilis. 2011. "Ethics." In *The Psychiatric Report: Principles and Practice of Forensic Writing*, edited by Alec Buchanan and Michael A. Norko, pp. 56–67. Cambridge, Cambridge University Press.

Peterson, E.E. and K.M. Langellier. 2006. "The Performance Turn in Narrative Studies." *Narrative Inquiry* 16: 173–80.

Porteous, C.A. and H.V. Robinson. 1915. "Some Notes on Expert Testimony by Alienists and Neurologists." *American Journal of Psychiatry* 71: 497–548.

Silva, J.A., R. Weinstock, and G.B. Leong. 2003. "Forensic Psychiatric Report Writing." In *Principles and Practice of Forensic Psychiatry*, edited by Richard Rosner, pp. 31–6. London: Arnold.

Stedman, H.R., G. Alder Blumer, and H.B. Howard. 1922. "Obituary: Walter Channing, M.D., LL.D." *American Journal of Psychiatry* 78: 491–3.

Weiss, K.J. 2015. "John H. Wigmore on the Abolition of Partisan Experts." *Journal of the American Academy of Psychiatry and the Law* 43: 21–31.

Wills, C.D. 2008. "The CHESS Method of Forensic Opinion Formulation: Striving to Checkmate Bias." *Journal of the American Academy of Psychiatry and the Law* 36: 535–40.

Wills, C.D. and L.H. Gold. 2014. "Introduction to the Special Section on DSM-5 and Forensic Psychiatry." *Journal of the American Academy of Psychiatry and the Law* 42: 132–5.

Zemishlany, Z. and Y. Melamed. 2006. "The Impossible Dialogue between Psychiatry and the Judicial System: A Language Problem." *Israel Journal of Psychiatry and Related Sciences* 43: 150–58.

CHAPTER 8

The Evolution of Forensic Training

Debra A. Pinals and Reena Kapoor

INTRODUCTION

Forensic psychiatry is a specialty in medicine that conjures up images of courtroom dramas but requires conscious attendance to professional ethics and rigor. As a subspecialty of psychiatry, it is geared to interface with the legal system, and with those complexities has experienced evolving trends in how the specialty is taught. As of 2015, forensic psychiatry training takes place in forty accredited forensic psychiatry fellowship programs across the country (Accreditation Council for Graduate Medical Education 2015a). The total number of forensic fellowship programs has fluctuated over the years. Data from the Accreditation Council for Graduate Medical Education (ACGME) from between 2001 to 2015 indicates that the total number of programs has ranged from thirty-eight in the 2011–2012 academic year to forty-five during the 2005–2006 academic year, with total numbers of residents ranging from about seventy to eighty.

Although the numbers of forensic psychiatry graduates may seem small compared to general specialties in medicine, the group of individuals who complete advanced training in forensic psychiatry learn skills that are often critical in some of society's most complex arenas. For example, following the training year, these individuals work as psychiatrists in public mental health settings, court clinics, forensic psychiatric hospitals, jails, and prisons. Many go on to work as private practitioners conducting critical evaluations related to disability, workers compensation, psychiatric malpractice and even system reviews in class action litigation and federal oversight activities. Some are drawn to leadership and administrative roles. Some return to clinical practice, enriched by the knowledge obtained during the training year. Additionally, as the field of forensic psychiatry has emerged as a well-rounded psychiatric subspecialty, forensic psychiatrists have increasingly been recognized in contributing to policy across a variety of frontiers, including significant landmark legal case decisions through amicus briefs, and commentary on statutory trends through the American Psychiatric Association's Council on Psychiatry and the Law (see e.g. Bonnie, Appelbaum, and Pinals 2015, Pinals et al. 2015).

Despite being what many would consider a unique field of medicine, as a subspecialty, forensic psychiatry must adhere to the larger trends faced by the medical specialists, including the sea changes that have been occurring in the approach to graduate medical education. Though the regulation of medical education is not new, advancement in efforts aimed at measuring outcomes, technological advances, and increased public scrutiny on health care delivery have contributed to a need for increasingly rigorous standardization related to education of medical residents and expectations of medical specialists. With these trends, graduate medical education programs have become focused on measurable methods of teaching skills, domains of knowledge, and attitudes residents must acquire in their training years.

Forensic psychiatry training has similarly moved from "learning on the job," to unregulated mentoring, to more recent codification of procedures and milestones to delineate the training and learning processes and outcomes. This chapter bears witness to the history and evolution of this training movement.

THE ROAD TO SUBSPECIALTY ACCREDITATION

The practice of forensic psychiatry began long before its recognition in 1992 by the American Board of Psychiatry and Neurology (ABPN) as a formal subspecialty of psychiatry. Figure 8.1 delineates important events in the field's evolution. The earliest reports of psychiatrists testifying in American courts date back to the nineteenth century, when psychiatrists gave opinions based on clinical expertise, without having any formal training in how to interface with the legal system. This practice continued until the latter half of the twentieth century. In the 1950s and 60s, medical and legal professionals who were interested in the interface between law and psychiatry began to organize into groups, and a few medical schools began training programs in forensic psychiatry, primarily using the apprenticeship model. By 1969, the field had progressed enough to form a professional organization, the

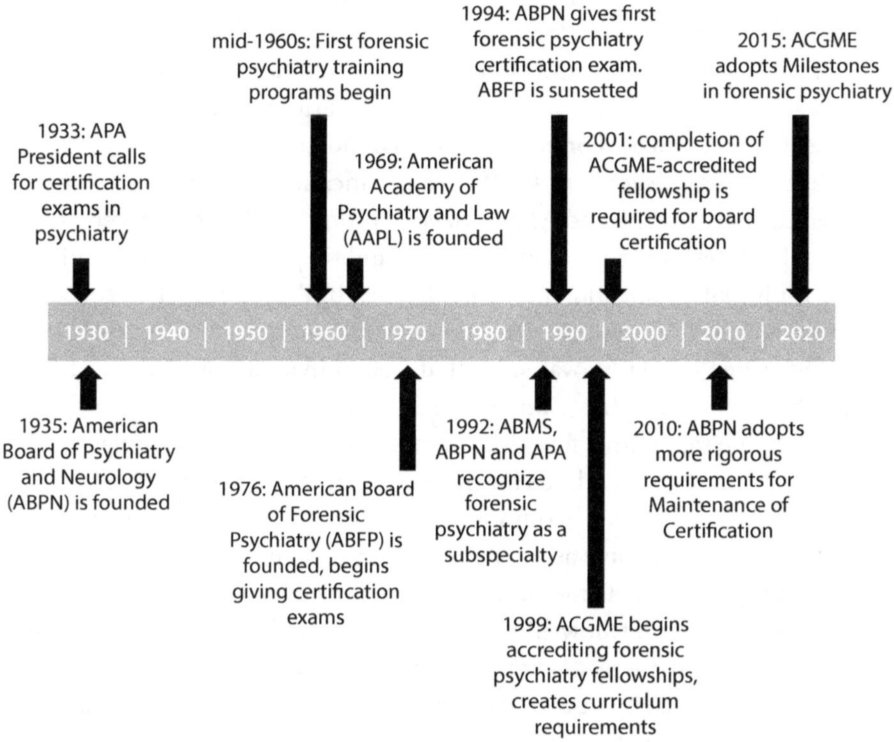

FIGURE 8.1 Landmark Events in Forensic Psychiatry Education.

American Academy of Psychiatry and the Law (AAPL). The mission of AAPL was (and remains today) to advance the body of knowledge in psychiatry and the law and to facilitate the exchange of ideas between members. Although AAPL members were required to be American Psychiatric Association (APA) members as well, the organizations were independent in their missions and governance.

In the early years of AAPL, members debated about whether to pursue formal training standards and subspecialty accreditation for forensic psychiatry. Opponents were concerned about misuse of board certification by attorneys and expert witnesses, while proponents perceived a heightened esteem for the profession from formal subspecialty recognition. After agreeing to pursue subspecialty status, a group of AAPL members approached the APA and American Board of Medical Specialties (ABMS) about subspecialty certification in the 1970s. The reception they received was lukewarm. The APA's Board of Trustees declined to create a certification board for forensic psychiatry, and the ABMS was concerned about the increasing number of medical subspecialties, requiring rigorous justification for any new area of special competence (Zonana 2012, 154). Because of this resistance, forensic psychiatrists were forced to look outside the usual pathways to medical specialty recognition in their effort to create an accreditation process.

In 1976, AAPL joined together with the American Academy of Forensic Sciences (AAFP) and the Forensic Sciences Foundation to create the American Board of Forensic Psychiatry (ABFP), a certification organization that was independent of the APA and ABMS. Several prominent forensic psychiatrists formed the initial governance of the ABFP, and they created written and oral exams for initial certification in the field. The ABFP gave its first certification exam to ten psychiatrists in 1976 and yearly exams thereafter. Between 1976 and 1994, when the ABFP was sunsetted, 260 individuals obtained certification in forensic psychiatry (Zonana 2012, 158).

Around the same time, forensic psychiatrists themselves were also working to create uniform standards for training in the subspecialty. In 1982, they formed the Accreditation Council on Fellowships in Forensic Psychiatry (ACFFP), whose mission was to establish clear goals and objectives for forensic fellowships, as well as methods for assessing educational outcomes. The Council required each fellowship program to submit documentation describing the content and methods of the training it offered. In addition, the ACFFP required a periodic site visit of each program by two experienced forensic psychiatrists in order to ensure the quality of the educational experience (Rosner and Sadoff 2015, 37).

By the mid-1980s, forensic psychiatry had developed processes for board certification and fellowship accreditation, but the fight for formal recognition as a medical specialty continued. The American Board of Psychiatry and Neurology (ABPN) and ABMS were still reluctant to recognize additional subspecialties, instead emphasizing the importance of broad clinical training in psychiatry. However, the ABPN did hold a conference to consider subspecialty accreditation requests in 1986, which the AAPL Medical Director and ABFP President attended. Following this conference, the ABPN echoed earlier critiques of forensic psychiatry: that the discipline did not yet have a clearly defined knowledge base or training curriculum. Despite continued lobbying by AAPL and the ABFP, another five years passed before the ABPN voted to recognize forensic psychiatry as a specialty in 1991. In 1992, the ABMS approved the ABPN's recommendation, and forensic psychiatry joined child/adolescent, geriatric, and addiction psychiatry as a formally recognized subspecialty.

The ABPN gave its first certification exam in 1994 and officially took over the ABFP's role as the organization responsible for board certification in forensic psychiatry. Similarly, the Accreditation Council on Graduate

Medical Education (ACGME) took over the process of fellowship accreditation from the ACFFP. Both the ABFP and ACFFP were sunsetted in 1994. The ACGME has since remained the organization that is responsible for the accreditation of any residency within medicine. Generally, completion of an ACGME-accredited residency allows the trainee to sit for the National Board examination in one's field. The ACGME performs its accreditation function through the work of its Residency Review Committees (or "RRC"s). The RRC for psychiatry oversees the adoption and implementation of required training components in general psychiatry and all of its subspecialties, including forensic psychiatry. For a residency or fellowship to be accredited, programs must apply to the ACGME and be reviewed by the RRC, using data from external reviews of program application materials and observational field visits.

Since it began accrediting forensic psychiatry fellowships, the ACGME has instituted many policies that have shaped the manner in which forensic psychiatrists obtain their initial fellowship training. The ACGME works alongside the American Board of Psychiatry and Neurology to develop standards for board eligibility and certification. This, too, has evolved. For example, between 1994 and 2000, psychiatrists could take the forensic board exam without completing a fellowship program, but in 2001 the ACGME began requiring completion of a one-year fellowship prior to board eligibility. In addition, the ACGME created rigorous accreditation procedures, "core competencies," and "Milestones" for all medical specialties that have added significant responsibilities to forensic training programs. At the same time, the ABPN has repeatedly revised its requirements for maintenance of certification—initially only a multiple-choice exam every ten years—and increased its expectations of diplomates over the years. The result of all these changes is that forensic education is now a robust industry, requiring constant attention from psychiatrists, trainees, and administrative professionals to ensure its smooth functioning.

DEVELOPING A STANDARDIZED CURRICULUM FOR FORENSIC PSYCHIATRY TRAINING

Early efforts to train forensic psychiatrists were based on an apprenticeship model, as psychiatrists with expertise in legal matters were relatively rare, and many medical schools had just one such individual who was qualified to train others. Apprenticeship experiences were often supplemented with interdisciplinary seminars including psychiatrists, attorneys, judges, psychologists, and professors. A 1973 survey of academic medical centers found that 81% of medical schools offered a training experience in psychiatry and the law, primarily based on lectures, discussions, and seminars (Sadoff 1974). Fewer than half of the schools included practical experiences, such as trips to institutions involved in law and psychiatry, in their programs. Only 25% of the medical centers considered their offerings adequate. Almost all of the programs were interested in communicating with other teachers of forensic psychiatry to share ideas and create a richer training experience.

In response to the growing demand for educational materials in forensic psychiatry, AAPL and AAFS members began to develop didactic curricula and recommended clinical experiences for training programs. An AAPL committee of experienced forensic psychiatrists led the preliminary efforts, meeting between 1979 and 1981 to craft recommendations. The committee's work eventually led to a 1982 report by the Joint Committee on the Accreditation of Fellowship Programs in Forensic Psychiatry, which established requirements for training programs. The report identified several core areas in which trainees were required to have didactic and clinical experiences:

- civil forensic psychiatry;
- criminal forensic psychiatry;
- legal regulation of psychiatry;
- special issues in forensic psychiatry (including assessment of dangerousness, psychopathic personalities, amnesia, and others);
- correctional psychiatry; and
- basic issues in law.

In addition, fellows were required to study landmark cases (as designated by the ABFP) and have regular clinical supervision with an experienced forensic psychiatrist. Training in law, research, and teaching were also required (Joint Committee on Accreditation of Fellowship Programs in Forensic Psychiatry 1982, 291).

Following the Joint Committee report, the ACFFP used the committee's standards to evaluate and accredit training programs across the United States. Fellowship programs grew from approximately fifteen in 1980 to twenty-eight in 1990. During this early stage of subspecialty development and fellowship accreditation, forensic psychiatry was free to define training standards as it saw fit. The field was not overseen by an umbrella agency of medical specialties, nor was it bound by requirements common to all disciplines. Therefore, the Joint Committee's initial requirements for training programs included many criteria that were unique to forensics. For example, training programs were required to have an attorney on faculty, and fellows were required to complete a minimum number of criminal and civil forensic evaluations during the fellowship year (Joint Committee on Accreditation of Fellowship Programs in Forensic Psychiatry 1982, 21).

When forensic psychiatry was recognized as a formal subspecialty by the ABPN in 1992, fellowship accreditation underwent major changes. Training programs that had been evaluated only by forensic psychiatrists now moved to a model of national accreditation by the ACGME, which utilized a standard system that applied to all branches of medicine. The accreditation process was further complicated in 1999, when the ACGME adopted a system of "core competencies" that would be required of residents in all medical specialties. The six core competencies are:

- medical knowledge;
- patient care;
- interpersonal and communication skills;
- professionalism;
- systems-based practice; and
- practice-based learning and improvement.

These six competencies were intended to capture the essential knowledge, skills, and attitudes that all physicians must acquire before completing residency training.

Adapting the early training goals of forensic psychiatry to the new ACGME domains led to some growing pains among programs, as several of the core competencies were not a natural fit for forensic work. For example, programs debated how best to create standards for "patient care" in a fellowship where trainees were explicitly being taught that forensic evaluees are not "patients" in the traditional sense. Similarly, the category of "medical knowledge" needed to be expanded into "medical and legal knowledge" to adequately encompass the goals of the fellowship. "Interpersonal communication" skills included not just the traditional medical role of patient–physician communication, but also courtroom testimony, written forensic reports, and consultation with legal professionals.

Despite these initial challenges, the use of ACGME core competencies quickly became routine, and forensic psychiatry adapted to the complex system of accreditation that the Council instituted for fellowships. Forensic psychiatry programs are now overseen by the academic institution's general psychiatry residency and its Graduate Medical Education committee. In addition, the ACGME oversees all psychiatry and subspecialty programs through its Residency Review Committees (RRCs) as described above.

The ACGME's accreditation requirements serve the purpose of creating some uniformity across fellowship programs that vary in size, location, and clinical focus. In forensic psychiatry, the Association of Directors of Forensic Psychiatry Fellowships (ADFPF) meets twice yearly at the AAPL and APA Annual Meetings. In addition to discussing practical matters, such as whether forensic psychiatry fellowships should join the Electronic Residency Application Service (ERAS) or participate in the "match," the ADFPF seeks to foster a dialogue among training programs. The ADFPF also provides feedback to the ACGME and American Association of Directors of Psychiatry Residency Training (AADPRT), who periodically make inquiries about forensic psychiatry training topics.

Recently, the ACGME has presented forensic training programs with a new challenge: adapting to its updated Next Accreditation System (NAS). NAS aims to shift the focus of resident evaluations away from qualitative assessments ("honest, hard-working, well-liked," etc.) and toward measurable assessments of skills ("able to perform forensic interview, conduct risk assessment, testify in uncomplicated cases," etc.). In some ways, the new system is easier for programs to navigate, as it eliminates some paperwork requirements and site visits by the ACGME every five years. However, it has also required the assessment of "Milestones," in which programs evaluate trainees every six months and report the results to the ACGME. Forensic psychiatry adopted thirteen Milestones in 2015, which are described in Table 8.1.

Although forensic training and accreditation have changed substantially in recent years, their aims remain remarkably similar to the goals and objectives first outlined by the field's pioneers in 1982. Modern forensic training has grown in scale and complexity, and trainees now have many more avenues to explore the field—national and international conferences, professional journals, videotaped mock trials, online education—than the early practitioners enjoyed. However, the heart of forensic training is still the acquisition of knowledge and skills about the intersection of psychiatry, law, ethics, and public policy. Training programs continue to focus on these content areas, but as the specialty has matured, educators have also become more thoughtful about the developmental process of becoming a forensic psychiatrist. As Pinals (2005) posited, forensic trainees go through stages of professional and personal development, progressing through stages of grief (for the treatment role) and self-doubt, ultimately achieving mastery of the field's knowledge base and their professional identities. Likewise, forensic education has undergone a similar process of maturation since its early, with many more stages of development yet to come.

Looking ahead, the ACGME is focused on developing outcome measures

TABLE 8.1 ACGME Milestones in Forensic Psychiatry

Core Competency	Content Area	Milestones
Patient care	Patient care	Provides psychiatric care in a forensic setting
	Procedural skills	Conducts a forensic psychiatric evaluation in criminal and civil settings
		Communicates the results of a forensic psychiatric evaluation through written and oral reports
Medical knowledge	Knowledge of the law and ethical principles as they relate to the practice of forensic psychiatry	Basic knowledge of the legal system, sources of law, and landmark cases relevant to forensic psychiatry
		Basic knowledge of civil law as it relates to forensic psychiatry
		Basic knowledge of criminal law as it relates to forensic psychiatry
		Knowledge of ethical principles as they relate to forensic psychiatry
	Knowledge of clinical psychiatry especially relevant to forensic psychiatry	Knowledge of the particular psychiatric and behavioral presentations commonly encountered in the practice of forensic psychiatry
		Knowledge of the assessment of particular psychiatric and behavioral presentations commonly encountered in the practice of forensic psychiatry
Systems-based practice	Patient/evaluee safety and the health care team	Medical errors and improvement activities
		Communication and patient/evaluee safety/risk
		Regulatory and educational activities related to patient/evaluee safety/risk
	Resource management	Costs of care and resource management
	Consultation to medical providers and non-medical systems	Provides recommendations as a consultant and collaborator
Practice-based learning	Development and execution of lifelong learning through constant self-evaluation	Self-assessment and self-improvement
		Evidence in the clinical workflow
	Teaching	Development as a teacher
		Observable teaching skills

Core Competency	Content Area	Milestones
Professionalism	Compassion, integrity, respect for others, sensitivity to diverse patient populations, adherence to ethical principles	Compassion, reflection, sensitivity to diversity
		Ethics
	Accountability to self, patients, colleagues, legal systems, professionals, and the profession	Fatigue management and work balance
		Professional behavior and participation in a professional community
		Ownership of patient care and/or responsibility for forensic evaluation
Interpersonal and communication skills	Relationship development and conflict management	Relationship with patients and evaluees
		Conflict management
		Team-based care or evaluation
	Information sharing and record keeping	Accurate and effective communication with team
		Effective communications with patients, evaluees, and others
		Maintaining professional boundaries in communication

that can help identify whether a particular resident has truly acquired the field's essential skills. Outcome measures are examined utilizing numerous tools, and programs are free to develop their own innovative ways of demonstrating the outcome of acquisition of the core competencies.

MAINTENANCE OF CERTIFICATION

With the recognition of forensic psychiatry as a subspecialty of psychiatry, the provisions related to education and training of lifelong learners applies. As such, the American Board of Medical Specialties (ABMS) has established an evolving set of requirements related to Board Certification, and in more recent years, related to Maintenance of Certification (MOC). As noted above, through the work of the American Board of Psychiatry and Neurology (ABPN), psychiatrists and subspecialists are able to obtain certification status that demonstrates that the individual has exhibited basic competencies. The ABPN cites as one of its goals a mechanism of accountability, a demonstrable credential that shows the physicians who have the certification are of sound quality (ABPN 2015a). In recent years, the medical field has seen a great deal of pressure related to ensuring high-quality standards and ongoing establishment of sufficient knowledge among practicing medical professionals. As such, all medical specialties have some form of MOC requirements, though each discipline in medicine has generated its own standards. There have been some studies that have shown that one's board certification status is directly correlated with improved practice (Bach et al. 2004; Holmboe et al. 2008; Lipner, Hess, and Phillips 2013; Hawkins et al. 2013).

Time-limited certification began in the mid-1990s, and along with this change came variations in approaches to ongoing certification as a whole. For psychiatry, the MOC program is comprised of four key parts (ABPN 2015b). Each one requires ongoing activities. The four components are:

- Professionalism and Professional Standing;
- Lifelong Learning (CME) and Self-Assessment (SA);
- Assessment of Knowledge, Judgment, and Skills; and
- Improvement in Medical Practice (PIP).

The first component, professionalism and professional standing, requires diplomates to maintain an active and unrestricted medical license to practice medicine. The second component of lifelong learning and self-assessment continues the tradition of requiring ongoing medical education of physicians (which is typically also seen in licensure requirements across the states). It adds, however, an element of self-assessment, which involves taking an approved assessment measure to help one identify areas of weakness that require further study and review. In forensic psychiatry, the American Academy of Psychiatry and the Law produced a written self-assessment examination beginning in 2012, and this has subsequently been followed by an online version. Many specialty organizations have done the same, and there are products available, generally for a fee, for individuals to complete their self-assessment requirement. Over time, these self-assessment tools have been required to be linked to continuing medical education activities as well, with attached educational credits. The third component, within psychiatry and its subspecialties, requires demonstrable cognitive expertise, as evidenced by passage of a written examination in the field and subspecialty every ten years. For expediency, it is possible to combine when these are taken (e.g. psychiatry and forensic psychiatry exam taken at the same time), but to date, they are separate examinations, and for a forensic psychiatrist to be considered a diplomate, he or she must maintain certification in psychiatry to maintain certification in the subspecialty of forensic psychiatry. A committee of the ABPN develops questions, which are revised over time.

The final component of MOC is for the physician to demonstrate ongoing attention to quality and "Performance in Practice," or PIP. This standard is often considered a more complicated standard but is in fact consistent with quality improvement activities that are typically utilized in settings such as hospitals and clinics. It involves two components, the first being a review of one's clinical treatment approaches through examination of patient medical records, and the second being the solicitation of feedback from peers. The clinical module of chart review is to be done on five patients and then repeated within three years on the same or other five patients. Forensic psychiatrists can choose what aspect of their work they wish to review. For example, a private practice forensic psychiatrist might choose to look at his work conducting independent medical examinations for disability insurance companies. By using a standard checklist such as the one developed by the American Academy of Psychiatry and the Law (AAPL), the psychiatrist can look at five disability reports and determine if his or her individual practice follows the outline of recognized practice guidelines. AAPL has developed several of the PIP forms that can be used for work on areas where practice guidelines exist (i.e., competence to stand trial assessments, disability assessments, and criminal responsibility assessments). Where there are deficits identified through these chart reviews, practitioners make an effort to improve and then reassess their own performance within three years.

The other component of the PIP modules includes the requirement that the physician would seek feedback from others on their work. This feedback module has evolved to require feedback from professional peers (which in forensic psychiatry may include attorneys). Patient or evaluee feedback had also been a requirement but is now optional according to the ABPN.

The evolving trend toward MOC activities has changed the landscape of forensic learning. True to its intended mission, it has furthered the need to ensure a package of evidence to demonstrate that the physician has engaged in lifelong learning and remains qualified to practice in the subspecialty. As with the rest of medical subspecialties, forensic psychiatrists have had to gear up to these standards. AAPL has been instrumental in helping its members and others by producing a self-assessment examination, PIP module assistance through checklist forms, and feedback forms that are relevant to forensic practice. In this way, the subspecialty is remaining current with the expectations of other physician groups. That said, the requirements continue to shift as the new standards of "maintenance" become a fabric of ongoing certification. Thus, forensic psychiatry teaching and learning continues to evolve.

TEACHING FORENSIC PSYCHIATRY TO OTHER LEARNERS

Beyond training psychiatrists to become forensic specialists, the field has evolved to ensure that forensic psychiatry training is a core part of any residency training curriculum. Early iterations of this included a focus on what topics and skills a resident in psychiatry should master during their early training years. The assessment of dangerousness and commitability, participation as an expert witness, the evaluation of competence to stand trial and criminal responsibility, as well as understanding family law and the nuances related to informed consent were suggested by Bloom and colleagues as needed components of residency training (1980). Methods of training residents that included attendance at law school and observation of courtroom testimony by other experts were topics that Lewis described as important early learning approaches (2004).

General psychiatry residencies now must have a forensic experience. Specifically, the ACGME requires that residents "experience evaluating patients' potential harm to themselves or others, appropriateness for commitment, decisional capacity, disability, and competency" (Accreditation Council for Graduate Medical Education 2015c). Core curriculum development in general residency programs includes a variety of efforts to expose budding psychiatrists to the field of forensic psychiatry (Marrocco et al. 1995; Williams et al. 2014). There are evolving trends in this area. For example, programs may have rotations in forensic hospitals or at correctional facilities (Fisher 2014; Jha et al. 2014)). Pinals also suggested that training psychiatrists on community forensic work, such as specialty courts, police diversionary activities, and the like, would be helpful to patients who find themselves between forensic, criminal, and public mental health systems (Pinals 2014). Training in forensic topics has also been identified as important in Child and Adolescent Psychiatry residency training (Wills 2011).

In addition to training psychiatrists on forensic topics, an important area of growth is in training non-medical professionals on topics related to forensic psychiatry. Learners of forensic psychiatry can also benefit from being engaged in training others, such as police officers, lawyers, and judges. Training of police in models such as Crisis Intervention Team training also can benefit from instruction by local clinical providers (Watson and Fulambarker 2012). When they participate as instructors, there can be an opportunity for forensic psychiatrists to learn and educate at the same time. Interdisciplinary training can have the benefit also of increasing knowledge and trust and better outcomes in service delivery when groups that often work in parallel engage in cross-training.

Other evolving standards of training in forensic psychiatry domains involves bringing other disciplines together in the forensic training experience (Mela and Luther 2013). For example, the ACGME requires that an attorney and a forensic psychologist must be part of a fellowship training experience (ACGME 2015b, requirement II.C.1). This cross-disciplinary exposure enriches the learning experience by bringing in other perspectives and sharing varying approaches to problem-solving in forensic cases. Given that forensic psychiatry is unique in its work that requires attorney interaction and frequently involves interaction with psychologists and forensic psychologists, requiring this type of training interface is a logical recognition of the reality of the work done in the field.

FUTURE DIRECTIONS

Forensic psychiatry is, relatively speaking, a young specialty, although it has rapidly evolved and matured as a discipline. As it approaches its 50th anniversary of formalization (if one marks its beginning as around the time of AAPL's inception) one can see the growth, including adaptation to outside regulatory forces, training expectations, and legal standards. As the courts have looked more deeply at issues of expert witness testimony and standards utilized (e.g. standards for expert testimony), and forensic practice guidelines have emerged (AAPL 2015), the world in which a forensic psychiatrist operates has become increasingly sophisticated, rigorous, and demanding. Other disciplines, such as forensic psychology, forensic social work, and even forensic nursing have taken stock and developed similarly, making for a climate in particular settings where professionals are well-poised to work with court-involved individuals and/or conduct assessments and testify to their findings. Roles have similarly evolved. For example, one state (Massachusetts) has begun to systematically hire social workers on criminal cases to assist public defenders.

Public mental health systems play a large role in funding forensic psychiatry fellowship training. Correctional systems also are often funders for such activities, and other public settings, such as the Veterans Administration, are beginning to look at forensic fellowship training as a helpful component to build a workforce to assist in the care of complex justice-involved populations with behavioral health needs. Thus, very often, forensically-trained clinicians are now finding work in settings such as forensic or civil state mental health hospitals, jails, prisons, community mental health centers, specialty court and other diversionary clinical services, Forensic Assertive Community Treatment programs, Assisted Outpatient Commitment clinics, and the like.

In the experiences of the authors, these trends have widened the scope of exposure of forensic trainees and the need to help them understand the contextual factors and environments in which they work. Whereas fifteen years ago fellowships were highlighted for training in forensic evaluation activities, now, in addition to the critical import of imparting knowledge to trainees in those endeavors, it is also apparent that exposure to public policy, administration, and work with individuals with the most challenging behavioral histories and histories of violence is critical. There are many patients who are in the public mental health system who have complex conditions involving early trauma, serious mental and medical illnesses, substance use and fractured social bonds. They may have behaviors including violence. When no one else is available to help treat them, forensic psychiatrists are often called upon to assist. The knowledge gained about the relationship between mental illness and violence, the ability to assess risk, and then the formulation of a treatment plan bring together skill-sets that are unique and valuable. Even in the world of civil forensic psychiatry, a sophisticated evaluator functioning in a private practice can sway a legal case in one direction or another.

The social responsibility of the forensic psychiatrist remains strong in the need to strive for honesty and objectivity in coming to the fairest conclusions in forensic evaluation work. This remains of the utmost importance to those impacted by a judge's ultimate decision. Thus, as the field has advanced, one can see the nuanced growth and trending in training and education of the learner. Organizations like AAPL can help keep the profession, and the professionals who do the work, grounded. This educational home remains a critical line to new knowledge and skills. Although much has happened to date in forensic training, undoubtedly we are still in the early phases of this fascinating evolution.

REFERENCES

Accreditation Council for Graduate Medical Education. 2015a. "Number of Accredited Programs Academic Year 2015–2016 United States." Accessed November 30, 2015. https://www.acgme.org/ads/Public/Reports/Report/3.

———. 2015b. "Program Requirements for Graduate Medical Education in Forensic Psychiatry." July 1, 2015. Accessed November 18, 2015. https://www.acgme.org/acgmeweb/Portals/0/PFAssets/ProgramRequirements/406_forensic_psych_07012015_1-YR.pdf.

———. 2015c. Program Requirements for Graduate Medical Education in Psychiatry." *ACGME*. Accessed November 15, 2015. http://www.acgme.org/acgmeweb/Portals/0/PFAssets/ProgramRequirements/400_psychiatry_07012015.pdf.

American Academy of Psychiatry and the Law. (AAPL). 2015. Accessed December 1, 2015. http://www.appl.org.

American Board of Psychiatry and Neurology (ABPN). 2015a. "Frequently Asked Questions." Accessed November 30, 2015. http://www.abpn.com/faqs/.

———. 2015b. "American Board of Psychiatry and Neurology, Maintenance of Certification, Program Requirements." *ABPN*. Accessed November 11, 2015. http://www.abpn.com/maintain-certification/maintenance-of-certification-program/program-requirements/.

Bach, P.B., H.H. Pham, D. Schrag, R.C. Tate, and J.L. Hargraves. 2004. "Primary Care Physicians Who Treat Blacks and Whites." *New England Journal of Medicine*. 351 (6): 575–84.

Bloom, J.D., J.D. Kinzie, and J.H. Shore. 1980. "Residency Curriculum in Forensic Psychiatry." *American Journal of Psychiatry*. 137 (6): 730–2.

Bonnie, R.J., P.S. Appelbaum, and D.A. Pinals. 2015. "The Evolving Position of the American Psychiatric Association on Firearm Policy (1993–2014)." *Behavioral Sciences and the Law* 33(2–3): 178–85. doi: 10.1002/bsl.2179.

Fisher, C.E. 2014. "General Psychiatric Residents and Corrections: Moving Forensic Education Beyond the Classroom." *Academy of Psychiatry* 38 (6): 680–4. doi: 10.1007/s40596-014-0216-6.

Hawkins, R.E., R.S. Lipner, H.P. Ham, R. Wagner, and E.S. Holmboe. 2013. "American Board of Medical Specialties Maintenance of Certification: Theory and Evidence Regarding the Current Framework." *Journal of Continuing Education in the Health Professions* 33, Fall: 7–19.

Holmboe, E.S., Y. Wang, T.P. Meehan, J.P. Tate, S.Y. Ho, K.S. Starkey, and R.S. Lipper. 2008. "Association Between Maintenance of Certification Examination Scores and Quality of Care for Medicare Beneficiaries." *Archives of Internal Medicine* 168 (13): 1396–403.

Jha, M.K., B.S. Fuehrlein, C.S. North, and A.M. Brenner. 2014. "Training Psychiatry Residents at Correctional Facilities." *Academic Psychiatry* 39 (1): 123–4.

Joint Committee on Accreditation of Fellowship Programs in Forensic Psychiatry. 1982. "Standards for Fellowship Programs in Forensic Psychiatry." *The Bulletin of the American Academy of Psychiatry Law* 10 : 285–92.

Lewis, C.F. 2004. "Teaching Forensic Psychiatry to General Psychiatry Residents." *Academic Psychiatry* 28 (1): 40–6.

Lipner, R.S., B.J. Hess, and R.L. Phillips. 2013. "Specialty Board Certification in the United States: Issues and Evidence." *Journal of Continuing Education in the Health Professions* Fall : S20–35.

Marrocco, M.K., J.C. Uecker, and J.R. Ciccone. 1995. "Teaching Forensic Psychiatry to Psychiatric Residents." *Bulletin of the American Academy of Psychiatry and the Law.* 23 (1): 83–91. PMID: 7599375.

Mela M. and G. Luther. 2013. "Law and Psychiatry Seminar: An Interprofessional Model for Forensic Psychiatric Training." *Academy of Psychiatry*. 37 (6): 421–5. doi: 10.1176/appi.ap.12070129.

Pinals, D.A. 2005. "Forensic Psychiatry Fellowship Training: Developmental Stages as an Educational Framework." *Journal of the American Academy of Psychiatry and the Law* 35 : 317–23.

———. 2014. "Forensic Services, Public Mental Health Policy, and Financing: Charting the Course Ahead." 2014. *Journal of the American Academy of Psychiatry and the Law* 42 (1): 7–19.

Pinals, D.A., P.S. Appelbaum, R. Bonnie, C.E. Fisher, L.H. Gold, and L.-W. Lee. 2015. "American Psychiatric Association: Position Statement on Firearm Access, Acts of Violence and the Relationship to Mental Illness and Mental Health Services." *Behavioral Sciences and the Law* 33(2–3): 195–8.

Rosner, R., and R.L. Sadoff. 2015. "The Modern Era of Forensic Psychiatry." In *The Evolution of Forensic Psychiatry: History, Current Developments, Future Directions*, edited by Robert L. Sadoff, pp. 33–40. New York: Oxford.

Sadoff, R.L., J.W. Thrasher, and D.W. Gottlieb. 1974. "Survey of Teaching Programs in Law and Psychiatry." *The Bulletin of the American Academy of Psychiatry Law* 2: 67–72.

Watson, A.C. and A.J. Fulambarker. 2012. "The Crisis Intervention Team Model of Police Response to Mental Health Crises: A Primer for Mental Health Practitioner." *Best Practices in Mental Health* 8 (2): 71.

Williams J., E. Elbogen and A. Kuroski-Mazzei. 2014. "Training Directors' Self-assessment of Forensic Education within Residency Training." *Academy of Psychiatry* 38 (6): 668–71. doi: 10.1007/s40596-014-0078-y.

Wills, C.D. 2011. "Forensic Education for Child-and-Adolescent Psychiatry Residents." *Academic Psychiatry* 35 (4): 256–9.

Zonana, H. 2012. "Forensic Psychiatry." In *The American Board of Psychiatry and Neurology Looking Back and Moving Ahead*, edited by Michael J. Aminoff and Larry R. Faulkner, p. 151. Arlington, Virginia: American Psychiatric Publishing.

SECTION 3

Changes in the Traditional Evaluative and Consultative Roles of the Forensic Psychiatrist and Psychologist

CHAPTER 9

Consultation to Civil and Criminal Courts

Barry W. Wall

INTRODUCTION

Traditionally, there were significant obstacles to improving the quality of forensic consultation to civil and criminal courts. Judges and attorneys were more likely to question the general evidentiary value of psychiatric expert opinions compared to other fields for several reasons. They included distrust of psychiatrists in general, the perception that behavioral sciences conclusions were unreliable, and rulings that psychological and psychiatric matters were understandable by common knowledge and therefore did not need expert evaluation. Courts were also often unwilling to set limitations for qualifications for expert witnesses in any field (Curran, McGarry, and Shah 1986). In a 1986 textbook on the developing fields of forensic psychiatry and forensic psychology, William Curran wrote:

> In the long history of the common law's use of expert consultation, the legal system itself—the consumer and patron of forensic science expertise—has been stubbornly unsupportive of quality standards for forensic psychiatrists ... Legal impediments to attracting the best of behavioral scientists to cooperate with the law courts have long existed, and their removal has often met resistance from the bench and bar until very recent times ... Until quite recent decades, conditions have not been much better on the professional side of psychiatry and psychology. The complexities and demands of interdisciplinary law-related service roles have discouraged and retarded the development of forensic training programs for

> the field. As a result, standards of professional quality have lagged behind other subspecialties. The busy practitioners, often without formal forensic training, have shaped and dominated the service aspects of the field. Most crucial of all, perhaps, has been the lack of support for research (Curran, McGarry, and Shah 1986, 1).

The American Board of Psychiatry and Neurology (ABPN) first recognized forensic psychiatry as an area of sub-specialization in 1992 (American Academy of Psychiatry and the Law website). Particularly since then, it has evolved into a specialized discipline. Developments within the field of forensic psychiatry, in medicine as a whole, and outside the profession have produced considerable change in the expectations of the courts, as well as the scope and functioning of the forensic consultant in traditional court contexts. These changes have been brought about by the fields of forensic psychiatry and psychology, technological and scientific advances, legal developments, and societal change such as the lessening of psychiatric stigma and the influence of consumer movements. While many functions of the expert witness remain the same as in years past, this chapter surveys how change has impacted expert witness practice.

QUALIFICATIONS AND CHARACTERISTICS OF EXPERT WITNESSES

Since the 1990s, courts have generally come to expect that forensic mental health specialists have additional education, training and certification in comparison to the non-forensic specialist. There is a common expectation that, for example, the forensic psychiatric expert complete a fellowship training program, pass the ABPN certification examination for "Certification in the Subspecialty of Forensic Psychiatry," and maintain both general and forensic subspecialty certification. The establishment of certified training programs in forensic psychiatry and psychology have contributed to the legal system's expectation that the expert witness possess specific qualifications and training to opine on forensic matters in court.

Unfortunately, the focus on training and certification can translate into clinical experience being given less consideration these days. Some experts now enter forensic practice without engaging in the care and treatment of patients at all, or they do not see the importance of developing concomitant clinical experience over time. Treating patients and retaining a fundamental clinical identity remains a matter of integrity and should not be overlooked by the forensic specialist, or by the courts.

ADMISSIBILITY OF TESTIMONY AND USE OF PRIOR TESTIMONY

Many jurisdictions have changed admissibility standards for scientific evidence over the years in an attempt to improve the utility of forensic sciences at court. The *Frye* test (*Frye* 1923), known as the general acceptance standard, served as the primary standard on admission of scientific testimony until the 1970s. In 1975, Congress established the Federal Rules of Evidence to guide admissibility of evidence at court. In 1993, the United States Supreme Court reviewed these standards in *Daubert v. Merrell Dow Pharmaceuticals, Inc.*, and held that the admissibility of scientific evidence depends on its scientific validity (*Daubert* 1993). Arguably, the shift away from *Frye* allows judges to better assess the overall validity of evidence, the precision and power of estimates, and the applicability and relevance of expert testimony (Glancy and Saini 2009).

The expert psychiatric witness now must be able to withstand *Daubert* challenges at court, and Gutheil and Bursztajn (2003) offer recommendations on doing so. Despite *Daubert*'s intent to strengthen forensic science, judges at the trial court level may admit testimony under the ruling with a great deal of latitude. A successful *Daubert* challenge sometimes can be better predicted by reviewing the decision history of a particular judge instead of by looking at the rulings made in similar cases within the same jurisdiction (Scott 2013).

In addition to addressing the validity of scientific expert testimony by courts, the American Medical Association (AMA) and states have attempted to limit "bad" expert testimony. Such efforts stem from the belief of non-expert physicians that expert witnesses cross state lines to deliver inaccurate testimony, and then return home having no accountability to anyone. AMA policy adopted in 1998 states that giving medico-legal testimony by a physician expert witness is considered the practice of medicine and that such testimony be subject to peer review (AMA 1998). In Florida, the out-of-state expert witness must apply for a certificate from the Florida Board of Medicine to provide expert testimony in that state (Florida Board of Medicine).

Although income is not the determining factor in Maryland's 20% attesting witness rule, it is relevant to credibility, so an expert should be prepared to provide the percentage of his or her income that is derived from medico-legal testimony (Daily Record 2002). Another approach to limit egregious testimony is to hold expert witnesses accountable in civil liability for "carpetbagging" (Gutheil 2006).

Electronic access to an expert witness's prior testimony is now more readily available. Attorneys can gather a great deal of information about an opposing party's expert prior to deposition. Attorneys seek such information to gain a tactical advantage during deposition or trial. Attorneys may also find information that could be used to discredit their own experts, such as inaccuracies as to qualifications or different testimony being given in a different lawsuit with similar facts. Some attorneys may find personal information about an expert to ensure that the expert is aware that the attorney has thoroughly researched him or her as a form of intimidation (Brennan and Dilenschneider 2009). Websites such as www.idex.com, www.dri.org, www.atla.org, and www.trialsmith.com help locate past testimony.

Electronic internet recordings of testimony are also more readily available. Some expert witness depositions and relevant materials are appearing on websites such as YouTube. Yahoo, Google and AltaVista have tabs that allow users to search for video. Expert psychiatric witnesses need to keep in mind that searches for electronic/video material on the internet have become a part of life as an expert witness.

CHANGES AFFECTING THE TRADITIONAL ROLES OF THE EXPERT PSYCHIATRIC WITNESS

Ethical Guidelines, DSM and Practice Guidelines, and Culture

The role of the expert psychiatric witness is to ethically provide scientific, clinically accurate testimony to answer the legal question at hand, when possible. Forensic assessment, forensic report writing, and oral testimony remain foundational elements of practice in the discipline.

There are several excellent reviews and literature contributions on psychiatric assessment, forensic report writing, testimony, and psychiatric consultation to the courts (AAPL 2015; Greenfield and Gottschalk 2008; Griffith, Stankovic, and Baranoski 2010; Griffith and Baranoski 2011; Melton 2007; Wettstein 2010). Work and research in each area have modernized practice since the early 1990s.

Contributions to ethics in forensic psychiatry continue to shape the field. The American Academy of Psychiatry and the Law adopted Ethics Guidelines for the Practice of Forensic Psychiatry in 1987 (American Academy of Psychiatry and the Law 2005), which emphasizes the difference between physician–patient relationships and examiner–examinee relationships. Expert psychiatric opinions may harm the examinee in service to the law, yet the forensic psychiatrist must adhere to the ethics principle of striving for honesty and objectivity. Appelbaum's truth-oriented stance toward ethics addresses the need for both subjective and objective truth-telling, as well as balancing truth against the evaluee's rights and dignity (Appelbaum 2008). There are comments on the practical futility of searching for truth and objectivity in forensic report writing (Griffith, Stankovic, and Baranoski 2010). Ethics contributions in the psychiatric literature offer competing, complementary and sometimes conflicting models of ethical practice, but all have contributed to the field's professional aspirations (American Academy of Psychiatry and the Law 2005; Martinez and Candilis 2009).

Practice guidelines began being developed in the 1990s, and they emphasize evidence-based practice (Glancy and Saini 2009). In addition to shaping medicine, they are finding their way to the courtroom. Their use as standards of care in medical malpractice trials is problematic because of the sheer volume of such guidelines and in the wide variation in the parties creating them (Zonana 2008). Nevertheless, they have become important considerations for the expert witness, as they may affect the witness's role, findings on the admissibility of evidence, and trial outcomes (Recupero 2008).

The American Psychiatric Association's Diagnostic and Statistical Manual of Mental Disorders advises that its use for forensic purposes can result in misuse or misunderstanding of the manual. But, of course, the DSM is used forensically. The adoption of the Fifth Edition creates new forensic problems for the expert witness. Misunderstanding of the alternate model for personality disorders, the promotion of other paradigm shifts in psychiatric diagnosis, and the use of paraphilia diagnoses in sexually violent predator commitment cases are examples of issues that the expert witness may need to address (Frances 2010; Slovenko 2011; First and Halon 2008).

Another arena that increasingly impacts the practical work of the forensic psychiatric expert is culture. Cultural competence demonstrates the ethical principles of respect for persons, beneficence, non-maleficence, and justice (Hoop et al. 2008). The psychiatric Cultural Formulation, introduced in DSM-IV, is an ethnographic framework that assists in creating patient-oriented narratives in general psychiatric practice. The need for cultural sensitivity is amplified in forensic populations since culture, gender, race, and ethnicity relate to many of the inequities in correctional settings and in the practices of the American criminal justice system, including excessive incarceration of minorities and barriers to treatment. Accounting for cultural issues pertaining to language, notions about perceptual phenomena, and different expressions of mental illness can play an important role in evaluating criminal defendants' competency to stand trial and criminal responsibility (Layde 2004).

Culture can impact treatment recommendations, and racial and gender discrimination can also serve as a basis for civil claims of emotional suffering. Carter and Forsyth (2009) describe the direct and specific effects of racism, which has particular relevance in civil lawsuits alleging racial discrimination and harassment. Available research in this area impacts forensic practice.

Despite public perception to the contrary, research suggests that some racial minorities consider all other alternative causes before attributing an ambiguous event to discrimination. Legal avenues to redress racial discrimination may not always be clear, so cases may be more difficult to prove than cases of gender discrimination. Some research indicates that subtle and ambiguous racial encounters can exact a greater emotional toll than more blatant acts of discrimination. In addition, the psychological impact of racial discrimination does not neatly map onto DSM 5 criteria for Post-Traumatic Stress Disorder. Carter and Forsyth offer a guide to the forensic assessment of the psychiatric and emotional impact of race-based encounters. It is important to assess racial identity ego statuses, understand the target's subjective perception of the alleged event, and assess functional impairment rather than focus on a specific diagnosis. Once again, the examiner's race and culture may influence the assessment, and cultural consultation and training may be necessary.

The interplay between the ethnicity of the examiner, the examinee, and the interaction between dominant and nondominant ethnic groups in the legal system can all affect examiner neutrality. Forensic specialists should consider race, culture, and ethnicity in forensic evaluations. Examiners should seek consultation with a colleague or someone with cultural expertise when assessing or treating a person from a particular cultural background. Psychiatrists have increasingly recommended that the Cultural Formulation and theories from cultural psychiatry should enrich forensic practice (Aggarwal 2012).

Despite its shortcomings, improving quality in the field of forensic practice is an important focus of research (Scott 2013). The development of ethical and practice guidelines is improving the quality of assessment, report writing, and testimony of the expert psychiatric witness. Attention to the impact of culture on forensic practice also improves forensic consultation.

Forensic Assessment

As noted above, understanding and incorporating factors pertaining to gender, culture, race, and ethnicity in forensic formulations is gaining widespread acceptance. The impact of cultural factors on medical and mental health care is increasingly recognized at a time that the American population becomes more diverse. Available evidence indicates that members of ethnic minority groups experience mental illness in different ways, receive disparate care compared with white Americans, and can therefore have different health care outcomes (Hicks 2004). These disparities have relevance in forensic practice since there are greater proportions of ethnic minority groups in correctional and forensic treatment settings, and because racial, ethnic, and cultural issues can receive great attention in these settings.

The literature reveals important differences between dominant and non-dominant groups that have clinical and forensic relevance. Hicks (2004) provides an excellent review of the impact of race and ethnicity on diagnosis, risk assessment, involuntary commitment, competency and criminal responsibility, evaluation of children, and tort issues. Clinicians may render a certain diagnosis based in part on whether a person is white or African American. African Americans may be more commonly misdiagnosed, not receive proper attention to affective symptoms, be given higher doses of antipsychotic medication, or receive unnecessary antidepressant or other psychotropic medications. Members of ethnic minority groups may present with different signs and symptoms of mental illness, and may communicate their distress differently from dominant groups. Clinicians can overpredict inpatient violence by non-whites and underpredict it by whites, although there is no clear evidence of the same in discharged patients. African Americans are hospitalized involuntarily more often than whites, although reasons for this can be practical rather than due to bias. There can be correlations between ethnicity and history of violent behavior in certain groups. The overwhelmingly disproportionate use of the death penalty in cases involving an African American defendant and white victim, compared to cases involving a white defendant and an African American victim, has received wide attention and sensitizes forensic practice. It is important to consider pertinent ethnic and cultural factors during assessment to avoid inaccurate forensic assessments that can adversely affect legal and treatment outcomes.

Whether to make electronic recordings of interviews has been debated over the years, and an AAPL task force on video-recording concluded that making recordings is acceptable but not mandatory. There has been a rise in systematic data-gathering tools, including scales to assess symptoms and mental status. As forensic assessment instruments have been developed, the validity of tests on certain populations, the strengths and limitations of actuarial tests, and the adjunctive nature of such tests has become increasingly important to the field. In response to these and other considerations, AAPL has developed a Practice Guideline for the Forensic Assessment, which reviews legal and psychiatric issues relevant to forensic assessment and offers practical guidance to performing such evaluations (American Academy of Psychiatry and the Law 2015).

Forensic Report Writing

The forensic psychiatric report may constitute the expert's sole work product in consulting to courts. Forensic psychiatrists continue to rely on face-to-face examination of the evaluee, reviewing collateral information from legal and medical records, and conducting third-party interviews to obtain and then interpret data to offer an expert opinion. Empirical development has described the content of forensic reports in different settings. Research has measured how frequently courts follow psychiatric recommendations. Theoretical developments have included analyses of the psychiatric narrative (Buchanan and Norko 2013) and conceptualizing report writing as performative narrative (Griffith, Stankovic, and Baranoski 2010).

Testimony and Courtroom Consultation

The expert's ability to appear authoritative on the opinions expressed and to be able to convince the fact-finder of the correctness of the opinion has always been central in the decision to use expert testimony. The components of effective expert testimony, including the relationship between confidence, credibility, and knowledge, have been a focus of research (Cramer and Brodsky 2009; Parrott and Neal 2015). Studies have also found differential effects based on experts' gender, either in favor of men or in favor of women (Parrott and Neal 2015; Recupero and Christopher 2015; Neal and Guadagno 2012). Results broadly point to how gender, race and culture of the judge, juror and expert witness may affect court rulings. Juror decision-making may be influenced by perceptions of expert witnesses (Neal and Guadagno 2012). In addition to viewing expert testimony as a way of educating and imparting knowledge, there is discussion of the performance aspect of testimony. Being an expert witness involves appearing and sounding professionally expert, and performance in the courtroom is critical to that image (Griffith and Baranoski 2011).

The role of the expert forensic witness for courts is not necessarily limited to testimony. Attorneys increasingly seek out forensic specialists to advise them and to participate in aspects of litigation, either in addition to or instead of providing testimony. Non-evaluative consultation roles, such as assisting one side to prepare its case or to aid in the cross-examination of an opposing expert, are appearing more frequently. Trial consultants and juror consultants can use research findings to aid in witness preparation to improve juror perception of confidence. Consultants can advise attorneys to add questions and otherwise coach expert witnesses to provide more effective testimony (Cramer and Brodsky 2009).

DEVELOPMENTS IN THE BIOMEDICAL SCIENCES

Forensic psychiatry, like other medical fields, increasingly uses an evidence-based approach (Glancy and Saini 2009). Advances in behavioral genetics and structural and functional neuroimaging studies are reaching the courtroom, and now have evidentiary implications in criminal and civil adjudication (Appelbaum and Scurich 2014). Courts are becoming more receptive to using newly evolving scientific data to support diagnostic conclusions, both in arguments for compensation and for mitigation in sentencing. Behavioral genetic data and structural imaging can be paired with each other as well as with neuropsychological testing. References to neuroscience in court cases are occurring more frequently as evidence that genetic and other biologic variables contribute to the risk of criminal behavior.

Even though biologic explanations are being introduced more often, how such explanations influence court decisions remains difficult to anticipate. There are some indications that neuroscience is used to reach opinions, such as in recent United States Supreme Court rulings pertaining to juvenile justice, discussed below. The use of neuroscientific evidence in the legal system may ultimately allow for fairer and more accurate legal findings. However, such information may also mislead jurors. Studies of the impact of such data on legal outcomes are mixed (Appelbaum and Scurich 2014). To address the challenges that are raised in the interface between law and neuroscience, the John D. and Catherine T. MacArthur Foundation created the *Law and Neuroscience Project* in 2007, as well as the *Research Network on Law and Neuroscience* in 2011 (Law and Neuroscience 2015). There are now publications on a variety of "neurolaw" topics including responsibility, sentencing, evidence, lie detection, psychopathy risk assessment, addiction, and juvenile issues (Jones and Shen 2012). The search for neurobiological factors underlying affective behavior can impact forensic assessment of conditions such as intellectual disability disorder and autism spectrum disorder. Increasingly, neuroimaging as well as genetic evaluation of intellectual disabilities can point toward etiology (Moeschler 2008; Pandey et al. 2004).

The integration of neuroscientific knowledge in forensic neuropsychiatric practice now obligates the expert to expand his knowledge base (Silva 2009). In the coming years, neuroscientific advances will clearly play a more prominent role in some courtroom deliberations, even though the utility of such information is unclear. When structural and functional differences in brains or genetic variances are linked to differences in individuals' ability to control their impulses, rather than the person making poor choices, they may appear to be convincing mitigators in criminal responsibility or proof of damages in civil matters. But identifying possible neural underpinnings of legally relevant capabilities and capacities does not render them indisputable, and there is no indication that they can actually address why a particular act or a specific type of damage has occurred. Even if such information helps establish pathology, it will only tend to support probabilities for certain kinds of behaviors. There is concern that information from brain imaging and genetic studies is not yet sufficiently mature for the courtroom and may mislead jurors into adopting overly deterministic concepts of criminal behavior.

By all indications, the influence of neuroscience on legal decision-making appears to be growing. However, decisions involving the use of neuroscientific evidence may stem from aligning other determinants about behavior with such findings instead of with brain functioning.

DEVELOPMENTS IN CHILD AND ADOLESCENT FORENSIC PSYCHIATRY

Although still not recognized as a formal subspecialty by the ABPN, progress continues in standard settings for forensic evaluations, training, and credentials in child and adolescent forensic psychiatry. The field encompasses diverse issues including juvenile justice, child custody, a wide range of abuse and neglect, and personal injury. Legal developments, advances in research including neuroscience, the trend to treat violent adolescent offenders as criminally responsible adults, and scrutiny of evaluation techniques for sexual abuse are examples of factors that have prompted change in child and adolescent psychiatric practice. A major change in the past twenty years has been the large increase in research based on quantifiable descriptive data of forensic populations, although studies using comparison or control groups remain relatively rare (Ash and Derdeyn 1997, Kraus and Thomas 2011).

Because of the juvenile justice system's original focus on helping instead of punishing youth, many of the due process procedures and rights for the adults in criminal court historically were not thought necessary in juvenile proceedings. Since the 1990s, public pressure emphasizing social protection over juvenile rehabilitation has resulted in implementation by courts and legislators of many features of criminal court into the juvenile justice system, as well as waiving more youth into adult courts (Penn and Thomas 2005; Kraus and Thomas 2011). This policy shift helped renew research in many areas. Research findings on developmental immaturity point out how juveniles can have impaired understanding and appreciation of Miranda rights, with younger individuals demonstrating the most impairment, how it can affect ability to understand and participate meaningfully in adjudication, and how developmental IQ relates to risk (Grisso et al. 2003; Viljoen, Zapf, and Roesch 2007). Contemporary, evidence-based protocols for treating youths who sexually offend are also now available. School bullying and cyberbullying have received a great deal of attention in both general media and professional literature (Bernet and Freeman 2011). Such developments obligate the expert to expand his knowledge base when consulting to juvenile court for competency to understand Miranda rights, competency to stand trial, waiver or transfer hearings, and in considering whether a child should remain in a facility or can return home.

The best interests of the child standard prevails in child custody, and these evaluations as well as parenting capacity remain thorny topics. Ethics and appropriate forensic methods for interviewing children and parents have received more attention over the years, including discussions of examiners identifying their own areas of potential conflict or bias. Problem areas in custody and parenting evaluations include assessing allegations of child sexual abuse, domestic violence, and "parental alienation" (Gould and Martindale 2007). Parental alienation has been controversial since its inception in 1985. An effort to codify it as a diagnosis in the DSM-5 was not successful, and courts are able to deal with a child's "malignity" against a parent without invoking mental illness (Houchin et al. 2012).

There are about three million annual reports of child abuse and neglect in the United States, about two thirds of which are screened for investigation or assessment (Kraus and Thomas 2011). Psychiatric evaluations are now routinely conducted in conjunction with psychologists, pediatricians, and social workers. The child's statements may be the only source of information in sexual abuse cases because there are often no witnesses and no physical findings. This makes sexual abuse cases in particular vulnerable to criticism, so attention is paid in the literature to use techniques that do not lead or prompt the child in a way that undermines or calls into question the answers or observations (Kraus and Thomas 2011). Assisting the court in determining what happened to the child, making recommendations regarding placement or treatment, and providing an opinion on termination of parental rights requires adequate education and training, understanding of the legal issues and care system, and keeping abreast of current forensic methods for assessing youth.

The expanding body of research suggests that childhood trauma and adverse experiences can lead to a variety of negative health outcomes, including substance abuse, depressive disorders, and attempted suicide among adolescents and adults (Dube et al. 2001). For example, the Adverse Childhood Experiences Study addressed the effects of various forms of child maltreatment and household dysfunction by collecting retrospective information from 17,337 adults in a health maintenance organization. In showing the relationship of specific adverse childhood experiences to the lifetime prevalence of suicide attempts, Dube et al. (2001) found 9.1% for individuals who experienced child sexual abuse and 2.4% for individuals who did not experience child sexual abuse. Children exposed to domestic violence can also be considered victims of child maltreatment. Such children, by virtue of their experience in the home, are psychologically maltreated and are also at high risk for physical abuse and some risk for sexual abuse (Holden 2003).

Minority youth are overrepresented in foster care and the juvenile justice system, in part a reflection of minority health care disparities similar to the adult system discussed above. There is increasing emphasis on cultural competency in forensic juvenile evaluations, which includes identifying, understanding and accepting cultural differences. Cultural factors can impact recommendations for a specific case. In a custody evaluation, the expert may wish to factor in one parent's willingness to support the child's involvement in the cultural traditions of the other parent. In juvenile court cases, referral to a treatment setting that is culturally competent may increase the likelihood of completing treatment (Kraus and Thomas 2011).

Scientific studies of the adolescent brain appear to be influencing landmark legal decisions. In the past decade, several United States Supreme Court cases that have banned or restricted the use of capital punishment or life without parole of juveniles convicted of serious crimes have mentioned scientific studies, including *Roper v. Simmons*, *Graham v. Florida* and *Miller v. Alabama*. In these cases, the court referenced findings from studies of brain development to support the position that adolescents are less mature than adults, which mitigates criminal responsibility. In *Miller*, the justices grounded their reasoning in developmental neuroscience, and specifically mentioned juvenile immaturity in executive functioning, such as appreciating the long-term consequences of actions, impulse control, and risk taking behavior. Since the deliberations of Supreme Court justices are not public, it is unknown how much neuroscience findings actually influenced its decision, as opposed to science simply adding validity to an argument based on "common sense" (Steinberg 2013).

CRIMINAL COURTS

Consulting to criminal courts in particular is impacted by the current shortcomings in the mental health and medical systems. The expert psychiatric witness is increasingly called upon in criminal courts to address care, treatment, and risk management of persons with mental illness due to inadequate treatment availability. A growing number of defendants judged incompetent to stand trial are unable to receive needed mental health care because of critical shortages of state hospital psychiatric beds and funding. Many persons with mental illness therefore end up in jails and prisons that lack the resources to provide adequate care and treatment. Forensic psychiatry and psychology have become relevant in providing care and treatment recommendations for persons in jails, prisons, and forensic treatment facilities. Judges are concerned about violence risk, which they weigh against the trend to return patients to their home communities. Addressing treatment resources will require better funding and integrating mental health capabilities within jails and prisons, courts, long-term and short-term hospitals, and communities. These matters now routinely pull the forensic expert into the courts.

The field of violence risk assessment has made considerable progress. Beginning in the 1960s, assessing dangerousness became necessary out of the developing need to distinguish between patients needing voluntary or involuntary treatment based on treatment advancements, the effects of deinstitutionalization, and legal decisions defining dangerousness as the criterion for involuntary treatment. In that era, the accuracy of predicting violence was distinctly below chance (Norko and Baranoski 2005; Norko and Baranoski 2008; Buchanan et al. 2012). Since the 1990s a distinct body of violence risk assessment research has emerged. Contemporary research correlates substance abuse and several demographic variables to be significant risk factors for violence, while mental illness represents a modest risk factor for violence. While actuarial predictors of future violence have greater statistical accuracy than clinical methods alone, combining actuarial and clinical methodologies predicts risk better than chance and is sensitive to the effects of treatment and clinical intervention (Douglas and Skeem 2005; Norko and Baranoski 2008).

Risk assessment and clinical management have emerged as central elements of all mental health practice (Mullen 2000; Buchanan et al. 2012). For the forensic expert, these elements now have a more significant role in discharge of persons with mental illness from prison and return to the community, death penalty cases, release of insanity acquittees, and aid in sentencing. Risk assessment can also play a major role in *Sell* hearings for pre-trial detainees. While the newer statistical approaches improve researchers' ability to describe what is and is not possible in predicting psychiatric violence, low base rates limit the ability of current assessment methods to prevent actual offending. Further research and newer methodologies are needed to improve detection of future risk of violence by psychiatric patients (Buchanan 2008).

Court decisions have impacted cases involving intellectual disability. In *Atkins v. Virginia*, the United States Supreme Court held that imposing the death penalty on intellectually disabled persons is cruel and unusual, citing evolving standards of decency and national consensus. The court's decision left the definition of intellectual disability to the states. Not defining intellectual disability suggests that as neuroscience advances our understanding of etiologies, such definitions may change. Similarly, the American Psychiatric Association replaced the term "mental retardation" with "intellectual disability" in order to focus on adaptive functioning and less on IQ.

Cultural factors increasingly impact criminal court proceedings. A criminal defendant's cultural history and milieu may deepen the context of his or her behavior at the time of an offense. Cultural assessments can therefore impact responsibility proceedings or mitigate sentencing (Boehnlein, Schafer, and Bloom 2005). Since the defense can raise all issues relevant to his or her circumstances in the sentencing phase, cultural evaluation and formulation can be powerful at this stage.

NEWER ROLES OF THE CONSULTING FORENSIC PSYCHIATRIST AND PSYCHOLOGIST

New loci make use of the forensic psychiatrist's knowledge base. Testimony in Veterans' Courts, the general military system, immigration courts, drug courts, mental health courts, special courts at Guantanamo, Catholic annulment courts, and religious organizations requesting assessment of problematic sexual behavior of clergy are all topics covered in other chapters. They illustrate the expansion of the forensic expert's consultative role to legal and other organized administrative systems. Advocacy for patients and for the professions by providing legislative consultation is yet another newer role for the forensic professional. Immigration clinics increasingly assist detained immigrants before immigration courts, by challenging confinement as well as conditions of confinement in federal court. Forensic cultural assessment now has a strong role in immigration clinics and courts. Cultural anthropology, war trauma, and knowledge of the limits of mental health treatment in a person's home country can provide a fuller assessment that can aid the legal system in determining whether to grant immigration asylum or to prevent deportation.

CONCLUSION

At this point in the history of forensic psychiatry and psychology, most legal professionals have sufficient skills to identify qualified, ethical practitioners in the field. This is in no small part because the emphasis on ethics, training, accreditation, and performance has strengthened the professional identity of the forensic specialist. The quality of forensic assessment, report writing, and testimony is also improving within the field. Despite ongoing shortcomings in forensic work, evidence-based practice, research, and neuroscience advances impact the functioning of the expert witness largely for the better.

In addition to relying on advances in medicine to construct and improve upon forensic expertise, creating culturally-sensitive narratives about people to explain findings and opinions is an important consideration as well (Griffith, Stankovic, and Baranoski 2010). This chapter surveys many of the advances in the field, including advances in research and neuroscience and acknowledgment of limitations in some methodologies. No matter how much further they evolve, science and technology alone cannot answer all questions pertaining to human behavior. As Griffith and Baranoski (2011) write, "Our activity is both informative and performative, drawing on observations culled from several other disciplines." Integrating scientific findings with the performance aspects of the field while maintaining an ethical framework requires the forensic psychiatric expert to hold paradox and maintain a cognitive dissonance.

In our discipline, the objective world of science and the subjective world of performance lie atop one another. They are different, yet occupy the same space.

REFERENCES

Aggarwal, N. 2012. Adapting the Cultural Formulation for Clinical Assessments in Forensic Psychiatry. *Journal of the American Academy of Psychiatry and the Law* 40 (1): 113–8.

American Academy of Psychiatry and the Law. 2005. Ethics Guidelines for the Practice of Forensic Psychiatry. Accessed May 31, 2015, http://www.aapl.org/ethics.htm.

———. 2015. "AAPL Practice Guideline for the Forensic Assessment." *Journal of the American Academy of Psychiatry and the Law* 43 (2) Supplement.

———. ABPN Certification in the Subspecialty of Forensic Psychiatry. Accessed July 10, 2015, http://www.aapl.org/abpn.htm.

———. Directory of Forensic Psychiatry Fellowships. Accessed July 10, 2015, http://www.aapl.org/fellow.php.

American Medical Association. 1998. H-265.993 Peer Review of Medical Expert Witness Testimony. Accessed July 11, 2015, https://www.ama-assn.org/ssl3/ecomm/PolicyFinderForm.pl?site=www.ama-assn.org&uri=/resources/html/PolicyFinder/policyfiles/HnE/H-265.993.HTM.

Appelbaum, P. 2008. "Ethics and Forensic Psychiatry: Translating Principles Into Practice." *Journal of the American Academy of Psychiatry and the Law* 36 (2): 195–200.

Appelbaum, P. and N. Scurich. 2014. "Impact of Behavioral Genetic Evidence on the Adjudication of Criminal Behavior." *Journal of the American Academy of Psychiatry and the Law* 42 (1): 91–100.

Ash, P. and A. Derdeyn. 1997. "Forensic Child and Adolescent Psychiatry: A Review of the Past 10 Years." *Journal of the American Academy of Child and Adolescent Psychiatry* 36 (11): 1493–1502.

Bernet, W. and B. Freeman. 2011. "Forensic Psychiatry." *Child and Adolescent Psychiatric Clinics of North America* 20 (3): xv–xvii.

Boehnlein J., M. Schaefer, and J. Bloom. 2005. "Cultural Considerations in the Criminal Law: The Sentencing Process." *Journal of the American Academy of Psychiatry and the Law* (33) 3: 335–41.

Brennan, M. and D. Dilenschneider. 2009. *Finding and Researching Experts and Their Testimony*. 2nd ed. White Paper. Accessed July 11, 2015 http://www.lexisnexis.com/documents/pdf/20071211111707_large.pdf.

Buchanan, A. 2008. "Risk of Violence by Psychiatric Patients: Beyond the 'Actuarial Versus Clinical' Assessment Debate." *Psychiatric Services* 59 (2): 184–90.

Buchanan, A., R. Binder, M. Norko, and M. Swartz. 2012. "Resource Document on Psychiatric Violence Risk Assessment." *American Journal of Psychiatry* 169 (3) Supplement: 1–10.

Buchanan, A. and M. Norko. 2013. "The Forensic Evaluation and Report: An Agenda for Research." *Journal of the American Academy of Psychiatry and the Law* 41 (3): 359–65.

Carter R. and J. Forsyth. 2009. "A Guide to the Forensic Assessment of Race-Based Traumatic Stress Reactions." *Journal of the American Academy of Psychiatry and the Law* 37 (1): 28–40.

Cramer, R. and S. Brodsky. 2009. "Expert Witness Confidence and Juror Personality: Their Impact on Credibility and Persuasion in the Courtroom." *Journal of the American Academy of Psychiatry and the Law* 37 (1): 63–74.

Curran, W., L. McGarry, and S. Shah (eds). 1986. *Forensic Psychiatry and Psychology: Perspectives and Standards for Interdisciplinary Practice*. Philadelphia: F.A. Davis Company.

The Daily Record. 2002. "Revisiting the Rules on Professional Medical Witnesses." http://thedailyrecord.com/2002/12/19/revisiting-the-rules-on-professional-medical-witnesses/.

Daubert v. Merrell Dow Pharmaceuticals, Inc. 509 U.S. 579 (1993).

Douglas, K. and J. Skeem. 2005. "Violence Risk Assessment: Getting Specific About Being Dynamic." *Psychology, Public Policy, and Law* 11 (3): 347–83.

Dube, S., R. Anda, V. Felitti, D. Chapman, D. Williamson, and W. Giles. 2001. "Childhood Abuse, Household Dysfunction, and the Risk of Attempted Suicide Throughout the Life Span Findings From the Adverse Childhood Experiences Study." *Journal of the American Medical Association* 286 (24): 3089–96.

First, M. and R. Halon. 2008. "Use of DSM Paraphilia Diagnoses in Sexually Violent Predator Commitment Cases." *Journal of the American Academy of Psychiatry and the Law* 36 (4): 443–54.

Florida Board of Medicine. Expert Witness Certificate. Accessed July 28, 2015, http://flboardofmedicine.gov/licensing/expert-witness-certificate/.

Frances, A. 2010. "The Forensic Risks of DSM-V and How to Avoid Them." *Journal of the American Academy of Psychiatry and the Law* 38 (1): 11–14.

Frye v. United States 293 F. 1013 (D.C. Cir 1923).

Glancy, G. and M. Saini. 2009. "The Confluence of Evidence-Based Practice and Daubert Within the Fields of Forensic Psychiatry and the Law." *Journal of the American Academy of Psychiatry and the Law* 37 (4): 438–41.

Gould, J. and D. Martindale. 2007. *The Art and Science of Child Custody Evaluations.* New York: Guilford Press.

Greenfield, D. and J. Gottschalk. 2008. *Writing Forensic Reports: A Guide for Mental Health Professionals.* New York: Springer.

Griffith, E. and M. Baranoski. 2011. "Oral Performance, Identity, and Representation in Forensic Psychiatry." *Journal of the American Academy of Psychiatry and the Law* 39 (3): 352–63.

Griffith, E., A. Stankovic, and M. Baranoski. 2010. "Conceptualizing the Forensic Psychiatry Report as Performance Narrative." *Journal of the American Academy of Psychiatry and the Law* 38 (1): 32–42.

Grisso, T., L. Steinberg, J. Woolard, E. Cauffman, E. Scott, S. Graham, F. Lexcen, N.D. Reppucci, and R. Schwartz. 2003. "Juveniles' Competence to Stand Trial: A Comparison of Adolescents' and Adults' Capacities as Trial Defendants." *Law and Human Behavior* 27: 333–63.

Gutheil, T. 2006. "Psychiatric Expert Witnesses in the New Millennium." *Psychiatric Clinics of North America* 29 (3): 823–32.

Gutheil, T. and H. Bursztajn. 2003. "Avoiding Ipse Dixit Mislabeling: Post-*Daubert* Approaches to Expert Clinical Opinions." *Journal of the American Academy of Psychiatry and the Law* 31 (2): 205–10.

Hicks, J. 2004. "Ethnicity, Race and Forensic Psychiatry: Are We Color-Blind?" *Journal of the American Academy of Psychiatry and the Law* 32 (1): 21–33.

Holden, G. 2003. "Children Exposed to Domestic Violence and Child Abuse: Terminology and Taxonomy." *Clinical Child and Family Psychology Review* 6 (3): 151–60.

Hoop, J., T. DiPasquale, J. Hernandez, and L. Roberts. 2008. "Ethics and Culture in Mental Health Care." *Ethics & Behavior* 18 (4): 353–72.

Houchin, T., J. Ranseen, P. Hash and D. Bartnicki. 2012. "The Parental Alienation Debate Belongs in the Courtroom, Not in DSM-5." *Journal of the American Academy of Psychiatry and the Law* 40 (1): 127–31.

Jones, O. and F. Shen. 2012. "Law and Neuroscience in the United States." In *International Neurolaw*, edited by Tade Spranger. Berlin: Springer-Verlag.

Kraus, L. and C. Thomas. 2011. "Practice Parameter for Child and Adolescent Forensic Evaluations." *Journal of the American Academy of Child and Adolescent Psychiatry* 50 (12): 1299–312.

Law and Neuroscience. 2015. "History: Phase I (2007–2011)." Accessed July 21, 2015. http://www.lawneuro.org/history.php.

Layde, J. 2004. "Cross Cultural Issues in Forensic Psychiatry Training." *Academic Psychiatry* 28 (1): 34–9.

Martinez, R. and P. Candilis. 2009. "Ethics." In *The Psychiatric Report: Principles and Practice of Forensic Writing*, edited by Alec Buchanan and Michael Norko, pp. 56–67. Cambridge: Cambridge University Press.

Melton, G. 2007. *Psychological Evaluations for the Courts: A Handbook for Mental Health Professionals and Lawyers*. 3rd ed. New York: Guilford Press.

Moeschler, J.B. 2008. "Genetic Evaluation of Intellectual Disabilities." *Seminars in Pediatric Neurology* 15 (1): 2–9.

Mullen, P. 2000. Forensic Mental Health. *British Journal of Psychiatry* 176: 307–11.

Neal, T. and R. Guadagno. 2012. "Warmth and Competence on the Witness Stand: Implications for the Credibility of Male and Female Expert Witnesses." *Journal of the American Academy of Psychiatry and the Law* 40 (4): 488–97.

Norko, M. and M. Baranoski. 2005. "The State of Contemporary Risk Assessment Research." *Canadian Journal of Psychiatry* 50 (1): 18–26.

———. 2008. "The Prediction of Violence; Detection of Dangerousness." *Brief Treatment and Crisis Intervention Advance Access* 8 (1): 73–91, doi:10.1093/brief-treatment/mhm025.

Pandey, A., S. Phadke, N. Gupta, and R.V. Phadke. 2004. "Neuroimaging in Mental Retardation." *The Indian Journal of Pediatrics* 71 (3): 203–9.

Parrott, C. and T. Neal. 2015. "Differences in Expert Witness Knowledge: Do Mock Jurors Notice and Does It Matter?" *Journal of the American Academy of Psychiatry and the Law* 43 (1): 69–81.

Penn, J. and C. Thomas. 2005. "Practice Parameter for the Assessment and Treatment of Youth in Juvenile Detention and Correctional Facilities." *Journal of the American Academy of Child and Adolescent Psychiatry* 44 (10): 1085–1098.

Recupero, P. 2008. "Clinical Practice Guidelines as Learned Treatises: Understanding Their Use as Evidence in the Courtroom." *Journal of the American Academy of Psychiatry and the Law* 36 (3): 290–301.

Recupero, P. and P. Christopher. 2015. "Gender Bias and Judicial Decisions of Undue Influence in Testamentary Challenges." *Journal of the American Academy of Psychiatry and the Law* 43 (1): 60–8.

Scott, C. 2013. "Believing Doesn't Make It So: Forensic Education and the Search for Truth." *Journal of the American Academy of Psychiatry and the Law* 41 (1): 18–32.

Silva, A. 2009. "Forensic Psychiatry, Neuroscience, and the Law." *Journal of the American Academy of Psychiatry and the Law* 37 (4):489–502.

Slovenko, R. 2011. "The DSM in Litigation and Legislation." *Journal of the American Academy of Psychiatry and the Law* 39 (1): 6–11.

Steinberg, L. 2013. "The Influence of Neuroscience on US Supreme Court Decisions About Adolescent's Criminal Culpability." *Nature* June 20: 513–18.

Viljoen J.L., P. Zapf, and R. Roesch. 2007. "Adjudicative Competence and Comprehension of Miranda Rights in Adolescent Defendants: A Comparison of Legal Standards." *Behavioral Sciences and the Law* 25 (1): 1–19.

Wettstein, R. 2010. "The Forensic Psychiatric Examination and Report." In *The American Psychiatric Publishing Textbook of Forensic Psychiatry*, edited by Robert Simon and Liza Gold, pp. 175–206. Washington DC: American Psychiatric Publishing.

Zonana, H. 2008. "Commentary: When Is a Practice Guideline Only a Guideline?" *Journal of the American Academy of Psychiatry and the Law* 36 (3): 302–5.

CHAPTER 10

Veterans' Courts and the VA's Veterans Justice Outreach Initiative

Emily A. Keram

INTRODUCTION

The nature of recent military engagements, improved recognition of the mental health needs of veterans, and the impact of service-related psychiatric illness on criminal behavior have created new opportunities for forensic psychiatrists. Policies have been developed within state courts and legislatures, as well as the Department of Veterans Affairs that address the needs of justice-involved veterans.

JUSTICE-INVOLVED VETERANS

Approximately 30% of recent combat veterans suffer "invisible wounds," including post-traumatic stress disorder (PTSD), traumatic brain injury (TBI), military sexual trauma (MST), and major depression (Tanielian et al. 2008). Rates of co-morbid substance use disorders range from 21% to 35% (Petrakis, Rosenheck, and Desai 2011). PTSD and its related factors are associated with increased risk of criminal justice contact (Yager, Laufer, and Gallops 1984). Combat veterans may also experience homelessness (Greenberg and Rosenheck 2008), unemployment (Western, Kleykamp, and Rosenfeld 2006), and relationship problems (Riggs et al. 1998), increasing their risk for contact with the criminal justice system.

Approximately 200,000 veterans were incarcerated in U.S. jails in 2007, roughly 10% of the total inmate population (Elbogen et al. 2012). One study demonstrated that jail screening for PTSD among incarcerated veterans was as high as 39% (Saxon et al. 2001). It is currently estimated that almost 20% of veterans meet diagnostic criteria for PTSD (Tanielian et al. 2008). Combat veterans present with more severe symptoms of PTSD (Kaylor, Wing, and King 1987). There is a strong positive correlation between the presence and severity of PTSD in veterans and increased rates of arrest and conviction (Calhoun et al. 2004). However, only half of Afghanistan and Iraq veterans referred for mental health services after deployment actually sought and received treatment (Hoge, Auchterlonie, and Milliken 2006; Milliken, Auchterlonie, and Hoge 2007).

Problem-solving alternative dispositions such as Mental Health and Drug Treatment Courts have been shown to decrease rates of recidivism (McNiel and Binder 2007) and improve psychological well-being, substance use abstinence, and quality of life (Cosden et al. 2005). Using these courts as a model, the first Veterans Treatment Court (VTC) was established in Buffalo, N.Y. in 2008 (Russell 2014). The Buffalo VTC inspired other jurisdictions across the country to develop similar collaborative approaches to treatment and disposition, focusing on supervision of the veteran with the goals of reducing recidivism and long-term costs to taxpayers and increasing public safety, while helping veterans lead sober, healthy, and productive lives (Russell 2014).

The Department of Veterans Affairs (VA) also responded to the needs of justice-involved veterans. In 2009, the VA implemented the Veterans Justice Outreach (VJO) initiative to partner with the criminal justice system in identifying veterans who would benefit from treatment as an alternative to incarceration. VJO facilitates access to care for justice-involved veterans by referring the veteran to VA and community treatment and services. VJO's mission is to prevent homelessness, improve social and clinical outcomes, facilitate recovery, and end recidivism.

The number of VTCs in the United States grew rapidly after their establishment in 2008. In June 2014 there were 220 VTCs nationally (Justice for Veterans). The VA's VJO provides services to veteran defendants in VTCs as well those in jurisdictions that do not maintain a separate docket for veterans. A Veterans Justice Outreach Specialist, typically a social worker, is assigned to every VA facility providing clinical services to liaise between criminal courts, local VA treatment centers, and appropriate resources in local communities (Clark et al. 2010).

Forensic psychiatrists may interface in VTCs in a variety of contexts.

Those with previous experience in Mental Health or Drug Treatment Courts may lend their expertise during the planning and early implementation phases of new VTCs. Forensic psychiatrists who are members of the VTC team that reviews the docket weekly may provide expertise and recommendations regarding suitability for admission to the VTC, diagnosis and treatment, risk factors for recidivism and other unwanted behaviors, court reporting requirements, and management of counter-transference between VTC team members and the veteran defendant. Community-based forensic psychiatrists may be called upon by the court, defense attorneys and the prosecution for a variety of assessments relating to suitability for, and court requirements during, VTC participation. They may also be called upon to provide expert reports or testimony in jurisdictions where proof of a nexus between military service, mental illness, and criminal behavior is mandated by state legislation. VA psychiatrists, whether forensically trained or not, do not typically participate directly in VTCs. However, they may be called upon to submit treatment records, participate in treatment planning, and document ongoing compliance with treatment.

VETERANS' COURTS

Creating Relationships

Establishing partnerships and subsequent collaborative planning precede the implementation of VTCs. In addition to the judge, defender, and prosecutor, the VTC team may include the local VA VJO Specialist, County Veterans Service Officer or VA Benefits Administration (VBA) Benefit Specialist, a forensic psychiatrist, probation officers, jail personnel, and Veteran Mentors. During the planning process the roles and responsibilities of team members should be delineated (Russell 2014).

The VA VJO Specialist may provide a veteran defendant with referrals to VA and community-based resources. The Specialist also helps educate team members on issues facing veterans. The county Veterans Service Officer or VA Benefit Specialist may assist the defendant veteran in identifying and applying for local, state, and federal entitlements and assistance. As noted above, a forensic psychiatrist may serve both an educational and consultative role for the treatment team, assisting in the development of preferred treatment plans and court requirements, and fostering awareness of counter-transference problems and their management. A probation officer provides compliance reports. Jail staff may develop screening procedures to identify veterans during booking, as many VTCs rely on a sequential-intercept model for case-identification (Blue-Howells et al. 2013). They may also assist in monitoring veteran functioning and compliance with in-custody requirements, such as participation in mental health or recovery services.

Veteran Mentors serve a vital role in many VTCs. They are usually combat veterans from the community who volunteer to support veteran defendants during the pendency of the criminal proceedings. Many have overcome significant difficulties, including criminality, in their own readjustment to civilian life. Mentor support may take the form of providing transportation to court and treatment; role-modeling successful community re-entry after military discharge; promoting camaraderie; and offering an empathic ear. Defendant veterans feel a special connection to Veteran Mentors based upon their shared military experience (Hawkins 2010). The Veteran Mentor may be able to assist and influence the defendant veteran when civilian members of VTCs are not successful. Many VTCs develop a Veteran Mentor training program or handbook, which provides education about the legal system, the role of Veteran Mentors, diagnosis and treatment of common problems, and VA and community resources. Many Veteran Mentor programs make their trainings and handbooks available online (California Veterans Legal Task Force; Buffalo, NY Veteran's Court).

Court Format

During the planning stages, VTC team members should decide the format of the court. Jurisdictions should be aware of legislation that may govern aspects of VTCs (see below). Several VTCs and allied organizations publish policies and procedures online, providing guidance to jurisdictions planning such courts (Buffalo Veterans Treatment Court, Florida Office of the State Courts Administration 2014, and Veterans' Courts Harris County Texas).

Resources and referrals will determine the interval of court sessions, the size of the docket, and whether the VTC team will meet prior to each session to review the defendants' progress and plan future requirements. Because identification of veteran defendants may be difficult, consideration should be given to allowing them to be referred to the VTC at any point in the criminal process, including probation. The VTC team must decide whether their court will function as pre-trial diversion or require defendants to plead guilty to the charges prior to entering court, with the understanding that a sentence may be suspended and charges dismissed upon successful completion of court requirements. There is some evidence that the leverage conferred by requiring a plea is associated with higher compliance and graduation from VTCs (McMichael 2011). However, VTCs should be aware of online reporting procedures in their jurisdiction, as online records may have long-term consequences. Concerned jurisdictions may prefer to offer pre-trial diversion to veteran defendants offering a lengthy period of court-ordered treatment and monitoring in lieu of a jail sentence or probation (Russell 2014).

Criteria should be established to determine defendants who will initially participate in the VTC while serving time in jail as opposed to being placed directly on probation. Parameters for determining the interval of status hearings and overall length of VTC participation should also be addressed. In planning most issues, the VTC team should provide for as much flexibility as possible to allow for determinations to be made on a case-by-case basis. VTCs, like all multi-disciplinary ventures, require patience and fortitude on behalf of everyone involved (Russell 2014).

Eligibility

One of the most important tasks during VTC planning is defining eligibility criteria for veteran defendants. Factors to consider include psychiatric diagnosis; conditions of military service; whether there is a nexus between diagnosis and military service; and whether there is a nexus between diagnosis and alleged criminal behavior. Nationally, eligibility criteria vary widely in VTCs. Some jurisdictions, such as the Buffalo VTC, accept veterans regardless of their diagnosis or service conditions. Other courts restrict eligibility to veterans who, for example, served in combat, qualify for VA services, or have certain psychiatric diagnoses (Russell 2014).

The nature of the alleged criminal conduct is one of the most important factors considered in determining eligibility. No VTC accepts serious violent crimes such as rape or murder. The Buffalo VTC accepts veteran defendants charged with any nonviolent felony or misdemeanor. Common charges include driving while intoxicated, theft, and drug possession. Violent crimes are evaluated on a case-by-case basis, with the District Attorney's office ultimately deciding on eligibility. In more serious offenses, for example, domestic violence, veterans are accepted if their behavior has changed proximate to their service as opposed to those with a prior history of violence. Consideration is also given to the fact that both PTSD and traumatic brain injury (TBI) are associated with irritability, anger, and behavioral dyscontrol (Russell 2014). Some VTCs, such as Los Angeles County, accept only veterans facing felony charges (Santa Cruz 2012). Individual VTCs determine how to weigh factors such as prior criminal record and victim's wishes in establishing eligibility criteria (McMichael 2011).

The judicial response to successful completion of VTC requirements varies within and between jurisdictions. Outcomes range from complete removal of charges to a case-by-case determination of disposition. The Buffalo VTC provides removal of charges to its graduates. Results in some jurisdictions are bound by statute. In California, for example, convictions for violent crimes and driving while intoxicated remain on the record (California PC 1170.9).

Legislation

Several states have passed legislation affecting VTCs and veteran defendants. Some states take an active role in defining VTC structure, eligibility, treatment, and monitoring. Other legislatures limit their authority to circumscribed matters regarding veteran defendants generally.

Illinois

Illinois' Veterans and Servicemembers Court Treatment Act of 2010 (Illinois Public Act 096-0924) provides comprehensive requirements for VTCs. All veterans are eligible for court referral provided they had an other than dishonorable discharge. A history of combat duty is not required. Illinois grants the prosecution the discretion to accept both pre- and post-adjudicatory veteran defendants. Both the prosecution and court must approve admission to the VTC. The defendant must demonstrate willingness to participate in a treatment program. Defendants must be excluded from VTCs if they have been convicted of a violent crime within the past ten years. Violent crimes include murder, sexual assault, aggravated assault, armed robbery, arson, kidnapping, stalking, or any offense involving discharge of a firearm resulting in serious bodily injury or death. Defendants failing to complete a VTC program within the prior three years are also excluded.

Illinois requires VTCs to work closely with jail and VA clinicians in assessing risk, treatment needs and available resources. The court may order outpatient, inpatient, residential, or custodial substance use disorder treatment; counseling; compliance with medication; and all follow-up treatment recommendation.

Failure to meet the conditions of Illinois VTCs may result in modification of the terms of participation, revocation of participation, and prosecution or sentencing. Grounds for violation, termination, or discharge may include treatment non-compliance, failure to respond to treatment, and additional criminal conduct. Successful completion of VTC may result in dismissal of the original charges, termination of sentencing, or discharge from other sanctions related to the original prosecution

Florida

The T. Patt Maney Veterans' Treatment Intervention Act of 2012 amended pre-existing chapters of Florida's mental health and criminal codes (Florida Office of the State Courts Administration 2014). Local jurisdictions may establish a separate Military Veterans and Service Members Court Program. Florida provides pre-trial and post-conviction opportunities for participants. The state requires a nexus between psychiatric status and military service and is liberal in extending eligibility to those suffering from mental illness, traumatic brain injury, substance use disorder, or a "psychological problem." The statute directs courts considering acceptance of a defendant to consider the individual's criminal history, military service, substance use disorder treatment needs, mental health treatment needs, amenability to services, and the recommendations of the prosecution and victim. Unlike Illinois, weighing of these factors is left to the discretion of the court rather than specified by law (FL Stat § 394.47891 (2014)).

Florida excludes more charges than does Illinois. In addition to charges prohibited by Illinois, ineligible charges are expanded to computer pornography, poisoning, abuse of a dead human body, aircraft piracy, treason, and deployment of a destructive device or bomb. Defendants accused of a felony may be excluded if they rejected a prior offer of VTC participation on the record at any time before trial or previously entered a court-ordered veterans' treatment program. As in Illinois, Florida provides for a broad range of acceptable treatment options and sanctions if conditions of participation are not met. Felony charges may be dismissed upon successful completion of a pre-trial intervention program and arrest records for dismissed charges may be expunged (FL Stat § 948.08 (2014)).

Florida's statutory options for management of non-veterans charged with misdemeanor possession of a controlled substance or drug paraphernalia are extended to those accepted into a pretrial veterans' treatment intervention program. Referral to pretrial substance use disorder education and treatment approved by a drug court is allowed for defendants who have not previously been convicted of a felony nor been admitted to a previous pretrial program. The court must decline referral to pre-trial diversion if the prosecution establishes, by a preponderance of the evidence, that the defendant was involved in dealing or selling controlled substances (FL Stat § 948.16 (2014)).

With respect to conditions of probation or community control, Florida allows courts to mandate treatment for veterans and military servicemembers with service-related mental health issues. Courts are directed to give preference to treatment programs through the VA or Florida Department of Veterans' Affairs (FL Stat § 948.21 (2014)).

California

The California legislature has a long history of recognizing the association between combat trauma and criminal behavior. First enacted in 1982,

California Penal Code §1170.9 directs courts to consider treatment rather than incarceration when sentencing a defendant who serves or has served in the military, who may otherwise be sentenced to county jail or state prison. PC 1170.9 does not mention VTCs, allowing those jurisdictions without the resources to establish such courts to offer its benefits to all California justice-involved veterans (California PC 1170.9).

California requires a nexus between a mental disorder, military service, and criminal conduct. Like Florida, California allows for a broad understanding of mental health consequences of military service, including "mental health problems." Courts are allowed to use existing resources to obtain an assessment to aid in the determination of the relationship between psychiatric distress, military service, and criminal behavior.

The veteran must plead guilty or be convicted, be eligible for probation, and agree to participate in the program. Appropriate treatment must be available. The court may order the defendant into local, state, federal, or private nonprofit treatment for a period of time not to exceed that which the defendant would have served in jail or prison. The law specifies that sentence credits will be granted to a defendant placed in residential treatment for the time spent in the facility. Preference is given to treatment programs that have a history of successfully treating veterans for sexual trauma, TBI, PTSD, substance use disorders, or other problems regardless of their affiliation with the VA.

California specifically recognizes the judicial interest in restoring to the community a defendant who acquired a criminal record due to a mental health disorder stemming from military service. Restorative provisions of the statute may be granted after a hearing, with fifteen days' notice provided to the prosecution, defense, and victim. The defendant must show substantial compliance with the conditions of probation and successful participation in court-ordered treatment that addressed the service-related mental health issue. Defendants must also demonstrate that they do not represent a danger to the community and that they have derived significant benefit from court-ordered education, treatment, or rehabilitation. Factors demonstrating significant benefit may include completion and degree of participation in education, treatment, and rehabilitation; progress in formal education; development of career potential; leadership and personal responsibility efforts; and contribution of service in support of the community.

California allows for far-ranging restorative provisions to eligible defendants. The court may order early termination of probation, cancellation of fines (with the exception of victim restitution), and reduction of an eligible felony to a misdemeanor. Eligible participants may petition for expungement of their record in accordance with state law. Additionally, the defendant does not have to disclose the arrest, the dismissed action, or the conviction that was set aside when information regarding prior arrests or convictions is sought under oath. (Defendants applying for a law enforcement position must disclose this history.) The court may order the sealing of police and court records related to the dismissed action. The dismissal precludes any future action based on the conduct charged. The legislature did restrict or prohibit restorative provisions in certain circumstances. A conviction that was set aside may be considered as a prior conviction in future prosecutions. Convictions in a dismissed action may also be considered a conviction when two or more convictions may lead to revocation or suspension of a driver's license. Finally, the defendant's DNA profile will not be removed from the state data bank by dismissal of an action involving conviction on an eligible offense.

VETERANS JUSTICE OUTREACH

Over a two-year period (fiscal years 2010 through 2012) VJO Specialists had contact with 37,542 veterans (Finlay et al. 2016). Results of a nationwide survey of VJO Specialists showed that they staffed 98% of the 168 known VTCs, dockets, and tracks (McGuire, Clark, and Blue-Howells 2013). They also serviced jurisdictions that lacked such programs. Forty-two percent of VTCs were staffed in person on a weekly basis, 27% on a bi-weekly basis, and 30% on a monthly basis. VJO Specialists covered four courts by telephone due to distance or infrequency of court sessions. On average, VJO Specialists spent eleven hours each month in court for either team meetings or court sessions (McGuire, Clark, and Blue-Howells 2013).

The courts' criteria for veteran admission generally paralleled the VA's mission of serving veterans of all eras. Sixty-four percent of courts allowed admission of veterans ineligible for VA services. This population constituted an average of 14% of the caseload of those courts. VJO Specialists were involved in many aspects of court functioning, including planning and implementation. They strongly supported direct involvement of other VA services in VTCs, such as Vet Center Counselors and Benefits Specialists. Defendant veterans were more likely to follow through with referrals when other VA staff were present in court. Over half of the courts had an active Veteran Mentor program, with another 21% having a program in development. There were a total of 851 active Veteran Mentors nationally, with an average of nine mentors per court. In keeping with the primary VJO mission of providing liaison services and education, VJO Specialists functioned as mentor program coordinators in only 8% of VTCs. The majority of mentor program coordinators were volunteers or Veteran Service Officers (40%). The VA does not advocate for the VJO Specialist to assume the role of mentor program coordinator as mentors supplement, but primarily function outside VJO's principal mission (McGuire, Clark and Blue-Howells 2013).

VJO Specialists reported that the average length of involvement in the courts for misdemeanants was fifteen to eighteen months and slightly longer for felons. Sixty-nine percent of participants successfully completed the court requirements and recommended health care treatment programs. Terminations were due to death, repeated non-compliance, disappearance, transfer, voluntary separation, or illness (McGuire, Clark and Blue-Howells 2013).

Fifty-nine percent of VTCs evaluated program functioning. Forty-nine percent kept a database that recorded baseline clinical, social, and criminal justice characteristics of veterans. VJO Specialists reported that 21% of courts had a formally approved evaluation process, usually as a funding requirement. Courts that did not conduct program evaluation most frequently cited lack of funding, staff, or expertise to conduct such assessments. Several VJO Specialists noted that the National Association of Drug Court Professionals (NADCP) published a model evaluation program that could easily be adapted to VTCs. The survey noted the rapid expansion of VTCs with the result that VJO Specialists were near or at capacity for staffing them. Collection of evidenced-based results of VJO involvement was encouraged, in part to support requests for additional federal funding of the VJO Initiative (McGuire, Clark and Blue-Howells 2013).

VTC RESEARCH

Demographics

The largest study of justice-involved veterans in contact with a VJO Specialist found that males aged forty-five and above comprised the majority of VTC veteran defendants (62%). Twenty-three percent were less than thirty-five years old. Four percent were female. Most were white (59%) or African American (32%). Forty percent were single and 37% were divorced/separated. Twenty-one percent were homeless and 45% had a service-connected disability rating (Finlay 2016).

Diagnoses

VJO Specialist contact with a justice-involved veteran was associated with 88% having a subsequent VA treatment visit. Most veterans (90%) were diagnosed with a disorder. Seventy-seven percent were diagnosed with at least one mental health disorder and 71% were diagnosed with at least one substance use disorder. Forty-seven percent were diagnosed with more than one mental health disorder, 46% with more than one substance use disorder, and 58% with dual diagnoses. The three most common non-substance-related diagnoses were depressive disorders (57%), PTSD (37%), and anxiety disorders (22%). Fifty-seven percent of veterans were diagnosed with alcohol use disorder, 13% with opioid use disorder, and 36% with other drug use disorders (Finlay 2016).

Use of Treatment Services

Ninety-seven percent of veterans diagnosed with a mental health disorder entered treatment within one year of their contact with a VJO Specialist. Seventy-two percent of veterans diagnosed with a substance use disorder entered substance misuse treatment. Entry into treatment was associated with being older, white, homeless, and having only one mental disorder. Treatment engagement, defined as six or more outpatient visits or inpatient/residential treatment, was 79%. Treatment engagement was associated with being female, between ages 25 and 54, and being Asian. Veterans in urban areas and homeless veterans were also more likely to engage in treatment. Having a service-connected disability rating and being dually diagnosed were also associated with engagement in treatment. Veterans with VJO Specialist contact were more likely than similarly diagnosed non-justice-involved veterans to engage in treatment. Court-ordered treatment likely accounted for some of this difference. Native Americans were less likely to enter care after a VJO contact, suggesting the need for targeted outreach to this community (Finlay 2016).

Symptom and Functional Improvement

Veterans who participate in VTC-ordered treatment have been shown to experience improvement in mental health and overall functioning. Measures of PTSD symptoms, sleep, substance use, depression, emotional well-being, and overall energy improve significantly during VTC involvement and treatment. Veterans also reported improvement in recovery orientation, family relations, social connectedness, and social functioning. Most measures showing improvements between pre-treatment and six months also showed further improvement or maintenance of gains between six and twelve months. At the twelve-month post-treatment follow-up, improvements were maintained in PTSD, depression, substance misuse, emotional well-being, and family functioning (Knudsen and Wingenfeld 2016).

Service Component Effectiveness

VTC services that predicted positive treatment outcomes included mentoring, PTSD treatment, psychiatric medication, and substance use disorder treatment. The presence of a Veteran Mentor program improved social connections. Trauma treatment was associated with improvements in PTSD, depression, and overall functioning. Inpatient substance use disorder treatment predicted improvement in substance misuse and sleep hours. Psychiatric medication was associated with improvements in depression, emotional lability, psychosis, and functioning (Knudsen and Wingenfeld 2016).

CHANGES IN THE SCOPE OF FORENSIC PRACTICE

As a result of the development of VTCs and the VJO Initiative, there has been an expansion of the scope of expertise courts seek from forensic practitioners in the VA and community-based settings. For example, as a condition of a veteran defendant's admission, many VTCs require expert opinion regarding the nexus between military service and the mental health issue related to the alleged criminal conduct. The evaluation of this nexus within the VA was previously the purview of VHA administrative personnel. Additionally, courts may rely on the expertise of forensic practitioners to develop treatment plans and to assist the VTC team in managing counter-transference issues. Thus, VA and community-based forensic practitioners must develop familiarity with mental health consequences of military service, tailoring treatment plans to a justice-involved population, the policies of VTCs, and relevant state statutes.

CONCLUSION

Veterans of all eras, regardless of service conditions, have been shown to have high rates of untreated mental health and substance use disorders. Additional factors, including homelessness and unemployment, further place veterans at risk for contact with the criminal justice system. Following the success of mental health and drug courts, the first VTC was established in 2008. The number of such courts has grown dramatically since that time. Many state legislatures have responded to the treatment needs of justice-involved veterans by passing laws supporting VTCs. A key component of VTC is a Veteran Mentor program, as peer support is associated with improvements in veterans' attitudes, behavior, and social functioning. The VA has responded to the needs of justice-involved veterans by implementing a VJO Initiative to link veterans to treatment and other resources in the community. Participation in a VTC is associated with improved mental health and functional outcomes. With the development of VTCs and the VJO Initiative, forensic practitioners in VA and community settings have new opportunities to provide expertise. As a result, they must be familiar with mental health consequences of military service, the policies of various VTCs and relevant state statutes.

REFERENCES

Blue-Howells, J.H., S.C. Clark, C. van den Berk-Clark, and J.F. McGuire. 2013. "The US Department of Veterans Affairs Veterans Justice Programs and the Sequential Intercept Model: Case Examples in National Dissemination of Intervention for Justice-Involved Veterans." *Psychological Services* 10 (1): 48–53.

Buffalo Veteran's Court and Veteran Mentor Handbook. Accessed October 10, 2015. www.nadcp.org/sites/default/files/nadcp/Buffalo%20Mentor%20Handbook_0.pdf.

Calhoun, P.S., L.A. Malesky Jr, H.B. Bosworth, and J.C. Beckham. 2004. "Severity of Posttraumatic Stress Disorder and Involvement with the Criminal Justice System." *Journal of Trauma Practice* 3 (3): 1–16.

California Penal Code §1170.9.

California Veterans Legal Task Force, Veterans Treatment Courts Mentor Training Program. Accessed October 10, 2015. http://www.cvltf.org/veterans-treatment-courts-mentor-training-program.html.

Clark, S.C., J.H. Blue-Howells, J. Rosenthal, and J. McGuire. 2010. *10NC1 Homeless Program VJO strategic plan, FY 2012–2016*. Washington, DC: Department of Veterans Affairs.

Cosden, M., J. Ellens, J. Schnell, and Y. Yamini-Diouf. 2005. "Efficacy of a Mental Health Treatment Court with Assertive Community Treatment." *Behavioral Sciences and the Law* 23 (2): 199–214.

Elbogen, E.B., S.C. Johnson, V.M. Newton, K. Straits-Troster, J.J. Vasterling, H.R. Wagner, and J.C. Beckham. 2012. "Criminal Justice Involvement, Trauma, and Negative Affect in Iraq and Afghanistan War Era Veterans." *Journal of Consulting and Clinical Psychology* 80 (6): 1097–102.

Finlay, A.K., D. Smelson, L. Sawh, J. McGuire, J. Rosenthal, J. Blue-Howells, C. Timko et al. 2016. "US Department of Veterans Affairs Veterans Justice Outreach Program Connecting Justice-Involved Veterans With Mental Health and Substance Use Disorder Treatment." *Criminal Justice Policy Review* 27 (2): 203–22.

FL Stat § 394.47891 (2014).

FL Stat § 948.08 (2014).

FL Stat § 948.16 (2014).

FL Stat § 948.21 (2014).

Florida Office of the State Courts Administration. 2014. Veterans Resource Guide for the Florida State Court System. Accessed October 10, 2015. http://www.flcourts.org/core/fileparse.php/266/urlt/VETERANS_RESOURCE_GUIDE.pdf.

Greenberg, G.A. and R.A. Rosenheck. 2008. "Jail Incarceration, Homelessness, and Mental Health: A National Study." *Psychiatric Services* 59 (2): 170–7.

Hawkins, M.D. 2010. "Coming Home: Accommodating the Special Needs of Military Veterans to the Criminal Justice System." *Ohio State Journal of Criminal Law* 7: 563–849.

Hoge, C.W., J.L. Auchterlonie, and C.S. Milliken. 2006. "Mental Health Problems, Use of Mental Health Services, and Attrition From Military Service After Returning From Deployment to Iraq or Afghanistan." *JAMA* 295 (9): 1023–32.

Illinois Veterans and Servicemembers Court Treatment Act, Public Act 096-0924.

Justice for Veterans, Veterans Treatment Court History. Accessed October 10, 2015. http://justiceforvets.org/vtc-history.

Kaylor, J.A., D.W. King, and L.A. King. 1987. "Psychological Effects of Military Service in Vietnam: A Meta-analysis." *Psychological Bulletin* 102 (2): 257–71.

Knudsen, K.J. and S. Wingenfeld. 2016. "A Specialized Treatment Court for Veterans with Trauma Exposure: Implications for the Field." *Community Mental Health Journal* 52 (2): 127–35.

McGuire, J., S. Clark, and J.H. Blue-Howells. 2013. "An Inventory of VA Involvement in Veterans Courts, Dockets, and Tracks." VA Veterans Justice Programs. Accessed October 11, 2015. http://www.cvltf.org/files/103430755.pdf.

McMichael, W.H. 2011. "Battle on the Home Front: Special Courts Turn to Those Who Served to Help Troubled Vets Regain Discipline, Camaraderie." *ABA Journal*. Accessed October 11, 2015. http://www.abajournal.com/magazine/article/the_battle_on_the_home_front_special_courts_turn_to_vets_to_help_other_vets/.

McNiel, D.E. and R. L. Binder. 2007. "Effectiveness of a Mental Health Court in Reducing Criminal Recidivism and Violence." *The American Journal of Psychiatry* 164 (9): 1395–403.

Milliken, C.S., J.L. Auchterlonie, and C.W. Hoge. 2007. "Longitudinal Assessment of Mental Health Problems Among Active and Reserve Component Soldiers Returning From the Iraq War." *JAMA* 298 (18): 2141–8.

Petrakis, I.L., R. Rosenheck, and R. Desai. 2011. "Substance Use Comorbidity Among Veterans with Posttraumatic Stress Disorder and Other Psychiatric Illness." *The American Journal on Addictions* 20 (3): 185–9.

Riggs, D.S., C.A. Byrne, F.W. Weathers, and B.T. Litz. 1998. "The Quality of the Intimate Relationships of Male Vietnam Veterans: Problems Associated with Posttraumatic Stress Disorder." *Journal of Traumatic Stress* 11 (1): 87–101.

Rodriguez, J.A. and C. Wang. "Primer to Veterans' Courts in Harris County, Texas." Accessed June 5, 2016. http://docplayer.net/1464911-Primer-to-veterans-courts-in-harris-county-texas.html

Russell, R.T. 2014. "Veterans Treatment Courts." *Touro Law Review* 31: 385–401.

Santa Cruz, N. 2012. "O.C.'s Combat Veterans Court Helps Ex-Warriors Fix Their Lives." *Los Angeles Times*, March 26. Accessed October 10, 2015. http://articles.latimes.com/2012/mar/26/local/la-me-oc-veterans-court-20120326.

Saxon, A.J., T.M. Davis, K.L. Sloan, K.M. McKnight, M.E. McFall, and D.R. Kivlahan. 2001. "Trauma, Symptoms of Posttraumatic Stress Disorder, and Associated Problems Among Incarcerated Veterans." *Psychiatric Services* 52 (7): 959–64.

Tanielian, T., L.H. Haycox, T.L. Schell, G.N. Marshall, M.A. Burnam, C. Eibner, B.R. Karney, L.S. Meredith, J.S. Ringel, and M.E. Vaiana. 2008. *Invisible Wounds of War. Summary and Recommendations for Addressing Psychological and Cognitive Injuries*. Rand Corporation, Santa Monica, CA.

Western, B., M. Kleykamp, and J. Rosenfeld. 2006. "Did Falling Wages and Employment Increase US Imprisonment?" *Social Forces* 84 (4): 2291–311.

Yager, T., R. Laufer, and M. Gallops. 1984. "Some Problems Associated with War Experience in Men of the Vietnam Generation." *Archives of General Psychiatry* 41 (4): 327–33.

CHAPTER 11

Legislative Consultation and the Forensic Specialist

Michael A. Norko

Forensic mental health specialists are well-positioned to influence the development of new legislation and the amendment of existing laws by virtue of their knowledge of case law and statutes, their experience with various matters related to the justice system and the legal regulation of psychiatry, and their clinical and/or research expertise in mental health. Such influence may be mediated through professional organizations, government agencies, or legislative liaisons or lobbyists. Forensic specialists may also interact directly with legislators as voting constituents or members of various interest groups.

This is not to imply, however, that such influence comes easily or that successes are routinely or expediently achieved or maintained. Nelson Cruikshank (a labor leader and lobbyist) noted in a presentation to the American Orthopsychiatric Association in 1966 that the adoption of constructive legislation is "a long and demanding process"; for example, it took fifty years for compulsory health insurance to be enacted as the law of the land from the time of the first proposed model legislation in 1915 (Cruikshank 1968). While Cruikshank also believed that skilled professionals had unique advantages to offer to legislators, he cautioned "Be not weary in well doing" (Cruikshank 1968, 73). Eric Redman took 300 pages to describe the federal legislative process that established the U.S. Public Health Corps (Redman 1973).

More recently, Kevin Sullivan (a former Connecticut state legislative leader and Lieutenant Governor) advised that "What we get, or do not get, from government has everything to do with how we approach the institutional, political, and personal processes involved" (Sullivan 2008). Cruikshank had advocated "the art of friendly persuasion" as the appropriate methodology for legislative advocacy (Cruikshank 1968, 67). Sullivan agrees with this idea, noting that changing policy is about building bridges, as well as building arguments. The former requires developing personal relationships, the latter requires a "focused, consistent, emotionally compelling" message that advances the "rhetoric of fairness, opportunity and personal responsibility embedded in our political culture" (Sullivan 2008, 12).

Psychiatrist Robert Becker has recently decried the loss of federal legislative support for community psychiatry, which was established in the mid-1960s, as a result of emerging federal fiscal policies and commercial economic interests in ensuing decades. He criticizes the loss of community services and the increased incidence of incarceration of people with psychiatric disabilities. As he urges, "If psychiatry does not rise up in protest to defend publicly the needs of its patients, we will have no grounds to disparage society's choices" (Becker 2015, 1099).

Irwin Perr (a former President of the American Academy of Psychiatry and the Law) similarly challenged forensic psychiatrists in 1979 to participate actively in the legislative process because without scientific input governmental decisions could not be responsible, even if responsive to other voices. As he stated, "Forensic psychiatrists, themselves acutely aware of the interaction of government power and social policy, must be alert to the need for professional input into the decision-making process" (Perr 1979, ix).

This chapter explores these themes regarding the involvement of forensic specialists in legislative and policy-making processes. It does so by noting the work of forensic professionals in legislative initiatives described in the literature and by illustrating legislative processes that involve significant sociopolitical topics: competence to stand trial, civil commitment, involuntary medication, the management of sexual offenders, involuntary outpatient commitment, and gun control legislation. Forensic professionals are often called upon to contribute to local and national legislative efforts. It would be beyond the scope of this chapter to explore local efforts in a state by state fashion, but I will begin with some notable illustrations of local contributions from my own state.

EARLY INFLUENCE ON LEGAL REFORMS IN CONNECTICUT

Much of the early work in reforming mental health legislation in Connecticut was accomplished with the significant input of Howard Zonana, who founded the Law & Psychiatry Division in the Department of Psychiatry at the Yale School of Medicine in 1975 and immediately embarked on the task of incorporating legislative activity into the work of forensic psychiatry (Norko 2010). Zonana was part of the group that worked on the 1976–77 revision of civil commitment law in Connecticut. This resulted in Public Act 77-595, which included provisions for: specific components required of independent physician examinations of the individual; the opportunity for the individual to choose voluntary status at a commitment hearing; re-evaluation of commitment after one year; a right to a probable cause hearing for individuals admitted under emergency certificates; and a duty of the hospital to discharge a person under emergency commitment who ceased to meet the standards for that commitment. Zonana similarly contributed to the development of child commitment statutes in Connecticut from 1978 to 1981, resulting in Public Acts 79-511, 81-247, and 81-472, codified at Connecticut General Statutes § 17a-75 to 17a-80. Zonana worked on drafting a revised competence to stand trial statute after the previous one had been declared unconstitutional, resulting in Public Act 81-365. Following the Hinckley verdict and the national debate about the insanity defense in the early 1980s, Zonana worked as a member of the Law Revision Commission Advisory Committees on the Insanity Defense and Psychiatric Security Review Board Legislation (1982–85), which resulted in the creation of Connecticut's Psychiatric Security Review Board. The Board was modeled after one in Oregon, but with some significant differences.

In 1983, two significant cases were decided advancing the rights of civilly committed patients to refuse medication (*Rennie v. Klein*; *Rogers v. Commissioner of Dep't of Mental Health*). At the time, Connecticut law permitted the involuntary medication of any involuntarily committed patient. Zonana worked with a group of psychiatrists, attorneys and judges for many years to attempt to create a new schema permitting due process for involuntary medication determinations. When years of discussion with advocates and the treaters failed to generate a consensus, a senior legislator forced a compromise that was written in seventy-two hours and resulted in Public Act 93-369. The Act established two different involuntary medication procedures, each an altered version of what the two sides had advanced unsuccessfully over years of debate, neither of which was truly satisfying at the time to anyone (Norko 2010). This is a fitting illustration of Sullivan's observation that "lawmakers … are less policymakers than they are policy diagnosticians and policy deciders. In other words, they make imperfect choices among imperfect options based on imperfect information under imperfect circumstances" (Sullivan 2008, 11).

SEX OFFENDER LEGISLATION

The history of legislation related to sex offenders began in the 1930s with the enactment of "sexual psychopath" laws designed to treat and cure sex offenders or keep them committed for the maximum criminal sentence period if they were not cured (APA 1999). By 1960, such laws had been enacted in twenty-five states, but by 1970, the "optimism of earlier decades that psychiatry held the cure to sexual psychopathy no longer shone so brightly" (APA 1999, 11). In 1977, the Group for the Advancement of Psychiatry concluded that these laws were a poorly conceived and failed socio-legal experiment that did not achieve clinical goals of treatment and research, and that they should be repealed (GAP 1977, 935–42). Courts, the American Bar Association, The President's Commission on Mental Health and the public also developed concerns about the laws (APA 1999). By 1985, all but six of those states had repealed such laws or no longer enforced them regularly (Brakel 1985, 740).

A horrific crime in Tacoma, Washington in 1989 was followed in 1990 by Washington's Community Protection Act. The Act provided for the first sex offender registration in the country, as well as for special commitment procedures for "sexually violent predators," as the Act referred to them. Kansas and Wisconsin enacted nearly identical laws soon thereafter. By the end of the decade, fifteen states had enacted such laws (WSIPP 2005). Over the subsequent decade, six more jurisdictions developed such laws (ATSA 2010).

The National Association of State Mental Health Program Directors (NASMHPD) adopted a position statement about civil commitment of sexually violent criminal offenders in 1997 (NASMHPD 1997) following the 5-4 decision of the U.S. Supreme Court earlier that year in *Kansas v. Hendricks* finding such commitment laws constitutional (*Kansas v. Hendricks* 1997). NASMHPD noted, "The Court's conclusion that the civil commitment of dangerous sex offenders who do not have a mental illness is constitutional does not necessarily mean that such laws represent good policy" (NASMHPD 1997). Instead, the Association recommended that concerns about violent sex offenders should be addressed through the criminal justice system.

Concern about these statutes had also prompted the APA to create the Task Force on Sexually Dangerous Offenders in 1994, chaired by Howard Zonana and including forensic psychiatrists Gene Abel, John Bradford, Steven K. Hoge, and Jeffrey Metzner. An interim report was released in 1996, with the final report released in 1999 (APA 1999). The report concluded:

> In the opinion of the Task Force, the sexual predator commitment laws establish a nonmedical definition of what purports to be a clinical condition without regard to scientific and clinical knowledge. In so doing, legislators have used psychiatric

> commitment to effect nonmedical societal ends that cannot be openly avowed. In the opinion of the Task Force, this represents an unacceptable misuse of psychiatry. (174)

The Task Force recommended instead that legitimate societal concerns for punishment and incapacitation were rightfully achieved through customary sentencing procedures and the criminal justice system.

The Connecticut Committee to Study Sexually Violent Persons overlapped with the final work of the APA Task Force, having been convened by the Governor in the summer of 1998. The Committee represented a broad range of stakeholders, including three forensic psychiatrists (Howard Zonana, Michael Norko, and Patrick Fox), and was co-chaired by the Director of Forensic Services of the Department of Mental Health and Addiction Services (DMHAS), Gail Sturges, an experienced forensic social worker. The committee invited testimony from three experts: W. Lawrence Fitch JD on sex offender legislation; John Bradford MD on sex offender treatment; and Dennis Dornan Ph.D. on evaluation, risk assessment and recidivism of sex offenders. (Fitch and Bradford were both members of the APA Task Force.) The committee ultimately recommended against enacting a sexual offender commitment law, instead suggesting a criminal justice approach to the problem, including longer sentences and longer periods of supervision under parole (Report of the Committee 1999). The presence of forensic mental health professionals on this committee was critical at multiple junctures to repeatedly buttressing the arguments against civil commitment. The legislature took up these recommendations in Public Act 99-02, June Special Session. One part of this legislation created a new definition of "persistent dangerous sexual offender" which empowered the courts to "sentence such person to a term of imprisonment and a period of special parole which together constitute a sentence of imprisonment for life" (CGS § 53a-40(i) 1999).

Thus, forensic mental health professionals in Connecticut were able to help spare the public mental health system the "misuse of psychiatry" (APA 1999, 174) adopted in so many other jurisdictions. In its 1997 position statement, NASMHPD had also acknowledged the reality that states would adopt such civil commitment statutes despite their drawbacks. Therefore, the position statement was also an effort to mitigate the risk of such statutes to public mental health systems by a variety of measures designed to separate the mental health agencies—and their resources—from the responsibilities for commitment of sexual offenders who did not have mental illnesses. In the late 2000s mental health professionals responsible for their public forensic systems were divided among those whose states had avoided or rejected sexually violent predator commitment laws and those who, regardless of their opinion about such laws, nonetheless were responsible for administering the resultant programs. Those who had such programs wanted to try to establish professional standards for implementing them in ways that attempted to attain the best possible practices. Those who did not have such programs argued that publishing such standards would undermine their efforts to avoid burdensome statutes that had been rejected by professional organizations and were already decreasing in popularity, in part because of their potential for continually expanding costs. The result was a decision not to elaborate upon the 1997 position statement, despite considerable effort invested in drafting a white paper on the topic in 2007.

The APA Task Force concluded that "sexual predator commitment laws represent a serious assault on the integrity of psychiatry" and that "psychiatry must vigorously oppose these statutes in order to preserve the moral authority of the professional and to ensure continuing societal confidence in the medical model of civil commitment" (APA 1999). Some forensic specialists, including psychiatrists, are in the difficult position of implementing such laws in a manner as consistent with professional ideals as possible despite professional condemnation of them. Other forensic specialists must remain vigilant to "expectations of simple and simplistic relief" of societal fears in the wake of new high-profile tragic events (Norko 2000, 287) and stay prepared to participate in emerging legislative processes.

OUTPATIENT COMMITMENT LAWS

One of the outcomes of increasing deinstitutionalization from the 1960s through the 1990s was a growing number of patients in the community who did not accept the need for treatment but also did not meet stricter involuntary hospitalization criteria that developed during this time. The result was a highly visible subpopulation of individuals who were not treated effectively in the community and who became caught in the revolving door of brief repeated hospitalizations or, worse, incarcerations. States began to develop outpatient commitment statutes in the 1980s to cope with this situation (APA 1999).

In 1987 the APA issued a Task Force Report on Involuntary Commitment to Outpatient Treatment. The report made legislative recommendations for criteria for outpatient commitment, including severe mental disorder, likelihood of harm to self or others or substantial deterioration, lack of capacity to make informed decisions regarding treatment, recent hospitalization and failure to comply with aftercare, a detailed plan describing the outpatient treatment, a "reasonable prospect" that the plan will be effective, and the treaters' agreement to accept the patient and the plan (APA 1987).

In 1996, the Connecticut DMHAS proposed legislation for outpatient commitment with criteria similar to those proposed by the APA Task Force, but without a requirement for lack of capacity or treaters' explicit agreement to the plan (CGA 1996). The bill permitted involuntary medication without the patient's informed consent if the absence of medication created a "direct threat of harm." Medication would be administered in a manner and place that is "clinically appropriate, safe and consistent with the dignity and privacy of the respondent" (CGA 1996).

In testimony at a public hearing before the legislature's Judiciary Committee, psychiatrist and Commissioner Albert Solnit acknowledged his reluctant support for the measure (given his long-standing support for individual liberties), noting that the bill would provide added safety for patients, their families and the public (Judiciary Committee 1996, 3). Psychiatrist Kenneth Marcus, DMHAS Medical Director, provided testimony that thirty-six states had such laws, the bill was tailored very narrowly to deal with violence and public safety, and it would affect a small number of patients (OLR 1996; Judiciary Committee 1996, 10). Howard Zonana testified as a member of the committee that developed the proposal. Psychiatrist Roger Coleman testified on behalf of the Connecticut Psychiatric Society in favor of the proposal (Judiciary Committee 1996). There was much testimony from consumers and advocates in opposition to the bill, and members of the Judiciary Committee had many challenging questions for Marcus and others. In the end, the Judiciary Committee did not pass the bill on for consideration by the General Assembly, but another bill included a provision to study the matter further (Public Act 96-215, Sec. 2). That study did not result in subsequent legislation for outpatient commitment, nor did DMHAS propose such legislation again.

In 1999, the APA's Council on Psychiatry and Law published its first Resource Document on Mandatory Outpatient Treatment. The stated purpose was to assist state psychiatric societies working on drafting legislation related to mandatory outpatient treatment (MOT) (Council 1999). The APA later updated this Resource Document in 2000. By that time, forty-one jurisdictions had enacted statutes permitting MOT, although only eighteen were using the statutes (Gerbasi, Bonnie, and Binder 2000). The document noted the mixed reviews in the literature regarding the effectiveness of MOT, but concluded that there were reasons to continue to support MOT for a subset of patients when certain criteria were met. It also concluded that MOT "concentrates the attention and effort of the providers," enhancing the services provided to the patient (Gerbasi, Bonnie, and Binder 2000, 141). The criterion of lack of capacity for informed consent from the 1987 recommendation was replaced with a criterion of lack of treatment compliance (Gerbasi, Bonnie, and Binder 2000, 136). The document contrasted its emphasis on need for treatment with the approach taken in most states linking MOT primarily to dangerousness to self or others (Gerbasi, Bonnie, and Binder 2000, 136). Importantly, the Resource Document acknowledged that in MOT programs, clinicians needed training in order to manage the dual role of therapy and social control—a basic tension that was clearly evidenced by conflicting testimony in Connecticut in 1996.

By the time the APA Resource Document was published in 2000, another clinical-social-political dimension was in ascendency—the Recovery Movement in mental health care. Proposals for outpatient commitment resurfaced in Connecticut in 2000, but advocates proposed other strategies to address the problem of repeated clinical deteriorations associated with treatment non-compliance. One such strategy was funded that year—the Peer Engagement Specialist Project. In this project persons with lived experience of mental illness were provided with training and hired to offer support and engagement to clients who were having difficulty living successfully in the community (Rowe 2013). In 2003, the President's New Freedom Commission strongly promoted the vision and principles of recovery and set out a national agenda to achieve important goals (Hogan 2003). The 2000s saw the gradual implementation of recovery principles in public mental health care across the country in varying degrees. In 2009 Connecticut was the only state to receive a grade A from NAMI—in the subcategory of Consumer & Family Empowerment. On overall grade, Connecticut was tied with five other states with a B grade, the highest mark given to any state (NAMI 2009).

In 2012, S.B. 452 was introduced in the Connecticut legislature, permitting probate court appointment of a conservator to authorize involuntary medication to a client after discharge from the hospital. NAMI-CT opposed this approach as antithetical to recovery values and individual autonomy in testimony before the Judiciary Committee (NAMI-CT 2012). The bill did not survive the committee's consideration. The next year, in line with the substantial development of recovery values in the Connecticut public mental health system, Yale psychologist Michael Rowe advocated peer engagement, citizenship-based approaches, and mental health outreach as viable and preferable alternatives to outpatient commitment in an editorial (Rowe 2013).

In the aftermath of the Sandy Hook tragedy in December 2012, the Connecticut General Assembly created a Bipartisan Task Force on Gun Violence Prevention and Children's Safety (A Safer Connecticut 2013). The

DMHAS Commissioner, Patricia Rehmer, MSN, provided testimony to the Mental Health Services Group of this task force in January 2013. In her testimony, Rehmer noted that forty-four states had some form of involuntary outpatient commitment but that many states did not implement the laws due to budgetary constraints (Rehmer 2013). She expressed concern that such a law would inhibit some people from seeking care and could deprive others engaged in treatment of needed resources. Ultimately the Mental Health Group of the task force recommended mental health first aid training for school staff, further study of mental health services available for adolescents and young adults, and case coordination initiatives in probate courts (A Safer Connecticut 2013).

Following the Sandy Hook shootings, the Helping Families in Mental Health Crisis Act of 2013 (H.R. 3717 2015) was introduced in Congress by Rep. Tim Murphy of Pennsylvania. The Act sought to expand and better coordinate mental health services through the country. One of the provisions of the bill required states to pass involuntary outpatient commitment laws. This raised concerns in Connecticut for DMHAS as well as for Senator Chris Murphy, who referred to that provision as a "nonstarter" (Ferris 2015). In the current version of the bill, H.R. 2646, co-sponsored by Rep. Eddie Bernice Johnson of Texas, this provision has been modified to reflect financial incentives for such programs, but not penalties for failure to establish them (Moran 2015). The 2015 bill is strongly supported by the APA (APA 2015).

Yet the idea of outpatient commitment remains controversial as its social control vector runs counter to expanding recovery sensibilities. Forensic psychiatrist Alexander Simpson has noted that it is possible to deliver mandated treatment and attend to recovery principles by informing patients fully, enhancing their "sense of voice," and treating them with respect (Simpson 2015, 49). Manchak and colleagues have studied mandated treatment relationships in 125 mental health court participants in relation to voluntary treatment relationships. They report that in mandated treatment clients experience significantly greater therapist control but that the quality of the relationships remains affiliative and autonomy-granting (Manchak, Skeem, and Rook 2014). Nonetheless, Connecticut officials will continue to monitor the progress of H.R. 2646 in relation to the recovery-oriented approach promoted by DMHAS.

GUN CONTROL LEGISLATION

During the last several decades, federal and state gun control legislation has been directed at persons with psychiatric disabilities, often following tragic events. In the Gun Control Act of 1968, Congress created prohibitions of firearm possession by persons "adjudicated as a mental defective or committed to any mental institution" (codified at 18 U.S.C. § 922(d)(4)). The Brady Handgun Violence Prevention Act (named for White House Press Secretary James Brady who was shot in 1981) was introduced in Congress in 1987 and passed in 1993. It required the creation of the National Instant Criminal Background Check System (NICS), "a national system that checks available records on persons who may be disqualified from receiving firearms" (FBI 2015) on the basis of prohibitions in 18 U.S.C. § 922. Following the Virginia Tech shootings in 2007, Congress passed the NICS Improvement Amendment Act of 2007, which required states to comply with reporting of prohibited individuals with both financial incentives and penalties for failure to do so.

That Act also represented a failed opportunity to correct the unfortunate language of "mental defective" (Norko and Baranoski 2014). An action paper introduced by three Connecticut forensic psychiatrists (Victoria Dreisbach, Ezra Griffith, and Michael Norko) was passed in the APA Assembly in 2008, directing the APA's Department of Government Relations (DGR) to work with Congress to eliminate the term (Norko and Dreisbach 2008). Although no Congressional action has taken place to date, the FBI did agree to change its use of the term, except for quoting federal law (Norko 2008). The APA position is that "Congress must take action to stop labeling Americans as 'mental defectives'" (APA 2010). Seven years after the Action Paper, with continued advocacy by the DGR, the alternative language proposed by the APA has made its way into two bills: the Safer Communities Act of 2015 (H.R. 2994, Section 1738); and the End Purchase of Firearms by Dangerous Individuals Act (H.R. 2917). In a similar situation, Congress did change the language of "mental retardation" in Rosa's Law in 2010 (Social Security Administration 2013), so we can remain hopeful that the mental defective language will also change in the near future with continued advocacy.

The Connecticut General Assembly had required state officials to report prohibited persons to NICS in Public Act 05-283, signed into law more than two years before the passage of the NICS Improvement Amendment Act of 2007. This necessitated a memorandum of understanding among the state police, DMHAS, the judicial branch and the FBI, which was finalized in November 2006. Thereafter DMHAS and the judicial branch began reporting individuals to NICS who were found incompetent to stand trial or not guilty by reason of mental disease or defect, or who were civilly committed to a psychiatric hospital or had a conservator appointed for them. More than 27,000 such individuals were reported for adjudications from 2003 to 2012 (Norko and Baranoski 2014, 1620).

Prior to these NICS-related actions, Connecticut had taken other actions in the wake of tragic shootings. In March 1998, an employee of the Connecticut Lottery killed four fellow employees and himself at work, in an apparent state of depression (CNN 1998). Within three months, the Connecticut General Assembly passed Public Act 98-129, which required reporting to the state police of individuals who had been civilly committed. Such individuals had already been prohibited from gun possession for twelve months in Public Act 94-1, but that prohibition relied on an honor system of individuals acknowledging their commitments on permit applications. Gail Sturges, then DMHAS Director of Forensic Services, worked with the state police and the state Department of Information Technology to create a "black box" system that would maintain the confidentiality of civil commitment data (the other relevant adjudications were matters of public record under Connecticut law) and of gun permit applications, and only notify the state police and DMHAS when a match occurred between a disqualifying adjudication and an issued or requested gun permit (Norko and Baranoski 2014).

Continued concern over the Lottery shootings, amplified in April 1999 by the Columbine shootings, led to further legislation in 1999. A proposal was circulated calling for psychiatrists to evaluate individuals to make a determination as to whether they were safe to have a gun. The mental health community resisted this idea, arguing that there were no scientific data on which such a determination could be made by mental health professionals and that the measure was stigmatizing to persons with psychiatric disabilities. Instead, Connecticut became the first state to permit gun seizures by law enforcement officers when an individual posed "a risk of imminent personal injury to himself or herself or to other individuals" regardless of mental health concerns (Public Act 99-212, codified at § 29-38c(a)). The seizure is accomplished via warrant and the judge is to consider recent threats or acts of violence, acts of cruelty to animals, reckless use of firearms, history of use of physical force against others, prior involuntary confinement in a psychiatric hospital, and illegal use of substances or abuse of alcohol. Thus, the law was crafted to target risky situations without targeting people with psychiatric disabilities *per se*. Preliminary data are consistent with this idea. In a study of 764 warrants from October 1999 through July 2013, 20% of the 700 men and 30% of the sixty-four women (23% total) had histories of involuntary hospitalization (Norko and Baranoski 2014). Current multi-university research efforts, led by Jeffrey Swanson, are underway to compare the outcomes of the Connecticut law with a similar law passed in Indiana in 2006 following a tragic shooting in that state (Parker 2010).

Following the Sandy Hook shootings in December 2012, the Connecticut

General Assembly passed Public Act 13-3, which provided for substantial new firearms control measures. The most significant components of that Act for mental health were the provisions in Sections 10 and 11 requiring that individuals who voluntarily admitted themselves to a psychiatric hospital would be prohibited from gun ownership for six months. Because voluntary admission does not involve a mental health adjudication, no records of such admissions were previously kept and there was no database allowing state police to regulate gun permits on the basis of voluntary psychiatric admissions. These provisions were an addition to the NICS-based prohibitions and a surprise to the mental health community, which had had no opportunity to comment on these ideas as they were never discussed in a public hearing or otherwise opened to discussion.

The new law required DMHAS officials to create another "black box" data system so that confidential records of voluntary psychiatric admissions were not simply released to the police. It also required a mechanism for each of the thirty-two hospitals with psychiatric services to report this data regularly to DMHAS. Since the initiation of the data system, matches of voluntary admissions with gun permits (current, surrendered or in application) has remained steady at about 3% (Norko and Baranoski 2014).

Psychiatrists have posed multiple objections to the bill (see Ackerman 2014, for example), including that it deters individuals from seeking needed psychiatric treatment, especially among people who do not wish their psychiatric admissions reported to the government (for various reasons, including celebrity) and those who are required to use a handgun in their employment (law enforcement, security personnel). Some psychiatrists have argued that the restriction would make more sense clinically if applied to those who are involuntarily held on Physician's Emergency Certificates (PEC, an involuntary fifteen-day hold based on a single physician determination) rather than voluntary patients (Beckler 2014).

Neither the voluntary admission process nor the emergency certificate process contains the kind of due process ordinarily associated with deprivation of a Constitutional right, in this case based on the Second Amendment. However, in a 2012 decision, the United States Court of Appeals for the First Circuit noted in dicta that temporary prohibitions might be constitutionally permissible pending further proceedings or if the individual had the ability to recover the suspended right through subsequent proceedings (*U.S. v. Rehlander*, 2012, 49). Thus, the constitutional concern about the lack of due process in the voluntary admission prohibition may not ultimately be problematic.

The concerns raised by psychiatrists about the prohibition continue to arouse discussion. A proposal was submitted during the 2015 legislative session to have psychiatrists make individual assessments about which voluntarily patients were unsafe to possess firearms. This raised the same concerns about the scientific basis for such determinations as had been raised in 1998, when forensic professionals successfully argued against the idea. One possible direction to pursue would be to repeal the voluntary admissions prohibition, but grant psychiatrists an exception to confidentiality in order to make a report of any patient not covered by NICS prohibitions (i.e., voluntary or PEC admissions) under the provisions of the gun seizure statute in situations of risk of imminent personal injury. Once again, this would represent a non-stigmatizing mechanism for dealing with the matter, through existing mechanisms. This will be the work for future legislative advocacy. Forensic psychiatrist Liza Gold has noted the examples of Indiana and Connecticut that allow the removal of firearms in dangerous situations without reference to mental illness *per se*. She encourages psychiatrists to take an active role in multidisciplinary public health approaches to reducing gun violence:

> By supporting a focus on dangerousness and violence risk assessment rather than on mental illness, we can help steer the national discussion toward nondiscriminatory approaches to reducing gun violence ... We should look for opportunities to shape social policy and legislative initiatives so as to include a role for violence risk assessment, with or without mental illness, in the effort to reduce firearms-related death and injury (Gold 2013, 341–2).

CONCLUSIONS

Forensic mental health professionals have made significant contributions to the evolution of legislation related to topics in mental health, as described here. Many other state and federal legislative initiatives involving forensic mental health input could be described in these and other relevant areas, but this would extend the discussion beyond the limits of this chapter.

It is important to note, however, that these contributions of forensic specialists have been the result of substantial and long-sustained efforts. One illustration of this point is found in the work of forensic psychiatrist Robert Weinstock, who continues to document psychiatrists' efforts to revise and clarify California's *Tarasoff* ruling forty years after its first release (Weinstock et al. 2014).

Successful legislative interventions require effectively translated communication to the right people at the right time (Whiteford 2001). That communication entails the presentation of science and clinical experience in an emotionally compelling manner and a tolerance of imperfection in the process and its outcomes (Whiteford 2001; Sullivan 2008). The responsible use of government power and the development of social policy require the input of the unique skills and perceptions of forensic specialists (Perr 1979) who are keenly aware of the vagueries, challenges and successes in the application of law at the personal level.

Perhaps even more critical to the potency of legislative contributions of forensic specialists are the humanistic goals at the center of the healing professions and the societal obligations inherent to the healing mission. This responsibility is not a theoretical abstract; it is a mandate to be considered and practiced in a serious fashion. As Simone Weil observed:

> It is the aim of public life to arrange that all forms of power are entrusted, so far as possible, to [those] who effectively consent to be bound by the obligation toward all human beings which lies upon everyone, and who understand the obligation.
>
> Law is the totality of the permanent provisions for making this aim effective. (Weil 1998, 137–8)

It is the privilege of forensic mental health professionals to attempt to contribute to such provisions. It is also their burden, which can entail sacrifice and suffering; the work is often long and difficult and the outcomes can be disappointing and even painful. My own recent efforts at leading a multi-agency effort to adopt statutory provisions for dealing with defendants who are found not competent to stand trial and not restorable on serious charges illustrate this point. After two years of research, study, and discussion within a carefully planned and deliberately inclusive consensus-building methodology, we failed at the very end to achieve unanimous support for the final product, scuttling hundreds of hours of work and a solution desired by nearly all of the involved agencies. One lesson learned is that the forensic professional can lead a group toward a desired destination, but actually arriving depends not on the quality of the journey but in knowing that the entire entourage wants to finish together in the end.

Given such realities, it can be a significant challenge to heed Cruikshank's advice to "be not weary in well doing" (Cruikshank 1968, 73). To the willing I offer Kent Keith's stronger encouragement for such occasions: "What you spend years building may be destroyed overnight. Build anyway" (Keith 1968).

REFERENCES

Ackerman, S. 2014. Mentally Ill Not Inherently Dangerous. Ct post. November 15, 2014. http://www.ctpost.com/opinion/article/Ackerman-Mentally-ill-not-inherently-dangerous-5895280.php. Accessed October 12, 2015.

APA (American Psychiatric Association). 1987. *Involuntary Commitment to Outpatient Treatment: Report of the Task Force on Involuntary Outpatient Commitment.* Washington D.C.

———. 1999. *Dangerous Sex Offenders—a Task Force Report of the American Psychiatric Association.* Washington DC.

———. 2010. *Offensive and Stigmatizing References to the Mentally Ill in Gun Law.* January 2010.

———. 2015. Letter to Representatives Murphy and Johnson in support of the Helping Families in Mental Health Crisis Act. http://psychiatry.org/psychiatrists/advocacy/federal-affairs/comprehensive-mental-health-reform. Accessed October 11, 2015.

A Safer Connecticut. 2013. Bipartisan Task Force on Gun Violence Prevention and Children's Safety. https://www.cga.ct.gov/asaferconnecticut/. Accessed October 11, 2015.

ATSA (Association for the Treatment of Sexual Abusers). 2010. Civil Commitment of Sexually Violent Predators. http://www.atsa.com/civil-commitment-sexually-violent-predators. Accessed October 10, 2015.

Becker, R.E. 2015. "Policies and Consequences: How America and Psychiatry Took the Detour to Erewhon." *Psychiatric Services* 66: 1097–100.

Beckler, A.L. 2014. "Post-Newtown gun law has a mental health loophole, critics say." *The CT Mirror*. February 14, 2014. http://ctmirror.org/2014/02/14/gun-law-has-a-mental-health-loophole-critics-say/. Accessed October 12, 2015.

Brakel, S.J., J. Parry, and B.A. Weiner. 1985. *The Mentally Disabled and the Law*. 3rd ed. Chicago: American Bar Foundation.

CGA (Connecticut General Assembly). 1996. Raised Bill No. 5821, An Act Concerning Outpatient Commitment.

CNN. 1998. "We Love You Matt—but Why?" March 8, 1998. http://www.cnn.com/US/9803/08/lottery.killings/index.html. Accessed October 12, 2015.

Council on Psychiatry and Law, American Psychiatric Association. 1999. Mandatory Outpatient Treatment Resource Document. https://www.google.com/url?sa=t&rct=j&q=&esrc=s&source=web&cd=1&cad=rja&uact=8&ved=0CCAQFjAAahUKEwjBptqki7vIAhUEMj4KHbtxBDQ&url=http%3A%2F%2Fwww.psychiatry.org%2FFile%2520Library%2FPsychiatrists%2FDirectories%2FLibrary-and-Archive%2Fresource_documents%2Frd1999_MandatoryOutpatient.pdf&usg=AFQjCNFjiF1VQe_R9DhI8iQK4W8_OlxPRg. Accessed October 11, 2015.

Cruikshank, N.K. 1968. "How to Win Friends and Influence Legislators." *American Journal of Orthopsychiatry* 38: 67–75.

FBI. 2015. National Instant Criminal Background Check System Fact Sheet. https://www.fbi.gov/about-us/cjis/nics/general-information/fact-sheet. Accessed October 12, 2015.

Ferris S. 2015. Dem Senator Eyes Changes to "Draconian" Provision in Mental Health

Bill. The Hill. http://thehill.com/policy/healthcare/242891-dem-senator-eyes-changes-to-draconian-provision-in-mental-health-bill. Accessed October 11, 2015.

GAP (Group for the Advancement of Psychiatry). 1977. Psychiatry and Sex Psychopath Legislation: The 30's to the 80's. Formulated by the Committee on Psychiatry and Law.

Gerbasi, J.B., R.J. Bonnie, and R.L. Binder. 2000. "Resource Document on Mandatory Outpatient Treatment." *Journal of the American Academy of Psychiatry and Law* 28: 127–44.

Gold, L.H. 2013. "Gun Violence: Psychiatry, Risk Assessment, and Social Policy." *Journal of the American Academy of Psychiatry and Law* 41: 337–43.

Hogan, M. 2003. Keynote Address. President's New Freedom Commission on Mental Health: Transforming the Vision. The Carter Center. https://www.cartercenter.org/documents/1701.pdf. Accessed October 12, 2015.

H.R. 3717. 2013. https://www.congress.gov/bill/113th-congress/house-bill/3717. Accessed October 12, 2015.

H.R. 2646. 2015. https://www.congress.gov/bill/114th-congress/house-bill/2646/text. Accessed October 11, 2015.

Judiciary Committee Hearing Transcript for March 22, 1996.

Kansas v. Hendricks. 1997. 521 U.S. 346.

Keith, K.M. 1968. The Paradoxical Commandments. Available at http://www.paradoxicalcommandments.com/. Accessed October 17, 2015.

Manchak, S.M. J.L. Skeem, and K.S. Rook. 2014. "Care, Control, or Both? Characterizing Major Dimensions of the Mandated Treatment Relationship." *Law and Human Behavior* 38: 47–57.

Moran, M. 2015. "Mental Health Reform Bill Reintroduced Into House." *Psychiatric News* 50 (13): 1,35.

NAMI (National Alliance on Mental Illness). 2009. Grading the States—A Report on America's Health Care system for Adults with Serious Mental Illness. http://www2.nami.org/gtsTemplate09.cfm?Section=Grading_the_States_2009. Accessed October 12, 2015.

NAMI–Connecticut. 2012. Testimony before the Judiciary Committee March 29, 2012 Opposing SB 452—An Act Concerning the Care and Treatment of Persons with Psychiatric Disabilities. https://www.google.com/url?sa=t&rct=j&q=&esrc=s&source=web&cd=1&cad=rja&uact=8&ved=0CB4QFjAAahUKEwjV34_DjrvIAhWFNT4KHZOjBNo&url=https%3A%2F%2Fwww.cga.ct.gov%2F2012%2FJUDdata%2Ftmy%2F2012SB-00452-R000329-Daniela%2520Giordano-%2520NAMI-TMY.PDF&usg=AFQjCNEvmjGoDkCqgcy_XW1Vy7Z8bWKt5w. Accessed October 11, 2015.

NASMHPD (National Association of State Mental Health Program Directors). 1997. Position statement on laws providing for the civil commitment of sexually violent criminal offenders. http://www.nasmhpd.org/content/position-statement-laws-providing-civil-committment-sexually-violent-criminal-offenders. Accessed October 10, 2015.

Norko, M.A. 2000. "Dangerousness: A Failed Paradigm for Clinical Practice and Service Delivery." *Journal of the American Academy of Psychiatry and the Law* 28: 282–9.

———. 2008. Letter to the Editor. *Journal of the American Academy of Psychiatry and the Law* 36: 428–9.

———. 2010. "Commentary: The Dynamic Evolution of Forensic Psychiatry at Yale and the Zonanian Sphere of Influence." *Journal of the American Academy of Psychiatry and the Law* 38: 577–80.

Norko, M.A. and M. Baranoski. 2014. "Gun Control Legislation in Connecticut: Effects on Persons with Mental Illness." *Connecticut Law Review* 46: 1609–31.

Norko, M.A. and V.M. Dreisbach. 2008. "Letter to the Editor." *Journal of the American Academy of Psychiatry and Law* 36: 269–70.

OLR (Office of Legislative Research, CT General Assembly). 1996. Outpatient Commitment Task Force. October 4, 1996.

Parker, G.F. 2010. "Application of a Firearm Seizure Law Aimed at Dangerous Persons: Outcomes From the First Two Years." *Psychiatric Services* 61: 478–82.

Perr, I.N. 1979. "President's Message; Laetrile, Legislation, and Chicken Soup." *Bulletin of the American Academy of Psychiatry and the Law* 7: ix–xi.

Redman, E. 1973. *The Dance of Legislation*. New York: Simon & Schuster.

Rehmer, P. 2013. Testimony Before the Mental Health Services Group of the Bipartisan Task Force on Gun Violence Prevention and Children's Safety, January 29, 2013. www.ct.gov/dmhas/lib/dmhas/legislative/lt1.29.13a.pdf. Accessed October 11, 2015.

Rennie v. Klein, 720 F.2d 266 (3rd Cir. 1983).

Report of the Committee to Study Sexually Violent Persons. 1999. Submitted to Governor John G. Rowland, State of Connecticut, February 10, 1999.

Rogers v. Commissioner of Dep't of Mental Health, 458 N.E.2d 308 (Mass. 1983).

Rowe, M. 2013. "Alternatives to Outpatient Commitment." *Journal of the American Academy of Psychiatry and Law* 41: 332–6.

Simpson, A.I.F. 2015. "Commentary: Civil Commitment and its Reform." *Journal of the American Academy of Psychiatry and Law* 43: 48–51.

Social Security Administration. 2013. Change in Terminology; "Mental Retardation" to "Intellectual Disability." Federal Register 78: 46499–502.

Sullivan, K.B. 2008. "A Public Policymaker's Response: Weisleder and Meyer on Legislator Decision-making." *Journal of the American Academy of Psychiatry and Law* 36: 10–12.

U.S. v. Rehlander. 2012. 666 F.3d 45 (1st Cir).

Weil, S. 1998. *Writings Selected with an Introduction by Eric O. Springsted.* Maryknoll, NY: Orbis Books.

Weinstock, R., D. Bonnici, A. Seroussi, and G.B. Leong. 2014. "No Duty To Warn In California: Now Unambiguously Solely A Duty To Protect." *Journal of the American Academy of Psychiatry and Law* 42: 101–8.

Whiteford, H. 2001. "Can Research Influence Mental Health Policy?" *Australian and New Zealand Journal of Psychiatry* 35: 428–34.

WSIPP (Washington State Institute for Public Policy). 2005. Involuntary Commitment Of Sexually Violent Predators: Comparing State Laws. Document No. 05-03-1101.

CHAPTER 12

Forensic Practice and Religion: Context and Change

John L. Young

INTRODUCTION

Both as academic disciplines and as aspects of everyday life, psychiatry's dealings with religion and with the law have been harmonious in some ages and in others considerably more turbulent. There are currently enough significant developments to suggest that we are living in a period of growing mutual understanding characterized by a shared culture of responsible curiosity and mutually respectful regard for diverse values. Such is the case for the mainstream at least, despite the reactions of the inevitable noisy fringe groups (Dupre 2008).

This chapter is an endeavor to identify and describe some relevant and interesting religious realms of operation for forensic mental health expertise. Ours is a time of changes that open new opportunities and alter the older arenas in ways that demand wider vision and deeper sensitivity.

We begin with an examination of Christianity's early roots in phenomena of healing, noting how the founding church's leaders were intimately involved with miraculous cures. We then see how during the early twentieth century the apparent effects of the church's decreasing secular hegemony included a withdrawal from involvements that threatened the leadership's sense of security. They expressed this in part by formatting several centuries-old intertwining legal customs into a detailed formulation or code of canon law. Included among its provisions was the restriction of the clergy from the practice of the healing arts, such as they were at the time.

The Second Vatican Council (1962–65) initiated a much-needed revision of the Code of Canon Law, promulgated in 1983. It was quite thoroughly reworked and it dropped the restriction on clergy medical practice, only to begin experiencing a phenomenon that proved orders of magnitude more embarrassing than could ever result from any medical practice by clergy. Addressing the scandalous sexual abuse by clergy members calls for involvement of forensic mental health expertise, a need finally acknowledged by the responsible officials. Consultation is also needed to assist the recruitment and guidance of clergy in formation.

In addition, we update the church's marriage tribunals' use of experts to support the validity and usefulness of their decisions. Forensic experts in psychology or psychiatry with an interest in religion are almost routinely needed in order to evaluate claims of serious psychological deficit(s). Here one can contribute significant help in alleviating emotional suffering.

We conclude with accounts of two group experiences designed to show medical professionals' pathways to experiencing the spiritual dimension inherent in their clinical work. These can serve as models for the creative applications awaiting discovery by religiously or spiritually interested forensic mental health professionals.

THE ANCIENT CHURCH

Today's Roman Catholic Church's early history is immersed in a tradition that is unabashedly positive about healing, whether it be physical, spiritual, or both. Well-accepted tradition dating at least to the second century has it that the evangelist Luke was a physician (Fitzmyer 1981). Not one of Jesus's original disciples, Luke first appears in Paul's Letter to the Colossians (4:14) as "the beloved physician." Luke's gospel supports in some of its details the claim to medical authorship: for example, the detailed description of a fever (4:38) and of a paralysis (5:24–25). Also, Luke portrays Jesus responding most sensitively to the chronically hemorrhagic woman who touched his garment, receiving an instant cure because of her strong faith (8:43–48). Luke's account states simply that no one had been able to heal her, whereas the version by Mark elaborates in a strikingly colorful way that the woman had long suffered much from many physicians and spent all her means and was only getting worse. The importance of this omission on Luke's part lies in the fact that Mark's Gospel is Luke's chief written source (Stuhlmueller 1968).

Luke also authored the Acts of the Apostles as a sequel to his Gospel. It is a narration of the apostles' early experiences as the Church very gradually took shape. Luke recounts that as Peter opened his first public speech, he led with a reminder to his audience of the miracles performed by Jesus (2:22), invoking them as part of the basis for his authority to address the crowd. Luke (2:41) reported that about three thousand responded by receiving baptism. Shortly after, Peter and John, in the presence of a crowd entering the Temple for evening prayer, drew attention by their healing of a well-known lame beggar just outside the Temple (3:1–10). With the newly healed beggar still clinging to him, Peter spoke to the amazed crowd, by then greatly swollen. This time he again invoked the continuing power of Jesus as the explanation for the healing. At this point, according to Luke, the number of people baptized grew to five thousand.

Thus the positive association of physical curing and healing with growth in the faith has deep roots indeed in the Church's early formative years. One later development illustrating this is the canonical requirement of two miracles in order for a person to be declared a saint. Usually these consist of curing individuals suffering from recognized incurable illnesses. Of course, the testimony of properly qualified medical expert witnesses is necessarily included in the process, usually over many decades.

Another positive connection between the healing arts and traditional Catholic consciousness finds expression in the naming of patron saints for many kinds of health workers as well as for sufferers living with a variety of medical conditions. A heartwarming touch is evident in this custom, encouraging faith to continue growing despite a painful grim prognosis by holding up an encouraging model for contemplation. Similarly for hardworking caregivers; some of them at least may look to the example of a patron saint to help combat the stressors inherent in their occupations. In general the Vatican declares these titles in response to requests from diverse sources often literally over the centuries. They traverse many areas outside medicine, for example cities and countries. Some practices may be admittedly over-emphasized and verging on misguided idolatry. Neglect of this potentially helpful resource is probably more common. In either case its practice allies the Church with medicine in general.

A PUZZLING PROHIBITION: NO MEDICAL HEALING BY CLERGY

Over the course of nearly its first two millennia, the Roman Catholic Church's rules for governing and relating to her members arose gradually. Christian and pagan influences on the shape of church law converged and grew together after the Roman Empire became Christian. Then, under the influence of the Renaissance, beginning in the thirteenth century with the rise of the universities, Roman law came to be re-understood and appreciated. It intertwined with Church law, both developing over the succeeding centuries. Meanwhile, in England the law evolved by following the decisions of courts, rather than the academic conversations in the schools, giving rise to today's common law. For Church law, the first global set of provisions or canons, 2,414 in number, were crystalized into a single volume, the "Code of Canon Law" or "Codex Juris Canonici." Promulgated in 1917, it is generally referred to as simply "the 1917 Code."

The year 1917 was most definitely not a quiet one for most of the western world. For the Catholic Church in particular, it marked the last stage of a painful political and military decline that ended in the humiliating loss of the territory that had been the Papal States. This also meant a serious waning of diplomatic influence. As they suffered decreasing control over temporal matters, the Church leadership naturally and properly sought to organize from within to gain whatever control was still possible. In this context the 1917 Code defined how and by whom a virtual universe of affairs would henceforth be arranged and managed. The Code delves into minute detail regarding roles, status, qualifications and duties of Church members, top to bottom, and each of the seven sacraments, including matrimony, as will become evident below.

The 1917 Code includes 383 canons devoted to governing the clergy. Naturally they vary considerably in length and in the seriousness of their subject matter. Their mere number would again suggest a strong need for power or control. One provision in particular is rather surprising, in view of the Church's long-standing traditions inculcating deeply held positive connections with medicine and healing as described above. It is Canon 139, and it specifies that without the pope's specific permission, known as an apostolic indult, members of the clergy may not practice medicine or surgery. Also, they are not to hold higher political office. Why? By way of explanation the canon labels these activities as unbecoming (*indecora*) or foreign (*aliena*) to the clerical state.

The context of this puzzling law offers some clarification. For example, although the pope himself must grant permission for clerics to run for high public office or practice medicine or surgery, only the local bishop's permission is required to run for lower political offices. Similarly, clergy are not to take part in boisterous hunting, but they are free to hunt alone or in small private parties. They are to stay away from unbecoming spectacles but are free to enjoy the more modest productions. Also fitting this pattern, the Code recognizes several varieties of military commitments and rules each one as in or out for clergy. However, a few roles are ruled out entirely, such as butcher or executioner.

The 1917 Code of Canon Law, then, appears to portray a felt need on the part of those in charge to impose dictates to a minute and intrusive degree. Yet one can also readily see a desire to appeal to the reader or subject's powers of reason by repeatedly offering a phrase or clause of explanation. The Code can be seen as a whole that is abundantly humane and sympathetic, a needed support for trying times. Any human document, especially a somewhat long one, is bound to have some difficult passages. In this way the perplexing provision in Canon 139 may be, if not fully understood, at least respected at face value. There are two outstanding examples of such respect (Lynch 1985, 224). One is the Rev. Robert F. Drinan, a Jesuit priest and lawyer from Massachusetts who served for a decade in the U.S. Congress but obediently declined to run again in 1980 when he received word through the Jesuit Superior General, Rev. Pedro Arrupe, that he no longer had the permission of Pope John Paul II to run for Congress. During the same election season, a Norbertine priest from Wisconsin, Robert J. Cornell, obeyed when he received word from the apostolic delegate (pope's representative) to the U.S., Archbishop Jean Jadot, that he also was not to run again for Congress.

Most of the commentaries offer little by way of explanation of the Church's reasons for excluding its priests from functioning also as physicians. In evaluating possible explanations one would do well to remember the state of the medical arts in 1917. In the U.S. it was a time of contention among several schools or traditions: allopathic, homeopathic, osteopathic, chiropractic, and even naturopathic. The Flexner Report, with its documentation of the need for specific reforms to American medical education practices, was just beginning to make its weight felt.

When Pope John XXIII convened the Second Vatican Council in 1963 he included a call for a revision of the 1917 Code of Canon Law. He quite possibly had the wisdom to foresee the seismic changes that he was setting into motion as he called for *aggiornamento*. As the Council's first session came to its end in March of 1963, the pope appointed the first members of the Pontifical Commission for the Revision of the Code of Canon Law. Sagaciously, the appointed group suspended its work until after the Council completed its own work in late 1965. The new Code was ready in 1983. It maintained much of the character of the 1917 version, with added attractive qualities including enhanced recognition of the dignity of the human person, the importance of local communities, and the roles of laypersons and the need for consultation. Although most of the clerical role restrictions remained, both in letter and in spirit, the clause in Canon 139 requiring an apostolic indult for clerics to practice medicine or surgery disappeared. The commentaries make only passing mention of this change, offering no speculation regarding its significance. Evidently the prohibition itself had lost its significance. Present or absent, it no longer seemed puzzling.

A PERPLEXING PROBLEM: THE CLERGY SEXUAL ABUSE SCANDAL

Just as the church was announcing the 1983 revision of its Code of Canon Law, the first signs were appearing of the clergy sex abuse scandal that would grow gradually and inexorably to reach historic proportions. It was to continue well over the next three decades (McGreevy 2004). To say the least, it was soon clear that the carefully wrought rules of Canon Law that attempted to govern every aspect of clerical formation and conduct had missed something of vital importance. It is also clear that forensic psychiatry and psychology are of critical relevance for addressing several aspects of the scandal.

For example, the 1983 Code added requirements not in the 1917 version for psychological screening of applicants for clerical studies. It also calls for additional expert consultation to those in charge of formation programs when indicated. It is obvious that seeing to the new canon law provisions can be a worthwhile and satisfying area for the services of forensic mental health expertise. Even though many seminaries had been using psychological screening and expert consultation for up to two decades by 1983, all too many individuals at risk of being or becoming sex abusers had already been accepted into and completed their clerical formation programs. This reality serves to accentuate the urgency of involving more interested forensically trained experts in a very worthwhile preventive function.

For all too many years it was quite easily possible for a cleric of any denomination to live as a serial abuser, so deferential were the criminal trial courts to crossing the first amendment wall between church and state (Young and Griffith 1995). In a major shift, dramatically marked in Boston in 1982 (Gautier, Perl, and Fichter 2012), the criminal and civil courts finally began to demonstrate that they were learning from the clergy sex abuse scandal no longer to be so deferential to the religious establishment. From this development it follows that these courts will require experts to assess the validity of accusations of clergy sexual abuse as well as risk assessment.

Inevitably some small number of sexual abuse accusations proves to be false. Owing to the high personal and emotional costs of lodging accusations in most situations, these are a very tiny minority. This is fortunate considering the high price inevitably exacted of those falsely accused, at least two bishops among them. They can be difficult to tease out from among all the valid claims due to the strong pressures to find reasons or excuses to exonerate accused clergy. Here lies an especially important challenge for the forensic mental health professional. Private firms are actively providing competent and thorough professional assessments at the individual and diocesan levels. In a forward-looking move, the Conference of U.S. bishops has added the appropriate expertise to its staff. As the latter turn over, more will be required over time.

As an important aside there are many who quite naturally believe that the celibacy requirement is significantly to blame for the problem. This does not seem to be currently supported as a generality by the evidence. However, the possibility of indirect causality is not ruled out for a significant number of cases. Relevant examples include findings of strong feelings of loneliness in younger priests leaving their priesthood within five years and among substance-abusing clergy (Haggett 2005). It is also worth remembering that clergy sexual abuse is present across the globe and among virtually all the denominations (Benyei 1998). Correspondingly, celibacy is by no means essential to priesthood. It became a requirement only in the twelfth century in response to a severe need to upgrade the seriously deteriorating quality of discipline among clerics of the Latin Church at the time. It was never in place for the eastern or Orthodox churches, most of whose clergy are married today. Once ordained, they do not marry, and celibacy is a requirement for their bishops.

Interestingly, it appears more likely than not that the proportion of clergy sexual abusers is substantially below that of all adult men (Lakeland 2006). The absolute numbers are on the decline, since possibly as early as 1990. This is probably due to many factors, including results of better screening and training beginning to show their effects. Of course, the pool of potential offenders shrinks and ages over time. Nevertheless, at the present time we are apparently experiencing a shortage of experts for screening and rehabilitation including risk assessment.

Most observers agree that the crisis could be entering the beginning stages of resolution, as reflected by well-written narratives covering the scandal's historical course (McGreevy 2004). In the U.S., bishops are becoming less uncomfortable with formulating local and national rules and practices intended to alleviate those conditions that have worsened the problem as well as to encourage the forces for resolution (McGreevy 2004). According to widely-held public opinion, this apparent tendency towards accepting a fuller responsibility needs to be supported and encouraged. Especially important is the need to back up resolutions and other statements with effective action. Interested forensic mental health experts are especially suited by their experiences to provide in consultation their advice for promoting continued positive episcopal policies and procedures.

Forensic mental health experts who enter this realm may expect to encounter some engaging challenges. For example, administrators who refer clergy for assessment and potential treatment might tend, in their habitual and well-intended zeal to protect confidentiality, to provide inadequate histories and insufficient documents that fail to convey the seriousness of what has happened. This of course vitiates the professional expert's effectiveness. On the other hand, disclosures by clergy of confidential information concerning congregants' behavior may turn out even in secular court not to be permissible (Griffith and Young 2004). These situations are all variants of the "two hats" double loyalty or dual role relationships situation (Strasburger, Gutheil, and Brodsky 1997).

Such dilemmas demand utmost attention of the sort that forensic psychiatrists and psychologists are duly trained to recognize and apply. The distinction between appropriate and inappropriate disclosures tends to prove especially challenging and complex when more than one party involved have clerical status. Multiple role relationships give rise to issues, sometimes not so subtly. An example is the case of a therapist who is working out of devotion to her church, providing therapy to a clergy member who is a student in formation, and discovers that the superior in charge wants to have information that the therapist considers protected. A situation such as this would be likely to benefit from a forensic consultation.

MARRIAGE ANNULMENT CONSULTATION

Before he addressed the issue of sexual abuse by priests in advance of his first trip to the U.S. in 2015, Pope Francis surprised many with another announcement that was sure to be of keen interest to Americans, Catholic or not, regarding the Church's treatment of its divorced members. He famously proclaimed an end to the expectation that divorced Catholics who remarried without having an annulment of the first marriage were to abstain from receiving the Eucharist. Yet only a year earlier he had officiated in Rome at a marriage ceremony for twenty couples. These were not celebrities as one might expect. Rather, they were ordinary people known to have such ordinary faults as being divorced and cohabitating before marrying. He did this immediately before a Synod of Bishops was to meet in Rome for discussions on family matters (Povoledo 2014). The pope also announced that the annulment process itself would be expedited. This was to be accomplished by dropping the long-standing requirement of automatic review by an outside tribunal of decisions in favor of nullity. This may not prove to be a major change since confirmation by the appeal court appears lately to be virtually routine. According to the Vatican's annually released statistics, it was around 99% in the U.S. in 2012. In addition, tribunals are to accelerate the current pace of serious efforts to reduce further any financial obstacles that impair access to their proceedings.

Part of that cost arises from the frequent need of experts to apply psychiatric or psychological expertise to address whether a particular requested annulment is justified. Regarding experts, canon 1574 of the 1983 Code provides:

> The services of experts must be used whenever their examination and opinion, based on the laws of art or science, are required in order to establish some fact or to clarify the true nature of some thing by reason of a prescription of the law or a judge.

The expert works with three other parties: the judge, the advocate who argues for the annulment, and the defender of the matrimonial bond. True to their inheritance from ancient Roman law as described above, all four are engaging in a joint collaborative search for the truth, wherever it may lie (Young and Griffith 1985). In contrast to our familiar common law-based adversarial process the judge, the expert, and the lawyers for and against granting an annulment are collaborating in a joint search for a just outcome. The mental process involved can be quite varied, depending on the facts and documents of any given case. The hearings are *ex parte*, and the judge is responsible for a prompt written decision laying out fully the facts found and aspects of the law leading to the conclusion.

The expert's work involves primarily the study of relevant documents, along with discussion with the advocate whose work includes interviewing the moving party and, whenever possible, the other spouse and collateral witnesses who have worthwhile information and experience to contribute. Most often the issues of concern are the ability to understand (due discretion) and carry out (due competence) the duties of the married parties to each other and any children (Young and Griffith 1991). Often enough, as experts gain experience with tribunals they may find their way to be quite effective in working with engaged couples to enhance the quality of their preparation and decrease the risk of avoidable problems.

Aside from Pope Francis's recent promulgations, this area of involvement of the forensic mental health professions with law and religion has seen major change. In fact, in 2000 the Canon Law Society of America saw fit to produce a fresh text and commentary, with a new translation of the code itself from the Latin. The first edition had appeared in 1985. As of this writing, after fifteen more years, no third edition has appeared. If anything, the expert's value is as emphatically affirmed as ever. This is evident from simply browsing the annual proceedings of the conventions of the Canon Law Society of America.

Another major change is the drop in number of annulments applied for as well as the number granted. Peaking shortly after the 1983 code was promulgated, the number of U.S. annulments granted declined to levels not seen in nearly fifty years. Correspondingly, the divorce rate in the U.S. has now gone into a little appreciated and poorly explained decline (Miller 2014). There are multiple reasons being proposed for this change, which may indicate that none of them is quite satisfactory. Whatever its causes, the decline in divorce rate would seem to have some degree of significance for the striking drop-off in annulments, as reported annually, over nearly three decades. Despite the decline, the tribunals continue to require the collaboration of experts. An articulate and detailed case for this, along with many practical suggestions, appeared recently (Jorgensen 2004).

INTERVENTIONS RELIGIOUS OR SPIRITUAL

In this final section I describe and comment on two rewarding experiences or ministries, with the intention of encouraging the reader to imagine yet further possibilities.

Not long before this writing I was preparing to move on after twenty-one years' service as a maximum security-based attending psychiatrist when a colleague, a devout Hindu, made what seemed an unusual request, one with potential for quite broad application. What she suggested was that she and a few other colleagues wanted to continue our association by having me lead a regular monthly gathering where we could relax and share freely some of our deeper concerns. Called a spiritual interest group initially, it gradually evolved in the clear direction of spiritual support, and its informal name shifted accordingly. Over its eighteen-month lifetime I sometimes heard the expression "spiritually hungry."

To help prepare for this project, I consulted with knowledgeable and spiritually mature friends and colleagues. Some had helpful structuring suggestions and questions. Others provided some wise suggestions of titles by authors such as Thomas Merton and Henri Nouwen. I gathered a few well-selected volumes to provide some structure in case it was needed. It soon became clear that it was not, but the reading did offer some worthwhile content. Somewhat more helpful were scattered essays from several medical journals on such humane topics as humility versus arrogance, mercy and integrity.

A few colleagues took notice and shared their sense of faith as demonstrated by popular songs and the words and actions of prominent individuals manifesting it on the daily newscasts. We deliberately kept the usual group structure with no restrictions on selection of topics for discussion, liberty to speak or not, low expectations regarding attendance, and the like. When it was feasible I took brief notes, preparing them promptly afterwards outside the group. This made it easy to assess overall quality and keep track of loose ends worth picking up at a subsequent meeting. I also made liberal use of e-mailed reminders and topical suggestions for upcoming meetings.

We tended to open with a brief and optional moment of attention to how each one (wanting to say so) was doing and feeling. Although many job- or hospital-related complaints were aired during some meetings, we suffered very little from any griping. Rather we enjoyed considerable success at keeping our freely shared complaints elevated to a level of insightful analysis that often enough arrived at practical suggestions. At one meeting we shared an uplifting Hindu sutra. We also made use of biblical passages when they seemed likely to be helpful. We turned to such well-worn issues as why good people suffer so often and the desirable qualities we'd like to develop in ourselves.

The spirituality support group diminished as each of its members moved on from the hospital to take advantage of other job opportunities, by no means an unusual occurrence among professionals employed in the health-related public sector. Very different is another model possibility for involvement of forensic mental health clinicians with a religious interest in exploring and developing.

As of this writing, I have fifteen years of experience as part of a twenty-year-old enterprise that takes place in rural western Connecticut at an abbey of contemplative Benedictine sisters called formally The Abbey of Regina Laudis (Queen of Praise). Among this community's enterprises is the Contemplative Medical Center (CMC), a modest wooden structure that had gone through other uses in the distant past until being turned to its current major use as a base for conducting afternoon plus evening retreats for groups of eighteen medical students and residents invited from nearby medical schools. At present there are three retreats per year.

Oversight of the CMC is by one of the sisters, a pediatric gastroenterologist before entering the abbey. Joining her is a nun who earned her Ph.D. in mammalian reproductive physiology after entering the abbey. Her training is fully utilized by the abbey's meat and dairy herds, sheep, and various other farm animals. Another sister, trained as an agronomist, contributes to the management of the 350-acre abbey farmland as well as to the structure for each retreat day. A core group of a dozen outside professionals, including me, is responsible for staffing the retreats, currently three per year, including recruitment of the retreatants. The core itself has developed over time, evolving to include some who became interested after attending several retreats. It meets on a monthly basis to plan for the retreats, and more importantly to share support in ways not unlike my former hospital spirituality project.

Students and residents at the two nearby medical schools receive invitations to the retreats by e-mail. In addition to practical advice and a notation that members of any faith or none are all welcome, the invitation describes the afternoon of work on the healing of the land as a spiritual experience that can be transferred to the broader medical work of healing. As the work draws to its close the retreat group moves on to the abbey church to attend the evening prayer sung by the sisters in the ancient Latin version. Generally a member of the core group explains the prayer with advice on entering into it as a spiritual experience. A hearty vegetarian dinner at the CMC precedes the evening's discussion, opening with a passage read from the Rule of Saint Benedict, as is customary for each calendar day. Without fail the discussions prove a more than worthwhile experience, as evidenced by what participants say spontaneously and by the number who come back for more of our retreat days or go on to pilgrimage their way back to the abbey on their own.

CONCLUSION

The purpose of this chapter is to encourage forensic mental health workers, primarily psychiatrists and psychologists, to broaden their horizons to incorporate and strengthen their religious perspective, leading them to expand their professional involvements to include both familiar traditional issues and fresh undertakings, limited only by their collective or individual imagination. In order to enrich their grasp of the context in which their efforts might flourish, this account opened with an historical discussion enlarging on the theme of change as it applies to the standard forensic agenda and might inform future developments.

Already the agenda includes psychological screening of clergy applicants, consultation to formation programs including teaching at various levels, assessment of accusations made against clerics, and various applications of risk assessment; also treatment for sex abusers and for their victims. Bishops may see a need for consultations on policy, as well as help to resolve disputes and misunderstandings. As with the entire chapter, this list is offered as a catalyst for readers' creativities.

And whatever involvements we undertake, we should proceed with compassion (Norko 2007).

REFERENCES

Benyei, C.R. 1998. *Understanding Clergy Misconduct in Religious Systems*. New York: Haworth Press.

Dupre, L. 2008. *Religion and the Rise of Modern Culture*. Notre Dame, IN: University of Notre Dame Press.

Fitzmyer, J.A. 1981. *The Gospel According to Luke*. Garden City, NY: Doubleday.

Gautier, M.L., P.M. Perl, and S.J. Fichter. 2012. *Same Call, Different Men: The Evolution of the Priesthood since Vatican II*. Collegeville, MN: Liturgical Press, pp. 112–47.

Griffith, E.E.H. and J.L. Young. 2004. "Clergy Counselors and Confidentiality: A Case for Scrutiny." *Journal of the American Academy of Psychiatry and the Law* 32 (1): 43–50.

Haggett, L. 2005. *The Bingo Report, Mandatory Celibacy and Clergy Sexual Abuse*. Freeport, ME: Center for the Study of Religious Issues.

Jorgensen, G.T. 2004. "The Role of the Expert in Tribunal Proceedings." *Canon Law Society of America Proceedings* 66: 137–51.

Lakeland, P. 2006. "Understanding the Crisis in the Church." In *Church Ethics and Its Organizational Context*, edited by Jean M. Bartunek, Mary A. Hinsdale and James F. Keenan, pp. 3–16. New York: Sheed and Ward.

Lynch, J.E. 1985. "The Obligations and Rights of Clerics." In *The Code of Canon Law: A Text and Commentary*, edited by James A. Coriden, Thomas J. Green and Donald E. Heintschel, pp. 224–5. New York: Paulist Press.

McGreevy, J.T. 2004. "The Sex Abuse Crisis: The View From Recent History." In *Governance, Accountability, and the Future of the Catholic Church*, edited by Francis Oakley and Bruce Russett, pp. 136–42. New York: Continuum.

Miller, C.C. 2014. "Divorce Surge Is Over, but the Myth Lives on." *New York Times*. 2 December, p. A3.

Norko, M.A. 2007. "People of the Whirlwind." *Journal of the American Academy of Psychiatry and the Law* 35 (3): 373–80.

Povoledo, E. 2014. "In Weddings, Pope Looks Past Tradition." *New York Times*. 15 September, p. A4.

Strasburger, L.H., T.G. Gutheil and A. Brodsky. 1997. "On Wearing Two Hats: Role Conflict in Serving as Both Psychiatrist and Expert Witness." *American Journal of Psychiatry* 154 (4): 448–56.

Stuhlmueller, C. 1968. "The Gospel According to Luke." In *The Jerome Biblical Commentary*, edited by Raymond E. Brown, Joseph E. Fitzmyer, and Roland E. Murphy, pp. 115–64. Engelwood Cliffs, NJ: Prentice-Hall.

Young, J.L. and E.E.H. Griffith 1985. "Experts in Church Courts: A Role Not Sacred." *Bulletin of the American Academy of Psychiatry and the Law*, 13 (4): 359–68.

———. 1991. "Understanding Due Discretion of Judgment in Catholic Marriage Courts." *Bulletin of the American Academy of Psychiatry and the Law* 19 (2): 109–18.

———. 1995. "Regulating Pastoral Counseling Practice: The Problem of Sexual Misconduct." *Bulletin of the American Academy of Psychiatry and the Law* 23 (3): 421–32.

CHAPTER 13

Management of Forensic Hospitals

Charles C. Dike

INTRODUCTION

The current concept of a forensic psychiatric hospital in the U.S. began taking shape in the late 1960s and early 1970s. Before then, forensic psychiatric patients (forensic patients) were housed in large state hospitals, most of which were built in the late nineteenth century. Forensic patients were admitted into designated or specialized units in state hospitals and shared space with civil patients. The massive depopulation of state hospitals in favor of community mental health agencies and treatment led to dramatic shrinkage in state psychiatric beds. For example, in 1955 there were 558,239 public (state and county) psychiatric beds available for a U.S. population of 164.3 million, compared to 52,539 public (state and county) psychiatric beds for a U.S. population of 269.4 million in 2005 (Torrey et al. 2008)

This exodus of psychiatric patients from public psychiatric facilities was associated with both an increase in homelessness and in arrests and incarceration of individuals with mental illness. This gradually but predictably led to a need for psychiatric facilities specialized in managing a unique group of psychiatric patients involved with the legal system and/or with the Department of Correction (DOC).

The management of forensic patients presents significant challenges regarding safety as most patients earn their place on the units through their high risk of danger to self and or others. In the past, staff depended heavily on the use of restraints and seclusion (RS) to maintain safety, but with regulations from the late 1990s significantly restricting the use of restraints and seclusions, forensic facilities must find alternative ways to manage aggression except for the extreme situations where RS could be used, albeit briefly, to prevent immediate risk of physical aggression.

Over the years, forensic psychiatric facilities have struggled with finding the right balance between providing adequate safety and security in and outside the facility while at the same time providing treatment. The pendulum tends to swing in the direction of more security and restrictions following high-profile and risky events committed by patients of forensic facilities, and toward more treatment following evaluation of the facilities by regulatory agencies (Scales, Phillips, and Crysler 1989). The development of a collaborative model of security-treatment rather than pendulum swings of the past is the aspiration of managers of forensic facilities.

Forensic facilities house individuals with refractory illnesses that often increase their risk of violence. Their lack of response or inadequate response to treatment continues to place them at risk. As a result, some spend decades in the hospital. Following the Civil Rights of Institutionalized Persons Act (CRIPA) in 1980 (42 U.S.C. § 1997 (1980), the *Olmstead* decision (*Olmstead*) in 1999, and subsequent investigations by the United States Department of Justice (USDOJ), forensic facilities now face increasing pressure to discharge patients to the "most integrated setting" in the community. Existing in parallel with the *Olmstead* decision is the Recovery Movement and recovery-oriented practice that works against the time-worn notion that individuals must recover first before being eligible for the community (see Chapters 2 and 5).

The legal and social pressures from deinstitutionalization and *Olmstead* are in tension with the public's intolerance for risk. Forensic facilities must work collaboratively with other state agencies to develop facilities and resources in the community that can adequately manage the risks posed by their patients.

In this chapter, I will discuss recent legal and social movements that influence admission, treatment, and discharge of forensic patients, changes in the environment of care, issues related to risk assessment and management, and challenges with management of the violent patient in the era of the Recovery Movement and active patient advocacy groups.

FORENSIC POPULATIONS IN PSYCHIATRIC HOSPITALS

Patients in forensic psychiatric settings generally fall under one of four categories: restoration of competency to stand trial; evaluation/treatment of insanity acquittees (those found not guilty by reason of mental disease or defect—NGRI); correctional inmates transferred to the hospital for evaluation, acute care or placement at end of sentence; and civil patients (either voluntary or involuntary) admitted due to agitation and risk of assault that cannot be managed in less restrictive environments. Most of the competency restoration patients, and inmates transferred from DOC for evaluation or treatment, will return to DOC following their stay in the hospital.

Forensic patients who were inmates in prisons (some in super-max conditions) and jails shortly before their hospitalization suddenly become patients in a psychiatric hospital and immediately become subject to the protections of the Patients' Bill of Rights (42 USC § 9501—Mental Health Rights and Advocacy—Bill of Rights). Custodial practices, such as single cell status, solitary confinement, group therapy in individual cages, and so on, that kept them and others safe in prison, no longer apply. Characteristics of these forensic patients can mirror those of non-psychiatric inmates in prisons, including intimidation, violence, exploitation and manipulation of others, as well as high potential for elopement from the hospital (Coid and Ullrich 2011).

But, even civil patients can be equally as challenging. They include: sex offenders with no major mental illness admitted at the end of their sentence in prison; patients with severe (and dangerous) personality disorders; and patients who insert and or swallow various objects, in addition to being physically aggressive.

Forensic facilities worry about patients absconding from the hospitals. An escape from a forensic facility, especially a maximum security setting, generates much public anxiety and uproar as such patients are usually believed, sometimes rightly so, to be dangerous. Stories of patients who escaped, sometimes during transportation to medical appointments, and subsequently acted violently in the community, though rare, concretize the fears of the public and scar all forensic patients. A formal process for assessing and managing risk of transportation outside the facility would likely provide added protection for staff and the public during such events (Dike, Nicholson, and Young 2015)

The dual risks of escape from a forensic facility and increased risk of violence in or outside the facility engenders a tendency for forensic institutions to be rigid in application of rules, and custodial in their interaction with patients. But forensic facilities are hospitals not correctional institutions, and as such are subject to the same criteria established by regulatory agencies, and/or mandated by government policies or statutes, that govern treatment practices and management in psychiatric institutions. Clinicians providing such mandated treatment need to attend to the special circumstances created by these mandates (Zonana and Norko 1993).

ENVIRONMENT OF CARE ISSUES

Effective treatment cannot be delivered in an environment with inadequate security that causes people to feel unsafe. Historically, the environment of care in forensic facilities focused on what materials should or should not be allowed into the facility, ratio of staff to patients, number of patients housed on a particular unit to prevent overcrowding, number of single rooms vs. dorms, and so on. More recently, however, there has been an increasing emphasis on the notion of trauma-informed care and trauma-sensitive environments. This is not altogether surprising given the findings of high levels of trauma, often from childhood, among psychiatric patients. The lifetime exposure to trauma for psychiatric patients has been reported to be 90% (Mueser and Rosenberg 2001). The rates are understandably higher for forensic psychiatric patients exposed to DOC where violence among prisoners is often experienced. Even offenders with no history of violence prior to prison may be released as violent offenders as a result of their exposure to high levels of violence while incarcerated. These patients come into forensic hospitals with their experience of trauma and propensity for violence (Kristine 2011).

Exposure to trauma is not limited to patients, as approximately 70% of nurses experience violence against their person in the course of their career (Abderhalden et al. 2002), with 20% of psychiatric nurses reporting intrusive memories of patient assault (Robinson, Clements, and Land 2003).

The National Center for Trauma Informed Care (NCTIC) recommends that services for psychiatric patients be provided in trauma-informed environments. A change in paradigm from the question, "What's wrong with you?" to "What happened to you?" will hopefully increase empathetic responses and interaction between staff and patients (SAMHSA/NCTIC 2015). Trauma-informed environments of care are meant to be comfortable, welcoming, and safe. For example, a calm milieu engenders calmness in patients, while a loud and chaotic milieu leads to irritability and agitation in patients whose stress levels are already high and frustration tolerance low. Units with calming colors and decorations with scenery generally associated with relaxation support the desired milieu.

Staff supervision at all levels is crucial. In intense environments, as forensic facilities are wont to be, supervision presents an opportunity: for an individual staff to vent to supervisor; for senior clinicians to hear first-hand what an individual staff member could be uncomfortable talking about in public; to identify potential problems early and intervene as necessary; for supervisors to remind individual staff members of new initiatives of the hospital.

A culture of respect for all is particularly important in a forensic facility, as a perception of disrespect, real or imagined, by a significant number of forensic patients has been a trigger for violence. Initiatives that encourage patients and staff to disavow violence, respect each other, and communicate and socialize peacefully drive home the point and keep the idea fresh in the consciousness of all.

Forensic hospitals cannot but be vigilant about objects that could be fashioned into weapons, reading or visual materials that could encourage or provoke violence, or clothing material with offensive writing that could invite an aggressive response.

The issue of access to the internet and worldwide web is one that forensic hospitals will have to confront in the near future. If hospitals are supposed to teach skills for success in the community, in an increasingly sophisticated electronic media age, it could be argued that not providing opportunities for patients to be computer-literate and to learn how to do research using the internet is tantamount to handicapping the patients. In addition, the internet provides a unique opportunity for social and family connections like never before, through Facebook, Twitter, Instagram, and the like, in addition to providing access to treatment interventions such as basic CBT or relaxation techniques.

But access to the internet presents a daunting challenge, most serious of which include decreased ability to monitor communications between legally held patients and their outside co-conspirators, and communications with victims of their crime. In addition, patients may engage in cyber-bullying or other forms of harassment without the knowledge of staff. Even if facilities are able to block undesirable material such as pornography or materials with extreme violence and gore, computer-savvy patients may be able to bypass the filters and gain access to these restricted sites.

MANAGEMENT OF ADMISSIONS AND DISCHARGES

Admissions to forensic facilities are unpredictable as they occur mostly through legal or court mandates/orders and, therefore, are largely out of the control of facility administrators. Court-involved individuals are mostly sent directly from courts to the forensic facility, sometimes without warning. Facility administrators must therefore develop processes and procedures for managing this unpredictable challenge, as the number of admissions could have a bearing on resources such as nurses or other staff needed to manage either a large number of admissions or any special circumstances a newly admitted individual would present.

Open communication between DOC and the forensic facility facilitates hand-off communication regarding treatment and special needs of an expected patient coming directly from DOC or via the courts, or returning to the DOC after treatment. Unplanned admission of patients during off hours poses specific challenges regarding availability of clinical information about them. An existing close collaborative relationship with DOC can be very helpful in such situations. For DOC inmates being transferred directly to a forensic facility for evaluation or treatment, there is ample time for exchange of relevant information before the transfer, including face-to-face (or video) meeting with the inmate and treatment staff as needed.

On occasion, urgent admission to the forensic facility is sought for a civil patient causing significant and unmanageable violence in the emergency department or on a general hospital unit. Admission of civil patients to a maximum security setting could attract the attention of legal advocates and, therefore, requires careful thought, planning, and monitoring. Unfortunately, the mere fact of admission to a maximum security forensic facility can label patients as extremely dangerous and subsequently decreases the willingness of outside agencies to accept them. This double stigma of being both mentally ill and dangerous is a valid argument for discouraging admission of civil patients to maximum security forensic hospitals.

In general, discharging forensic patients to the community presents unique challenges. Risk assessment and management is an integral element of work in a forensic hospital, especially as it relates directly to movement of patients outside the hospital. In *Jones v. United States* (1983), the U.S. Supreme Court ruled that an insanity acquittee could be committed to a forensic hospital indefinitely until he or she is no longer mentally ill and dangerous. Risk assessment for dangerousness therefore is at the crux of decision-making. (See Chapter 16 for a more complete discussion of risk assessment.)

However, *Olmstead* mandates discharge of persons with mental disabilities into community settings if: the state's treatment professionals have determined that community placement is appropriate; the transfer from institutional care to less restrictive setting is not opposed by the affected individual; and the placement can be reasonably accommodated, taking into account the resources available to the state and the needs of others with mental disabilities. The USDOJ has made it a priority to enforce *Olmstead* and has investigated and sued state hospitals out of compliance with the law, including forensic facilities (Bloom 2012).

Forensic facilities leadership must balance pressures to discharge patients with the dangers of potential violence in the community or in less restrictive settings. Consultation by forensic psychiatrists experienced in risk assessment and management is sometimes necessary for decisions about movement of patients within and outside the hospital grounds.

That said, patients admitted to maximum security settings for a significant amount of time should probably be stepped down to a less secure psychiatric unit/hospital before being discharged to the community. It would be important for them to demonstrate safety and self-management in a less structured and secure hospital environment before being gradually re-introduced into the community in a stepwise fashion with increasing degrees of freedom. If such a step-down process from the maximum security setting is not feasible, forensic hospitals are still tasked with teaching patients basic life skills such as shopping, banking, navigating bus routes, and so on, which have been lost due to prolonged institutionalization. Virtual reality technology and avatars that create life-like situations mimicking the scenarios described earlier are currently being researched. If successful, they will provide useful options not only for discharge planning, but also for management of hallucinations (Leff et al. 2014).

FORENSIC STAFF

Psychiatrist

The attending psychiatrist is the clinical leader of the treatment team in a forensic facility. It is generally not required that the attending or unit psychiatrist be a fellowship-trained forensic psychiatrist. In the absence of a forensic psychiatrist, however, access to one for consultation, education and supervision, and reviewing of forensic reports, might provide sufficient forensic oversight of staff.

In terms of medical care for patients, access to physicians or general practitioners, medical specialists, dentists, and other ancillary service providers is safer within the walls of the hospital as it avoids transportation of these patients to outside facilities with its attendant risks (Dike, Nicholson, and Young 2015).

Nursing Staff

The largest workforce in a forensic facility is the nursing staff. Working in a forensic facility is stressful, draining and demanding all at once. As the number of nurses willing to work in such stressful environments is lower than in non-forensic settings, overtime use is often high. Float staff from non-forensic units are either unwilling or unable to assist due to discomfort of feeling incompetent to work with forensic patient population, or hospital policies that bar them from working in forensic settings. To address this problem, Cyr and Paradis piloted the concept of developing forensic float nurses, a pool of nurses trained in working on forensic units, to assist with managing staff shortages or excessive overtime. The pilot study showed a dramatic decrease in overtime by 50% (Cyr and Paradis 2012).

Psychologists

Patients in forensic facilities often have serious mental illnesses largely refractory to psychotropic medication treatment, and complicated by cognitive deficits from developmental disorders, traumatic brain injuries, side effects of psychotropic medications, enduring effects of long-term abuse of illicit substances or alcohol, or a combination of these. Their behavioral excesses are characterized by disorganization, a tendency to disrupt the smooth functioning of the unit, or aggression.

An initial psychological evaluation soon after admission will inform the treatment team of the patient's basic psychological profile and triggers for violence. This would influence the development of behavioral guidelines and plans for working optimally with the patient. It could reasonably be argued that all challenging patients in a forensic facility need formal psychological or neuropsychological testing to better assist in formulating their care (see Chapter 15).

On occasion, more comprehensive behavioral techniques, for example positive behavioral support plans, or specialized psychological evaluations such as sex offender evaluations, would be warranted. Behavioral psychologists forming a behavioral intervention team can provide critical value as consultants to all units for developing and monitoring behavioral plans and interventions, as well as for supervising staff (see Chapter 15). In addition, a behaviorally based unit with a social learning program, a token economy system, reinforcement schedules, and other core behavioral interventions has shown promise at managing the most challenging of behaviors (Beck et al. 1991).

Psychoanalytic, psychodynamic, or other forms of psychotherapy can be useful in forensic hospitals. As individuals who committed heinous crimes regain their sense of reality orientation through treatment, dealing with the consequences of their actions could be overwhelming. Most become estranged from their family as a result of their crime. Given the dearth of financial and other resources in state facilities, it could be cost-effective for a standing psychotherapy service (or person) to provide psychotherapy across the facility, and to assign and supervise all referrals for psychotherapy to interested staff and trainees.

Social Workers

In addition to the traditional functions of social workers in discharge planning, and sometimes psychotherapy, they can be trained to provide specific forensic psychiatric evaluations. For example, at Connecticut Valley Hospital (CVH), social workers do restoration to competency evaluations, write court reports and testify in court, under supervision of a forensic psychiatrist.

Occupational and Rehabilitation Therapists

The importance of these professionals in a forensic facility cannot be overemphasized. Teaching forensic patients relaxation techniques, and other interventions to manage stress, anxiety, and agitation, will ultimately lead to a decrease in aggressive responses to these emotions, and an overall decrease in violence in the facility. The interventions include sensory modulation techniques, use of comfort rooms, alternative interventions for relaxation (tai chi, yoga, etc.), weighted blankets, exercise, art, recreation, music, and pet therapies, structured vocational engagements, and so on.

THE SERIOUSLY VIOLENT PATIENT

Sometimes forensic facilities admit patients whose degree of violence is extreme even amongst a population of violent patients. As a general rule, forensic staff are better able to cope with individuals whose violence is clearly the result of psychosis, and to some extent developmental disorders; many staff would put themselves at significant risk to manage them. On the other hand, patients whose violence is perceived as due to severe personality disorder evoke less patience from staff and trigger counter-transferential responses that could escalate the situation.

It is perhaps unfair to ask staff to manage individuals with severe personality disorder, some of whom have spent a significant amount of time in solitary confinement due to their unmanageable violence while in prisons. As these patients have the potential to disrupt the smooth and safe functioning of the entire facility beyond the unit of their current location, staff must engage creative approaches involving a variety of disciplines to keep all safe.

For some, the recommended psychopharmacologic algorithms (Glancy and Knott 2013; Stahl et al. 2014) for managing aggressive behavior, in addition to consultations by psychopharmacologists, have only provided partial relief. These are the individuals for whom behavioral psychologists develop positive behavior support plans and other behavioral interventions, occupational therapists administer sensory modulation interventions, and rehabilitation therapists provide an array of structured activities to occupy the patient and decrease arousal and agitation.

In addition to these interventions, the question of involvement of hospital security staff in managing the violent patient comes up from time to time.

For example, the Joint Commission recently posted on its leadership blog, "Hospital Security — Different Approaches to Mitigate Violence," which focused on the question of arming hospital security officers. According to the author:

> The Joint Commission standards do not specify whether security personnel should or should not be armed. Each hospital must examine its unique environment and develop appropriate policies and approaches to safeguard patients, staff and visitors ... Violent acts will never go away completely, but it's worth looking at all possible options to try and decrease them (Crafton 2015).

At the Whiting Maximum Security Service of CVH, agency police officers have been asked, on some occasions, to institute frequent "security" rounds on the unit. In extreme situations, they have been posted temporarily on all shifts of a unit housing a markedly dangerous patient. Of note, the presence of security staff on psychiatric units could either have a cooling effect on a particular patient's behavior or an escalating effect, depending on the patient's previous experience or the content of the patient's psychotic symptoms. The ability of security staff to use their special training in situations considered too extreme for clinical staff to manage can be helpful in some situations but also presents new challenges. Understanding which staff are in charge (clinical or security) in an evolving dangerous situation is one such challenge.

RESTRAINTS AND SECLUSION

Following the Hartford Courant reports of deaths that "occurred during or shortly after psychiatric or developmentally developed individuals were restrained or secluded" (Weiss 1998), the National Association of State Mental Health Program Directors (NASMHPD) released Position Statements

> to prevent, reduce, and ultimately eliminate the use of seclusion and restraint and to ensure that, when such interventions are necessary, they are administered in as safe and humane a manner as possible by appropriately trained personnel (Hester 2001, iv).

In addition, RS were never to be used for the purposes of discipline, coercion, or staff convenience, or as a replacement for adequate levels of staff or active treatment. RS are last resort measures that can only be used when there is an imminent or immediate risk of danger to self or others, and no other safe and effective intervention is possible.

Regulatory agencies such as The Joint Commission, Centers for Medicare and Medicaid Services (CMS), U.S. DOJ, etc., quickly adapted the NASMHPD Position Statement and generated standard measures for ongoing monitoring of hospitals. Forensic institutions, despite having the most dangerous and challenging patients, were not exempt from these requirements. Before then, it was common to see forensic patients in all forms of restraints, including ambulatory (2- or 4-point) and bed restraints, and with treatment plans that included periods of being in restraints. The most disturbed and violent patients were in restraints, usually ambulatory restraints, sometimes for years at a time. Staff were not trained in alternative interventions to de-escalate a patient's dangerous behavior, or accustomed to them. Further, the efficacy of these alternative interventions was not demonstrated to staff in a satisfactory manner.

The change from a culture that depended on RS for safety to one that is striving to eliminate their use completely even in forensic settings was and remains a herculean task. Education of staff on the benefits of decreased RS, such as less staff and patient injuries, safe hospital environment, and better therapeutic alliances with patients, may do little to decrease staff anxiety. Even now that the culture change has taken root, it takes only the admission of the next violent and frightening patient for the pressure to use RS to begin. Although the era of liberal use of RS is gone, real issues continue, as evidenced by the struggles to deal with people whose violence does not seem to respond to milieu, direction, behavioral interventions, medication, and so on. The presence of these "outliers" makes it difficult to completely eliminate RS (Whitehead and Liljeros 2011). Ongoing vigilance and monitoring are required if the goal of reducing the use of RS as much as possible is to be achieved.

RECOVERY MOVEMENT

The 1999 U.S. Surgeon General's Report on Mental Illness challenged all mental health services to become more consumer-oriented and to promote recovery. Before then, the term "people in recovery" had been applied mostly to those with alcohol and drug addictions. The 2003 U.S. Presidential New Freedom Commission consolidated the notion of recovery, stating in the report entitled *Achieving the Promise: Transforming Mental Health Care in America* that "… recovery from mental illness is now a real possibility. The promise of a New Freedom Initiative—a life in the community for everyone—can be realized." Recovery was defined as "the process in which people are able to live, work, learn and participate fully in their communities … the ability to live a fulfilling and productive life despite a disability" (President's New Freedom Commission on Mental Health 2003, Executive Summary, 7).

Recovery-oriented clinical practice includes person-centered care, which was highlighted by the 2001 Institute of Medicine Report titled *Crossing the Quality Chasm: A New Health System for the 21st Century*. The report affirms the patient as "the source of control" in treatment planning and interventions.

Patients are encouraged and empowered to make their own decisions with the recognition that they will make mistakes and fail sometimes as they embark on the journey to full self-determination, concepts that have been described as "right to fail" and "dignity of risk" (Deegan 1996). To support patients in the journey, it is recommended that treatment teams engage individuals with lived experience as peer supports because patients are more likely to identify with them (see Chapter 2). For forensic patients, peers include those with a history of incarceration in prison, substance or alcohol use problems, and physical aggression. Some forensic facilities do not allow visits by felons. However, these are the exact peers whom forensic patients need, especially if they have now become engaged citizens.

Recovery-oriented care has some significant challenges in forensic hospitals. For individuals under legal mandates to the hospital, an external judicial or administrative body often has control over their movement and sometimes influences treatment decisions as well. Also, a patient's decision to stop taking psychotropic medication could be difficult to justify if their history shows that serious criminal behavior results when they are actively psychotic. Therefore the freedom of choice to not take prescribed psychotropic medication would not be in the patient's or society's interest.

Despite the challenges described above, however, elements of the Recovery Movement that enhance patients' strengths, instill hope and respect patients' wishes and aspirations can be beneficial to forensic facilities. So also is the careful use of peers. The ramifications of the Recovery Movement in forensic settings are evolving and sure to influence care in the years to come.

INTERACTION WITH PATIENT ADVOCATES AND ATTORNEYS

Forensic clinicians often find themselves practicing in the middle of multiple adversarial agents. Patients' grievances are often channeled through their legal advocates, some of whom vigorously cross-examine staff members publicly during treatment team meetings. In the era of increasing advocacy for patients, facility administrators are tasked with responding to the concerns of patients' advocates in a timely fashion and with seriousness of purpose. Their concerns, complaints, and conflicts are best addressed in the context of advocates-management collaborations fostered through regular meetings between the facility clinical administrators and patients' advocates, legal and otherwise.

CONCLUSION

The evolution of inpatient psychiatric treatment that began in the 1960s, largely driven by mental health policies enacted by government, and consolidated in later years by patient advocacy movements, landmark legal decisions such as *Olmstead*, and focused investigation by various regulatory agencies, has shaped forensic hospitals of today. The challenge of increasing patient autonomy and person-centered care in a system that must also pay serious attention to safety and security has never been greater.

As the world becomes more technologically advanced, forensic hospitals will come under increasing pressure to relax restrictions on social media and other technological devices for patients, likely complicating risk management and the balance between treatment and safety even more. Forensic hospitals should anticipate these changes in the context of a more vocal patient advocacy and rights movement, and find creative ways to adapt without compromising safety.

REFERENCES

Abderhalden, C., I. Needham, T.K. Friedli, J. Poelmans, and T. Dassen. 2002. "Perception of Aggression Among Psychiatric Nurses in Switzerland." *Acta Psychiatrica Scandinavica* 106: 110–17.

Beck, N.C., A.A. Menditto, L. Baldwin, E. Angelone, and M. Maddox. 1991. "Reduced Frequency of Aggressive Behavior in Forensic Patients in a Social-Learning Program." *Hospital and Community Psychiatry* 42: 750–2.

Bloom, J.D. 2012. "CRIPA, *Olmstead*, and the Transformation of the Oregon Psychiatric Security Review Board." *Journal of American Academy of Psychiatry and the Law* 40: 383–9.

Coid, J. and S. Ullrich. 2011. "Prisoners with Psychosis in England and Wales: Diversion to Psychiatric Inpatient Services." *International Journal of Law and Psychiatry* 34: 99–108.

Crafton, M. February 2015. "Hospital Security—Different Approaches to Mitigate Violence." *Joint Commission Leadership Blog.* Accessed November 23, 2015. http://www.jointcommission.org/leadership_blog/hospital_security_different_approaches_to_mitigate_violence/.

CRIPA. 1980. 42 U.S.C. § 1997.

Cyr, J.J. and J. Paradis. 2012. "The Forensic Float Nurse: A New Concept in the Effective

Management of Service Delivery in a Forensic Program." *Journal of Forensic Nursing* 8: 188–94.

Deegan, P. 1996. "Recovery and the Conspiracy of Hope." Presented at "There's a Person Here," the Sixth Annual Mental Health Services Conference of Australia and New Zealand, Brisbane, Australia, 1996. Accessed November 24, 2015. https://www.patdeegan.com/pat-deegan/lectures/conspiracy-of-hope.

Dike, C.C., E. Nicholson, and J. Young. 2015. "Transporting Forensic Patients." *Journal of American Academy of Psychiatry the Law* 43: 4 (in print).

Glancy, G.D. and T.F. Knott. 2013. "Part III: Psychopharmacology of Long-Term Aggression—Toward an Evidence-Based Algorithm." *CPA Bulletin de l'APC* February 13–18.

Hester, T.W. March 2001. "Reducing the Use of Seclusion and Restraint Part II: Findings, Principles, and Recommendations for Special Needs Populations." *NASMHPD*. Accessed on November 28, 2015. www.nasmhpd.org//sites/default/files/Seclusion_Restraint_2.pdf.

Institute of Medicine Report. 2001. "Crossing the Quality Chasm: A New Health System for the 21st Century." Washington, DC. Accessed November 28, 2015. https://iom.nationalacademies.org/~/media/files/report%20files/2001/crossing-the-Quality-Chasm/Quality%20Chasm%202001%20%20report%20brief.pdf.

Jones v. United States. 1983. 463 U.S. 354.

Kristine, L.M. 2011. "Gangs and Violence in Prisons." In *Corrections*, edited by William J. Chambliss. SAGE Publications Inc. Accessed November 22, 2015. https://edge.sagepub.com/system/files/Ch12RennisonGangsandViolenceinPrisons.pdf.

Leff, J., G. Williams, M. Huckvale, M. Arbuthnot, and A.P. Leff. 2014. "Avatar Therapy for Persecutory Auditory Hallucinations: What Is It and How Does It Work?" *Psychosis* 6: 166–76.

Mueser, K.T. and S.D. Rosenberg. 2001. "Treatment of PTSD in Persons With Severe Mental Illness." In *Treating Psychological Trauma and PTSD*, edited by J.P. Wilson, M.J. Friedman, and J.D. Lindy, pp. 354–82. New York: The Guilford Press.

National Center for Trauma-Informed Care and Alternatives to Seclusion and Restraint. 2015. "Trauma Informed Care and Alternatives to Seclusion and Restraint." *SAMHSA*. Accessed November 23, 2015. http://www.samhsa.gov/nctic.

Olmstead v. L.C. 1999. 527 U.S. 581.

President's New Freedom Commission on Mental Health. 2003. "Achieving the Promise: Transforming Mental Health Care in America." Executive Summary. Rockville, MD. Accessed November 28, 2015. Govinfo.library.unt.edu/mentalhealthcommission/reports/report.htm.

Robinson, R.J., K. Clements, and C. Land. 2003. "Workplace Stress Among Psychiatric Nurses: Prevalence, Distribution, Correlates, and Predictors." *Journal of Psychosocial Nursing and Mental Health Services* 41: 32–41.

Scales, C.J., R.T.M. Phillips, and D. Crysler. 1989. "Security Aspects of Clinical Care." *American Journal of Forensic Psychology* 7: 49–57.

Stahl, S.M., D.A. Morrissette, M. Cummings, A. Azizian, S. Bader, C. Broderick, L. Dardashti, D. Delgado, J. Meyer, J. O'Day, G. Proctor, B. Rose, M. Schur, E. Schwartz,

S. Velasquez, and K. Warburton. 2014. "California State Hospital Violence Assessment and Treatment (CAL-VAT) Guidelines." *CNS Spectrums* 19: 449–65.

Torrey, E.F., K. Entsminger, J. Geller, J. Stanley, and D.J. Jaffe. 2008. "The Shortage of Public Hospital Beds for Mentally Ill Persons." *A Report of the Treatment Advocacy Center.* Virginia. Accessed November 28, 2015. www.treatmentadvocacycenter.org/storage/documents/the_shortage_of_publichospital_beds.pdf.

U.S. Department of Health and Human Services, U.S. Public Health Service. 1999. "Mental Health: A Report of the Surgeon General." Rockville, MD: *USDHHS, SAMHSA, CMS, NIH, NIMH.* Accessed November 28, 2015. Profiles.nim.nih.gov/ps/access/NNBBHT.pdf.

42 USC § 9501—Mental Health Rights and Advocacy—Bill of Rights 2010. Accessed November 22, 2015. http://www.gpo.gov/fdsys/pkg/USCODE-2010-title42/html/USCODE-2010-title42-chap102-subchapIV-sec9501.htm.

Weiss, E.M. 1998. "Deadly Restraint: a Hartford Courant Investigative Report (Five-Part Series)." *Hartford Courant*, October 11–15.

Whitehead, P.D. and F. Liljeros. 2011. "Heavy-Tailed Distribution of Seclusion and Restraint Episodes in a State Hospital." *Journal of American Academy of Psychiatry and the Law* 39: 93–9.

Zonana, H.V. and M.A. Norko. 1993. "Mandated Treatment." In *Clinical Challenges in Psychiatry*, edited by W.R. Sledge and A. Tasman, pp. 249–91. Washington, DC: American Psychiatric Press Inc.

SECTION 4

Forensic Practice in the Treatment and Care of Patients

CHAPTER 14

Forensic Psychotherapy: Psychodynamic Therapy with Offenders

Daniel Papapietro and Gwen Adshead

INTRODUCTION

Forensic Psychotherapy (Cordess and Cox 1995) was a joint venture between forensic psychiatry and the psychological therapies. It described the process of engaging a patient's curiosity about his life and his crime in an effort to identify and understand what conscious and unconscious emotional conflicts, issues, or impulses compelled him to do what he did. The aim of therapy was to contextualize both crime and mental illness within the narrative of a life. Twenty years later, psychodynamic psychotherapy continues to strive for an in-depth understanding of the forensic patient from earliest infancy forward. Through slow, deep, and thoughtful exploration it seeks to understand his issues of attachment, progress or impairment through normally expected developmental stages, and ultimately the nature of his adult sexual and emotional relationships to help understand why he offended, and whether he might one day in the future, under certain conditions, ever again at risk of reoffending.

A thorough understanding of the psychological factors that contributed to offending is an important outcome of treatment and can play an important role in how the individual gets psychologically better. Getting better consists of the patient being able to integrate the reality of his mental illness and the crime into his sense of self, allowing him to begin the process of understanding and accepting the painful reality of having a serious mental illness. It is especially critical for the patient to have a full and realistic understanding of having committed a serious crime if he is to acknowledge and accept the need for treatment. This acceptance is generally referred to as insight. The therapist's ability to understand the myriad factors leading to the crime can contribute to a thorough assessment of potential risk when the patient is considered for greater freedom and eventual transition out of the forensic hospital. How the patient understands their crime and mental illness, and how the treaters understand it, and the degree to which these conform to each other allows the professionals to explain to the courts and community what risk (if any) the patients poses; if that risk has reduced; and how (with sufficient treatment and supervision) they may one day be released from the hospital.

It is sometimes (but erroneously) suggested that psychodynamic psychotherapy is not appropriate for forensic patients; asserting either that people with psychotic disorders cannot benefit from psychodynamic psychotherapy, or because cognitively based therapies (CBT) are the only forms of therapy that have been shown to be effective for this or that disorder. The first argument is a distortion of old beliefs from the early days of psychoanalysis, when the emotional intimacy and intensity of daily individual sessions was clearly too much for people with psychosis (who did not have the benefit of medication). The second view, however, is a distortion arising out of the effects of twentieth-century health care economics.

Psychodynamic therapies have been increasingly excluded from mental health service provision because they are thought to be expensively lengthy. Health care administrators prefer short-term therapy packages, especially treatments that are manualized so that anyone can provide the treatment. Although cognitive-behavioral treatments are undoubtedly effective for many psychiatric disorders, there is little (or no) evidence that short-term CBTs are effective in people with severe long-term and co-morbid disorders (who make up the majority of forensic patients). There is, however, significant empirical data that indicates that psychodynamic therapy may be especially useful for people with severe and persistent mental illness, just like those that are admitted to forensic services (Hall et al. 1999; Leichsenring and Klein 2014; Bateman and Fonagy 2013; Leichsenring and Rabung 2011; Gibbs 2007). However, the old prejudices tend to persist because so many forensic professionals lack exposure to or training in psychodynamic theory and remain unaware of the empirical evidence base for its effectiveness.

In this chapter, we hope to provide a corrective view. We will give an overview of the psychodynamic theoretical framework as a basis for understanding the genesis of violent offending and how psychotherapy can help violent offenders recover their mental health and reduce their risk. We will discuss both individual and group approaches to therapy, and comment on ethical issues in forensic psychotherapy. We conclude by arguing that psychodynamic thinking is especially helpful to understand the *meaning* of violence for a perpetrator, which aids them in their recovery, and helps professionals to assess and manage their risk (Yakeley and Adshead 2013).

PSYCHODYNAMIC THEORIES OF OFFENDING

There are a few key concepts in psychodynamic theories that are relevant to understanding how violence occurs. The first concept is that unresolved distress from past relationships can be re-enacted in present relationships, especially those relationships that evoke memories of loss, trauma, dependence, vulnerability, and the need for care (Karon 2003). These unresolved early-life relationships, mixed with psychotic or manic distortion and projection, can contribute to lethal acting out. Another key concept is that, psychologically, people are not what they seem and that overt behaviors and language may function as defenses to cover up deeper meaning and significance of the crime. This is particularly true of symptoms of mental illness, which reflect conscious cognitive distortions, but also reflect an attempt to deal with inner psychological pain and loss of a sense of social reality. A third key concept is that of psychological defenses (sometimes referred to as coping mechanisms) necessary to maintain *psychological homeostasis* (i.e. that people develop internal psychological systems to regulate their distress). These "defenses" help people tolerate emotional distress related to fear and anxiety, and also to contain and control unconscious aggressive impulses.

Adults who are reliant on primitive defenses (those psychological processes necessary for infants, toddlers, and children but which have not evolved into more appropriate adult defenses of humor, displacements, or sublimation) are at risk for greater problems. Primitive defenses in adulthood detract conscious attention away from reality (including unconscious conflicts and impulses) and over time, under stress of mental illness, can fail, leaving the individual with no other appropriate or adequate coping or defense mechanism. As a result, the individual will "act out" emotional conflict and stress in order to maintain psychological homeostasis. These episodes of acting out simultaneous with loss of control of thinking and emotional dyscontrol due to severe mental illness can often have tragic consequences. For example, denial is a common defense against distress that may be useful in the short term; however, if the individual has no better coping mechanisms, this primitive defense will in the long term usually cause more problems (Levit 1993, 5; Finzi-Dottan and Karu 2006), especially when the defense (against unconscious, often primitive aggression) fails, leaving the individual with no better coping behavior available than acting out the aggression.

From a psychodynamic perspective, violence is not meaningless but has personal significance and salience for the offender (Yakeley and Adshead 2013). Violence may represent (a) a dysfunctional communication to a particular person or persons; (b) the repetition of an unresolved and usually traumatic relationship pattern; and/or (c) the defensive displacement of intolerable feelings of distress and fear onto someone else. What the violence perpetrator consciously feels or knows about their violence may be hard to assess if they are acutely mentally ill or in a state of denial and distress. The *unconscious* significance and meaning of the violence (in terms of past trauma or relived memory) will naturally be hard to assess, but is necessary for the individual (as much as he is capable) to understand that a driving force in the crime was in no small part his unconscious, unresolved issues. This helps to eliminate any chance the forensic patient can maintain a defense based on magical thinking that "the voices made me do it," and can further protect against future risk of offending.

TRAUMA AND OFFENDING

Psychodynamic psychotherapy explores the impact of trauma and loss on the development of mental functioning and interpersonal relating. This is important in forensic settings because so many forensic patients have substantial histories of emotional and physical traumas due to chaotic and dysfunctional families. Studies of prisoners have found that at least 30% have been raised in institutional care, usually because of abusive or neglectful parenting; and recent study of childhood adversity and violence perpetration in young offenders found a linear relationship between the numbers of violent offending and the extent of childhood adversity (Baglivio et al. 2014). Other studies have found a strong relationship between childhood trauma and violence; especially the experience of physical abuse. In one study of mentally disordered offenders in a high secure psychiatric hospital, 80% had experienced childhood abuse and/or neglect (Coid 1992), a figure that is at least four times higher than in the general population.

There is ample evidence that early relational trauma affects the developing sense of self and impairs the capacity for self-soothing that enables individuals to tolerate aloneness, fear, and frustration without becoming overwhelmed by distress (Schore 2001). Maltreatment and neglect influence the development of neural systems in the frontal cortex that regulate negative affects arising in the limbic system, principally anger and fear (Harvard Center on the Developing Child 2012). Early childhood maltreatment increases the risk of the development of a range of psychiatric disorders, including personality disorders as well as psychotic illnesses, and is also associated with increased risk of substance misuse and childhood conduct disorders, both of which are known risk factors for later adult violence.

Longitudinal research based on attachment theory has provided empirical evidence for psychodynamic hypotheses about the long-term sequelae of disrupted attachments in childhood. Insecurity of attachment is recognized as a risk factor for violence (Ogilvie et al. 2014) and is associated with childhood maltreatment and neglect. Attachment security promotes the development of the capacity to mentalize, which is the process whereby we learn to "read" other people's intentions accurately, and "see" other people as having minds like our own (Frith 2007). Failure to mentalize properly leads to a variety of dysfunctional behaviors (such as self-harm) and may be associated with acts of serious violence (Fonagy and Gwen 2012; Adshead et al. 2013).

Exposure to emotional, physical, or sexual traumas during childhood leads to a high level of cognitive and emotional deficits in all subsequent developmental stages which in turn affects people's impact to make and maintain healthy relationships, regulate their own distress, and manage physical sensations in their bodies. Traumatized people who cannot mentalize tend to manage stress through their bodies: through self-harm, eating disorders, or somatization disorder. Their physical complaints in adulthood often reflect their childhood developmental stage, so that abuse in early life to age five(+/–) (when basic bodily functions such as feeding/nurturing are vital) may manifest in various stomach and GI problems. Trauma in late childhood and teenage years may manifest in adulthood as vague head/thinking-related problems (dissociative, dizzy, migraines). Because puberty is a time of gender-role consolidation and identification, trauma at this time affects the development of healthy gender identity, erotic object choice, and the capacity for sexual intimacy.

FORENSIC PSYCHOTHERAPY: ASSESSMENT

Clearly the decision to offer a patient psychodynamic psychotherapy will be based on an assessment of their psychopathology, its relation to their offence, and their capacities for thinking and tolerating stress. Many patients may benefit from psycho-educational sessions about all types of therapy so they may learn what psychological change is about; and there are a number of interventions for emotional regulation and distress tolerance that may be useful for patients to complete before they start in psychodynamic work.

It is essential to consult the medical records before starting psychodynamic therapy, first, because many patients find talking about their mental states and experience difficult; second, because forensic patients have often been interviewed repeatedly and so find interviews stressful; and, third, because the records may indicate key risk indicators prior to the index offence, which may be relevant to current potential risk of aggression in hospital, and may forewarn against certain psychotherapy styles (for example: the overly casual, friendly approach may strike fear into the heart of one whose childhood trauma was perpetrated by a relative, neighbor etc., who may have ingratiated themselves into the patient's life; or the too-psychoanalytic approach of silence; or the use of what Volkan (1987) referred to as "noises of encouragement" for free association, which might agitate the paranoid patient who interprets the unfamiliar as dangerous. The paranoid patient needs to feel they understand what the therapist is thinking (or not thinking); they also need a degree of openness from the psychotherapist, a willingness to answer reasonable questions and a more supportive style, which does not turn every question back to the patient). Often the records show that the patient showed atypical and violent behavior early on in their life, well before the identified mental illness or the criminal history began, which reflects the extent of the patient's basic discomfort with the social reality of other people's minds. It is essential to understand as much as possible about the index offence: what occurred, how it occurred and the nature of the relationship with the victim, all of which may be relevant to the therapist's safety.

It is always helpful to review what therapy has already been tried, and if it was successful or not. It is helpful to get a sense of the patient's defense style: forensic patients typically use a range of immature defenses (Huband et al. 2014), and it may help to know that a patient uses projection or denial, although this will reveal itself through the course of psychotherapy. Any history of drop-out or therapy-interfering behaviors should be noted. A history of sexual abuse by professionals should raise alarm bells, as should direct attacks on professionals, including those not involved in therapy. Both idealizing and denigrating statements about previous therapists (or even psychotherapy or mental health professionals in general) should be treated with caution.

It may be helpful to offer an extended assessment before psychotherapy is offered. This can consist of four to six sessions so that the patient has an experience of sitting in the room with the therapist. It may also be helpful to consider offering small-group work before individual therapy, especially for those who have experienced extended abuse from a caregiver or parent.

PSYCHODYNAMIC THERAPY WITH FORENSIC PATIENTS: GETTING STARTED

It may be helpful to recap on some general aspects of psychodynamic therapy for patients and therapists. Psychodynamic therapy (either individual or group) entails making a relationship with a therapist and a willingness to explore one's psychological experiences, both past and present. Most people who engage in therapy want to understand themselves better, and successful therapy is associated with improved sense of agency and more coherent autobiographical competence (Adler, Skalina, and McAdams 2008; Holmes 1993). The therapeutic alliance is most important for effective outcomes, and success is most likely if the therapist and the patient can establish a rapport and a joint vision of what the therapeutic process is aiming at.

The therapist's role in psychodynamic psychotherapy includes making a secure space for reflection, discussion and exploration of past experience; helping patients develop their mentalizing skills; acting as an "accessory mind" that helps patients think rather than act; and judicious use of their own personality and personal experience. In terms of technique, therapists tend to let patients set the conversational agenda, and engage reflectively and supportively rather than educationally or in an advisory way.

Depending on the psychological structure of the forensic patient, the role of the psychotherapist may be as a "vitalizing object." LaMothe (2001) describes it this way:

> These objects, which represent interactional processes [between patient and psychotherapist], provide [patients] with subjective and intersubjective experiences of being alive and real, [So that] … therapy, at its best, becomes a collaborative process involving the construction of potential space so that the patient–by virtue of insight, integration, symptom removal, and self-reflection–is able to experience him- or herself as alive and real in the social and intersubjective realms of life.

In forensic psychiatric settings, psychodynamic therapy presents significant challenges for both patients and therapists. Patients may lack the capacity to make healthy attachments to others because their experience of childhood adversity causes an inability to trust and unresolved feelings of paranoia (which may have led to the index offence). They may also fear abandonment (and so exhibit avoidance or clingy dependency), or avoid any form of intimacy because of unresolved and persistent fear of abuse (and so denigrate and reject help offered as accusatory of their own feared—and real—helplessness).

Forensic patients tend to use immature defenses like projection, reality distortion and somatization because they have not developed the necessary psychological structures for managing painful and fearful affects. Developing more mature defenses involves letting go of old defenses, and for a time, being able to rely on the psychotherapist for necessary ego protection, and this process may be stressful. Because many (if not most) forensic patients have suffered childhood abuse from an apparently "trustworthy" person, engagement in psychotherapy can stimulate high levels of fear, both conscious and unconscious. Failure to engage is the most common way for patients to manage this fear, but physical attacks on the therapists (similar to the index offence) are not unknown.

When beginning psychotherapy with these patients, the primary goal will be simply to help the patient learn to tolerate what appears to be intolerable. Many patients have limited capacity to contain their anxiety on their own, and may have no self-soothing capacity at all. Those with borderline personality organization may previously have used sex, substances, cutting, and even abusive relationships to soothe their intolerable anxiety. Their acts of violence are often the result of overwhelming anxiety and related substance misuse, which, when combined with increasing distortion of reality (psychosis), adds up to a high risk of violence. Some patients may have used seduction or sexual relationships to manage their anxiety and fear of others' violence and may act in seductive ways with therapists, increasing the risk of sexual boundary violations. It is of interest that sexual boundary violations by professionals in secure settings typically involve male patients (often known sex offenders) and female professionals (Thomas-Peter and Garrett 2000).

The work of forensic psychotherapy is difficult for the patient and their resistance to it needs to be appreciated and respected. For the severely psychotic, paranoid, and disorganized patient, psychotherapy might begin with a five-minute check-in once or twice weekly, possibly for many months, until there is sufficient "evidence" for the patient that the psychotherapist takes this seriously, is patient and consistent, and is not going to abandon them, as perhaps real parental figures from childhood had done. Even then, weekly psychotherapy will be challenging and complicated. Depending on the patient's history and defense style, the psychotherapist might need to simply and slowly develop trust with the patient by being a constant, predictable, and reliable "object" whom the patient might initially begin to tolerate, and then gradually trust (Adshead 2003).

Work with forensic patients, especially those with personality disorder, can give rise to a wide variety of organizational dynamics involving the therapist (Norton and Hinshelwood 1996). These patients are often experienced by unit staff in diametrically different ways either as likeable or unlikeable. Very often the split these patients create are between team members, between unit staff and the treatment team, first shift staff against second or third shift, or between the unit and other units, and of course splits between treatment in general versus the administration goals of politics, policy, and containment.

Some forensic patients with severe and chronic psychopathology use social isolation in order to avoid becoming over-stimulated and more paranoid. They may be overlooked by staff, and rejected by their fellow patients, and so are often difficult to engage in any unit group or activity. The patient's way of interacting with the world is such that other people become almost invisible to them—other people are like furniture, just things to avoid and move around—and as a result they become invisible to others. These patients typically have committed offenses involving the assault, murder, or attempt to murder a parent. If these patients do start in psychotherapy, their negative symptoms, intractable auditory hallucinations, social isolation, and disorganized thinking may result in the psychotherapist never being able to find the patient up and ready for psychotherapy appointments, and staff also "forgetting" to have the patient up and ready. However, psychotherapy can be adapted to most patients, even those with severe mental disorders and a moderate level of developmental disorders.

GROUP THERAPY FOR FORENSIC PATIENTS

Regardless of diagnosis or clinical condition, group treatments are a primary modality in forensic settings, and forensic patients will all be invited to engage in group treatment as part of a prosocial experience. Forensic patients will regularly be invited to groups that address social skills building, psychoeducation groups on mental illness, medications, and legal issues related to their crime and acquittal. Group treatments may be especially useful for those patients who find the intimacy of individual psychotherapy too much for them to tolerate.

Psychodynamically-oriented group therapy offers therapy where the *process* of the group is the treatment itself. In these groups, patients slowly learn to expand their abilities to trust beyond just the group psychotherapist and to peers in the group. In forensic therapy groups, therapists try to help group members move from the passive to the active voice; a process first described by Cox (1986) in his similar work with offenders. Cox notes how the recovery process is accompanied by changes in language:

> "I don't know what you are talking about."
> "It wasn't me."
> "It was me, but I was mentally ill when I did it."

"I did it when I was mentally ill."
"I did it."

Cox (1976) refers to this process as a "scala integrata"; but it can also be seen as a series of steps along a Via Dolorosa. In this sense the recovery process for forensic patients can be very painful indeed, and therapists need to be aware of the risk of suicidal feelings emerging in treatment. Group therapy can also be seen as a way to help forensic patients develop better mentalizing skills; that is, to be better able to think about other people's minds, feelings and intentions (Adshead et al. 2013)

Group therapy also explores the extent to which the offender identity can be given up, or transformed into something which is not completely defined by the past offence. However, the group members and therapists are all aware that this is not completely up to them to decide, and so it may not be possible for these patients to leave that identity behind, even if the offence is now a decade or more ago. Society (either in the form of the Justice administration or the media) will not let them forget, and some of them have continuing and complex relationships with the families that they altered irrevocably by their actions.

Listening to others tell their story reduces the sense of shame and social isolation brought about by the offense, and enhances people's abilities to tell their story. What forensic group therapy aims to do is to help group members develop a more coherent narrative about their index offence (Adshead 2011), and demonstrate that they are more able to understand the importance of a 'secure' state of mind.

CONCLUSIONS

Forensic treatment is not simply getting a patient better in terms of having fewer symptoms, along with cooperation and compliance with treatment; nor is it about teaching offender patients to "parrot" learned accounts of how their mental illness caused them to offend, and how they will be compliant with meds forever in the future.

The best treatment helps an offender patient to come to terms with what they have done by understanding how they came to let themselves act so violently, and the impact on them and their victim(s). Treatment that does not include attention to the meaning of the offence for the offender is treatment that has overlooked vital risk-related issues. It will not be able to identify potential future situations or relationships that could precipitate some psychiatric decompensation and subsequent risk of dangerous behaviors. To know that about a patient one must know the patient well and thoroughly, and that kind of knowledge of another person can only be obtained through appropriate use of psychotherapy.

Whatever the challenges, psychodynamic treatment has much to offer the forensic patient for several reasons. First, the (usually) extended length of detention makes it possible to offer a long-term reflective space. Over time, the forensic patient can get to know himself and the therapist in a relationship that is based on *epistemic* trust (Fonagy, Luyten, and Allison 2015); that is, trust in which curiosity is supported and new ideas can be explored safely. Once that trust is established, the patient can start to explore the idea of their mind as a living dynamic system: the role of unconscious drives, feelings, and impulses; how this might have led to their acts of violence; and the impact of their offense on them, their families, and their future.

Second, psychodynamic psychotherapy in a forensic hospital can help patients think about their identity as offenders in a way that does not induce more shame and guilt, but does address themes of responsibility and agency. Current interventions for prisoners that address offending are not geared towards those with mental disorders; and most CBT interventions for mental health do not address offending or the meaning of offending. Psychodynamic therapy can address meaning and identity.

Third, psychodynamic theory has a moral discourse built into the concept of inner conflict. The original theory contains within it the idea of a transgressive self that is in conflict with itself, and assumes that irrationality is as important to mental life as rationality. Most interventions based on CBT assume a type of rational engagement with life, which fits poorly with the experience of forensic patients, whose lives (and offenses) rarely reflect rational social norms. Psychodynamic therapy, in contrast, is all too familiar with the destructive reality of the irrational.

REFERENCES

Adler, J.M., L.M. Skalina, and D.P. McAdams. 2008. "The Narrative Reconstruction of Psychotherapy and Psychological Health." *Psychotherapy Research* 18 (6): 719–34.

Adshead, G. 2003. "Three Degrees of Security." In *A Matter of Security: Attachment Theory and Forensic Psychiatry and Psychotherapy*, edited by F. Pfäfflin and Gwen Adshead, pp. 47–66. London: Jessica Kingsley.

Adshead, G. 2011. "The Life Sentence: Using a Narrative Approach in Group Psychotherapy with Offenders." *Group Analysis* 44 (2): 175–95.

Adshead, G., E. Moore, M. Humphrey, C. Wilson, and J. Tapp. 2013. "The Role of Mentalising in the Management of Violence." *Advances in Psychiatric Treatment* 19 (1): 67–76.

Baglivio, M.T., N. Epps, K. Swartz, M.S. Huq, A. Sheer, and N.S. Hardt. 2014. "The Prevalence of Adverse Childhood Experiences (ACE) in the Lives of Juvenile Offenders." *Journal of Juvenile Justice* 3 (2).

Bateman, A. and P. Fonagy. 2013. "Impact of Clinical Severity on Outcomes of Mentalisation-Based Treatment for Borderline Personality Disorder." *The British Journal of Psychiatry* 203 (3): 221–7.

Coid, J.W. 1992. "DSM-III Diagnosis in Criminal Psychopaths: A Way Forward." *Criminal Behaviour and Mental Health* 2: 78–94.

Cordess, C. and Cox, M. 1995. *Forensic Psychotherapy: Crime, Psychodynamics and the Offender Patient.* Vols 1 and 2. London: Jessica Kingsley Publishers.

Cox, M. 1976. "Group Psychotherapy in a Secure Setting." *Proceedings of the Royal Society of Medicine* 69 (3): 215.

———. 1986. "The 'Holding Function' of Dynamic Psychotherapy in a Custodial Setting: A Review." *Journal of the Royal Society of Medicine* 79 (3): 162–4.

Finzi-Dottan, R. and T. Karu. 2006. "From Emotional Abuse in Childhood to Psychopathology in Adulthood: A Path Mediated by Immature Defense Mechanisms and Self-Esteem." *The Journal of Nervous and Mental Disease* 194 (8): 616–21.

Fonagy, P. and A. Gwen. 2012. "How Mentalisation Changes the Mind." *Advances in Psychiatric Treatment* 18 (5): 353–62.

Fonagy, P., P. Luyten, and E. Allison. 2015. "Epistemic Petrification and the Restoration of Epistemic Trust: A New Conceptualization of Borderline Personality Disorder and Its Psychosocial Treatment." *Journal of Personality Disorders* 29 (5): 575–609.

Frith, C.D. 2007. "The Social Brain?" *Philosophical Transactions of the Royal Society B: Biological Sciences* 362 (1480): 671–8.

Gibbs, P.L. 2007. "The Primacy of Psychoanalytic Intervention in Recovery From the Psychoses and Schizophrenias." *Journal of the American Academy of Psychoanalysis and Dynamic Psychiatry* 35 (2): 287–312.

Hall, J., S. Caleo, J. Stevenson, and R. Meares. 1999. *Economic Analysis of Psychotherapy for Borderline Personality Disorder Patients.* Sydney: Centre for Health Economics Research, University of Sydney.

Harvard Center on the Developing Child. 2012. www.developingchild.harvard.edu/resources.

Holmes, J. 1993. "Attachment Theory: A Biological Basis for Psychotherapy?" *The British Journal of Psychiatry* 163 (4): 430–8.

Huband, N., C. Duggan, L. McCarthy, L. Mason, and G. Rathbone. 2014. "Defence Styles in a Sample of Forensic Patients with Personality Disorder." *Personality and Mental Health* 8 (3): 238–49.

Karon, B.P. 2003. "The Tragedy of Schizophrenia Without Psychotherapy." *Journal of the American Academy of Psychoanalysis and Dynamic Psychiatry* 31 (1): Special issue: 89–118.

LaMothe, R. 2001. "Vitalizing Objects and Psychoanalytic Psychotherapy." *Psychoanalytic Psychology* 18 (2): 320.

Leichsenring, F. and S. Klein. 2014. "Evidence for Psychodynamic Psychotherapy in Specific Mental Disorders: A Systematic Review." *Psychoanalytic Psychotherapy* 28 (1): 4–32.

Leichsenring, F. and S. Rabung. 2011. "Long-term Psychodynamic Psychotherapy in Complex Mental Disorders: Update of a Meta-analysis." *The British Journal of Psychiatry* 199 (1): 15–22.

Levit, D.B. 1993. "The Development of Ego Defenses in Adolescence." *Journal of Youth and Adolescence* 22 (5): 493–512.

Norton, K. and R.D. Hinshelwood. 1996. "Severe Personality Disorders. Treatment Issues and Selection for In-patient Psychotherapy." *The British Journal of Psychiatry* 168 (6): 723–31.

Ogilvie, C.A., E. Newman, L. Todd, and D. Peck. 2014. "Attachment and Violent Offending: A Meta-analysis." *Aggression and Violent Behavior* 19 (4): 322–39.

Schore, A.N. 2001. "The Effects of Early Relational Trauma on Right Brain Development, Affect Regulation, and Infant Mental Health." *Infant Mental Health Journal* 22 (1–2): 201–69.

Thomas-Peter, B. and T. Garrett. 2000. "Preventing Sexual Contact between Professionals and Patients in Forensic Environments." *The Journal of Forensic Psychiatry* 11 (1): 135–50.

Volkan, V.D. 1987. *Six Steps in the Treatment of Borderline Personality Organization.* New York: Jason Aronson.

Yakeley, J. and G. Adshead. 2013. "Locks, Keys, and Security of Mind: Psychodynamic Approaches to Forensic Psychiatry." *Journal of the American Academy of Psychiatry and the Law* Online 41 (1): 38–45.

CHAPTER 15

Positive Behavioral Supports for Managing Violence Risk in the Inpatient Forensic Setting

Tracey Sondik

Violence and aggression in an inpatient forensic setting are relatively common behaviors that threaten the safety and well-being of patients and staff who care for them. Data suggest that most psychiatric staff, including nurses, psychiatrists, and direct care mental health workers, have been assaulted by a patient or verbally threatened at least once in their career. Violence has a number of significant negative consequences including posttraumatic stress response in injured staff, staff burnout and turnover, lost wages, financial costs to institutions due to loss of time from work by staff, and decreased effectiveness of treatment (Hallet, Huber, and Dickens 2014; Antonius et al. 2010; Pragnell 2009; Morrison and Love 2003; McCann and Ball 2000).

Traditionally, inpatient settings have relied primarily on control measures in response to these problematic behaviors including the use of restraints/seclusions, medications, and aversive measures (punishment). Despite common use, these control measures, alone, have limited effectiveness in the treatment of violent patients and serve to keep patients institutionalized or warehoused in prisons and forensic inpatient settings. For patients, these measures do little to contribute to and may even retard the acquisition of the daily living skills, coping skills, and prosocial behaviors that are required for successful transition back into the community.

What has evolved in institutional settings is the need for treatment to reduce violence and aggression based on recommendations from Regulatory and Human Rights agencies including Office of Safety and Health Administration (OSHA), Department of Justice (DOJ), Centers for Medicare and Medicaid Services (CMS), and The Joint Commission on Accreditation of Healthcare Organizations (JCAHO). In addition, promising research has revealed that aggression and violence can be reduced in inpatient forensic settings utilizing evidenced-based treatment (Corrigan 1994; Donat 2003, 2005; LaVigna and Donnellan 2007; LaVigna and Willis 2012).

This chapter will present the emerging behavioral treatment strategies and models in institutional settings, beginning with an analysis of aggression in inpatient forensic settings and the complex interplay of internal (e.g. psychiatric condition, personality, poor emotion regulation, neurobehavioral factors) and external factors (e.g. crowded environment, management style of staff), leading to aggression and violence (Dickens, Piccirillo, and Alderman 2013; Meehan, McIntosh, and Bergen 2006).

The chapter will trace the progression of forensic inpatient interventions to manage aggression from traditional behavioral control measures, through behavioral management, to the renewed interest in the area of behavioral and psychosocial treatment (Gardner and Cole 1987; Hunter 2000). The research comparing effectiveness of various models will be presented, along with the advantages of integrating a positive behavioral approach including components of enhanced coping skills and positive programming for the patients, staff, and institutions.

AGGRESSION ON INPATIENT UNITS

The presence of aggression and violence in inpatient forensic settings is a significant problem that impacts the patients, staff, and therapeutic milieu. Aggression in inpatient forensic settings refers to a broad range of behaviors that include threatening or intimidating behavior, verbal assault, property destruction, throwing objects, physical assault directed at others, and aggression directed toward one self, including self-harm behaviors such as cutting or insertion. Violence can be considered a subset of aggression which describes a narrower range of behaviors that result in actual physical harm (Dickens, Piccirillo, and Alderman 2013). Episodes of aggression and violence are a regular occurrence in inpatient forensic psychiatric settings. Nursing staff are at highest risk for being physically assaulted by a patient in forensic settings resulting in staff absence, reduced productivity, low rates of job satisfaction, and increased stress level. Violent acts by inpatients cause bodily harm to staff and other patients, disrupt the therapeutic climate on the unit, and can leave patients and staff feeling angry, traumatized, and helpless (Newton et al. 2012; Hamrin, Iennaco, and Olsen 2009; Cornaggia et al. 2011; Dickens, Piccirillo, and Alderman 2013).

The relationship between aggression and violence and mental illness has been well established. Mental disorders including active psychosis, co-morbid substance abuse, organic brain disease, and personality disorders, in particular antisocial personality disorder, are all risk factors for violent behavior, along with criminal history (Rice and Harris 1997; Nijman et al. 1999; Hamrin, Iennaco, and Olsen 2009; Soliman et al. 2013). The high incidence of personality disorders in forensic settings is well established in the literature, with the most prevalent ones being Antisocial, Narcissistic, Borderline, and Paranoid Personality Disorders.

However, aggression and violence in inpatient settings cannot be explained by mental disorders alone. Researchers have determined a number of variables that contribute to aggression and violence in inpatient settings. These variables can be categorized into different models that suggest a complex interplay of patient and environment (Nijman et al. 1999; Duxbury and Whittington 2005; Hamrin, Iennaco, and Olsen 2009; Meehan, McIntosh, and Bergen 2006; Pulsford et al. 2013; Dickens, Piccirillo, and Alderman 2013).

1. Internal models of aggression focus on factors within the individual that predispose him to violence. These patient-related factors include mental illness, personality, alcohol and substance abuse, along with sex, age, history of violence, socioeconomic status, mental state, and non-compliance with medication.
2. External models of aggression examine the impact of environmental factors that contribute to aggression by patients including the layout of the ward (space, overcrowding, limited privacy), the unit routines including medication administration, mealtimes, and the lack of structured activities.
3. Interactional models examine the impact of patient/staff relationships. Studies suggest that poor staff and patient relationships, negative staff attitudes regarding patients, authoritarian behavior by staff, and use of controlling and coercive behavior can lead to increased patient aggression.
4. Finally, societal models look at the role of values and culture on violence in inpatient settings. Western values such as individualism, self-responsibility, and personal uniqueness may contribute to higher levels of violence in inpatient settings, especially in the United States (see Figure 15.1).

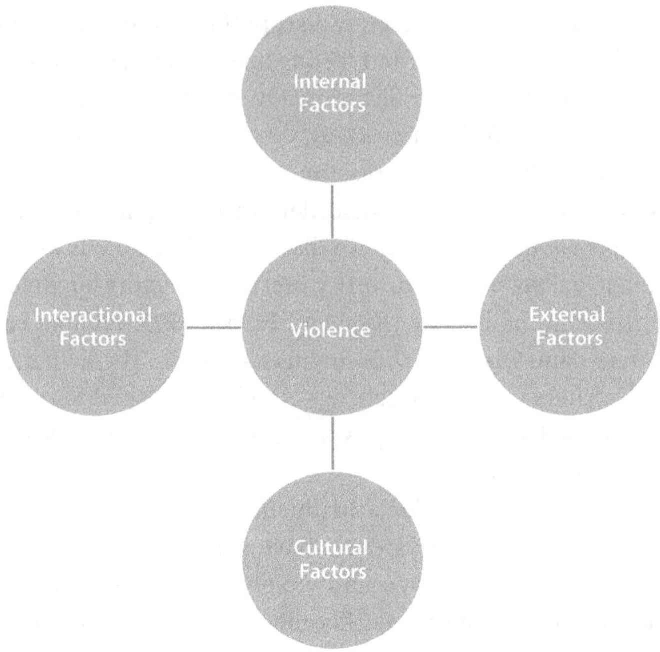

FIGURE 15.1 Integrated Model of Inpatient Aggression.

Using a multi-layered model to understand inpatient aggression is an important foundation in developing effective treatment strategies. However, traditional interventions in forensic inpatient settings have historically emphasized control and management over treatment, particularly in public-sector inpatient settings, which are often the only treatment option for severely mentally ill and frequently dangerous patients. These settings have significant resource limitations, lack access to treatment interventions, and have high levels of acuity, which can lead to an over-reliance on restrictive control interventions including restraints, seclusion, or the use of psychotropic medications to achieve sedation. The use of seclusion, restraints, and medication in forensic inpatient settings have been controversial issues with much debate in the literature as to whether they are valid therapeutic interventions, a form of necessary containment, or a form of punishment. Many researchers have concluded that seclusion and restraint can have significant negative physical and psychological effects on both patients and staff. Restraints, in particular, have been associated with injuries to staff and patients, and patient deaths. In addition, the over-reliance on restraints and seclusions in forensic inpatient settings decrease the focus on effective training and teaching skills development for patients to manage themselves successfully outside a forensic setting. Further, these containment strategies may actually increase aggression as it serves as a model for aggressive ways for staff and patients to interact (Sailas and Wahlbeck 2005; Donat 2003).

STRATEGIES FOR MANAGEMENT

During the past decade, there has been increased scrutiny around the use of coercive measures in psychiatric settings from regulatory bodies, authoritative organizations, and judicial reviews. New recommendations have been issued to improve the safety of seclusion and restraints when needed and increase the use of intervention strategies including verbal de-escalation and crisis management training with the end goal of reducing the need for restraints and seclusion. Most psychiatric facilities require formal training in the management of aggression and violence on a yearly basis. Many of these programs include prevention techniques, using a team approach, and crisis intervention. Regulatory and authoritative organizations have stopped short of recommending the complete removal of restraints and seclusions as an intervention for managing aggression and violence due to the risks of injuries to other patients and staff that can occur due to severe behavior (Donat 2003; Morrison and Love 2003; Sailas and Wahlbeck 2005; Recupero et al. 2011; Liberman 2011).

The interest in alternative interventions to decrease aggression and violence has evolved as a result of the regulatory and judicial movement toward restraint and seclusion reduction. These alternatives include both management procedures and treatment interventions. Management procedures focus on the reduction of psychiatric symptoms. These techniques temporarily cause a reduction in symptoms, but are not permanent. Examples include psychiatric medication or voluntary time out. Once the procedure is stopped, the behaviors and symptoms will come back. Even though management through medications alone is largely ineffective in sustaining permanent changes in patients, facilities continue to heavily rely on medication due to a variety of factors including an overdependence on biochemical theories for mental illness and aggression, pressure to come up with "quick fix" solutions to complex problems, and providing the least expensive treatment possible. A comprehensive approach to forensic inpatient treatment incorporates both treatment and management interventions to obtain the best outcomes. Researchers and clinicians have demonstrated that investing in treatment interventions focused on permanent change in patients including behavioral, psychological, psychosocial, and educational models can lead to improved care of forensic inpatients and reduced needs for control measures (Ball 1993; Hunter 2000).

BEHAVIORAL STRATEGIES TO REDUCE AGGRESSION

Research over the past several years has demonstrated the value of behavioral and psychosocial treatment interventions to reduce aggression and increase prosocial skill development in inpatient forensic populations. These programs will be reviewed including: (a) behavioral interventions, (b) cognitive-behavioral interventions, and (c) positive behavioral support plans, an integrated model that will be detailed in full below (Rice, Harris and Cormier 1992; Ball 1993; Hunter 2000; Corrigan 1994; McCann and Ball, 2000; Liberman 2011; LaVigna and Donnellan 2007; LaVigna and Willis 2012). Behavioral strategies have been utilized to reduce violent and aggressive behavior in inpatient forensic settings for more than half a century. Many of the procedures have been replicated over and over across different settings and patient populations, providing a valid and reliable treatment option for treatment teams working with aggressive and violent behaviors. Behavioral strategies are based on an education model and focus on the interaction between individuals, antecedents, and consequences of the behavior that they are engaging, and the effects of the behaviors (maladaptive or adaptive) in their environment. From a behavioral therapy perspective, aggression and violence are learned maladaptive behaviors over many years of reinforcement. These behaviors can be increased, reduced, modified, or eliminated through systematic application of antecedents and consequences to those behaviors

TABLE 15.1 Model of Behavioral Analysis

Setting Events and Vulnerabilities • Situations in the environment combined with the individual's deficits. • Broader setting events (i.e., unpredictability, medical conditions—e.g. unstable blood sugar, undiagnosed seizure activity, untreated sleep problems, medication side effects).
Antecedents and Triggers • What occurred immediately *before* the behavior? • *External* (e.g. a conflict earlier in the day) versus internal antecedents (e.g. feeling isolated and lonely influences behavioral choices). • Lifestyle issues (e.g. remote stresses, interpersonal relationships, problems accessing preferred activities). • *The "universal trigger" is often "enforcing rules," rather than giving flexible guidance.*
Precursors • What noticeable actions in body language came before the behavior of concern (e.g. pacing, pressured speech, rolling their eyes, clinching their fists)?
Maintaining Consequences • What occurred immediately *after* the behavior of concern? • How did the caregivers respond? Is there inadvertent reinforcement?

within the individual's environment. Behavioral interventions typically begin with an analysis of the behavior (Table 15.1).

Based on the behavioral analysis, interventions are selected that will likely reduce aggressive behavior. Once the interventions are implemented, data are collected to determine the effectiveness of the interventions; further modification of interventions may be required if the aggression continues. The behavioral analysis is the backbone of these well-known behavioral interventions:

1. **Environmental change** is a simple way to reduce aggression as the focus of change is on the environment rather than changing the patient. Examples of environmental change include the level of noise, light, sensory stimulation, routine, and staff modeling.
2. **Differential reinforcement** schedules have been widely used to reduce aggression and violence in inpatient settings. These schedules are designed to reinforce or reward the absence of aggressive behavior. The reinforcement can be applied when there is a decrease in the aggressive behavior, when the patient demonstrates a behavior that is incompatible with aggression, or for any behavior other than the aggressive ones. The reinforcers can be made more stringent over time until the aggressive behaviors are eliminated.
3. **Token economies** are another behavioral intervention that can be used both for individuals as well as a whole system (unit, hospital) as they work by creating an environment that is designed to motivate prosocial behaviors. Symbolic rewards (tokens, points, stickers) are provided after the completion of tasks and/or the absence of aggressive behavior. These can be exchanged for preferred items and privileges within the hospital setting.
4. **Response cost** refers to the loss of positive reinforcement when aggressive behavior occurs. However, this intervention must be done in a systematic manner so as not to be used punitively, which may lead to frustration and failure which could actually increase the aggressive behavior. An example of response cost might be the loss of specified privileges (canteen, access to recreation area, use of certain personal belongings, etc.) as a result of a specified behavior of concern occurring or a patient to go to a location (time-out) and ignoring the behavior to allow the patient to regain control. Aversive stimuli (electric shock, bad tasting or smelling substances, water mist) have been eliminated from virtually all forensic inpatient settings due to the deleterious psychological effects for patients (Ball 1993; Liberman 2011).

Cognitive-behavioral treatment approaches that focus on the modification of maladaptive cognitions have been effective in reducing depression, self-harm, and aggression associated with personality disorders in outpatient settings. Given the high prevalence of personality disorders in forensic psychiatric settings, these same treatment approaches have demonstrated efficacy for the forensic population as well (Allen, MacKenzie, and Hickman 2001; Morgan and Flora 2002). However, due to system barriers including time and resource limitations, inpatient forensic settings often resort to more traditional methods as described earlier including control and management. To address these system barriers, researchers and clinicians have developed some promising new cognitive-behavioral approaches for inpatient forensic settings including dialectical behavioral therapy, schema-focused cognitive therapy, and brief behavioral activation.

Many cognitive-behavioral treatments for forensic settings can be used in group formats, have manualized approaches that can allow for ease in implementation, and can be tailored to individual needs of the patients. Dialectical behavioral therapy added an additional goal to its curriculum, focusing on increasing emotional attachment, as many with personality disorders avoid or have frequent disruptions in their attachments. Further, they are approaches that can be modified for outpatient treatment and can be an important bridge between institutional treatment and community living (McCann and Ball 2000; Hopko et al. 2003; Berzins and Trestman 2004; Bernstein, Arnoud, and de Vos 2007).

Despite the successful outcomes that many of these behavioral and cognitive behavioral treatments have demonstrated with reduction of aggression/violence, diminished psychiatric symptoms, and improved social functioning, several barriers still remain in terms of actual implementation on a day-to-day basis. These include insufficient training for frontline mental health staff and nursing and resource limitations that are an ongoing reality for many forensic inpatient settings (Corrigan et al. 1994; Corrigan 1994; Donat 2003, 2005). The following section will describe new and comprehensive treatment approaches that address the individual patient, staff, and institution.

POSITIVE BEHAVIORAL SUPPORT MODEL

The use of an integrative Positive Behavioral Support (PBS) model can be an effective way to lead to improved care and treatment for patients while at the same time reducing problematic behaviors of aggression and violence in an inpatient forensic setting. A model for the systematic application of PBS in a forensic inpatient setting will be offered, including the key components that address the needs of the patient, staff, and institutional setting:

1. understanding the concepts, terms, and strategies for PBS;
2. identifying the functions that influence behavior;
3. measuring effectiveness with data collection and graphing;
4. regular hospital administrative oversight and review of PBS supports;
5. behavioral consultation team led by a senior behavioral psychologist;
6. comprehensive staff training;
7. transitioning PBS into a community re-entry treatment plan.

Positive Behavioral Support is a comprehensive approach that incorporates the science of applied behavioral analysis (ABA) in the support of patients with challenging behaviors including aggression and violence. It is a supportive approach that is centered around proactive and data-driven strategies based on a comprehensive assessment of an individual and environment (Carr and Sidener 2002; Horner 2000; LaVigna and Donnellen 1997; Lavigna and Willis 2012)

The primary focus of PBS is to improve the quality of life of the person receiving services, decrease problem behaviors by teaching new skills, and modify the environment to maximize positive outcomes (Association for Positive Behavioral Support (APBS: www.apbs.org).

PBS is considered a non-linear form of ABA in that it does not rely solely on the Antecedent-Behavior-Consequence contingency relationship described above in the behavioral therapy section. Instead, PBS is considered a multi-element, non-linear model that views behaviors as goal-directed and interconnected with physiology, situation, cultural and institutional factors, cognitions, and feelings.

Over the twenty years, a growing evidence base for PBS has developed indicating its effectiveness as a model for treating individuals with problem behaviors including severe behavioral problems, for high-rate behaviors, and for behavioral problems for individuals living in institutional settings. Further, research has demonstrated that PBS is a model that can be cost-effective, easily taught to direct care psychiatric staff, and can be an integral part of community living following discharge from an inpatient facility (Donnellan et al. 1985; LaVigna and Willis 2012; Grey and McClean 2007; McClean, Grey, and McCracken 2007).

PBS has a number of integral components that address individual and system factors (Carr 2007; LaVigna and Willis 2005). The foundation for a PBS plan is the development of a functional behavior assessment (FBA), a thorough and comprehensive method for understanding the function and meaning of a person's behavior. The functional assessment has several elements, including the traditional ABA concepts of setting events, antecedents and triggers, precursors, and maintaining consequences.

The functional assessment in PBS also includes psychological, neurobiological, medical, and social issues that may be influencing problem behaviors. Finally, the functional assessment provides a road map toward understanding the function of the behavior itself. Rather than just trying to render the challenging behavior obsolete, it is critical to understand the function of the person's behavior in their environment and apply this understanding toward the development and teaching of replacement or functionally equivalent skills (for example, using a calm voice to express one's feelings rather than yelling).

This functional approach also facilitates greater empathy and understanding toward a patient's challenging behavior. According to the PBS model, any behavior, whether adaptive or maladaptive, can be seen as having a distinct and important purpose (Lowry and Sovner 1991; Silka and Hauser 1997). Behaviors may start out adaptive and over time become maladaptive (for example, a young child's screaming when in pain may be adaptive then and continue into adulthood, screaming due to difficulty controlling emotional distress). The behavior may be a symptom of a medical disorder, side effect of a medication, or a result of a skills deficit secondary to cognitive limitations. The four primary functions of behavior described in Figure 15.2 provide a basic categorization system that effectively describes the purpose and meaning of most maladaptive behaviors.

Finally, a PBS functional assessment provides an extensive analysis of the environment to determine if there are any mismatches or triggers in the environment that may be causing or exacerbating challenging behaviors (for

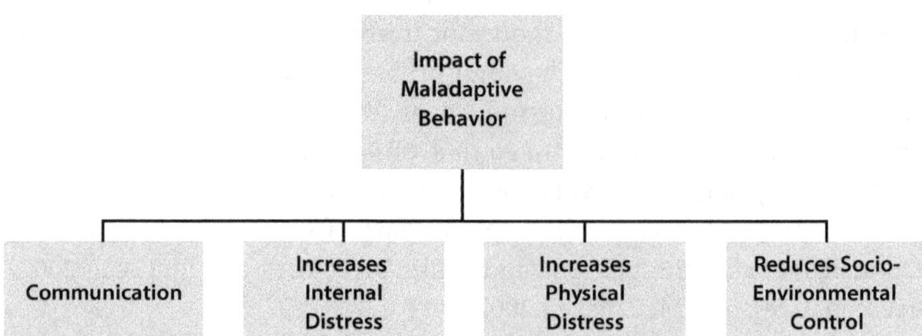

FIGURE 15.2 Maladaptive Behavior as a Driver of Disrupted Function. Based on Lowry and Sovner, 1991

TABLE 15.2 Elements of a PBS Plan

Critical Components
1. Ecological strategies—removing mismatches between individual's needs and their environment.
2. Positive programming—teaching general skills, functionally equivalent skills (replacement behaviors), and functionally related skills, coping and tolerance skills.
3. Focused support strategies designed to achieve rapid and efficient control over challenging behavior (e.g. using differential reinforcement of other behaviors).
4. Reactive strategies to reduce episodic severity (e.g. active listening).

Adapted from LaVigna and Willis 2005

example, a patient who becomes easily over-stimulated lives in a noisy area of a hospital ward). By understanding the meaning and function of the behavior from the patient's point of view, a PBS model is truly a person-centered approach to treating challenging behaviors.

A PBS plan is a multi-element approach that includes several strategies based on the functional assessment. The strategies include both traditional behavioral therapy interventions (e.g. a differential reinforcement schedule) along with innovative ways to teach new skills (see Table 15.2).

Most behavioral management and behavioral therapies focus on reactive strategies, which are the interventions implemented following a challenging behavior. The hallmark of a PBS approach is the emphasis on proactive strategies rather than reactive interventions. Proactive or positive strategies that are designed to:

1. increase emotional regulation through teaching functionally equivalent behaviors including coping strategies, self-soothing, healthy diversions, and opportunities to learn self-control;
2. increase prosocial skills and reciprocal relationships; and
3. build mastery, confidence, and self-esteem through participation in positive programming (see Table 15.3).

The focus on positive programming is key to improving patient's quality of life and producing sustainable changes in their overall behavior. A number of studies in forensic inpatient facilities have revealed that patients living in institutions with persistent mental illness spent most of their time in solitary or passive leisure activities such as sleeping, watching television, and personal care. Patients viewed their time in institutions as constraining and limiting in terms of future goals. Further, without active engagement, patients were more at risk for engaging in challenging behaviors (Farnworth, Nikitin, and Fossey 2004). Positive programming refers to the development of planned

TABLE 15.3 Guidelines for Promoting Functionally Equivalent Behaviors

Steps and Therapeutic Messages to Create Restructured Reinforcers

1. Serve the Same Purpose:
   - Putting feelings into polite words to communicate.
2. Get Reinforcement as Soon or Sooner:
   - Self-soothing with ice pack, rather than self-injurious behavior.
3. Receive as Much or More Reinforcement:
   - Caregivers quickly attend when he says "again please", as much as if he had expressed his demands with an outburst.
4. Just as Easy or Easier to Do:
   - Following directions in one to two steps is easier than refusing an appointment or missing an outing.

and scheduled activities that provide meaning to patients. Programs should have educational, skills development, vocational opportunities, or leisure/recreational value. Reinforcement can come from the satisfaction of completing the activity itself, the social interactions between patients, and the positive response provided by staff. Positive programming can assist in helping patients to bolster their mastery by learning new skills, self-esteem, and interpersonal effectiveness by developing new relationships, and self-esteem through positive reinforcement of their prosocial behaviors (for example, staff provides positive praise each time the patient is helpful). Aggression will be reduced as participation in positive programming increases. One cost-effective and innovative way to increase positive programming is the use of treatment malls, which are centralized areas in a hospital that offer a variety of treatment and leisure opportunities in a setting that approximates real-world settings. Patients can spend several hours in the treatment mall, attending groups, shopping in stores, going to the bank, and getting their hair cut in a salon. This treatment mall approach combines positive programming with skills development, making it an appealing option when looking toward community integration (Liberman 2011; Bopp et al. 1996; Webster, Harmon, and Paesler 2005).

The PBS model relies on data collection as an integral part of the functional behavioral assessment and for tracking outcomes. During the functional assessment, data collection can serve as a data probe to determine the most salient problem behaviors to address. PBS measures episodic severity, a term developed by LaVigna and Willis, which refers to a quantified measure of the intensity of a behavioral incident based on frequency, duration, and severity (for example, verbal aggression can be measured based on duration, rate, intensity on a scale from 1 to 5) (LaVigna and Willis 2005). Plans that track the episodic severity help provide more specific and socially valid data than simple frequency data.

Hospital clinical and administration leadership can play an important role in efforts to utilize effective treatment modalities such as PBS to reduce aggression and violence and the associated use of restraints and seclusion (Emerson and Emerson 1987; Donat 2002, 2003, 2005). Organizational management strategies are recommended to address the systems changes needed for successful implementation of PBS. The development of a formal case conference review is an important feature of this organizational approach. The case conference committee should be conducted with the purpose of reviewing cases that reach specific thresholds for the hospital in terms of episodic severity of aggression and required restraint and seclusion utilization (for example, patients that have had more than one restraint in the last thirty days). The committee should include administration leadership, clinicians including behavioral psychologists, nursing, and direct care staff. The committee then makes treatment plan recommendations, including, but not limited to, a PBS plan. The committee will continue to monitor and follow up regularly on these cases by tracking data, modifying treatment recommendations, and utilizing consultants for the most difficult cases that are not responding to current treatment.

The development of PBS plans require the expertise of a behaviorally-trained clinician including a clinical psychologist or master's-level behavioral analyst training in the PBS model. Traditionally in inpatient forensic settings, a psychologist assigned to a ward became responsible for the development, implementation, and monitoring of a plan. The psychologist had to rely on other members of the treatment team to observe and record data and implement strategies. This often restricted the positive benefit of the behavioral plan due to limited staffing resources, negative staff attitudes secondary to burnout, and lack of knowledge by staff regarding basic behavioral concepts. Therefore, the Department of Justice and other review agencies have recommended the development of a behavioral consultation team within the hospital setting to address the most challenging cases, provide staff training, and provide support for discharge transitions (Donat 2005).

A psychologist with specialty knowledge and training in behavioral methods leads the behavioral consultation team. Other members of the team can include doctoral-level clinical psychologists and master's-level behavioral analysts and paraprofessionals training in behavioral methods. The behavioral consultation team works directly with the treatment teams and patients to effectively develop, implement, and track a plan which may extend over several weeks to several months including transition to the community.

Training for frontline staff on behavioral and PBS methods can significantly enhance the effectiveness of PBS plans. Higher-level competency in behavioral methods leads to improved staff attitudes and reduced levels of occupational stress (Emerson and Emerson 1987; Donat 2005). A behavioral consultation team relies on well-trained staff members to effectively maintain PBS interventions. Without this critical link with the frontline staff, the effectiveness of PBS is weakened. Training of frontline staff can be done in a multi-stage manner, beginning with a global training for new employees that reviews the basic mission of PBS, concepts, and examples of treatment plans. Training for patient-specific plans should be conducted at a ward level by the behavioral consultation team and/or behavioral psychologist. For optimal performance in plan implementation, the training will include:

1. a summary of the functional behavioral assessment, training in utilization of positive programming, focused support strategies, and reactive strategies;
2. designation of roles for who is responsible in carrying out each component of the plan,
3. a plan for progress monitoring for accountability, including regular team meetings, review of data, and fidelity checks to ensure correct implementation of the plan.

Once patients are discharged into the community, treatment often drops off significantly. However, many of the same variables that contributed to an individual's increased risk for aggression remain, including neurobiological underpinnings, psychiatric symptoms, substance abuse relapse, and environmental stress. Without comprehensive treatment, patients may end up committing aggressive or violent acts leading to recidivism and possibly reinstitutionalization.

CONCLUSIONS

PBS plans can serve as an important bridge from inpatient treatment to community re-entry and reduce the risk of recidivism. Literature has demonstrated that PBS can be successfully applied in both institutional and community settings. Some studies have suggested that the most dramatic reduction of aggression occurred during the discharge community phase of a PBS plan (Berkman and Meyer 1988; LaVigna and Willis 2012). Many PBS plans can be easily modified for the community while still keeping the major proactive interventions, especially positive programming, and effective reactive strategies that have already proven to reduce aggression in that individual. Positive programming can be enhanced with more opportunities in the community to build self-esteem through educational, vocational, spiritual, and recreational programs. The community team direct care staff can be trained directly by the inpatient direct care staff, which can be a very effective training model.

Treatment for aggression and violence has evolved in forensic inpatient settings by utilizing methods grounded in behavioral sciences that are outcome-driven and address the complex interplay of individual and institutional factors leading to challenging behaviors. The PBS model offers an effective therapeutic approach to the care offered in inpatient forensic settings and can reduce aggression and recidivism and improve the quality of life for forensic patients.

REFERENCES

Allen, L.C., D.L. MacKenzie, and L.J. Hickman. 2001. "The Effectiveness of Cognitive Behavioral Treatment for Adult Offenders: A Methodological, Quality-based Review." *International Journal of Offender Therapy and Comparative Criminology* 45: 498–514.

Antonius, D., L. Fuchs, F. Herbert, J. Kwon, J. Fried, P. Burton, T. Straka, and Z. Levin. 2010. "Psychiatric Assessment of Aggressive Patients: A Violent Attack on a Resident." *American Journal of Psychiatry* 167: 253–9.

Ball, G.G. 1993. "Modifying the Behavior of the Violent Patient." *Psychiatric Quarterly* 64: 359–69.

Berkman, K.A. and L.H. Meyer. 1988. "Alternative Strategies and Multiple Outcomes in the Remediation of Severe Self-Injury: Going 'All Out' Nonaversively." *The Journal of the Association for Persons with Severe Handicaps* 13: 76–86.

Bernstein, D.P, A. Arnoud and M. de Vos. 2007. "Schema Focused Therapy in Forensic Settings: Theoretical Model and Recommendations for Best Clinical Practice." *International Journal of Forensic Mental Health* 6: 169–83.

Berzins, L. and R.L Trestman. 2004. "The Development and Implementation of Dialectical Behavior Therapy in Forensic Settings." *International Journal of Forensic Mental Health* 3: 93–103.

Bopp, J.H., D.J. Ribble, J.J. Cassidy, and R.A. Markoff. 1996. "Re-engineering the State Hospital to Promote Rehabilitation and Recovery." *Psychiatric Services* 47: 697–701.

Carr, E.G. 2007. "The Expanding Vision of Positive Behavior Support: Research Perspectives on Happiness, Helpfulness, Hopefulness." *Journal of Positive Behavior Interventions* 9: 3–14.

Carr, J.E. and T.M. Sidener. 2002. "On the Relation Between Applied Behavioral Analysis and Positive Behavioral Support." *The Behavior Analyst* 25: 245–53.

Cornaggia, C.M., M. Beghi, F. Pavone, and F. Barale. 2011. "Aggression in Psychiatry Wards: A Systematic Review." *Psychiatry Research* 189: 10–20.

Corrigan, P.W. 1994. "Differences Between Clinical and Nursing Inpatient Staff:

Implications for Training in Behavioral Rehabilitation." *Journal of Behavioral Therapy and Experimental Psychiatry* 25: 311–16.

Corrigan, P.W., E.P. Holmes, D. Luchins, J. Parks, A. Basit, E. DeLaney, and D. Kayton-Weinbert. 1994. "Setting Up Inpatient Behavioral Treatment Programs: The Staff Needs Assessment." *Behavioral Interventions* 9: 1–12.

Dickens, G., M. Piccirillo, and N. Alderman. 2013. "Causes and Management of Aggression and Violence in a Forensic Mental Health Service: Perspectives of Nurses and Patients." *International Journal of Mental Health Nursing* 22: 532–44.

Donat, D.C. 2002. "Employing Behavioral Methods to Improve the Context of Care in a Public Psychiatric Hospital: Reducing Hospital Reliance on Seclusion/Restraint and Psychotropic PRN Medication." *Cognitive and Behavioral Practice* 9: 28–37.

———. 2003. "An Analysis of Successful Efforts to Reduce the Use of Seclusion and Restraint at a Public Psychiatric Hospital." *Psychiatric Services* 54: 1119–23.

———. 2005. "Encouraging Alternatives to Seclusion, Restraint, and Reliance on PRN Drugs in a Public Psychiatric Hospital." *Psychiatric Services* 56: 1105–08.

Donnellan, A.M., G.W. LaVigna, J. Zambito, and J. Thvedt. 1985. "A Time-Limited Intensive Intervention Program Model to Support Community Placement for Person with Severe Behavior Problems." *Journal for the Association of Persons with Severe Handicaps* 10: 122–31.

Duxbury, J. and R. Whittington. 2005. "Causes and Management of Patient Aggression and Violence: Staff and Patient Perspectives." *Journal of Advanced Nursing* 50: 469–78.

Emerson E. and C. Emerson. 1987. "Barriers to the Effective Implementation of Habilitative Behavior Programs in an Institutional Setting." *Mental Retardation* 25: 101–6.

Farnworth, L., Nikitin, L., and Fossey, E. 2004. "Being in a Secure Forensic Psychiatric unit: Every Day is the Same, Killing Time or Making the Most of It". *British Journal of Occupational Therapy* 67: 430–8.

Gardner, W.J. and C.L. Cole. 1987. "Behavior Treatment, Behavior Management, and Behavior Control: Needed Distinctions." *Behavioral Residential Treatment* 2: 37–53.

Grey, I.M. and B. McClean. 2007. "Service User Outcomes of Staff Training in Positive Behaviour Support Using Person-Focused Training: A Control Group Study." *Journal of Applied Research in Intellectual Disabilities* 20: 6–15.

Hallett, N., J.W. Huber, and G.L. Dickens. 2014. "Violence Prevention in Inpatient Psychiatric Settings: Systematic Review of Studies About the Perceptions of Staff and Patients." *Aggression and Violent Behavior* doi: 10.1016/j.avb.2014.07.009.

Hamrin, V., J. Iennaco, and D. Olsen. 2009. "A Review of Ecological Factors Affecting Inpatient Psychiatric Unit Violence: Implications for Relational and Unit Cultural Improvements." *Issues in Mental Health Nursing* 30: 214–26.

Hopko, D.R., C.W. Lejuez, J.P. LePage, S.D. Hopko, and D.W. McNiel. 2003. "A Brief Behavioral Activation Treatment for Depression: A Randomized Pilot Trial Within an Inpatient Psychiatric Hospital." *Behavioral Modification* 27: 458–69.

Horner, R.H. 2000. "Positive Behavioral Supports." *Focus on Autism and Other Developmental Disabilities* Summer 15: 97–105.

Hunter, R.H. 2000. "Treatment, Management, and Control: Improving Outcomes

Through More Treatment and Less Control." *New Directions For Mental Health Services* 88: 5–15.

LaVigna, G.W. and A.M. Donnellan. 2007. *Alternatives to Punishment*. New York: Irvington Publishers.

LaVigna, G.W. and T.J. Willis. 2005. "A Positive Behavioral Support Model for Breaking the Barriers to Social and Community Inclusion." *Learning Disability Review* 10: 16–23.

———. 2012. "The Efficacy of Positive Behavioral Support with the Most Challenging Behavior: The Evidence and its Implications." *Journal of Intellectual and Developmental Disability* 37: 185–95.

Liberman, R.P. 2011. "Commentary: Interventions Based on Learning Principles: Can Supplant Seclusion and Restraint?" *The Journal of the American Academy of Psychiatry and Law* 39: 480–95.

Lowry, M. and R. Sovner. 1991. "The Functional Existence of Problem Behavior: a Key to Effective Treatment." *The Habilitative Mental Health Care Newsletter* 10: 59–63.

McCann, R.A. and E.M. Ball. 2000. "DBT With an Inpatient Forensic Population: The CMHIP Forensic Model." *Cognitive and Behavioral Practice* 7: 447–56.

McClean, B., I.M. Grey, and M. McCracken. 2007. "An Evaluation of Positive Behavioural Support for People with Very Severe Challenging Behaviours in Community-based Settings." *Journal of Intellectual Disabilities* 11: 281–301.

Meehan, T., W. McIntosh, and H. Bergen. 2006. "Aggressive Behaviour in the High-Secure Forensic Setting: the Perceptions of Patients." *Journal of Psychiatric and Mental Health Nursing* 13: 19–25.

Morgan, R.D. and D.B. Flora. 2002. "Group Psychotherapy with Incarcerated Offenders": A Research Synthesis." *Group Dynamics: Theory, Research, and Practice* 6: 203–18.

Morrison, E.F. and C.C. Love. 2003. "An Evaluation of Four Programs for the Management of Aggression in Psychiatric Settings." *Archives of Psychiatric Nursing* 17: 146–55.

Newton, V.M., E.B. Elbogen, C.L. Brown, J. Snyder, and A.L. Barrick. 2012. "Clinical Decision-making About Inpatient Violence Risk at Admission to a Public-Sector Acute Psychiatric Hospital." *Journal of the American Academy of Psychiatry and Law* 40: 2016–214.

Nijman, H.L.I., J.M.L.G. Campo, D.P. Ravelli, and H.L.G.J. Merckelbach.1999. "A Tentative Model of Aggression on Inpatient Psychiatric Wards." *Psychiatric Services* 50: 832–34.

Pragnell, S.J. 2009. "Behavioural Interventions for Self Injurious Behaviour: A Review of Recent Evidence (1998–2008)." *British Journal of Learning Disabilities* 38: 259–70.

Puslford, D., A. Crumpton, A. Baker, K. Wright, and J. Duxbury. 2013. "Aggression in a High Secure Hospital: Staff and Patient Attitudes." *Journal of Psychiatric and Mental Health Nursing* 20: 296–304.

Rice, M.E. and G.T. Harris. 1997. "The Treatment of Mentally Disordered Offenders." *Psychology, Public Policy, and Law* 3: 126–83.

Rice, M.E, G.T. Harris, and C.A. Cormier. 1992. "An Evaluation of a Maximum Security Therapeutic Community for Psychopaths and Other Mentally Disordered Offenders." *Law and Human Behavior* 16: 399–412.

Recupero, P., M. Price, K.A. Garvey, B. Daly, and S.L. Xavier. 2011. "Restraint and Seclusion in Psychiatric Treatment Settings: Regulation, Case Law, and Risk Management." *Journal of the Academy of Psychiatry and the Law* 39: 465–76.

Salias, E. and K. Wahlbeck. 2005. "Restraint and Seclusion in Psychiatric Inpatient Wards." *Current Opinion in Psychiatry* 18: 555–9.

Silka, V.R. and M.J. Hauser. 1997. "Psychiatric Assessment of the Person With Mental Retardation." *Psychiatric Annals* 27: 162–9.

Soliman, A., H. Sadek, H. Azzam, and H. Elkholy. 2013. "Risk Factors for Violence among Forensic Psychiatric Inpatients." *Middle East Current Psychiatry* 20: 1–5.

Webster S.L, S.H. Harmon and B.T. Paesler. 2005. "Building a Treatment Mall: a First Step in Moving a State Hospital to a Culture of Rehabilitation and Recovery." *Behavioral Therapy* 29: 71–8.

CHAPTER 16

Violence Risk and Forensic Practice: The Case of Preventive Detention

Alec Buchanan

Forensic psychiatrists assess and treat people whose mental disorders have led to their posing a risk of harm to others. Some of those people are the clients of psychiatric outpatient services and are living in the community. Others are detained in secure hospitals and prisons. The detention of many of the patients in secure hospitals in the U.S. has been authorized by the criminal courts. For others, the authority for their detention is "civil" and unrelated to criminal charges. Whatever the administrative mechanism, detention has usually been justified in whole or in part by reference to the risk that the individual poses to other people.

In the criminal justice system, using the risk of harm to others as a justification for restricting someone's liberty, for instance in assessing for bail or parole, is routine. It involves balancing not just harms but also risks of harms. The risk of harm to others has to be balanced against the harm that is inherent in depriving someone of their liberty. The harms deriving from violence have both short- and long-term aspects and extend beyond the immediate victim to the victims' families and the perpetrators. The harms involved in restricting a person's liberty are both material and abstract. Outside mental health, incarcerating some people to prevent harm to others is known as preventive detention.

When people are detained as part of their mental health treatment the situation is more complicated still. While managing the risk of harm to other people is an essential part of psychiatry, the primary task of mental health services is to provide care to an individual (Buchanan and Grounds 2011). The usual reason to admit someone to a psychiatric hospital is to facilitate this care. In some instances where someone's mental disorder leads them to pose a risk to others it is impossible to manage that risk, and hence adequately to address that person's clinical needs, in the community. Inpatient services, including secure inpatient services, exist in part to meet those needs.

These two functions of secure psychiatric hospitals, providing care to patients and preventing harm to others, have always been subject to conflicting social pressures. In the twentieth century patient advocates and civil rights campaigners pointed to the inappropriateness of many patients' placements in long-stay psychiatric hospitals and to the poor quality of the care that patients received there. The resulting pressure on policy makers contributed to the closure of large numbers of inpatient beds on both sides of the Atlantic. The extended lengths of stay of the relatively few remaining inpatients in secure psychiatric hospitals remain a focus of criticism.

At the same time, public, political, and press concern over psychiatric patient violence means that it is often difficult for patients who have acted violently to move from the hospital into the community, even when there are services to treat them there. While most clients of psychiatric services do not act violently and while suicide remains a greater risk than homicide, a small number of people with mental disorders present very significant risks of violence to others. Calls for "outpatient commitment" laws mandating treatment in the community for patients who present a risk of harm are one consequence of these concerns (Swanson, Swartz, and Mosely in press).

These conflicting pressures present psychiatrists with a dilemma from which improved violence risk assessment holds out the prospect of an escape. Instead of simply steering a middle course between the Scylla of long inpatient stays in psychiatric units that are increasingly unsuited to being homes for patients as well as places for treatment and the Charybdis of over-hasty discharge of patients with a history of violence, the hope is that clinicians will increasingly be able to distinguish those at greatest risk of acting violently and tailor discharge plans accordingly.

To the extent that violence risk assessment is up to the task, the majority of patients can then be rapidly discharged without the risk of their acting violently to other people because the "risky" patients will have been identified and kept in the hospital. Mental health services now make increasing use of risk assessment technology. This technology includes instruments consisting of structured interviews and rating scales. The use of these instruments is now supported by a large number of research studies showing better than random ability to predict violence. Some of the structured interviews and rating scales used in psychiatry are similar to approaches that were developed and remain in use in criminal justice.

Psychiatrists are obliged to put the needs of patients first. This distinguishes their work from that of the criminal justice system. Some aspects of the psychiatric management of violence risk nevertheless have parallels in criminal justice. The weighing of one form of harm against another, for instance, and the weighing of a risk of future harm (such as violence) against an actual, present harm (such as restricting a potential perpetrator's freedom), are features of risk management that are common to both systems. This chapter will review the experience of preventive detention on both sides of the Atlantic. It seeks to identify lessons from that experience for forensic psychiatry.

PREVENTIVE DETENTION AND CRIMINAL JUSTICE: ANGLO-AMERICAN PRACTICE

In 1895 the Gladstone Committee on Prisons concluded in respect of persistent offenders in England and Wales that "to punish them for the particular offence in which they are detected is almost useless." The Committee recommended segregating this group from the rest of the prison population. Persistent offenders would no longer be subjected to those aspects of prison life, such as hard labor and penal servitude, that were most clearly identified with punishment. They would, however, be imprisoned for longer. The Prevention of Crime Act that followed in 1908 provided for a "habitual criminal" to be sentenced to between five and ten years of imprisonment in addition to what he or she would have been sentenced to for the crime committed (see Advisory Council on the Treatment of Offenders 1963).

The government had made clear that the Act was intended to address the "persistent dangerous criminal" and not offenders who were merely "a nuisance rather than a danger to society" (see Forrester 2002). Yet between 1908 and 1911 it became apparent that the police in England and Wales, in presenting cases for indictment as habitual criminals, had developed their own interpretations of these terms and were presenting offenders for whom preventive detention had not been intended. At the end of that period further instructions were issued to the police that they should not present people for indictment under the new law unless they were over thirty and their offense had been "substantial and serious."

Fewer than 1,000 people were sentenced to preventive detention in the UK under the Prevention of Crime Act between 1909 and 1930. In addition to the newly introduced age restriction, judges seem to have regarded the new preventive sentences of between five and ten years made possible by the Act as too long. A government bill that provided an alternative preventive sentence of two to four years was never enacted, however. Concerns remained among politicians, if not among the judiciary, that extended preventive detention was necessary for three types of criminal: the "professional criminal" who lived by preying on the public, those who perpetrated fraud on the poor, and sexual offenders. The 1948 Criminal Justice Act permitted preventive sentences ranging from five to fourteen years, but addressed concerns over abuse by again restricting their use to defendants over thirty.

The principal criterion for a judge to address was whether it was "expedient for the protection of the public" that the offender be detained in custody for a substantial time. Supporters of the legislation intended to limit judicial discretion and, in particular, to address the judiciary's practice of reserving long sentences for the most serious crimes. The numbers sentenced to preventive detention increased but remained low; 261 defendants received such sentences in 1961. Psychiatric research conducted at the time suggested that the majority of detainees were "of the passive-inadequate type, feckless and ineffective in every sphere, who regard the commission of crime as a means of escaping immediate difficulties rather than a part of a deliberately antisocial way of life" (Advisory Council on the Treatment of Offenders 1963, para. 21). Few were found to be "of the seriously violent or aggressive type of personality."

The English experience of preventive detention was later reviewed by Brody and Tarling (1980). The authors concluded:

> The infrequency of really serious crimes of violence, their apparently generally random quality and the rarity of anything like a genuinely "dangerous type" offers little encouragement for a policy which aims to reduce serious assaults by selective incapacitation of those with violent records. (37)

Preventive detention in England and Wales was abolished by the Criminal Justice Act of 1967. Although in the years that followed it remained possible for courts to pass an "extended sentence" for certain persistent offenders, this legal provision was little used (Radzinowicz and King 1977).

On the continent of Europe, however, preventive detention had been used widely throughout this period. There the usual sentencing model followed a dual system where a period of punishment for what had been done was followed by a further period explicitly for the purpose of preventing future crime. In theory the second part of the sentence, because it was not designed for the purposes of punishment, was served under less exacting conditions. In the 1970s this was described by an Austrian academic quoted by Radzinowicz and King as an "Etikettenschwindel": a fraudulent trade description. An Italian detainee, moved from prison to an institution for preventive detention, commented, "I see no difference: the minestrone is just the same" (Radzinowicz and King 1977, 211).

In the United States, an array of "sexual psychopath" statutes aimed at dealing with "habitual offenders" by means of indeterminate sentences emerged in the first half of the twentieth century. By the 1970s here also, however, skepticism over the ability to diagnose dangerousness accurately and the possibility of medically curing criminal propensities had led to these statutes falling out of use. In recent years America's ongoing "wars" against terrorism and sex offenders have again seen the widespread use of preventive detention (Janus 2009; Yung 2010). Arguments that the detention of sex offenders should not count as preventive detention because they are receiving treatment have gained little traction outside the U.S. Supreme Court. Of over 3,000 people detained since 1990, only fifty had been released by 2012 (Schwab 2012).

In the last thirty years the legitimacy of incapacitation as a justification for imprisonment has been challenged by the "Just Deserts" movement, which emphasizes the role of retribution in sentencing. A number of U.S. states have nevertheless adopted "habitual offender" laws (White 2006; Sampsell-Jones 2010) that extend the period of imprisonment for repeat offenders beyond what would otherwise be warranted by their crime. Imposing consecutive rather than concurrent sentences on the basis of a defendant's past criminal record, a practice that achieves the same effect, is now commonplace (Allen and Laudan 2011). And dangerousness is taken into account in parole decisions. Although these measures are not labeled preventive detention, public policy continues to permit the widespread incarceration of convicted individuals beyond the period that the nature of their crime would otherwise permit.

Not infrequently, forensic psychiatrists are involved in risk assessment for the criminal courts (Buchanan and Norko 2011). This is the case both in the U.S. and internationally. Norval Morris (1994) wrote of what he regarded as a paradox:

> The psychiatric literature and the official statements of the organized profession of psychiatry stress the unreliability of psychiatric predictions while the courts increasingly rely on those same predictions by individual psychiatrists despite their admittedly prejudicial impact—an impact certainly greater than is justified by their validity. (244)

In 2016 the pressure on forensic psychiatrists to produce estimates of risk for both criminal justice and mental health purposes shows little sign of diminishing.

PREVENTIVE DETENTION AND CRIMINAL JUSTICE: CRITICISM AND CONTROVERSY

Questions concerning efficacy

Criminal justice theorists can be utilitarian or retributivist in outlook and the way in which they approach preventive detention differs. To a utilitarian, protecting the public by incapacitating those who have shown themselves likely to cause harm to other people is a legitimate purpose of criminal sentencing. Detention of a likely future perpetrator can contribute to doing the greatest good for the greatest number. To a pure retributivist, punishment should be allocated solely by reference to what the person has done, not what they might do in the future. The prevention of crime may be a useful by-product of imprisoning people but in a retributive scheme cannot be the justification for doing so.

In noting the limits on our ability to predict violence, Morris had argued that the term of punishment should not be extended by virtue of a prediction of dangerousness beyond that which could be justified as a deserved punishment in the absence of such a prediction. One potential corollary to this is that people who are detained for the protection of others, as opposed to those who are detained as punishment, should be detained in conditions better than prison. A more radical suggestion is that they should be financially compensated (Corrado 1996; Frankel 1970).

Avoiding utilitarian justifications for punishing people, however, does not prevent longer sentences for all repeat offenders. To some retributivists, prior crimes make the present offense more serious because the defendant can no longer claim his behavior was out of character. This can lead to these retributivists arriving at the same outcome as utilitarians, but for different reasons. While utilitarians would lengthen the sentence because prior criminality increases risk, these retributivists would do the same because repetition implies increased blameworthiness (for a discussion, see Duff 2001). Other retributivists have advocated alternative, civil processes when it is sought to prevent future acts of violence and the present offense is not serious enough to warrant incarceration (Robinson 2008).

However imposed and whatever the justification, preventive detention is less palatable when it is less discriminating. The degree to which it will be considered acceptable to detain some people for the protection of others will depend, in part, on the ratio of the number of people who have to be detained to the number of crimes prevented. Whatever approach is taken to the assessment of risk, the group who are detained will include a number of people, typically labeled "false positives," who would not have done the thing that detention was intended to prevent but who will have been detained alongside those who would have.

Attempts to establish how many such people any given approach to the prediction of violence will generate quickly run into methodological problems. One can never know whether an individual who has been detained would have committed a crime. Official statistics on crime are problematic because most crimes do not lead to conviction and high-rate offenders may be less prone to arrest and conviction than other offenders. Self-reports of criminal activity are subject to sampling biases and to offenders under-reporting for fear of the consequences of revealing illegal behavior, despite researchers' reassurances to the contrary (for a review, see Spelman 1994).

In addition, differences in sentencing policy across countries affect the way preventive detention is administered and make international comparisons very difficult. An "enhanced" sentence for burglary under Dutch law is comparable to the default sentence in the United States (Lochner 2010). It may be that many U.S. jurisdictions already benefit from the incapacitating effect of longer sentences without calling this preventive detention. Finally, the ratio of cost to benefit can be expressed using a range of different statistics, not all of which are straightforward for non-statisticians to understand.

The most convincing evidence for the efficacy of preventive detention emerges from studies where laws focus on particular crimes and particular groups. A "habitual offender" law adopted in the Netherlands in 2001 permitted a two- to three-year prison sentence for people with ten or more offenses (Vollard 2011). Although those sentenced under the law accounted for only 5% of the prison population, the rates of car theft and burglary fell by 40%. Evidence for preventive detention reducing the overall crime rate is much weaker. Testing of one method of predicting criminal offending suggested that a 20% reduction in the overall crime rate could be achieved only by sentencing all predicted high-rate offenders, including those convicted of non-serious offences, to prison terms of ten to twenty years (Spelman 1986).

Even this estimate, however, did not take into account that most convicted criminals commit fewer crimes as they get older. Preventive detention is often applied at a point in people's criminal careers when their rates of offending would have been declining anyway. When one group of researchers adjusted their model to assume an average criminal career of four to ten years, the projected decline in the number of robberies dropped to between 0.5 and

3.7% (Spelman 1986, Visher 1986). A different risk assessment scale, tested using different statistics, succeeded in explaining only 20% of the variance in reoffending and assigned only 45% of subjects to the correct (low, medium, or high) risk group (Greenwood 1982).

Questions concerning values

False positives, methodological problems related to the measurement of offending and the difficulty of describing the size of any effect are not the only hurdles in creating a system of preventive detention. It is also the case that no agreed method has emerged to ascribe value to the different variables. Detaining five people who would not have committed an offense is clearly a form of harm. But if preventive detention requires balancing, there has to be some agreement about how much harm detention causes. And preventing a serious act of violence presumably justifies more false positives than preventing a theft. How many more false positives does it justify? What false positive rate should be accepted?

These are judgments that require the application of moral values and the balancing of those values against each other. Being at liberty and safe from harm are things that different people seem willing to pay different amounts for (see Mossman and Hart 1993). It seems unlikely that any explicit algorithm could be agreed upon that would work in all difficult cases. On the other hand, saying that it is difficult to know what should be done with a prediction of violence is very different from saying that it is so difficult to know that there is never a reason to act on the prediction. In addition, preventive detention is in widespread use, albeit not always by that name. If these judgments are already being made, it seems preferable that they be made explicitly.

One infrequently studied approach to the problem of integrating the facts and values at play in any decision regarding preventive detention asks, "What would we say to a future victim who asks why the perpetrator was at large?" (see Duff 2001, 170–4). Duff is reluctant to see those committing nonviolent offenses detained to prevent future crimes and notes the unreliability of prediction. But he notes also that there are some who persistently commit serious assaults. What we could say to a future victim should depend, he argues, on several considerations. Among these are the safeguards attaching to preventive detention, the rights accorded to the person thus detained and the persistence of the perpetrator's future offending. Asking what we would say to a future victim puts the focus not just on empirical evidence but also on the values at issue.

The previous section suggested that the history of preventive detention is not the history of a rigorous search for a mathematical algorithm that will achieve the greatest good at the lowest possible cost. Instead, preventive detention has usually been directed inconsistently and with little advance evaluation of the likely effects. The history of its use suggests also that it has usually been more acceptable when those detained are seen as undesirable in ways unrelated to the risk that they pose. Foote's criticism of preventive detention was that it could only work if society was prepared to relegate to "second class citizenship" the group of people in which the false positives would fall (Foote 1970).

This is because the value judgments necessary to operate a system of preventive detention require placing a value on the rights of those being detained. It has been argued that the responses to the two most significant acts of terrorism in the United States in the past twenty-five years show that the rights of some groups of the population have been undervalued and that, as a result, those groups have been relegated to Foote's second class citizenship.

Timothy McVeigh's bombing of a federal building in Oklahoma City in 1995 was, at the time it was committed, the most serious act of terrorism in the history of the United States. McVeigh was not a militia member but attended militia meetings. He hoped to inspire a revolt against what he believed to be a tyrannical federal government. McVeigh's crime prompted some narrowing of the law of habeas corpus (through the Antiterrorism and Effective Death Penalty Act of 1996) but no significant use of preventive detention. The attack on the World Trade Center in New York in 2001, on the other hand, was followed by the detention of 5,000 foreign nationals in the United States over the following two years. Those detained were overwhelmingly Arab by ethnicity and Muslim by faith (see Cole 2009).

There are several possible explanations for why only one of these crimes was followed by widespread preventive detention. The first is that while no legal mechanism existed to detain militia supporters, legislation permitting the detention of foreign nationals in the United States was already in place in the wake of the World Trade Center attacks. A second possibility is that Islamic terrorists were seen by those implementing the policy as less capable of being deterred from conducting further attacks, a widely invoked justification for preventive detention in other situations (see Slobogin 2003–4).

A third possibility, however, relates to evidence that Arab and Muslim people were seen differently at the time many were being detained. Surveys in 2001 showed that even in areas of high illegal immigration from Central and South America, Arab immigrants elicited more prejudicial attitudes than immigrants from Mexico (Hitlan et al. 2007). It may be that those detained following the World Trade Center attacks were vulnerable because they belonged to an identifiable minority who were perceived negatively by the majority of the population. Preventive detention becomes more palatable when those detained are seen as "other" (Vars 2014, 3).

PREVENTIVE DETENTION AND FORENSIC PSYCHIATRY

The technological challenges facing those trying to reduce the numbers of false-positive errors are similar in psychiatry and the criminal justice system. The proportion of all of those detained that are false positives will depend, in part, on the quality of risk assessment. A risk assessment method that distinguished perfectly those who would be violent from those who would not would reduce the false positive rate to zero. The various approaches to risk assessment that are currently available, however, share similar, unspectacular, levels of accuracy: better than chance but much less than perfect. Because they have similar levels of accuracy, the number of false positives is not greatly affected by the choice of which one to use (see Buchanan 2008).

Instead, the principal source of variation in the number of false positives is the base rate of offending in the population as a whole. Over any given period, preventive detention where the base rate is 9.5% requires the detention of five false positives to prevent one crime (Buchanan and Leese 2001). This "number needed to detain" (NND) rises increasingly rapidly as the rate of the behavior that is sought to be prevented falls (see Figure 16.1). At the six-month prevalence of assault with a weapon or causing serious injury in the CATIE study the NND is 15. For every correct prediction of homicide in psychosis, one informed estimate is that there would be 2,000 false positives (Szmukler 2000).

In several respects, however, mental health is different. One difference was referred to in the introduction. In mental health, detention is not purely or even, in most cases, even partially justified by reference to the prevention of violence against other people. Instead, it is justified almost always by reference to the person's own interests, principally their health and safety. An NND of 15 may be unacceptable when that detention amounts to confinement and little more. But if detention involves and is justified by the provision of treatment, whether medical or psychological, rehabilitation and transfer to lower levels of restriction as someone's condition improves, the term "false positive" starts to appear something of a misnomer. Many people who are false positives in terms of whether they commit an offence will be "true positives" in terms of needing care and treatment.

The second reason that mental health is different is that the days when psychiatry was in a position to detain a large number of people ended with the closure of the large mental hospitals. The associated decline in inpatient bed

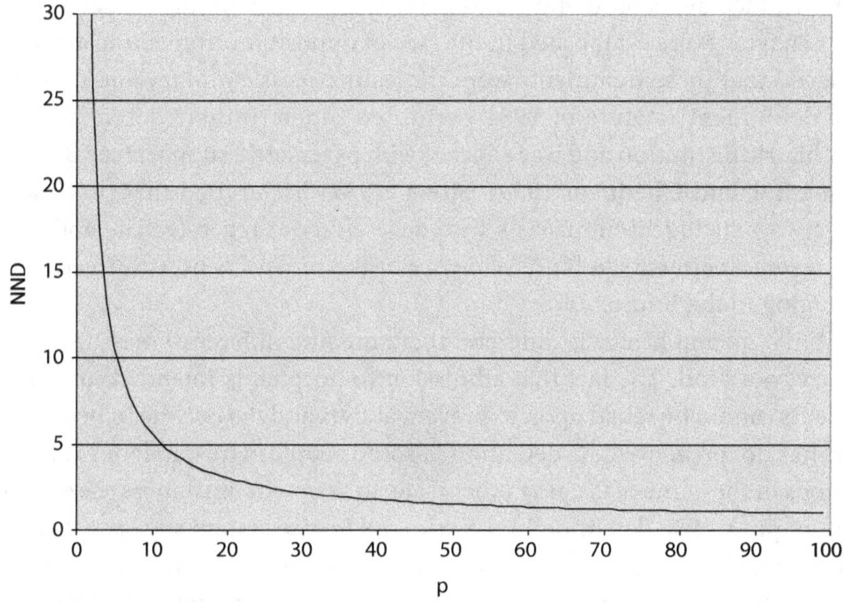

FIGURE 16.1 Relationship between Number Needed to Detain (NND) and prevalence (p) when sensitivity = 0.73 and specificity = 0.63. See Buchanan, *Psychiatric Services* (2008) 59: 184

numbers in the second half of the twentieth century was profound, on both sides of the Atlantic. Concern that the process had been taken too far may have contributed to the relative preservation of forensic inpatient services, particularly since 2000 (see Buchanan 2009). But the relative preservation of beds in forensic services notwithstanding, concern remains that there are now insufficient places for people whose illnesses leave them unable to lead independent lives and who, at times, pose a risk to others.

Each of these reasons why mental health is different requires qualification, however. Both qualifications suggest that the lessons of preventive detention in the criminal justice system have relevance to psychiatry. First, the relative preservation of forensic inpatient services, and its expansion as a proportion of the total psychiatric inpatient estate, suggests that psychiatry's role in detaining people for the protection of others has persisted even as its ability to provide inpatient care for those incapable of living independently has declined. Second, the fact that psychiatric detention is supposed to be for the benefit of the patient has not prevented past abuses.

Psychiatry's involvement with public safety in the United States has at times led to "warehousing," not treatment. Patients' right to refuse treatments that included aversion therapy and psychosurgery, often directed at antisocial behavior, were established in the face of opposition from clinicians who believed that these treatments were clinically necessary. Maryland's "defective delinquent" statute of 1951 permitted indeterminate detention in a psychiatric institution and was enacted with psychiatric support (see Boslow, Rosenthal, and Gliedman 1959). Stone (1984) has argued that psychiatry has always included enthusiasts who have either exaggerated the ability of its present treatments to "cure" violence or the prospects of such treatments emerging in the future.

While mental health is different, therefore, the difference may be one of degree, not kind. The fact that admission to hospital is intended to benefit patients cannot be relied upon to prevent abuses and the decline in bed numbers has not prevented the detention of some people in hospital for extended periods in the name of keeping others safe. In these circumstances the experience of preventive detention in the criminal justice system suggests that the way in which those being detained are perceived by the public, by the courts and by society as a whole will be crucial to the ways in which risk of harm to others is managed through detention in hospital. Psychiatric patients seem vulnerable to inappropriate detention by virtue of both their "otherness" and "undeterrability."

With regard to "otherness," one U.S. critic notes that preventive detention threatens an important libertarian message of the criminal law: if you obey the law, your liberty is secure. Civil commitment of persons with mental illness does not challenge this message because they are different:

> The condition of illness is the significant symbolic and ideological distinction, the jurisdictional condition which makes commitments of the mentally ill socially tolerable … the notion of illness is a distinguishing factor which serves to assure most people that they are not subject to being incarcerated; they believe that only those who are ill are subject to such restraint (Frankel 1970, 54).

The power of Frankel's "notion of illness" may account for the different ways in which homosexuality was treated by the law in the twentieth century.

Between the 1930s and 1960s "sexual psychopath" statutes, described in an earlier section of this chapter, permitted the detention in psychiatric institutions of people committed of certain classes of sexual offenses (see also the Introduction and Chapter 11). These statutes operated in twenty-nine U.S. states and the District of Columbia. Although they had usually been passed in reaction to notorious cases of sexual assault, they were applied to other cases also (Miller 2009; George 2015). In Michigan in the 1940s, noting that a risk to children should be "gravely considered" despite not finding evidence of pedophilia, two psychiatrists diagnosed sexual psychopathy in the case of a man arrested in a consensual homosexual act (see *People v. Chapman* 1942). Consensual homosexuality was the reason given for the detention of over 7% of persons detained in Nebraska between 1949 and 1956 (Caporale and Hamann 1957). By the time a second wave of sex offender commitment statutes emerged in the 1980s, on the other hand, consensual homosexual acts were less likely to be regarded as abnormal and had been removed from the usual systems of psychiatric classification. Consensual homosexuality was no longer used as a reason to detain.

Clients of psychiatric services are often described in the literature of jurisprudence as less amenable to deterrence. "Less susceptible to the force of reason," one reviewer has noted, "the mentally ill are less able to modify their behavior in response to the threat of criminal sanction" (Vars 2014, 21). There are no reliable data to this effect, however, and as a generalization it seems vulnerable (Morse 1982). People with psychoses can adhere to a set of values that reduce the deterrent effect of the law, but so do terrorists and gang members. People suffering from severe depression have symptoms that could be termed "impaired volition," but research suggests that drug users and drunk drivers do also. The notion of the "undeterrability" remains a powerful one, however, and has been used to justify the detention and compulsory supervision of criminal defendants with mental illness (see Slobogin 2012).

CONCLUSION

The role of risk assessment in criminal justice has changed over the past thirty years. From the end of the eighteenth century, Anglo-American criminal law had traditionally focused on the offender. The origins of crime were assumed to lie in his personality and the social conditions in which he lived (see Garland 1985). Today, whether the question relates to a security level, to a defendant's suitability for a non-custodial sentence or to the required level of monitoring of defendants, this focus on the individual is being replaced by an emphasis on groups, categories, and classes.

The techniques of risk assessment that the criminal justice system uses have evolved in line with this change in role. They have increasingly come to emphasize statistically selected risk factors that allow the allocation of an individual to a group or class. Over the same three decades, a "populist punitiveness," whereby politicians compete to provide ever more severe responses to criminal behavior, has been antipathetic to approaches, including medical ones, which seek to understand behavior and help people to change it.

One consequence in criminal justice has been increased rates of detention. One critic has argued in relation to statutes for the preventive detention of sex-offenders:

> The goal is waste management. Populist punitiveness is exceedingly hostile toward medicalization. The result is an important transformation of the sex offender from the most obvious example of crime as disease back to an earlier conception of crime as monstrosity. (Simon 1998, 456).

Instead of focusing on the offender, the aim has become the identification and isolation of what the U.S. Supreme Court, quoting the Kansas statute, described as "a small but exceedingly dangerous group" (see *Kansas v. Hendricks* 1997, 2077).

A 1999 Surgeon General's report noted that the stigma attached to mental illness had intensified over the past forty years (U.S. Department of Health and Human Services 1999). Since the report was published there has been no decrease in stigma, despite improved understanding of the causes of mental illness (Pescosolido et al. 2010). Public reaction may be driven in part by the continuing presence on the streets of towns and cities of large numbers of untreated and often homeless people suffering from mental illness (see Sharfstein 2012). But whatever their source, perceptions affect the way in which people with mental illness are treated.

Forensic psychiatry is engaged in the care of people who are detained in hospitals in order to prevent harm to others. Experience in the criminal justice system suggests that in addition to any risk they present, the way in which people are perceived is an important determinant of whether they will be detained, and for how long. Those who are seen as different from other people and as less amenable to being deterred by criminal sanctions have traditionally been particularly vulnerable. Forensic psychiatrists are responsible for ensuring not only that the risk posed by an individual is properly assessed, but also that stigma does not unnecessarily impede that person's treatment, discharge and community rehabilitation.

REFERENCES

Advisory Council on the Treatment of Offenders. 1963. *Report*. London: Her Majesty's Stationery Office.

Allen, R. and L. Laudan. 2011. "Deadly Dilemmas III: Some Kind Words for Preventive Detention." *Journal of Criminal Law and Criminology* 101: 781–802.

Boslow, H., D. Rosenthal, and L. Gliedman. 1959. "The Maryland Defective Delinquency

Law: Psychiatric Implications for the Treatment of Antisocial Disorders Under the Law." *British Journal of Delinquency* 10: 5–13.

Brody, S. and R. Tarling. 1980. *Taking Offenders out of Circulation. Home Office Research Study No. 64.* London: Her Majesty's Stationery Office.

Buchanan, A. 2008. "Risk of Violence by Psychiatric Patients: Beyond the 'Actuarial Versus Clinical' Assessment Debate." *Psychiatric Services* 59: 184–90.

———. 2009. "The Development of Out-Patient Services for Mentally Disordered Offenders in the United States and United Kingdom." *Japanese Journal of Forensic Mental Health* 4: 23–36.

Buchanan, A. and A. Grounds. 2011. "Forensic Psychiatry and Public Protection." *British Journal of Psychiatry* 198: 420–3.

Buchanan, A., and M. Leese. 2001. "Detention of People with Dangerous Severe Personality Disorders." *Lancet* 358: 1955–9.

Buchanan, A. and M. Norko. 2011. "Violence Risk Assessment." In *The Psychiatric Report*, edited by A. Buchanan and M. Norko, pp. 224–39. Cambridge: Cambridge University Press.

Caporale, D. and D.F. Hamann. 1957. "Sexual Psychopathy—a Legal Labyrinth of Medicine, Morals and Mythology." *Nebraska Law Review* 36: 320–53.

Cole, R. 2009. Out of the Shadows: Preventive Detention, Suspected Terrorists, and War. *California Law Review* 97: 693–750.

Corrado, M. 1996. "Punishment and the Wild Beast of Prey: The Problem of Preventive Detention." *Journal of Criminal Law and Criminology* 86: 778–814.

Duff, R. 2001. *Punishment, Communication and Community.* Oxford: Oxford University Press.

Foote, C. 1970. "Comments on Preventive Detention." *Journal of Legal Education* 23: 48–53.

Forrester, A. 2002. "Preventive Detention, Public Protection and Mental Health." *Journal of Forensic Psychiatry* 13: 329–44.

Frankel, L. 1970. "Comments on Preventive Detention." *Journal of Legal Education* 23: 53–6.

Garland, D. 1985. *Punishment and Welfare: A History of Penal Strategies.* Aldershot: Gower.

George, M. 2015. "The Harmless Psychopath: Legal Debates Promoting the Decriminalization of Sodomy in the United Sates." *Journal of the History of Sexuality* 24: 225–61.

Greenwood, P. 1982. *Selective Incapacitation.* Santa Monica: Rand.

Hitlan R., K. Carrillo, M. Zárate and S. Aikman. 2007. "Attitudes toward Immigrant Groups and the September 11 Terrorist Attacks." *Peace and Conflict. Journal of Peace Psychology* 13: 135–52.

Janus, E. 2009. *Failure to Protect. America's Sexual Predator Laws and the Rise of the Preventive State.* New York: Cornell University Press.

Kansas v. Hendricks, 117 S.Ct. 2072 (1997).

Lochner, L. 2010. *Education Policy and Crime.* NBER Working Paper No. 15894. Cambridge MA.

Miller, N. 2009. *Sex Crime Panic: A Journey to the Paranoid Heart of the 1950s*. Alyson: New York.

Morris, N. 1994. "'Dangerousness' and Incapacitation." In *A Reader on Punishment*, edited by R. Duff and D. Garland, pp. 241–60. Oxford: Oxford University Press.

Morse, S. 1982. "A Preference for Liberty: The Case Against Involuntary Commitment of the Mentally Disordered." *California Law Review* 70: 54–106.

Mossman, D. and K. Hart. 1993. "How Bad Is Civil Commitment? A Study of Attitudes Toward Violence and Involuntary Hospitalization." *Bulletin of the American Academy of Psychiatry and the Law* 21: 181–94.

People v. Chapman, 301 Mich 584 (1942).

Pescosolido, B., J. Martin, J. Long, T. Medina, J. Phelan, and B. Link. 2010. "'A Disease Like Any Other'? A Decade of Change in Public Reactions to Schizophrenia, Depression, and Alcohol Dependence." *American Journal of Psychiatry* 167: 1321–330.

Radzinowicz, L. and J. King. 1977. *The Growth of Crime*. London: Hamish Hamilton.

Robinson, P. 2008. *Distributive Principles of Criminal Law*. Oxford: Oxford University Press.

Sampsell-Jones, T. 2010. "Preventive Detention, Character Evidence and the New Criminal Law." *Utah Law Review* 3: 723–77.

Schwab, J. 2012. "Note. Due Process and 'the Worst of the Worst': Mental Competence in Sexually Violent Predator Commitment Proceedings." *Columbia Law Review* 112: 912–50.

Sharfstein, S. 2012. "Status of Stigma." *Psychiatric Services* 63: 953.

Simon, J. 1998. "Managing the Monstrous." *Psychology, Public Policy and Law* 4: 452–67.

Slobogin, C. 2003–4. "A Jurisprudence of Dangerousness." *Northwestern University Law Review* 98: 1–62.

———. 2012. *Preventive Detention in Europe, the United States and Australia*. Vanderbilt University Law School. Public Law and Legal Theory Working Paper Number 12-27. Available at http://papers.ssrn.com/sol3/papers.cfm?abstract_id=2094358.

Spelman, W. 1986. *The Depth of a Dangerous Temptation: Another Look at Selective Incapacitation*. Cambridge: Harvard Law School.

———. 1994. *Criminal Incapacitation*. New York: Plenum.

Stone, A. 1984. *Law, Psychiatry and Morality*. Washington, DC: American Psychiatric Press.

Swanson J., M. Swartz, and D. Mosely. In press. "Understanding Outpatient Commitment in Context: When Is It Ethical and How Can We Tell?" In *Care of the Mentally Disordered Offender in the Community*. 2nd ed., edited by A. Buchanan, L. Wootton. Oxford: Oxford University Press.

Szmukler, G. 2000. "Homicide Inquiries. What sense do they make?" *Psychiatric Bulletin* 24: 6–10.

U.S. Department of Health and Human Services 1999. *Mental Health: A Report of the Surgeon General*. Rockville, MD: U.S. Department of Health and Human Services, Substance Abuse and Mental Health Services Administration, Center for Mental Health Services, National Institutes of Health, National Institute of Mental Health.

Vars, F. 2014. "Fear of an Undeterrable Other." *Louisiana Law Review* 75: 1–28.

Visher, C. 1986. "The Rand Second Inmate Survey: A Reanalysis." In *Criminal Careers and "Career Criminals", Volume 2*, edited by A. Blumstein, J. Cohen, J. Roth and C. Visher, pp. 161–211. Washington, DC: National Academy of Sciences.

Vollard, B. 2011. *Preventing Crime Through Selective Incapacitation*. TILEC Discussion Paper DP 2011-001. Tilburg, Netherlands: Tilburg University.

White, A. 2006. "The Juridical Structure of Habitual Offender Laws and the Jurisprudence of Authoritarian Social Control." *University of Toledo Law Review* 37: 705–45.

Yung, C. 2010. "The Emerging Criminal War on Sex Offenders." *Harvard Civil Rights-Civil Liberties Law Review* 45: 435–81.

CHAPTER 17

The Mental Health System—Criminal Justice Interface Expanding Strategies for Therapeutic Jurisprudence

Madelon V. Baranoski

INTRODUCTION

Impetus for Change

Morning rush hour, a disheveled, street-worn man sits alone at a center table in the bustling coffee shop at the train station. As the line of morning commuter customers extends past his table, he taps one after another on the arm asking for change to buy coffee. A woman at another table gets up for more napkins; he grabs and gobbles her unfinished donut and drinks her coffee. Angry shouts for the manager punctuate the morning routine: "Get him out of here! Make him leave!" The out-of-place intruder shouts back; his gibberish and profanity frighten the customers who are left.

The police come, the man protests. He is arrested and locked up. At arraignment, he is sober but psychotic, incoherently asserting that he owns the town, that the judge will be punished, that he will bomb the court. He incurs another charge. The judge orders a competency to stand trial evaluation. He is found incompetent and sent for restoration to a state hospital. Two months later, he returns to court, reluctantly taking antipsychotic medication and adhering to courtroom protocol. He is released to the community, adjudication complete, at a cost of over $70,000 to the state. Less than two months later, in a different coffee shop, the situation is repeated.

This familiar scenario and the associated social and economic costs contributed to the national impetus to address what had become an untenable disconnection between the mental health access to service and the criminal justice system for persons with substantial mental illness who are not engaged in treatment and who disturb society. Different etiologies were proposed as the basis for the problem—deinstitutionalization, techno-urbanization, ease of access to drugs—but regardless of cause, available models for care and adjudication were inadequate to break the cycle of recidivism. Beginning in the 1980s, efforts that crossed boundaries between the mental health and criminal justice systems created new systems of services.

Strategies from therapeutic jurisprudence, the sequential intercept model, diversion programs, specialized courts, and specialized police programs have created new pathways for persons with mental illness. From mental health diversion programs, to mental health courts, to police interventions, programs crossed the usual boundaries among the mental health system, law enforcement, and the criminal justice system navigating the different purposes, regulations, and practices. These partnerships have been multidisciplinary; forensic psychiatry and psychology and social work have helped to define the issues and to shape the new and challenging interface between these systems. The changes have brought benefits, risks, and opportunities.

Diversionary programs have advanced from pilot initiatives into comprehensive frameworks that direct policy, research and treatment. In particular, the *sequential intercept model* proposed by Mark R. Munetz, M.D. and Patricia A. Griffin, Ph.D. (2006) provides a cogent and comprehensive analysis of intervention points from pre-arrest through prison release. In a thorough review of the development of diversionary programs, Munetz and colleagues describe the progression to an integrated model that identifies the "ultimate intercept—an accessible comprehensive effective mental health system focused on the needs of individuals with severe and persistent mental disorders—is undoubtedly the most effective means of preventing the criminalization of people with mental illness" (Munetz, Griffin, and Kemp in Yeager et al. 2013, 461). The underlying assumption in all of these programs is that treatment for persons with mental illness will be more effective than arrest, criminal adjudication, and incarceration.

Starting from the foundation of the inclusive and thorough descriptions of diversionary programs and their evolution well described by others (Munetz, Griffin, and Kemp in Yeager et al. 2013), this chapter examines the challenges of the mental health and legal partnership as well as the barriers to and risks in successful diversion. Finally it examines the emerging role for forensic psychiatry and psychology in mediation and policy development.

FROM DEINSTITUTIONALIZATION TO THE THERAPEUTIC GAP: THE CHALLENGE OF THE UNENGAGED

Deinstitutionalization has been proffered as the primary cause of the shift of psychiatric care from hospitals to prisons (Lamb and Weinberger 2005). The shift has been supported in many studies by examining the inverse correlations between number of psychiatric beds over time and the prevalence of mental illness among inmates. Lamb and Weinberger in 2005 described a decrease of 106% in psychiatric beds in the United States from 1955 through 2000 (from 339 beds per 100,000 populations to twenty-two beds per 100,000). During this same period, there has been an increase in prevalence of the mentally ill in prison (Lamb and Weinberger 2005).

In 1992, E. Fuller Torrey, noted psychiatrist and patient advocate, and his team published a report of state-by-state incarceration rates of persons with mental illness. The paper was intended as an indictment of the mental health system and its failure to effectively manage psychiatric patients in the community (Torrey et al. 1992):

> Clearly the fundamental flaw rests within public mental health services, the neglected and unwanted stepchild of American psychiatry, psychology, and psychiatric social work. (97)

Other professionals were equally critical of the mental health system. Legal advocates and consumer groups cited the widespread incarceration as a violation of civil rights and as failure to provide moral treatment of persons with mental illness. The term "criminalization of the mentally ill" became the shorthand reference to the inadequacies of the mental health system. Since then, the idea of *transinstitutionalization* has become a term of art referencing the failure of the system in the United States as the cause of a mass migration of persons from hospitals into prisons.

The research and clinical experience, however, indicate significantly more complicated circumstances. Indeed, the majority of persons with mental illness are never incarcerated. So the theoretical massive shift of the population of persons with mental illness from hospital to prison did not actually occur.

Deinstitutionalization through the laws that forced discharge of the hospitalized patients to the community, however, was a factor in the criminalization of the mentally ill; it created *the right to choose not to engage in treatment* and, in so doing, laid the foundation for an undertreated population vulnerable for arrest. The strict requirements for involuntary hospitalization of persons with mental illness (under *Baxstrom v. Herold*, in 1966—the United States Supreme Court decision requiring dangerousness for psychiatric commitment of inmates and state commitment laws) and the shift of management of psychiatric behaviors to families and the community created a *therapeutic gap—the lack of effective strategies and services for those with mental illness who are unengaged in and rejecting of treatment, who do not meet criteria for inpatient commitment, but whose function is too impaired to manage social demands in the community*. In the era of large psychiatric hospitals, patient choice in treatment was irrelevant; those with disruptive behaviors were removed psychiatrically, segregated into communities of their own. With deinstitutionalization, for those in the therapeutic gap, psychiatric services as usual are not sufficient for preventing arrest and incarceration.

Mental health and psychiatry have developed new approaches to service delivery specifically for those persons caught in the gap. Assertive Community Treatment Teams, for example, provide services to those who require intensive treatment and outreach beyond usual outpatient care. Pharmacological treatments have also improved, and the Recovery Movement has adopted expanded choice and self-determination, reframing expectations for those with mental illness.

All of these advances shrink the therapeutic gap. But many persons, particularly those with emerging mental illness and combinations of drug addictions, trauma, and social burdens, reject engagement or cannot access services. Anosognosia accounts for a significant number of persons with psychotic and mood disorders not seeking treatment and agreeing to medication (Torrey 2015; Orfei et al. 2007). For others, refusal to seek or remain in treatment or to comply with medication may be related to drug side effects, cost, and the remaining burdens of other social and human needs. Some may consider the cost-benefit analysis to be negative; relief of positive symptoms is only the first step toward productive adjustment and independent living. Housing, employment, social connections, fulfillment are still to be attained.

Not engaged in treatment, persons with mental illness manage; but when symptoms are manifest as disruptive behavior, the criminal justice system intervenes in the therapeutic gap with arrest and criminal adjudication. The criminal justice system becomes the default mediator representing society's interest even when the criminal magnitude is low. Once in the system, the synergy between mental illness and a criminal record magnifies the risk for recidivism and further marginalization.

Many other factors contribute to circumstances in which persons with mental illness get involved in the criminal justice system. The availability and adequacy of mental health services are among them, but even when services are available, social and personal instability from homelessness, unemployment, poverty, drugs, and pervasive marginalization impede engagement with services that could help. These factors have been well described. Often referred to as *criminogenic factors*, they are viewed as barriers to access to services, destabilizing factors, and sources of interpersonal chaos.

Resources to manage such personal and social burdens vary by community and by state. The lack of resources contributes to the therapeutic gap for persons with mental illness. When resources in a community are robust, however, persons' willingness and capacity to access them can still limit their effectiveness. People are free to refuse services as long as their suffering does not break a law or disrupt community life; when symptoms or distress cross that line, arrest follows and personal choice about accepting intervention ends. The intervention is a legal one. In the community, initiating, accepting, and participating in treatment require a personal buy-in; arrest, court involvement, and incarceration do not. Involvement in the criminal justice system is not voluntary, has no personal or financial eligibility requirements, and no waiting lists. These conditions make arrest a unique opportunity as a first entry or a re-entry into psychiatric treatment. Creative treatment strategies implemented in prison or in the community under court mandate are an opportunity to reduce the therapeutic gap.

CHANGE FROM PRISONS AND COURTS

In the United States, for decades following deinstitutionalization, options for treatment after arrest were limited to psychiatric services in prison when those services were available and when inmates accepted them. There were no mechanisms for referral to outpatient services under court supervision; psychiatric care and criminal adjudication were separated by law and practice. From a psychiatric perspective, the cycle of arrests and incarceration is iatrogenic and economically ineffective. From a consumer and family perspective, arrest and incarceration increase the burden and stigma of mental illness.

Misdemeanants with mental illness, however, also challenge the criminal justice system. Disruptive behavior in court and rapid and frequent recidivism even on minor charges block the judge's options for dispositions and strategies that judges can employ in a busy court. For example, in 1990 in a Connecticut survey, criminal court judges identified four challenges for dealing with "mentally ill misdemeanants": lack of access to assessment and services, risk to public, threat to civil liberties of the mentally ill." From the judges' point of view, "adjudicating persons with mental illness required new options" (Sturges and Baranoski 1997, 12–14).

Empirical evidence to drive change also came from the prevalence of mental illness among jail detainees and prison inmates. Rates between 6% through 24% have been reported in various studies since 1992—the wide variation in the reported prevalence relates to definitions of mental illness, sources of data, practices across states, and type of facility. Even the lowest estimates are greater than that reported in the general population. Even more relevant is the relationship between level of charge and presence of mental illness. In 2009, the Bureau of Prisons reported that among inmates, persons with mental illness were 2.7 times as likely as those with no mental illness to be misdemeanants, results that are consistent across studies (Torrey et al. 1992). Despite low-level charges, persons with mental illness require more services and often are not able to be assigned to usual programs focused on employment skills, education, and preparation for community re-entry. Persons with mental illness are often held in solitary confinement for disruptive behaviors and are at a greater risk for suicide (Metzner 2002; Hughes and Metzner 2015). Persons with untreated mental illness are also significantly more likely to recidivate than those who have access to treatment (McNeal and Binder 2007). In some reports examining the effects of mental illness and substance abuse combined, rates of re-arrest were three to four times greater than those with addiction alone (NAMI 2006).

The overall findings describe a group of persons falling through gaps in all systems, at great cost to the community and to the state. Despite at risk for being undertreated and ineffectively adjudicated, they are more expensive to manage in the health and criminal justice systems, the departments of correction, and their communities. The repeated cycling through arrest, emergency department visits, court appearances, and incarcerations is cost-ineffective, and counter-therapeutic. In states where competency evaluations and restoration apply in misdemeanor cases, the economic burden and therapeutic frustration are much higher.

COLLABORATION FOR CHANGE

The high cost and poor outcomes were powerful drivers of change and led to a partnership between systems that have different missions—the mental health system and the criminal justice system. In 1990, Steadman and colleagues established the National Coalition for the Mentally Ill in the Criminal Justice System (Steadman 1990b). It was the first collaboration among mental health, criminal justice, correction, and consumers that focused on how to divert persons with mental illness out of jail and into treatment.

What began as a cooperative exploration of common ground has developed into a myriad of strategies of collaboration, and sharing responsibility for and monitoring of persons with mental illness who are at risk for arrest or who do enter into the criminal justice system. Collectively termed diversionary programs have evolved into systems of interventions that forge new options for adjudication, for treatment, and for research.

Stakeholders and Common Ground

The Steadman Coalition and others like it initially focused on identifying stakeholders and common ground among them. Initial efforts to form productive partnerships were met with concerns about safety and disruption of community life. In Connecticut, one community expressed concerns about safety and requested a guarantee of "unfettered movement and convenience of citizens" before agreeing to participate in community meetings. The criminal justice and mental health systems also differed in their perception of persons with mental illness and arrests. Courts viewed persons with mental illness as revolving door defendants with frequent arrests, probation violations, and ineligible for alternative sentences and community services. Their initial preferred solution was long hospitalizations. Paradoxically, community mental health services were often out of the recidivism loop: arrest-incarceration-release-rearrest. When it occurred, the primary interface with the psychiatric system was through the emergency room if police brought arrestees in for an evaluation on the way to lock-up. Most mental health agencies were unaware of the magnitude of the problem: their patients were not getting arrested and those who were, were unlikely to have been treated. The agencies further worried about case findings that would overwhelm available services and personnel. The public viewed psychiatric patients as uniformly disruptive since their most memorable contact was related to the need to call police because someone was showing disruptive behavior. In the early meetings, consumers and families were reluctant to voice an opposing view for fear of being stigmatized and socially denigrated. The disparate views among the stakeholders indicated the extent of the therapeutic gap and the need for collaborative bridges across systems. Although common consensus was that the system was not working, collaboration among stakeholders was slow to develop. In lieu of system change and legislation, independent pilot projects emerged.

Boundary Spanners

One key role in forging and running these programs was the assignment of boundary spanners who understood the different systems involved (Steadman 1992). Boundary spanners were often social workers, attorneys, and in some cases wardens and police who provided liaison and trouble-shooting among the different agencies involved. They learned about the collaborating systems and working closely became the bridge that negotiated areas of conflict and concern. The most effective boundary spanners were those viewed as "insiders" by all systems, those who learned the professional jargons and routines that shaped the court, jail and mental health system in order to appreciate and address areas of concern. For example, in one diversionary program judges were afraid to allow persons in psychiatric crisis to go to the emergency department because they feared the hospital would release the person who would then be lost to court follow-up and put the community at risk. The boundary spanners, in this case a psychologist and psychiatric nurse, worked with both sides: they helped the hospital appreciate that the usual requirement for hospital admission (imminent risk of harm to self or other or grave disability) was too high a bar for the court that worried the discharged man would return to frightening persons in the local grocery. The spanners helped the court understand that law regulated involuntary hospitalization and that there were other levels of care that could help the man control his behavior. Using that one incident as a model, the spanners worked on a policy that allowed arrestees to be assessed at the hospital; but if the hospital was not going to admit, the court would be notified and the person brought back to court for a new disposition—diversion or jail. The plan allowed the most severely ill arrestees to be assessed at the hospital rather than being sent to jail and prevented an arrestee from falling back into the therapeutic gap—not needing hospitalization but still disruptive to the community. It also allowed the hospital to make clinical decisions about admission and not be forced to keep an arrestee who did not warrant hospitalization.

The role for boundary spanners was practical and productive but also raised issues of confidentiality, responsibilities, and risk management. What the early programs demonstrated was the need for policies that assured that collaboration did not erode the rights and the treatment of persons with mental illness. Examples of these issues are discussed below.

Boundary spanners brought more confidence in common ground among the courts, jails, and mental health agencies. Along with increasing pressure from consumer groups, diversionary programs emerged along two distinct pathways that share the common goal of treatment alternatives for those who are arrested. The first pathway was from the criminal justice system followed by the mental health system.

DIVERSION UNDER THE CRIMINAL JUSTICE SYSTEM: SPECIALIZED COURTS AND THERAPEUTIC JURISPRUDENCE

In the 1990s David Wexler, Ph.D. and Bruce Winick, Ph.D., professors of law at the University of Arizona and experts in mental health law, introduced the construct of therapeutic jurisprudence as a framework to acknowledge and study the impact that court decisions have on the well-being of defendants, families, and communities. They argued that legal decisions have broader effects than those recognized by the court as the fulfillment of justice:

> Therapeutic jurisprudence is the study of the effects of law and the legal system on the behavior, emotions, and mental health of people. It is a multidisciplinary examination of how law and mental health interact. According to this branch of jurisprudence, the processes used by courts, judicial officers, lawyers and other justice system personnel can impede, promote or be neutral in relation to outcomes connected with participant well-being such as respect for the justice system and the law, offender rehabilitation and addressing issues underlying legal disputes. (Wexler and Winick 1991, 981)

The concept has been expanded to include examination of the role of the court as a "problem solver," active in prevention and rehabilitation (Wexler 1990). Problem-solving courts fall under that rubric, although the first specialized courts existed long before declaration of the concept of therapeutic jurisprudence. Indeed, the earliest of these courts was the juvenile court in Chicago in 1889, which shifted focus from punitive adjudication to rehabilitation. The impetus came from religious leaders and child advocates who emphasized reform (Winick 2002).

More recent specialized courts include family courts, drug courts, domestic violence courts, community courts, and specialized treatment courts. What all specialized courts have in common are separate dockets with assigned judges and staff. Defendants who meet specific criteria appear before the court and receive alternative dispositions not usually available in the criminal court. In some cases prosecution is deferred; in others the defendant has to plead guilty. However, in no special court is the option of a trial available. And although rehabilitation and future adherence to the law is emphasized over the past wrongful behavior, the assumption of guilt is clear (Steadman, Morris, and Dennis 1995). Specialized courts emerge when a significant volume of types of cases is deemed underserved by usual practices (as with drug courts), or when societal pressures emphasize particular groups, as is the case with veterans' courts. Because not all legal options are available to the defendants, the ideal in specialized courts is to have very active preliminary legal representation available before the defendant decides to participate in the court docket.

Drug Courts

In 1989, the Dade County Miami criminal court established the first treatment court, a drug treatment docket (Bamberger 2002; Winick 2002). In Miami, judges noted that the court docket was clogged with nonviolent reoffenders on drug charges. The cycling through courts and jails was viewed as a failure of the system of justice that in part rests on personal deterrence. In the drug treatment court, defendants were given the opportunity to participate in treatment, with the judge as a member of the treatment team. Successful adherence to a set of conditions—compliance with urine testing, compliance with drug treatment, avoidance of arrests, and acceptance of extended court and probation monitoring—resulted in dropped charges and expunged records. The main objective of the court was reduction in recidivism.

The successful track record of drug courts in reducing recidivism, as most research shows (Spohn et al. 2001; Mitchell et al. 2012), supports its popularity. In 2000, just eleven years after the first drug treatment court started, over 600 drug courts operated in twenty-two states and by 2010, close to 1,600 such courts operated in thirty-nine states (Cooper 2001). Variations on the original model have included juvenile drug courts and drunk driving courts.

Mitchell and colleagues (Mitchell et al. 2012) conducted a meta-analysis of evaluations of drug courts for adults and juveniles. The results indicated that recidivism for adults going through drug court fell by half compared to those with similar offenses who did not participate in the program. For juveniles, however, there was no significant reduction in recidivism. The authors identify the need for further research to clarify factors associated with success and failure.

The findings are important to understand the complexity of substance abuse. Most drug courts exclude defendants with major mental illness (Hora 2002). In adolescents, drug use may be a symptom of emerging psychiatric disorder or may reflect a reaction to abuse or trauma. Success in drug courts is related to defendants' motivation to end addiction; the court enhances that motivation through positive reinforcement of the judges' involvement as well as the negative reinforcer of the potential for conviction and incarceration in the face of failure.

Mental Health Courts

In 1980 the first specialized court for persons with mental illness was created in Indianapolis, Indiana, by Judge Evan Dee Goodman in the Wishard

Memorial Hospital. The court combined probate hearings for civil commitment and a criminal docket for patients with mental illness charged with minor offenses. Except for a four-year hiatus from 1992 to 1996, the court has been in continuous operation (Goodale and Callahan 2013). The Indianapolis Court is one of a kind. In 1997, the first formal mental health court for misdemeanants began in Broward County, Florida (Petrila 2001). What made this court unique was the focus on defendants with mental illness arrested for minor crimes who were then committed to hospitals for treatment. Initially, upon release from the hospital, the defendants' court involvement was over. However, connected to therapy in the community, persons lost the therapeutic gains during inpatient stays, and criminal recidivism was common. The mental health court established a second court phase following defendants after discharge to encourage compliance with outpatient treatment, including taking medication. Although hospitalization was the most common first stop after arraignment, the discharged defendant was assigned to frequent court visits and extensive monitoring of their community treatment. The judge and court personnel are members of the interdisciplinary treatment team. The court's involvement serves as an external motivator to stay engaged as well as an external incentive to treaters to be creative in encouraging treatment.

A variety of mental health courts have evolved (National Criminal Justice Reference Service 1999). Almost all accept only misdemeanants and nonviolent offenders. They all include collaboration with mental health providers but many of the mental health courts employ their own social workers and contract for psychiatric services. The court oversees monitoring of substance use and of compliance with treatment; the judge receives reports from the providers. In many courts, the judge has face-to-face contact with the defendant, offering praise for adherence to the plan and stern encouragement when one falters. In some programs another arrest terminates participation and the defendant is referred to the criminal docket. In other mental health courts, re-arrests reset the program and lead to new assessments and higher levels of treatment and lengthens the period of monitoring. Some courts involve supervision by probation. With some variation in programming, mental health courts incorporate the "essential elements" defined by the Council of State Governments Justice Center: a specialized court docket with a problem-solving approach; judicial supervision of community-based treatment programs designed by court and mental health personnel, regular status hearings, and criteria defining completion or further adjudication (Thompson, Osher, and Tomasini-Joshi 2009).

Despite differences in programming, mental health courts harness treatment and medication as tools against recidivism, and in turn use the court

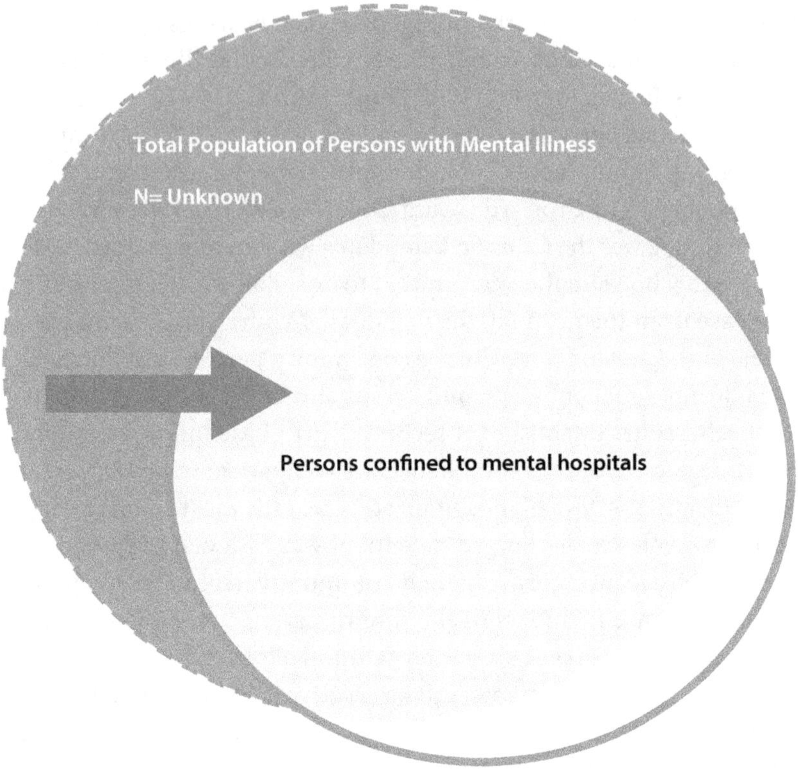

FIGURE 17.1 Psychiatric Treatment Services through 1955.
Before deinstitutionalization, persons with mental illness were primarily confined in large inpatient hospitals. Precise figures vary; by 1955 one in every 300 Americans was confined in a psychiatric institution (Decker 2013). Fuller Torrey (1997) sites the peak of institutionalization as 1955 when close to 560,000 Americans were hospitalized; the population of the United States was 165 million. Torrey dates the start of deinstitutionalization as 1955 with the common use of the antipsychotic and tranquilizer chloropromazine (Thorazine). During the era of lengthy hospitalization, the movement was primarily into confinement; disruptive persons, mentally ill or not, were removed from society. Arrest of persons with mental illness for petty disruptions was uncommon. Recidivism among persons with mental illness was rare.

to encourage and sustain engagement in mental health services. Successful participation in the program forestalls incarceration and in many cases, successful completion allows the charges to be expunged.

The effectiveness of mental health courts has been assessed through both qualitative and quantitative studies. Most studies report fewer jail days for defendants who complete the mental health court programming but effects on recidivism vary from reduction to re-arrest in a majority of graduates of

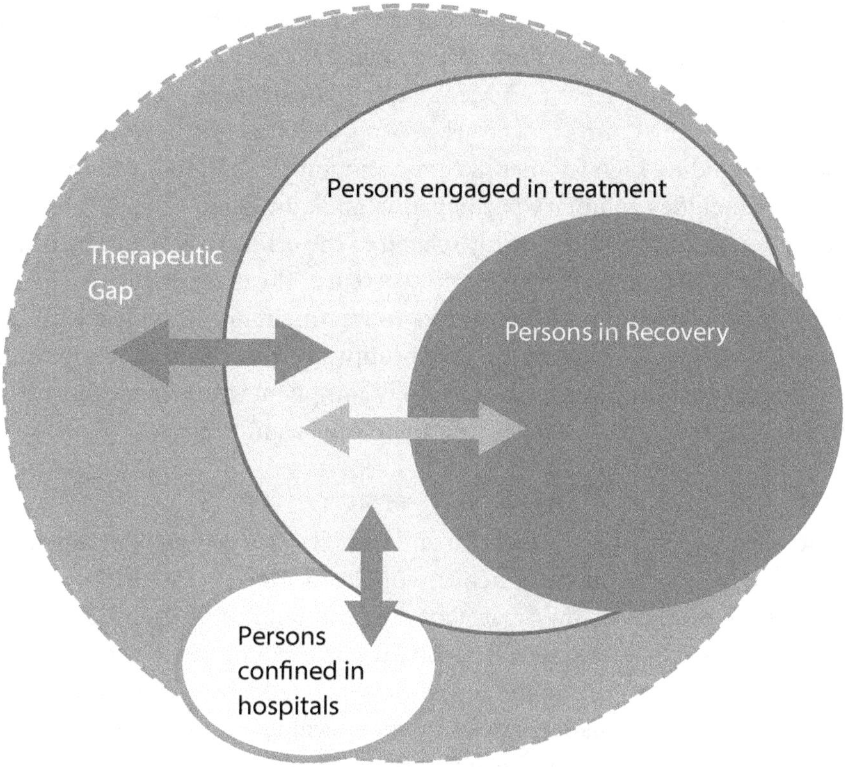

FIGURE 17.2 The Therapeutic Gap in Psychiatric Care.
Since deinstitutionalization, lengthy hospitalizations are reserved for those with the most severe psychiatric illness. In 1955 at the peak of institutionalization, there were 300 beds per 100,000 population. In 2010, the Treatment Advocacy Center (2015) reported a reduction to fourteen beds per 100,000. In 1955 for a U.S. population of 165 million, 495,000 beds were available. Now with a population over 320 million there are fewer than 50,000. The majority of persons with mental illness receive outpatient treatment; many receive their treatment in prison. The therapeutic gap (in dark blue) represents the population of persons with psychiatric disorders who are underserved or under-engaged. No longer are treatment and containment through long psychiatric hospitalizations a management option for disruptive persons in the community; arrest and incarceration are the default. (Treatment Advocacy Center 2015)

the program (Frailing 2010; Sarteschi, Vaughn, and Kim 2011; Turpin and Richards 2003; Stainbrook, Penney, Elwyn 2015). In a novel qualitative study of mental health court defendants' assessment of justice and fairness, Wales, Hiday, and Ray (2010) showed that defendants felt respected and validated in their interactions with the judges. They reported greater satisfaction with their experience in court than with their experience with treatment. The investigators acknowledged that participants in mental health courts are all voluntary and all agree that they have a mental illness.

The Bronx County New York Mental Health Court is an example of a subset of mental health courts that target persons with mental illness arrested for felonies, excluding high felonies like rape and murder. Eligibility for entry in that court includes voluntary participation and admission of guilt. The psychiatric condition must be broadly related to the criminal act, but the nexus is not at the level required for an insanity defense. The defendant, often incarcerated during a period of time, agrees to treatment and complies with the conditions set by the court. In the community, the defendants are monitored by frequent court appearances. Successfully compliant with all conditions, the defendant is often not convicted, and therefore has no record.

Variations in Court Supervised Diversion

In the absence of formal mental health courts, a number of states have developed court and mental health collaborations in which the courts and probation monitor the treatment and compliance of defendants with mental illness. For example, Connecticut has a court-supervised "jail re-evaluation initiative" under the Court Supportive Services Division of the State Department of Justice. Social workers evaluate nonviolent offenders with mental illness who have been incarcerated after arraignment for placement with service agencies contracted with by the department. The court monitors progress and compliance; re-incarceration is the likely option if the persons fails to engage. In this and similar programs, the criminal adjudication is unrestricted: defendants can take their case to trial or accept a deal. The program focuses on reducing incarceration during the pre-trial stage.

In other initiatives jurisdictions have programs modified for persons with psychiatric disorders. Again, in Connecticut, persons on a first arrest can apply for accelerated rehabilitation, which is deferred prosecution for eligible crimes (nonviolent, below specified levels of property destruction). The defendants agree to and serve one to two years of probation. With successful completion of the program, charges are dropped and purged from all records except one that records participation. Failure, particularly re-arrest during the probationary period, brings the charges forward for adjudication. Connecticut modified this program for persons with mental illness. Mental health accelerated rehabilitation allows persons with mental illness to apply regardless of past arrests. The probation includes compliance with mental health treatment, substance disorder treatment as needed, and at times residential services. In addition, persons with mental illness are eligible for this program twice; if successful, a record of convictions can be avoided.

What all of these programs have in common with mental health courts is judicial monitoring, time-specified treatment and oversight, and some alteration in the usual judicial process and the rights afforded in general to any defendant. The programs all include leveraged treatment; that is, external factors that mandate participation in treatment; treatment is a condition of the court programs, and the resolution of the case—either through termination of prosecution or probation—is determined on enrollment in the program. When defendants do not comply, the case is generally transferred to the regular court docket.

The risks and limitations of mental health courts arise from the complexity of mental illness and the law. Mental health courts require the voluntary participation of defendants; therefore, the defendants who are not able to give the informed consent required cannot be served. The sickest are left out of the option to participate and, therefore, face the court process as is. A related issue is the way in which courts view non-compliance as a defiant, voluntary choice when in many cases it is the natural course of the emergence of illness. Finally, mental health courts are status courts; that is, they define dockets by an immutable characteristic of the persons. In contrast, drug courts, domestic violence courts, and community courts are based on the type and level of crime.

Status courts are anathema to the American justice system. For example, the United States does not have courts based on socioeconomic or ethnic characteristics. The juvenile justice system does have separate courts, but youth are also defined by statute and the laws and punishments are different. The concept of mental health courts implies that those with mental illness warrant a different process of justice. The risk here is that persons with mental illness may be less able to voice and advocate for their own interests. They do warrant extra help to obtain the same level of fairness and justice. But attention to mental health issues cannot erode civil rights. Further, mental health courts must be designed to maximize the fair treatment of a person with mental illness and not be designed to coerce treatment.

MENTAL HEALTH SYSTEM DIVERSIONS: THE SEQUENTIAL INTERCEPT MODEL

A second pathway to diversion of those with mental illness from incarceration is under the direction of mental health systems, often administrated by the state department of mental health. These diversion programs are designed as outreach and engagement programs for persons after arrest and at any other point during involvement with the criminal justice system.

Although many programs began as an effort to divert defendants at arraignment (the first appearance in court), most have evolved to include other critical periods from lock-up at arrest through discharge from incarceration and probation.

Munetz and Griffin proposed the Sequential Intercept Model as a framework for developing policy and interventions to enhance treatment engagement and divert from the criminal justice system (Munetz and Griffin 2006). They identify five critical junctures, beginning with pre-arrest emergency services, through community supervision under probation and parole. Each of the five intercepts (pre-arrest; lock-up and early court hearings; incarceration and forensic commitments; re-entry from incarceration and hospitals; and community supervision under the criminal justice or forensic systems) involves the special needs of the person with mental illness and special requirements for effective engagement and treatment.

Mental health jail diversion programs have addressed some of these areas. Specifically, jail diversion clinicians provide assessment, referral treatment planning, and follow-up intervening at the point of arrest or arraignment. As mental health providers and not employees of the court, they are positioned to discuss treatment options independent from the disposition of the criminal case. Mental health diversion is not limited to a special docket; treatment is provided regardless of the plea entered by the defendant, and treatment is available even when the defense chooses not to link mental health issues to the criminal activity.

The goal of the early assessment is to provide to the judge alternatives to incarceration by offering a treatment and monitoring plan that the defendant has accepted. If the judge adopts the plan, then a three-way agreement outlines the process: the defendant agrees to engage in treatment, follow treatment recommendations, and give permission for the clinician to report compliance to the court. The mental health agency agrees to provide treatment, monitor progress, and report compliance to the court. The court agrees to the treatment plan derived by the mental health agency.

In most programs of mental health diversion, courts defer prosecution and monitor the case through continuances. At the court's discretion the charges may be dropped. If not, then the defendant decides with the defense attorney the best course of action—to accept a plea offer or to go to trial. In mental health diversion no legal options are prohibited.

When defendants are too psychiatrically impaired to enter into a diversionary agreement, jail diversion arranges and advocates for a hospitalization or a residential service. If the judge does not agree, defendants may be incarcerated. The diversion clinician works with the jail staff to institute treatment and negotiates with the court for release to community treatment when the defendant can express agreement. Treatment plans in mental health diversion focus on clinical needs and in the best practice, defendants are assigned to teams and clinicians who are expected to care for them after the court case is complete.

Because treatment transitions are associated with higher dropout rates, continuity of care is one advantage of mental health diversion over mental health courts. Others include the protection of civil rights, the wider application of services across court dockets, and the ability to serve persons with severe symptoms who cannot consent to treatment.

The disadvantages of mental health diversion include the resistance of courts to relinquish control over treatment. Related to that issue is that mental health diversion clinicians are outsiders in the court. Unlike mental health courts there are no specialized teams and therefore court personnel may be unfamiliar with and wary of the mental health community as a partner in their work. Connecticut addressed this issue through a statutory requirement that mental health diversion clinicians assess defendants with mental illness in all entry-level criminal courts. Connecticut is the only state with statewide diversion by statute.

A different and subtle effect of mental health diversion is the treating agency's inaccurate expectation of influence over the court process. The connection between the court and the service agency can be misunderstood. For example, the agency might view the court as required to follow the goals of the treatment team, or the diversion clinician as someone who can direct the court action. With proper training and ongoing case review, these challenges can be managed. The risk to breaches of confidentiality is always present at the interface between mental health and the criminal justice system. Protection of clinical privacy and of legal rights is an essential component of program design and training.

Community Reintegration

Return to the community is one of the critical intercepts in the Sequential Intercept Model. Incarceration disrupts families, employment, and community connections. For persons with mental illness the disruption is magnified. Rates of recidivism are highest in the first six months after release from incarceration. For persons with mental illness the re-arrest rates reach as high as 70% within the first year (Treatment Advocacy Center 2015). Although prisons have programming to address reintegration, persons with mental illness are often ineligible. They are often ineligible for parole because of their risk of reoffending.

Since 2000, programs focused on moving persons with mental illness out into the community before end of sentence have gained momentum. On parole, they are still under supervision and motivation for compliance with treatment is enhanced by the threat of retuning to prison. Addressing the criminogenic factors associated with recidivism, comprehensive re-entry programs combine housing and employment with mental health and substance abuse treatment to enhance stability and successful adaptation to community life (DeMatteo et al. 2013).

Since 2000 mental health parole and probation officers with special training and lower caseloads oversee the release and adjustment of persons with mental illness. As part of the treatment team, the officers collaborate with the mental health providers to encourage compliance and to monitor response to treatment.

Mental health parole and probation serve serious offenders as well as those with repeat minor charges. Supervision of those with a violent or sex offense is often more frequent and intrusive; parole and probation officers can determine where a person lives, works and socializes. In some cases, parole officers direct clinical treatment, requiring an agency to have more frequent sessions or add different groups. Although clinical agencies do not have to comply, failure to do so can result in the client on parole being reincarcerated. Another more recent development in the collaboration between mental health and criminal justice monitoring is the attendance of probation officers at sex offender treatment groups.

The success of this partnership is difficult to measure. Violations of probation and parole can be determined by many factors and outcome measures are difficult to collect. The consistent finding is that in the absence of substance abuse, persons in treatment for mental illness are significantly less likely to reoffend after release from incarceration. However, with substance abuse as a factor, recidivism rates with and without treatment are the same within states (National Institute on Drug Abuse 2014).

PRE-BOOKING DIVERSIONS: POLICE DISCRETION IN ARREST

Initial diversion programs were categorized as pre and post booking; that is, interventions that occur before or after arrest (Steadman 1990a). In prebooking diversion, the police take disruptive persons to emergency rooms or specialized treatment centers for evaluation in lieu of arrest, depending on statutory limits. This role for police is not new, and to some extent was a routine part of policing through the mid-1900s.

Evolution of Police Interventions with Persons with Mental Illness

Within the paramilitary organization of American police departments, police have significant discretion in whether to arrest or not when neither harm to victims nor destruction of property has occurred. The majority of municipal police calls do not end in arrest and many calls do involve interactions with persons with mental illness. What have evolved are the options police have in dealing with these situations.

Deinstitutionalization affected police work, not only because persons with mental illness were in the community; hospitalization was no longer an option that police could access on their own. Police themselves often initiated psychiatric hospitalizations, simply by dropping off disruptive or troubled persons at the state psychiatric hospital (Hollingshead and Redlich 1958; Torrey et al. 1992). Police viewed persons from lower socioeconomic status, those who were homeless or causing public discomfort and those who were at risk of victimization (like women and the elderly) as benefiting from institutional care (Hollingshead and Redlich 1958).

After deinstitutionalization, police dealt with more circumstances involving persons with mental illness and had to create options other than hospitalization and arrest (Bittner 1967). For example, "drunk tanks" and overnights in police lock-up provided temporal de-escalation; warnings and escorts out of town addressed public concern about odd behavior. Since there was no arrest, transport to and holding in the police station was not considered detention but rather a humane and preventive housing of someone too impaired to exercise good judgment. The difficulty was that without treatment, most persons with severe mental illness will not improve and so release back to the community was difficult. In the 1990 investigation by Torrey and colleagues, fourteen states reported that 40% of their jails held mentally ill persons without charges; and in six states over 60% of the jails detained persons with mental illness without arrest (Torrey et al. 1992). The jails had become surrogate hospitals for police. What began as an emergency or even benign intervention became in some states a long-term solution.

Jail detention without arrest, however, was not the norm; interactions between police and those with mental illness were part of routine policing especially in large cities. In 1980, Teplin and Pruett described police as "street corner psychiatrists," providing firm warnings and advice to those whose symptoms were escalating and recognizing when inpatient hospitalization was likely. Police were also aware when someone with mental illness was being victimized (Teplin and Pruett 1992)

Teplin's investigation was seminal, focused on identifying the "decision-making normative framework" police use to manage persons with mental illness in the community (Teplin and Pruett 1992, 139). Their investigation showed that factors like shortage of beds and stricter requirements for involuntary hospitalization affected police action. Decisions to arrest, involve the emergency department, or defer were "based less on the degree of psychiatric symptomatology than on the sociopsychological and structural factors" (Teplin and Pruett 1992, 154). The public involvement, area of town, and whether the symptoms were assessed as "bad, mad or eccentric" determined outcome (Teplin and Pruett 1992, 154). Public discomfort and disruption were more likely to end in an arrest, especially if the call for police intervention came from the public. Further, police are aware that they have control over arrest and lock-up but not over treatment and hospitalization (Kimhi et al. 1998).

From Neighborhood Cop to Mobile Police Force

Since the 1990s policing has evolved both in technology and regulations. Major change came when police radios, 911 networks, and police mobility reshaped policing. As policing grew more mobile and mechanized, the "cop walking the beat" grew less common. Familiarity with neighborhoods and with particular persons with mental illness decreased. Police were no longer street corner psychiatrists but emergency responders.

In addition, concerns about liability for false arrest and civil suits related to failure to act drove an increase in arrests as the primary response to disruptive behavior. Encounters with disruptive persons with mental illness or drug or alcohol intoxication were more easily managed with arrest and lock-up than with more time-consuming negotiations with hospital staff.

In 2000, reduction in psychiatric beds further reduced the reliability of hospitals as an effective police management strategy. Police were daunted by the rapid, and in their view inappropriate, release of persons back to the community after police brought persons to hospitals in lieu of arrests.

The police had first-hand experience with the therapeutic gap—persons not symptomatic enough to meet criteria for involuntary hospitalization but still impaired enough to disrupt others in the community. Police were the reluctant mediators between the unengaged mentally ill and the intolerant public. Law enforcement must respond to public disturbances and communities expect police to alleviate the disruption; arrest is a ready option under police control.

Community Policing, Partnerships, and Pre-Booking Diversion

In the period leading up to the establishment of community policing, police departments responded to increase in violence unrelated to mental illness. Gang violence, drug dealing and organized crime flourished and emergency response after the crime was not enough. Community policing—assigning police to neighborhoods and making them visible as problem solvers—was introduced as a return to effective strategies for police in preventing and solving crimes.

The community policing movement provided the backdrop for the pre-booking diversion strategy that Steadman and colleagues had recommended in the 1990s (Liberman 1969). Police in the neighborhood are aware of persons with mental illness and of local resources. In theory, community police become de facto monitors of symptoms and levels of function as well as of family and community tolerance and resilience. Such awareness offers opportunity for early intervention and crisis prevention.

The potential for community policing for pre-booking diversion relies, however, on available community mental health services and on willing consumers. When either is lacking, community policing highlights the therapeutic gap but cannot reduce it. For example, an investigation of policing in a community in Connecticut showed that community policing reduced drug dealing, school truancy, and gang-related activity but arrests of persons with mental illness did not decrease. Waiting lists for treatment, lack of beds, and refusal of treatment were identified as the barriers to effective outcomes (Codish and Baranoski 2004).

Although all diversionary models rely on the adequacy of mental health services, pre-booking diversion requires immediate access to all levels of service including emergency care, hospitalization, residential options, and effective engagement in outpatient interventions. In the absence of court mandated treatment or incarceration, police hand-offs must be to reliable and effective care options. Police departments recognize the value of partnerships with providers willing to assume responsibility for assessment and management of those with mental illness who do not warrant arrest (Goldstein 1987). Collaboration with mobile crisis clinicians has enhanced police options and shared responsibility for decision-making.

In the 1980s the Los Angeles Police Department formed co-responder teams with local mental health agencies with the goal of diverting persons into treatment in lieu of arrest (Reuland, Draper, and Norton 2013). Access to a full menu of treatment options and the willingness of the detainee to agree to treatment were essential to successful diversions. Similar programs have developed in large cities. Although police and mental health agencies

TABLE 17.1 Characteristics of Diversionary Programs from Pre-Arrest to Post-Incarceration

	Pre-Booking Police Diversion	Problem-Solving Courts	Mental Health Diversions	Re-entry Programming
Leadership/ Control	Police with mental health collaboration.	Judge-controlled post booking, post arraignment diversion.	Mental health agency with formal collaboration with courts.	Department of Correction; parole and probation.
Essential Features	Police discretion to refer to treatment in lieu of arrest; specialized teams or trained officers in liaison with embedded mental health clinician.	Specific court dockets for eligible clients who waive right to trial and pleading not guilty. Court refers to and oversees treatment. Charges dropped or ended on completion of program.	No specific docket; court-wide access to defendants with misdemeanors and low felonies. Three-way agreement: defendant, clinician, and court.	Connection with community services; monitoring of treatment by probation and parole.
Requirements	Extensive police training. Twenty-four hour access to mental health services/ inpatient and residential services. *Willing participant.*	Specific dedicated docket. Court-based clinicians, specific and trained legal and support staff. Probation and court involved in monitoring. *Willing, compliant, competent participant.*	Mental health clinicians assigned to courts but not under the court supervision. Immediate assessments and referrals to full menu of services. Availability of emergency hospitalization; liaison with jail clinicians.	Mental health probation and parole officers. Extensive mental health services with residential treatment options housing and employment services.
Advantages	Avoids arrest, court involvement, criminal record, and mandated treatment. After police referral, mental health in control of treatment.	Court involvement motivates compliance. Dropped charges avoid record. Resources come from mental health and court system.	No limitation on pleading options. Treated as clinical contact with seamless connection to services at end of court case.	Enhances engagement after incarceration. Additional housing resources; shared management of risk.
Risks / Limitations	Lack of mental health services and options limit diversion in every case. Costly to police departments for training and implementation. Embedded clinician threatens confidentiality.	Special effort to assure rights. Unavailable for those too symptomatic to agree and those who wish to plead not guilty. Threats to confidentiality. No formal transition once court case over leads to increased recidivism.	Requires buy-in from court personnel who are not specially trained. Resistance from judges.	Parole intrusion into treatment. Inconsistent response to non-compliance.
Program Examples	Memphis Model Crisis Intervention Teams (CIT)	New York and Florida mental health courts	Connecticut Jail Diversion Program	Connecticut Offender Re-entry Program

acknowledge the merits of these partnerships, budget cuts, lack of resources and psychiatric beds often result in discontinuation of the partnerships.

Crisis Intervention Teams—Police-Initiated Diversion and Crisis Management

In 1988, the Memphis Police Department in conjunction with the National Alliance on Mental Illness (NAMI) and the University of Memphis and University of Tennessee launched a program for crisis response to those with mental illness. Following the September 1987 police shooting death of a young man with mental illness who had aggressively responded to usual police action, the police and mental health community explored crisis intervention strategies (Vaughn 2014; Sadoff and Cronin 2015). The Crisis Intervention Team (CIT) expanded into the primary pre-booking diversion model in the United States.

Under CIT, police officers, often as a unit within the police force, are trained in de-escalation techniques, mental health assessment, and resource management. They are dispatched to calls that involve disruptive behavior, suicide threats, and family violence situations. An essential feature of the model is partnership with the local mental health agencies and the assignment of a CIT liaison clinician who accompanies police on calls and intercedes on their behalf to access services from local hospitals and residential services. Some police departments have "embedded clinicians," usually social workers who are hired by the municipality or police department.

The CIT model has expanded to international status and yearly conferences and ongoing training increase the scope of officer interventions that now include juvenile and school-based CIT policing.

Although popular, there have been no systematic investigations of its impact on diversion from arrest (Sadoff and Cronin 2015). Anecdotal accounts and community surveys expressing satisfaction with police as well as increased police satisfaction and comfort in interactions with persons with mental illness are cited as indicators of effectiveness (Bonfine, Ritter, and Munetz 2014; Ritter et al. 2011; Ritter et al. 2010). What is critical in the effectiveness in CIT interventions is the scope, effectiveness, and availability of mental health resources, including housing options and the willingness of participants to engage.

An emerging challenge to police departments is their capacity to train enough officers to cover multiple calls and the rapid deployment of CIT-trained officers to crisis situations. In a recent United States Supreme Court case, *City and County of San Francisco, California v. Teresa Sheehan* (135 S. Ct. 1765 2015), affirmation that police are responsible under the Americans with Disabilities Act and must offer accommodation to persons with mental illness (unless the situation poses threat of violence to others) underscored the challenge for police departments in addressing costs of training and civil litigation. In the San Francisco case, Ms. Sheehan was living in a mental health residential program. Police responded to an emergency call from the residence that a woman was in her room, had a knife, and needed to be transported to a hospital for admission. What transpired was a failed effort to interact with Ms. Sheehan who ordered police out of her room. They entered her room a second time; when pepper spray failed to subdue her, the police shot multiple times. She survived and brought suit against the police force and city. Although the United States Supreme Court held that the officers were justified in using potentially dangerous force, the Court emphasized the obligation that police have in responding to calls involving persons with mental illness. Although not stated, one accommodation is that of pre-booking diversion. Police can divert persons to treatment but when the person is unwilling, the situation can escalate as it did in the Sheehan case. Without special training in de-escalation, intended diversion can result in violence. Even when police are specially trained, a resistant person in the community cannot be managed in the same way as on an inpatient unit.

There are significant advantages to pre-booking a diversion for persons with mental illness and for the mental health system. The effective engagement of someone with untreated mental illness decreases the therapeutic gap without involvement in the criminal justice system. There is no arrest, no criminal record, and no external monitoring of treatment, level of care, or placement. The police intervene but the person remains a citizen with choices about his or her care.

There are risks and challenges in pre-booking diversion. Threats to confidentiality require constant vigilance about what information is shared with police. In addition, the rights of a person to refuse treatment and the stigma within mental health services of the client referred by police are areas that require training and monitoring.

THE EMERGING ROLE FOR FORENSIC PSYCHIATRY AND PSYCHOLOGY IN DIVERSION

Psychiatric disorders, although clearly biochemical in nature, are unique among medical conditions. Psychiatric disorders are evident in behavior, especially in interpersonal interactions. There are no scans, no blood tests, and no stress tests to identify the disorder, measure its severity, or track the effectiveness of treatment. More critically, serious psychiatric disorders affect personhood: one's perception, judgment, function, and capacity for intimacy. Perhaps most destructively, psychiatric disease affects the person's ability to recognize, accept, and manage his own illness. The burden, pain, and severity of other chronic diseases have a public face that evokes sympathy and even respect. Psychiatric disease also has a public face. Unfortunately, what others see does not capture the internal agony and distress experienced; rather, others perceive problem behaviors, incapacity, idiosyncrasies, and often threats. Behaviors that once were sequestered in state hospitals are now evident in the community.

Forensic psychiatry by its definition is at the interface of law and psychiatry; the forensic psychiatrist's role was primarily that of evaluator and consultant. On a case-by-case basis, the psychiatrist is a forensic expert to aid the court in its deliberations, to bolster the case of either side in the adversarial process, and to focus attention on psychiatric factors in sentencing. The role for forensic psychiatry in diversion and implementation of the sequential intercept model is much broader. Policy development, treatment, training and supervision of programs, and the protection of boundaries are critical areas that require the expertise of the forensically trained psychiatrist or psychologist.

Steadman identified the role for boundary spanners; forensic psychiatrists are the ultimate spanner bringing both theoretical and practical knowledge about disorders, risk assessment, and legal options and their consequences. They also bring an awareness of the pitfalls of these laws and police and mental health partnerships and how to avoid and manage them (Steadman 1992).

These are a few of the areas of potential conflict that can affect outcomes for persons with mental illness, the burden on the mental health systems, and the overreach of the court and police.

- *Definition of Success.* In the literature on outcomes related to mental health courts and diversion programs, reduction in criminal recidivism is primary. Engagement in treatment and reduction in symptoms are the primary goals for the mental health system. The view of the courts—especially mental health courts—that every behavior a mentally ill person does is a product of mental illness is wrong and dangerous. That view puts an inappropriate expectation on the mental health services. There are many factors that contribute to criminal behavior and focusing on mental illness alone impedes a comprehensive approach to successful integration in the community.
- *View of Failure.* A defendant who fails to comply with mental health treatment can be viewed as rejecting help and, therefore, as more "bad than

mad." Failure to comply is common in mental health treatment. Forensic psychiatrists view it as part of the trajectory of an emerging illness, the resistance to accepting that one is ill, or even evidence that the treatment is not working. The risk in the court is that failure on diversion can lead to pejorative views of the defendant's character.

- *Right of Refusal.* The introduction of mental health courts and diversion breaches the boundary between a private health matter and criminal involvement. Although the interface was created to help the mentally ill defendant, there is a risk that these interventions interfere with a defendant's right to keep mental health issues out of the court case. If refusal of treatment is viewed as a characterological flaw, then justice for that defendant with mental illness is threatened *because* the diversion program exists.
- *Rush to Judgment.* Busy courts that have diversion programs or mental health dockets risk using these options as an expeditious and presumably harmless way to move mentally ill defendants through the system. For example, one man who had been through the diversion system before, got connected with treatment and did no jail time, was arrested on charges related to stealing a bicycle from a teenage boy who was shopping with his father. Police recovered the bike several blocks away. The father gave police an eyewitness account and named the man who frequented that shopping area, panhandling and talking to himself. The man had previous arrests related to taking carts from shoppers. In court, the judge, prosecutor and public defender agreed that diversion into mental health court was the best option—it had worked before. The diversion clinician in collecting mental health records discovered that the man was hospitalized when the bike was stolen. A forensic psychiatrist intervened when the court had planned to continue with the diversion "to give a refresher about staying in treatment." Because incarceration was not being considered, court personnel saw little harm in encouraging continued treatment. These good intentions violated civil rights and eroded the valuable separation between the roles of the court and of treatment.
- *Worthy vs. Unworthy Clients.* Role confusion also occurs on the mental health side. Providers can view the court's demands as intrusive. Court-mandated clients are at risk for being viewed as the less deserving. Indeed, clients arrested on sex offenses, regardless of how psychiatrically compromised they are, often cause discomfort and resistance in their treaters. When the court orders treatment, clinicians can be confused about their responsibility, the limits to confidentiality, and their role as treater versus agent of the court.

The new interface with the court can also be misunderstood as a clinical tool. For example, a clinician with a difficult client who was reluctant to take medication attended one of the mental health court sessions, asked to speak in court, and requested that the judge send her client to jail "so he can learn his lesson." The judge did not comply and the already meager therapeutic alliance was destroyed.

The interaction with probation and parole can be more complicated. In one case a clinician insisted to a probation officer that her client be violated on probation for missing a treatment session. In the request, the clinician noted, "He only comes to sessions when it benefits him." The clinician explained that she believed she was responsible to probation and the court for assuring the client's attendance. In this case the treatment relationship was impeded by the clinician's role confusion; she became a court monitor rather than therapist.

The role for forensic psychiatry includes that of navigator and teacher across the court and treatment interface. Program development and legislative initiatives will benefit from the input and oversight of experts in psychiatry with an understanding of the law. Moreover, forensic psychiatry has developed within its specialty a body of knowledge about the subset of persons whose manifestations of their psychiatric disorder put them at risk for arrest. They overlap with those caught in the therapeutic gap, for which new interventions and engagement are required. Jail diversion programs are a major first step in developing the engagement of persons in the gap.

CONCLUSION

All forms of jail diversion are leveraged care models that entice those unengaged or inadequately engaged into treatment in lieu of the usual criminal adjudication. The research, although still scant, has shown promising effects. Recidivism, although reduced in rate and frequency, is still unresolved. What the research suggests and clinical experience indicates is the complexity of criminal involvement for persons with mental illness and addiction. Improving collaboration between the criminal justice system and the mental health system has been a major step toward the idea of seamless assessment, treatment and follow-up for persons with mental illness. What is still lacking are the collaborations and interventions that can address the criminogenic factors and maintain the relevant engagement of persons with mental illness after the leverage of the criminal justice system expires.

A serendipitous side effect of efforts in jail diversion and the partnerships between mental health and criminal justice is the recognition of a special sub-group of persons with mental illness defined not by diagnosis but rather by interplay between their illness and society. This interplay invites research and policy to define forensic patients in a different way—not by a current connection with police, courts or corrections, but rather by a pattern of behaviors that put them at risk for falling into the therapeutic gap and the criminal justice system.

REFERENCES

Bamberger, P.S. 2002. "Specialized Courts: Not a Cure-All." *Fordham Urban Law Journal* 30 (3): 1091–5.

Bittner, E. 1967. "Police Discretion in Emergency Apprehension of Mentally Ill Persons." *Social Problems* 14 (3): 278–92.

Bonfine, N., C. Ritter, and M.R. Munetz. 2014. "Police Officer Perceptions of the Impact of Crisis Intervention Team (CIT) Programs." *International Journal of Law and Psychiatry* 37 (4): 341–50. doi: 10.1016/j.ijlp.2014.02.004.

City and County of San Francisco, California, et al. Petitioners v. Teresa Sheehan, Respondent. 2015. 130 Supreme Court. 1765.

Codish, K. and M.V. Baranoski. 2004. "Community Policing and Citizen Satisfaction: Setting Goals for Law Enforcement." Report to New Haven City Council.

Cooper, C.S. 2001. In *2000 Drug Court Survey Report: Program Operations, Services and Participant Perspectives*. Washington, DC: U.S. Department of Justice.

DeMatteo, D., C. LaDuke, B.R. Locklair, and K. Heilbrun. 2013. "Community-based Alternatives for Justice-involved Individuals with Severe Mental Illness: Diversion, Problem-solving Courts, and Reentry." *Journal of Criminal Justice* 41 (2): 64–71. doi: 10.1016/j.jcrimjus.2012.09.2012.

Decker, H.S. 2013. *The Making of DSM-III: A Diagnostic Manual's Conquest of American Psychiatry*. New York: Oxford University Press.

Frailing, K. 2010. "How Mental Health Courts Function: Outcomes and Observations." *International Journal of Law and Psychiatry* 33 (4): 207–13. doi: 10.1016/j.ijlp.2010.06.001.

Goldstein, H. 1987. "Toward Community-oriented Policing: Potential, Basic Requirements, and Threshold Questions." *Crime and Delinquency* 33 (1): 6–30.

Goodale, G. and L. Callahan. 2013. "What can We Say about Mental Health Courts Today?" *Psychiatric Services* 64: 298–300.

Hollingshead, A.B. and F.C. Redlich. 1958. *Social Class and Mental Illness: A Community Study*. New York: John Wiley & Sons.

Hora PF. 2002. "A Dozen Years of Drug Treatment Courts: Uncovering Our Theoretical Foundation and the Construction of a Mainstream Paradigm." *Substance Use & Misuse* 37 (12–13): 1469–88. http://www.tandfonline.com/doi/full/10.1081/JA-120014419

Hughes, K.C. and J.L. Metzner. 2015. "Suicide Risk Management." In *Oxford Textbook of Correctional Psychiatry*, edited by Robert L. Trestman, Kenneth L. Appelbaum, and Jeffrey L. Metzner. New York: Oxford University Press.

Kimhi, R., Y. Barak, J. Gutman, Y. Melamed, M. Zohar, and I. Barak. 1998. "Police

Attitudes toward Mental Illness and Psychiatric Patients in Israel." *Journal of the American Academy of Psychiatry and the Law* 26 (4): 625–30.

Lamb, H.R. and L.E. Weinberger. 2005. "The Shift of Psychiatric Inpatient Care From Hospitals to Jails and Prisons." *Journal of the American Academy of Psychiatry and the Law* 33 (4): 529–34.

Liberman, R. 1969. "Police as a Community Mental Health Resource." *Community Mental Health Journal* 5 (2): 111–20.

McNeal, D.E. and R.L. Binder. 2007. "Effectiveness of a Mental Health Court on Reducing Criminal Recidivism and Violence." *American Journal of Psychiatry* 164 (9): 1395–403.

Metzner, J.L. 2002. "Class Action Litigation in Correctional Psychiatry." *Journal of the American Academy of Psychiatry and the Law* 30 (1): 19–29.

Mitchell, O., D.B. Wilson, A. Eggers, and D.L. Mackenzie. 2012. "Assessing the Effectiveness of Drug Courts on Recidivism: A Meta-analytic Review of Traditional and Non-traditional Drug Courts." *Journal of Criminal Justice* 40 (1): 60–71. doi: 10.1016/j.jcrimjus.2011.11.009.

Munetz, M.R. and P.A. Griffin. 2006. "Use of the Sequential Intercept Model as an Approach to Decriminalization of People With Serious Mental Illness." *Psychiatric Services* 57 (4): 544–9.

NAMI. 2006. "Grading the States: A Report on America's Healthcare System for Serious Mental Illness." 3.12.2016. www2.nami.org/gtstemplate.cfm?sectiongrading_the_states

National Criminal Justice Reference Service. 1999. "Diversion Programs: An Overview." Accessed September 21, 2015. www.ncjrs.gov/html/ojjdp/9909-3/div.html

National Institute on Drug Abuse. 2014. "Drug Use, Crime, and Incarceration." *Drug Addiction in the Criminal Justice System*. Accessed July 10, 2015, www.drugabuse.gov.

Orfei, M.D., R.G. Robinson, G.P. Prigatano, S. Starkstein, N. Rusch, P. Bria, C. Caltagirone, and G. Spalletta. 2007. "Anosognosia for Hemiplegia after Stroke Is a Multifaceted Phenomenon: a Systematic Review of the Literature." *Brain* 130: 3075–90. doi:10.1093/brain/awm106.

Petrila, J. 2001. "Preliminary Observations from an Evaluation of the Brownard County Mental Health Court." *Court Review* 37 (Winter): 14–16.

Ritter, C., J. Teller, M. Munetz, and N. Bonfine. 2010. "Crisis Intervention Team (CIT) Training: Selection Effects and Long-Term Changes in Perceptions of Mental Illness and Community Preparedness." *Journal of Police Crisis Negotiations* 10(1–2): 133–52.

Ritter, C., J.L.S. Teller, K. Marcussen, M.R. Munetz, and B. Teasdale. 2011. "Crisis Intervention Team Officer Dispatch, Assessment, and Disposition: Interactions with Individuals with Severe Mental Illness." *International Journal of Law and Psychiatry* 37 (1): 30–8.

Rueland, M., L. Draper, and B. Norton. 2013. "Developing a Statewide Approach to Specialised Policing Response (SPR) Programme Implementation" In *Policing and the Mentally Ill: International Perspectives*, edited by Duncan Chappell, 3–18. Boca Raton: CRC Press.

Sadoff, R.L. and G. Cronin. 2015. "Forensic Psychiatry in Law Enforcement: A Practitioner's Perspective." In *The Evolution of Forensic Psychiatry: History, Current Developments, Future Directions*, 283–92. New York: Oxford University Press.

Sarteschi, C.M., M.G. Vaughn, and K. Kim. 2011. "Assessing the Effectiveness of Mental Health Courts: A Quantitative Review." *Journal of Criminal Justice* 39 (1): 12–20. doi: 10.1016/j.jcrimjus.2010.11.003.

Spohn, C., R.K. Piper, T. Martin, and E.D. Frenzel. 2001. "Drug Courts and Recidivism: The Results of an Evaluation Using Two Comparison Groups and Multiple Indicators of Recidivism." *Journal of Drug Issues* 31 (1): 149–76.

Stainbrook, K., D. Penney, and L. Elwyn. 2015. "The Opportunities and Challenges of Multi-site Evaluations: Lessons from the Jail Diversion and Trauma Recovery National Cross-site Evaluation." *Evaluation and Program Planning* 50 (June): 26–35. doi:dx.doi.org/10.1016/jevalprogplan.2015.01.005.

Steadman, H.J., S.M. Morris, and D.L. Dennis. 1995. "The Diversion of Mentally Ill Persons from Jails to Community-Based Services: A Profile of Programs." *American Journal of Public Health* 85 (12): 1630–5.

Steadman, H.J. 1990a. *Jail Diversion for the Mentally Ill: Breaking Through the Barriers*. Seattle: National Coalition for the Mentally Ill in the Criminal Justice System.

———. 1990b. *Effectively Addressing the Mental Health Needs of Jail Detainees*. Seattle, Wash.: National Coalition for the Mentally Ill in the Criminal Justice System.

———. 1992. "Boundary Spanners: A Key Component for the Effective Interactions of the Justice and Mental Health Systems." *Law and Human Behavior* 16 (1): 75–87. doi: http://www.jstor.org/stable/1393988.

Sturges, G. and M.V. Baranoski. 1997. "The Status of Jail Diversion in Connecticut." *Annual Report to the Connecticut Department of Justice and General Assembly*. Connecticut Department of Mental Health and Addiction Services. 2–29.

Teplin, L.A. and N.S. Pruett. 1992. "Police as Streetcorner Psychiatrist: Managing the Mentally Ill." *International Journal of Law and Psychiatry* 15 (2): 139–56.

Thompson, M., F. Osher, and D. Tomasini-Joshi. 2009. "Improving Response to People with Mental Illness: The Essential Elements of a Mental Health Court." *Council of state Governments Justice Center/Criminal Justice Mental Health Consensus Project*. www.justicecenter.csg.org/mentalhealthconsensus. Accessed January 19, 2016.

Torrey, E.F. 1997. *Out of the Shadows: Confronting America's Mental Illness Crisis*. New York: John Wiley & Sons.

———. 2015. "Impaired Awareness of Illness: Anosognosia." *Mental Illness Policy Org*. Accessed November 23, 2015. http://mentalillnesspolicy.org/medical/anosognosia-studies.html.

Torrey, E.F., J. Stieber, J. Ezekiel, S.M. Wolfe, J. Sharfstein, J.H. Noble, and L.M. Flynn. 1992. *Criminalizing the Seriously Mentally Ill: The Abuse of Jails as Mental Hospitals, a Joint Report of the National Alliance for the Mentally Ill and Public Citizen's Health Research Group*. Washington, DC: Public Citizen's Health Research Group.

Treatment Advocacy Center. 2015. "No Room at the Inn: Trends and Consequences of Closing Public Psychiatric Hospitals." *Office of Research and Public Affairs*. Accessed July 12, 2015. http://www.tacreports.org/bed-study.

Turpin, E. and H. Richards. 2003. "Seattle's Mental Health Courts: Early Indicators of Effectiveness." *International Journal of Law and Psychiatry* 26 (1): 33–53.

Vaughn, R. 2014. "Crisis Intervention Team: The Memphis Model." Memphis Police

Department. Accessed September 20, 2015. http://www.memphispolice.org/crisis_intervention.htm.

Wales, H.W., V.A. Hiday, and B. Ray. 2010. "Procedural Justice and the Mental Health Court Judge's Role in Reducing Recidivism." *International Journal of Law and Psychiatry* 33 (4): 265–71. doi:10.1016/j.ilp.2010.06.009.

Wexler, D.B. 1990. *Therapeutic Jurisprudence: The Law as a Therapeutic Agent*. Durham: Carolina Academic Press.

Wexler, D.B. and B.J. Winick. 1991. "Therapeutic Jurisprudence as a New Approach to Mental Health Law, Political Analysis, and Research." *University of Miami Law Review* 45 (5): 979–1008.

Winick, B.J. 2002. "Therapeutic Jurisprudence and Problem Solving Courts." *Fordham Urban Law Journal* 30 (3): 1055–71.

Yeager, K., D. Cutler, D. Svendsen, and G.M. Sills. 2013. *Modern Community Mental Health: An Interdisciplinary Approach*. New York: Oxford University Press.

CHAPTER 18

Community Forensic Services as an Integrated Treatment Model

Reena Kapoor and Madelon V. Baranoski

INTRODUCTION

In the early years of forensic psychiatry, the profession acted largely in response to the needs of the legal system. Psychiatrists consulted with attorneys, formed opinions, wrote reports, and testified in court, all in the service of helping to answer legal questions related to mental health. What happened to evaluees after the legal question was answered—how and where they were treated, whether they were restored to health, how best to manage future risk—was not the province of forensic psychiatrists. Such matters were largely left to general psychiatrists and criminal justice agents.

Had it not been for the desire of forensic psychiatrists to obtain formal subspecialty recognition from the American Board of Medical Specialties (ABMS), this division of labor between general and forensic psychiatrists may have remained intact. However, in the 1970s, the ABMS opined that forensic psychiatry's lack of a defined patient population was a barrier to subspecialty recognition. The field considered how best to respond to this critique, ultimately identifying patients in correctional institutions and high-security psychiatric hospitals as its target patient population. This adoption of a patient population paved the way for the field's formal recognition. Subspecialty accreditation for forensic psychiatry was granted by the ABMS in 1992 (Zonana 2012).

Despite the formal adoption of correctional treatment into forensic psychiatry's mission, the American Academy of Psychiatry and the Law (AAPL) maintained its focus primarily on forensic assessment, reports, and testimony. AAPL annual meetings are, to this day, more focused on forensic evaluations and courtroom-related issues than on the treatment of forensic populations. The lack of emphasis on treatment may have initially reflected the field's ambivalence about accepting correctional and forensic hospital treatment into its mission, but it may also have resulted from a general lack of scientific inquiry into treating forensic populations. For example, one recent study found that articles about correctional psychiatry or the criminal justice system comprised just 9 of the 158 papers published in *Psychiatric Services* and 3 of 155 in the *American Journal of Psychiatry* in 2015 (Appelbaum 2015). Similarly, the American Psychiatric Association (APA) has identified the advancement of correctional psychiatry as a priority for over forty years (APA 1974), but correctional institutions still struggle to recruit competent mental health professionals. In short, forensic treatment remains an underserved area, and forensic populations remain somewhat marginalized, stigmatized both by serious mental illness and by criminal justice involvement.

Although research into best practices for treating forensic patients is just emerging, psychiatry's understanding of the forensic population's needs has evolved over the past three decades. Initial theories about the relationship between mental illness and criminal justice involvement focused on the "criminalization hypothesis," linking the increase in the justice-involved mentally ill population to the closure of state hospitals (Lamb and Weinberger 2005). According to that proposition, the population of psychiatric patients was presented as languishing in the streets after the large-scale deinstitutionalization of the 1960s, and over time they were arrested for small crimes related to manifestations of mental illness. This simple "criminalization" hypothesis has been replaced with a more complex understanding as psychiatry's body of knowledge has expanded. Current ideas about the relationship between mental illness and criminal justice involvement acknowledge that, for a subset of persons with mental illness, simply treating the psychiatric illness is inadequate to reduce criminal recidivism. Persons with mental illness are still over-represented in criminal justice settings, but many factors other than mental illness—poverty, homelessness, antisocial attitudes, substance use disorders—also contribute significantly to criminal behavior.

Over time, psychiatrists have increasingly recognized that treatment as usual may not be effective for forensic patients, many of whom come from the therapeutic gap described in Chapter 17. These patients had limited access to treatment or did not accept treatment until after arrest, and the criminal justice system incentivized treatment as an alternative to incarceration. Evaluation of evidence-based practices in mental health care such as Assertive Community Treatment (ACT), cognitive behavioral therapy (CBT), and dialectic behavioral therapy (DBT) has demonstrated that these interventions successfully reduced symptoms, but they did not affect criminal recidivism (Rotter and Carr 2013; Case et al. 2009; Skeem et al. 2009). Even mental health courts and jail diversion programs were more effective in connecting persons to treatment than preventing future arrests (Sarteschi, Vaughn, and Kim 2011). Also ineffective was the tendency for mental health programs to disown responsibility for reducing arrests; once symptoms were managed, the mental health system considered their obligation met. As jail diversion programs and collaborative efforts between criminal justice and mental health programs grew, however, responsibility for improved outcomes was thrust upon psychiatry. The need for specialized forensic psychiatric and psychological expertise in treatment increased.

In this chapter, we propose a model that seeks to enhance psychiatry's understanding and treatment of justice-involved persons with serious mental illness, bringing forensic populations into the mainstream mission of community mental health treatment. We recognize that there are several challenges that must be overcome in this mission: identifying a target treatment population, obtaining adequate resources to provide meaningful care, integrating forensic expertise into non-forensic treatment teams, and overcoming non-therapeutic attitudes. We address several of these challenges in the chapter, aiming to create an integrated treatment model for outpatient forensic populations. We propose, further, that the integration of forensic expertise improves psychiatric care for all patients.

IDENTIFYING A TARGET TREATMENT POPULATION

One of the first challenges of treating forensic populations is identifying which patients are considered "forensic." Most patients in community treatment settings have at least one risk factor for violence or self-harm, so using these criteria to identify forensic patients may not yield a specific subpopulation. As a practical way of defining and narrowing the patient population, many forensic programs accept only those referred by a criminal justice agency and who will have ongoing legal oversight. This approach has its merits, as it clearly defines a target population and allows treatment teams to collaborate with the referring agency. However, the approach also runs the risk of over- and under-identifying patients who need the specialized services of a forensic treatment team. Some patients referred by a criminal justice agency may not pose a significant risk of violence (e.g. a man with depression who engaged in credit card fraud), while others may pose significant risk but have no arrests or convictions (e.g. a man who has made repeated unwanted sexual advances to other patients in a psychiatric unit).

Sometimes decisions about which patients are labeled "forensic" are made based simply upon administrative factors and the availability of resources. For example, many state-funded mental health agencies require a diagnosis of "serious mental illness" (SMI) for service eligibility, typically accepting patients with schizophrenia or other psychotic-spectrum disorders. However, some diagnoses—borderline personality disorder, developmental disabilities, impulse control disorders—may fall into a gray zone of diagnostic seriousness but are related to high rates of arrest. Treatment programs are left to make clinical judgments about whether the patient fits into their existing services, especially when they are referred by probation and through jail diversion initiatives. Depending on the availability of treatment services, the patient's level of interest, and the severity of presenting symptoms, such patients may or may not be accepted into community forensic treatment.

Another criterion for identifying forensic patients involves the type of criminal offense. Many forensic programs were initially designed to serve patients who had committed relatively small criminal offenses, such as trespassing or breach of peace. Patients with serious violent crimes, such as murder or weapons offenses, were excluded because of safety concerns. Sex offenders were also typically excluded from outpatient mental health settings, being civilly committed instead to specialized inpatient programs (Miller, Amenta, and Conroy 2005) or referred to criminal justice-led Sex Offender Programs (U.S. Probation 2015). Although persons with serious charges are often incarcerated on lengthy sentences, they return to the community in need of psychiatric services; some programs have decided eligibility based on previous arrests, even when prison sentences have been served.

These rudimentary methods of identifying forensic patients are understandable, given current resource limitations and the large number of patients needing to be screened for treatment eligibility. Clinicians sometimes do not have the time to consider every referral in detail and to perform the type of complex risk assessments that would best identify patients needing specialized services. However, we suggest that, where possible, an approach to identifying high-risk individuals that considers factors beyond diagnostic categories and type of criminal offense should be employed to identify forensic patients and create meaningful treatment plans. This approach is consistent with the Risk-Needs-Responsivity (RNR) approach outlined by Andrews and Bonta in 2010, structuring treatment plans around individual needs rather than what the mental health system could easily provide.

The traditional approach to identifying patients for forensic services is outlined in Figure 18.1. This model includes those at the intersection of mental illness and the criminal justice system.

Our proposed approach aims to move beyond the inclusion of only patients with SMI diagnoses and criminal justice involvement, acknowledging that violence risk may occur independently of arrests and criminal convictions. Thus, the "ideal" patient population served by forensic services is found at the intersection of violence risk and mental illness, not at the intersection of criminal justice involvement and mental illness. This approach is depicted in Figure 18.2.

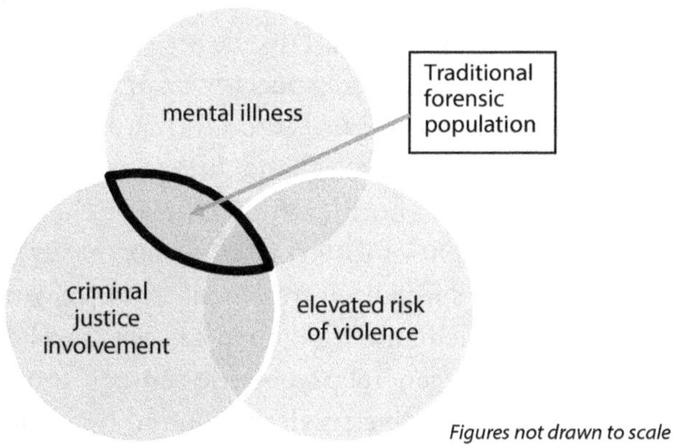

FIGURE 18.1 Traditional Method of Identifying Patients for Community Forensic Services.

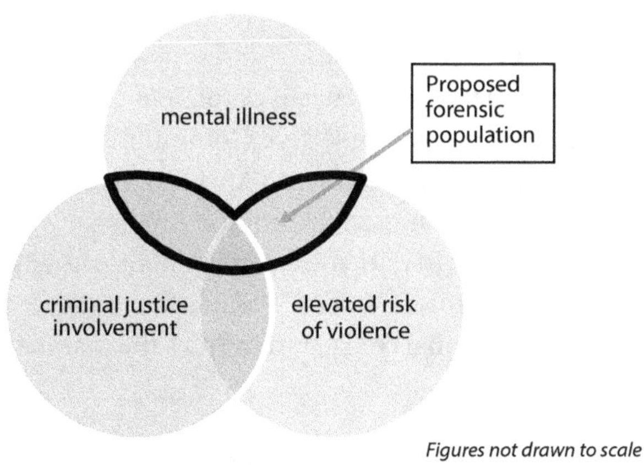

FIGURE 18.2 Proposed Method of Identifying Patients for Community Forensic Services.

As a practical matter, the difference between the two approaches is that, in the latter method, forensic expertise will be applied more broadly than its current mandate of serving only justice-involved patients. By this method, psychiatry rather than the law will decide which patients require forensic expertise and specialized services. Several service delivery models can be employed to accomplish this objective. These models are discussed in the following section.

MODELS OF COMMUNITY FORENSIC TREATMENT: TO INTEGRATE OR NOT TO INTEGRATE?

There is little doubt that applying forensic expertise to psychiatric treatment system can enhance the quality of care. However, when developing forensic services, every mental health system must decide how to implement the treatment program, choosing to create a subspecialty team dedicated to forensic patients or to embed forensic expertise into all treatment settings. These approaches have been termed "parallel" and "integrated" models, respectively (Tighe, Henderson, and Thornicroft 2002, 100). The parallel model has the added potential benefit of fostering clinical expertise and providing intensive treatment, but specialized treatment teams may never be able to expand enough to meet demand. Integrated services can better serve to enhance forensic expertise in general psychiatric settings, though they may not be able to provide the intensive services required by some patients. In the best-developed treatment systems, both methods are employed, using a mixed model of direct care and consultative services by forensic psychiatrists. This dual approach creates the broadest impact of forensic expertise on treatment provision.

Specialized Forensic Teams

Two evidence-based models of specialized outpatient treatment are relevant to forensic populations: Forensic Assertive Community Treatment (FACT) teams and Assisted Outpatient Treatment (AOT). Both models require significant resources and are designed to provide intensive treatment to the patients most in need of care. In both models, patients are legally mandated to comply with outpatient treatment. In FACT teams the mandate comes from a probation officer or the criminal court, and in AOT the mandate comes from the probate (civil) court.

Forensic Assertive Community Treatment (FACT) Teams

FACT teams were adapted from the traditional Assertive Community Treatment (ACT) team model, aiming to provide intensive outpatient services and reduce the cycle of homelessness, hospitalization, and arrest that plagues many forensic patients. As in ACT teams, patients are followed closely and frequently evaluated outside of mental health clinics. However, FACT teams differ from ACT teams in a few key aspects. FACT programs typically have (1) enrollees with criminal justice involvement, (2) referrals primarily from a criminal justice agency, and (3) a close partnership with a criminal justice agency (Lamberti, Weisman, and Faden 2005). In some cases, probation or parole officers are embedded within the treatment team and monitor compliance. Although initially promising, longer-term outcomes of FACT teams have yet to be evaluated. A few studies have attempted to evaluate FACT outcomes, but methodological limitations make it difficult to draw conclusions from the data (Morrissey 2014; Morrissey, Meyer, and Cuddeback 2007). FACT programs are widely employed, but their evidence base lags behind the pace of implementation.

Assisted Outpatient Treatment (AOT)

Assisted outpatient treatment, also known as outpatient commitment, has been adopted by forty-five states to serve clients with severe mental illness who have histories of non-compliance with medication, resulting in frequent hospitalizations and high risk for violence. Under commitment through civil court proceedings, persons meeting guidelines (varying by state) are mandated to comply with treatment and medication. Non-compliance results in hospitalization, including involuntary hospitalization. Although not designed specifically to serve forensic patients, many of the committed individuals have criminal justice involvement.

Research has demonstrated AOT's effectiveness in reducing hospitalizations in New York (Swartz et al. 2009). Other states showed similar reductions (Esposito, Westhead, and Berko 2008; Swartz et al. 1999). Some investigations have also demonstrated that AOT reduces arrests and incarceration (Gilbert et al. 2010; Esposito, Westhead, and Berko 2008; Swartz, Swanson, and Hiday 2001), violence and disruptive behaviors (New York State Office of Mental Health 2005; Phelan et al. 2010), and victimization of the committed clients (Hiday et al. 2002).

The success of AOT relies on adequate numbers of qualified staff to provide intensive outpatient treatment and access to inpatient beds when needed. The practice of AOT is sustained, intensive treatment. Although clients are the ones committed to treatment, the mental health system is also mandated to treat under these programs. In contrast to traditional mental health programs, non-compliance with treatment leads to a higher level of care and not to discharge or potential arrest.

INTEGRATING FORENSIC EXPERTISE INTO GENERAL PSYCHIATRY PRACTICE

Forensic psychiatry's body of knowledge is relevant to clinical care beyond just the identified forensic population, and there are advantages to incorporating this expertise into the general practice of psychiatry. Forensic expertise can aid in focusing treatment, increasing its relevance to clients, and improving risk assessment and management. Specifically, forensic training enhances a clinician's history taking, use of collateral data, appreciation of community resources and contextual influences on behavior, attention to mental health law and medical ethics, and familiarity with research on risk assessment and management. In a more nuanced way, forensic training engenders an appreciation for the complexity of clients' lives beyond diagnosis and symptoms. Forensic cases demonstrate that the confluence of circumstances, more than diagnoses, shapes behavior, function, and violence risk.

The incorporation of forensic expertise into general psychiatric practice can be accomplished through consultation to general treatment teams and through forensic psychiatrists treating patients directly. In community mental health centers, forensic psychiatrists are among the physicians on the treating teams, often assigned to care for high-risk clients with particularly vexing symptoms and histories. The teams and clients benefit from the expertise, and the forensic psychiatrists bolster their credibility in forensic work. The forensic psychiatrists can also provide consultation through several programs.

Risk Management Rounds

Routine case presentations of high-risk clients in rounds provide both consultation and training. Forensic psychiatrists demonstrate ways to think about risk and treatment that shape thinking and assessments. Rounds that include all team members, including case managers and para-professionals, contribute to group cohesion and a shared mission to foster engagement of resistant clients. The risk management rounds serve to manage counter-transference, allaying clinicians' isolation, fears, and helplessness. The rounds can engender respect and empathy, especially for clients who are viewed as "more bad than mad." In the same way, rounds can also identify risks that are unrecognized and minimized. Rounds are enhanced by periodic updates on clients who were previously presented in detail.

Team-Embedded Forensic Experts

In mental health centers with a cohort of forensic psychiatric experts, forensic psychiatrists can be assigned to teams for consultation, participation in team rounds, supervision, liaison with the court and probation/parole, and direct assessments of high-risk clients. The close collaboration between the expert and the team shares the burden and provides a rich opportunity for teaching and supervision. Through the sustained, close interaction with the team, the forensic psychiatrist can observe the team's strengths and weaknesses and identify educational and training needs. This method uses forensic experts efficiently; forensic psychiatrists can be embedded in more than one team and can help balance assignment of cases, based on risk and special needs. Being part of frontline delivery of services, the embedded forensic expert can also advise administration on relevant policy and procedures.

Risk rounds and embedded forensic experts can be blended with the specialized teams. The best model depends on many factors, including the size of the agency, available experts, and connection with criminal justice agencies. The goal is twofold: first, to make forensic expertise accessible and incorporated as standard of care, and second, to view all clients as benefiting from that expertise.

GOALS AND KEY FEATURES OF COMMUNITY FORENSIC TREATMENT PROGRAMS

Principles of Care

Mental health clinicians help forensic patients to live safely in the community. The primary goal is to improve the health of the patient, but forensic clinicians will also help patients to navigate the criminal justice system successfully, including complying with probation/parole mandates and avoiding behavior that could lead to re-arrest. In addition, clinicians must also be mindful of public safety and take reasonable steps to protect others from foreseeable harms caused by their patients (*Tarasoff* 1976).

When engaging forensic patients, clinicians take a significantly different approach from criminal justice agents. Knowledge about the legal system is necessary for clinicians to understand their patients' circumstances, but clinicians must be careful not to adopt the monitoring and policing functions of the criminal justice system. Instead, successful approaches to working with mentally ill offenders are based on building patients' strengths and helping them to understand the relationship between their illness and criminal behavior. The Good Lives Model of Offender Rehabilitation (Ward, Mann, and Gannon 2007) and the Risk-Needs-Responsivity Model (Andrews and Bonta 2010) are programs that, although not specifically designed for offenders with mental illness, utilize this individualized, strengths-based treatment approach. Clinicians can build upon these programs and tailor them to the needs of persons with mental illness, recognizing that all patients—whether justice-involved or not—have unique interests, abilities, and aspirations that will shape the course of their treatment. Designation as a "forensic" patient does not change this bedrock principle of mental health care.

Components of a Treatment Program

Community forensic treatment, whether organized as a specialized program or embedded in general psychiatric practice, utilizes a multidisciplinary approach to the management of high-risk patients. Forensic treatment programs offer psychotherapy, medication, case management, housing, and vocational supports. These components are included in many intensive psychiatric treatment programs, such as ACT teams, but forensic treatment programs also include some unique features.

"In-Reach" Into Prisons and Secure Hospitals

Many patients find that leaving a correctional institution or forensic psychiatric hospital provokes anxiety and fear. They may be uncertain about where to live, how to reconnect with family and friends, or how to adapt to technological advances after many years of institutionalization. For persons with mental illness, these challenges are often amplified. Forensic clinicians can help to reduce anxiety and ease patients' transition to the community by providing "in-reach" services in prisons and secure hospitals. Clinicians meet clients months (or even years) prior to the patient's release, and they offer counseling about issues commonly faced by people returning to the community. The counseling sessions can be done individually or in groups involving several soon-to-be-released patients. In addition to easing the emotional burden faced by patients, clinicians can also help ensure they are connected with community mental health providers, planning for their arrival well in advance and obtaining necessary resources.

Access to Varying Levels of Psychiatric Care

Successful community forensic treatment offers a range of psychiatric services: traditional outpatient appointments, day hospitals, residential treatment, crisis management, emergency care, and inpatient facilities. This continuum of care is necessary to manage risk on a day-to-day basis. For example, a patient with schizophrenia and a history of assault may begin to exhibit symptoms that are similar to those he displayed just prior to his last violent episode. The clinician recognizes that the patient's risk of violence is elevated, even though he may not meet civil commitment criteria or require involuntary hospitalization. Access to a higher level of care, such as a day hospital or short-term residential placement, can greatly help to monitor the patient and manage the risk. Without these services, clinicians may be forced to wait until the patient's symptoms reach a much higher level before intervening, thereby managing the violence risk less effectively.

Housing Programs

As with other types of psychiatric patients, stable housing is beneficial to forensic patients. However, finding adequate housing can be a challenge, as communities are often reticent to have individuals perceived as "criminals" or "crazies" in their midst. The challenge is even greater for patients convicted of sex crimes or identified on Sex Offender Registries, as community members can easily find detailed information about their criminal histories online. Forensic treatment programs must work diligently with communities to confront stigma and create a safe place for patients to live. Answering the public's questions at town hall meetings, meeting privately with community leaders, and developing relationships with local landlords can all be helpful in this effort.

Vocational Programs

Many criminal offenders experience difficulty finding work, as job applications typically require disclosure of criminal convictions. Persons with mental illness are doubly disadvantaged, marked both by a criminal record and symptoms of mental illness. Nonetheless, employment is an important component of forensic treatment programs. Meaningful work can enhance self-esteem for patients, provide necessary income, and foster a greater sense of community integration. Vocational programs for forensic patients have not yet been studied in detail, but innovative approaches, such as that employed in the Connecticut Department of Mental Health and Addiction Services (DMHAS), are being developed. In the DMHAS program, employment specialists attend weekly rounds with the forensic treatment team. They also meet individually with patients to assess their vocational skills and goals, and they conduct group programs focused on résumé building, interview skills, and conflict resolution. Employment goals are integrated into the mental health treatment plan from the outset.

Interventions to Address Criminogenic Needs

Untreated mental illness is not the only cause of criminal recidivism, and effective treatment programs must address other factors that contribute to destabilization and lead to arrest. For forensic clients, some criminogenic needs are common. Homelessness, unemployment, and substance use are common targets for intervention for all clients, not only for those involved in the criminal justice system. However, other needs are particular to those who are at risk for re-offense, and specialized interventions have developed through the use of forensic expertise.

Specialized approaches for offenders with mental illness address the "antisocial cognitions" that contribute to recidivism (Rotter and Carr 2013). In a review of cognitive-behavioral approaches, Rotter and Carr identified those that began in correctional settings and were then applied in community treatment. Although many approaches were designed for offenders with no mental illness, some have been modified for those with psychiatric impairments and show promise in reducing criminal recidivism. For example, Reasoning and Rehabilitation, an effective intervention for non-mentally ill offenders, was modified for persons with mental illness (R&R2M). The modified version reduced disruptive behaviors in patients in a forensic hospital (Young and Ross 2007). Moral Reconation Therapy (MRT) and Interactive Journaling are treatment interventions used in some mental health courts, but their effects have not been evaluated (Rotter and Carr 2013; Rotter and Olson 2010). These approaches target thinking and reactivity associated with antisocial cognitions.

Other interventions have focused on modulation of affect and reduction of impulsivity. For example, in one Veterans Administration Medical Center, a group called the Three Cs for veterans with post-traumatic stress disorder and other affective disorders focuses on the recognition and control of emotional flare-ups associated with aggression. The three Cs are "catch it, check it, correct it," referring to the rise of disruptive emotion that drives impulsive and disruptive behavior.

Focus on Staff Wellness

Clinician burnout can be heightened when working with forensic patients. The patients have often perpetrated serious violent offenses, but they, just as often, have been the victims of horrific life events. For clinicians, listening to patients' stories and helping them to work through traumatic events can be challenging, causing sadness, fear, anger, and disgust. Because of the strong emotions that arise in the course of treatment, forensic programs must pay extra attention to the wellness of clinicians and other staff. Clinical rounds and individual supervision may be places where treatment providers can share feelings and obtain support, but in some circumstances, creating a dedicated time for clinicians to process emotions can also be helpful. This focus on staff wellness in forensic settings mirrors the methods used in other therapeutic approaches for difficult clients, such as DBT.

Applying Risk Assessment and Management Strategies as Standard of Care

Risk assessment and management are inherent requirements of general psychiatry, and they are even more important when working with forensic populations. Forensic psychiatrists have expertise in risk assessment, not only for violence, but also for risk of suicide and risks of functional decline. Their specialized skills, measures, and techniques—traditionally used to complete forensic evaluations, write reports, and testify in court—can also be applied to enhance clinical care in general psychiatry. Specifically, forensic psychiatrists can foster the use of collateral information and structured risk assessment tools to enhance clinical judgment. In addition, clinicians with forensic training appreciate that risk is dynamic and reactive to environmental circumstances, disease trajectory, changes in treatment, and reactivated trauma responses. An initial risk assessment at intake is not informative without constant update and sensitive exploration.

Forensic expertise is relevant to management strategies as well. Types and frequency of monitoring, transitions across levels of care, and the integration of substance abuse treatment into psychiatric care are familiar strategies in forensic psychiatry. In addition, forensic psychiatrists are knowledgeable about law, ethics, and public policy related to mental health care. When working with forensic patients, this broad-based, multidisciplinary perspective can enhance treatment planning and risk management.

CLINICAL CHALLENGES OF COMMUNITY FORENSIC TREATMENT

The advantages of psychiatric care informed by forensic expertise are many, but the forensic focus also brings challenges. The therapeutic alliance between patients and clinicians can be strained and complicated by the additional factor of criminal justice involvement, and the course of treatment is not always smooth. We discuss several common challenges in forensic treatment below.

Clinician Attitudes About Forensic Clients

The "forensic" label can evoke concerns and biases about risk, about forced treatment and increased clinical responsibility, and about the injustice of dedicating scarce resources to clients who are avoiding consequences of their illegal actions. For clinicians, these attitudes often arise from and are enhanced by lack of resources, training, effective interventions, and role models. The negative counter-transference can be particularly strong for clients labeled as sex offenders, child molesters, child abusers, or violent. These labels can impede engagement, compliance, and effective risk assessment and management.

The designation of "forensic client" was initially based on legal involvement. The nomenclature had no scientific or diagnostic relevance, but the label often directed placement and even treatment. Often a client in general psychiatry is, at the point of arrest, perceived as different, perhaps more complicated, more risky, and less deserving. The integration of forensic psychiatry expertise can alter that perception and the effect on treatment in two critical ways.

First, forensic expertise helps treaters to recognize legal involvement as a clinical matter related to the new burdens borne by the client. The arrest and label of forensic client does not convert a deserving "mad" client into an undeserving "bad" one. The risk level does not automatically increase because a client is labeled forensic; rather, the previously unidentified risk is now recognized and can be managed.

In a subtler effect, forensic expertise translates the relationship between law and medicine: the legal process is based on invented principles, and medicine on the discovery of natural order in disease and health. Therefore, a forensic label is not the same as a diagnosis. They differ in how they impact treatment. For example, a labeled sex offender indicates only that someone has been convicted of a sex offense. Treatment cannot be based on the label "sex offender," since the label does not inform the etiology, the frequency, or the absolute nature of the person's behavior. Further, someone without the label of sex offender may be someone who simply has not been convicted. The lack of a label does not equate to the absence of deviant behavior.

Applying this understanding of the law and medicine, a forensic psychiatrist on a treatment team can help to correct misperceptions of the relevance of forensic labels as well as misperceptions about their absence. Clients not connected to the criminal justice system also require risk management and a focus on problem behaviors that put them at risk for future arrests. Forensic psychiatrists can help clinicians modify their perceptions of "forensic clients" to include all those who exhibit problem behaviors and potential for violence exacerbated by substance abuse, non-compliance, and resistance to engagement.

Converting Leveraged Care Into a Therapeutic Approach

Clients mandated by courts, probation, and parole are often treated in community mental health centers. Many have never been in treatment before; others have been in treatment but were non-compliant. Court-mandated treatment forcibly engages clients formerly in the therapeutic gap

(Chapter 17)—persons in need of treatment who either do not have access to treatment or who have not engaged in treatment. The failure to engage can come from anosognosia or rejection of treatment as irrelevant or with a lower priority than other social and environmental demands. Forced into treatment, these clients are often unfamiliar with the process and enter to avoid the alternative of incarceration. Many do not see a need for treatment and do not appreciate the negative effects of their symptoms.

Leveraged care can be a barrier to treatment and engagement. The transference to the treaters can be one of policing, aligned with the court. The counter-transference can also be a barrier to engagement. Clinicians feeling forced to treat patients who do not want treatment may view the mandate for treatment as a "dump" of bad behavior onto the mental health community. Patients on probation for violent offenses or sexual deviance present even greater challenges. In these cases, counter-transference becomes a bigger hurdle, enhanced by higher risks and a sense of responsibility for outcomes.

Forensic psychiatry has expertise in risk assessments and management, consultation with staff, and liaison with the legal community that is constructive in these cases. Forensic expertise can go further, however, and foster engagement that converts leveraged care into a therapeutic intervention. The therapeutic approach redefines the forced treatment as a vehicle for addressing the clients' needs from their point of view.

Focusing therapy beyond diagnosis and medication compliance to issues of priority for the client provides a hook into engagement. Often what clients identify as needs such as homelessness, unemployment, poverty, social isolation, and detachment, if met, do reduce criminal recidivism. Further, problem-solving that focuses on clients' priorities enhances compliance, conveys respect, and builds a therapeutic alliance.

Another therapeutic technique engages the client through acceptance of the clients' goals as related to the criminal justice involvement. For example, a client mandated to treatment by probation may fear returning to incarceration. The therapeutic focus will be on staying out of jail (the client's goal) rather than on complying with probation (probation's goal). Although the required behaviors are nearly identical, the therapeutic manipulation of purpose can enhance the client's control and buy-in.

This therapeutic approach works even when the clients' stated goals seem unrelated to therapy. For example, a client diverted to treatment by the court may want to argue with the attorney or take issue with the judge's decision. Although, at first glance, not a desirable goal, the therapeutic manipulation focuses on the wish to be heard and respected. Allying with the client around that goal can support engagement and can reintroduce medication as a means to be calm enough and organized enough to participate in defense and voice opposition in a constructive manner. This approach takes time, genuine interest, and enough knowledge of the criminal justice system to strategize with the client.

Tensions Between Client Desires and Public Safety

In successful community forensics programs, patients may spend months or years outside of institutions. As patients mature, the focus of their care shifts. Whereas the initial treatment focus may have been on survival and basic needs—shelter, financial support, resolution of legal involvement—over time patients progress in their lives and begin to take an interest in school, work, and romantic relationships. Clinicians work with patients on addressing these issues, but sometimes the patient's goals conflict with public safety. For example, a patient with a history of sexual violence involving teenagers may wish to attend high school or college classes, and the patient's interests in getting an education must be weighed against the potential risk posed to the community.

Interdisciplinary team meetings, both with and without the patient present, are often helpful in sorting through these difficult decisions. Risk management rounds are also good places to discuss the tensions and decide how best to balance them. In many cases, clinicians can work with patients to identify the risks involved in activities like college classes or romantic relationships, proactively engaging them in the process of risk management. When patients feel respected and involved in planning for their futures, rather than simply being told not to do something by an oversight agency, they are more likely to modify their behavior. Moreover, clinicians and patients alike can be guided to appreciate that protecting the public is in the clients' best interest, preventing the conflict that arises from a sense of a divided mission.

Collaborating with Criminal Justice Agencies

There are many reasons why individuals with mental illness find themselves on probation or parole. For some—typically those who have repeatedly committed "nuisance" crimes related to symptoms of mental illness—probation is used as a method of monitoring and encouraging compliance with mental health treatment. For others, probation and parole provide necessary oversight during the high-risk period following long incarcerations for serious violent crimes. In some states, particular crimes or legal designations, such as being a registered sex offender or a sexually violent predator, are accompanied by long periods of probation and other restrictions (e.g. electronic GPS monitoring, residency and work restrictions). Thus, forensic patients are very likely to interact with probation or parole officers at some time, and clinicians must develop strategies to work collaboratively with these agencies.

Collaboration between mental health clinicians and criminal justice agents is complicated by threats to confidentiality, boundary issues, and potential erosion of the benefits of treatment. Without guidance and structure, interactions with the criminal justice system can polarize a treatment team. Clinicians can over-identify with the policing role and ally with the legal monitors. Other treaters may ally with the client against the courts and probation. Either position erodes therapeutic effectiveness and team cohesion. However, avoiding collaboration with probation or parole officers is also problematic, potentially creating a split that increases clients' acting out and exacerbates symptoms.

Forensic expertise can guide the collaboration to maximize benefit to clients and support the treatment team. Although protocols can be established for interactions with probation and parole, individual cases present unique complications that demand critical analysis and decisions based on the knowledge and application of psychiatric, legal, and ethical principles. Ongoing forensic consultation can help sort through the complex issues as they arise.

Another risk of collaboration with probation, parole, and courts is the potential for clinicians to view criminal justice interventions as clinical tools. Clinicians may wish for an arrest to teach their patient a lesson, incarceration to teach acceptance of responsibility, or probation violation to force treatment compliance. These desires are understandable, but they are examples of clinicians misunderstanding the purpose, boundaries, and risks of the mental health–criminal justice collaboration. The risks of collaboration are bidirectional. Professionals in the criminal justice system can also misunderstand how the collaboration works. For example, probation officers may request access to clinical records or treatment groups, or a criminal court judge may order that a defendant be prescribed medication as part of a jail diversion program. These requests are boundary crossings, intruding into the province of mental health professionals.

Mental clinicians and criminal justice agents must be mindful that familiarity with the other system does not make experts on either side. When done well, cooperation can benefit clients and advance goals of both the mental health and the criminal justice systems. However, the interface is complicated and fraught with challenges. Availability and infusion of forensic expertise is a critical asset that maximizes the benefits of collaboration and manages the risks.

FUTURE DIRECTIONS

Forensic psychiatry has evolved in scope and expertise, transforming from a specialty focused primarily on assessment and consultation to one that takes an active role in the treatment of forensic populations. Advances in psychiatry, neuroscience, and the law continue to shape the field's evolution. Future directions will combine those implemented by design and those forced upon the discipline by other factors. Areas ripe for further development include:

- *Additional Research Into Treatment Efficacy.* Many of the interventions developed to reduce recidivism in criminal offenders are currently in the early phases of study. Additional research into their efficacy and the adaptations necessary for offenders with mental illness is crucial to expanding psychiatry's knowledge base and enhancing treatment approaches.
- *Dynamic Risk Assessment Models Appropriate for Outpatient Treatment.* One novel approach to risk management is incorporating client opinion in how individual risk has changed and what would help reduce the risk. Incorporation of risk assessment models into AOT and FACT teams offers a way to improve outcomes.
- *Modification of the Recovery Movement for Forensic Clients.* The Recovery Movement is a powerful force shaping psychiatry (Barber 2012). However, many of the pillars of Recovery cannot apply to forensic clients without modification. For example, "freedom to fail" is a central tenet in Recovery; failure for forensic clients can result in incarceration, another arrest, and even threats to public safety. Modified to "freedom to start anew," "freedom to forgive myself," or "right to another chance" might be substituted and carry the same message of self-determination. Such modifications can extend eligibility and acceptance of forensic clients into treatment settings.
- *Development of Forensic Peer Services.* The success of peer services as part of the Recovery Movement establishes a role for the involvement of clients in nurturing recovery in others. However, forensic clients are often not eligible. Development of forensic peers can extend the effectiveness of this intervention to those who have criminal involvement. Participation in peer interventions can help patients to increase a sense of belonging and will support successful community integration.
- *Reduction of Stigma of Mental Illness.* Forensic psychiatry is positioned to address stigma from the advantage of knowledge of law, risk, and management strategies. Eminent forensic psychiatrists provide measured and corrective responses to media frenzy after violent tragedies, but the stigma of mental illness remains a destructive force against community integration for many clients. Effective treatment models for those with significant

criminal histories can reduce risk for violence, isolation, and ostracism.

- *Training and Education.* Although forensic psychiatry is a subspecialty, its relevance to general psychiatry is significant. A stronger presence of forensic psychiatry expertise and methods in medical school curricula, clerkships, and residency can maximize the integration of forensic expertise into general psychiatry.

CONCLUSION

Forensic psychiatry is an established subspecialty with an identified patient population, a particular mission, qualified experts, and unique interventions. However, forensic psychiatry does not exist in a silo; the principles learned from working with patients involved in the criminal justice system are relevant to all psychiatric practice. Indeed, forensic patients are a broader group than just those with active legal charges. They can be identified not only by their legal involvement, but rather by characteristics of their disorders, their functional abilities, and their risk. Different models incorporate forensic expertise into clinical practice. Some use specialized treatment programs, and others integrate forensic principles into general psychiatry. Regardless of the model chosen, including forensic expertise in clinical care provides many advantages, allowing treatment systems to improve risk management, support and educate staff, and solidify psychiatry's mission of providing quality patient care.

REFERENCES

Andrews, D.A. and J. Bonta. 2010. "Rehabilitating Criminal Justice Policy and Practice." *Psychology, Public Policy, and Law* 16: 39–55.

APA (American Psychiatric Association). 1974. "Position Statement on Medical and Psychiatric Services in Correctional Institutions." Approved by the Board of Trustees Feb 9, 1974.

Appelbaum, K. 2015. "Correctional Psychiatry: The APA and Where Do We Go From Here?" Presented at the 2015 AAPL Annual Meeting, Ft. Lauderdale, FL. October 22, 2015.

Barber, M.E. 2012. "Recovery as the New Medical Model for Psychiatry." *Psychiatric Services* March 2012. doi: 10.1176/appl.ps.201100248.

Case, B., H.J. Steadman, S.A. Dupuis, and L.S. Morris. 2009. "Who Succeeds in Jail Diversion Programs for Persons with Mental Illness? A Multi-site Study." *Behavioral Sciences and the Law* 27: 661–74.

Esposito, R., V. Westhead, and J. Berko. 2008. "Florida's Outpatient Commitment Law: Effective but Underused." (letter). *Psychiatric Services* 59: 328.

Gilbert, A.R., L.L. Moser, R.A. Van Dorn, J.W. Swanson, C.W. Wilder, P.C. Robbins, K.J. Keator, H.J. Steadman, and M.S. Swartz. 2010. "Reductions in Arrest under Assisted Outpatient Treatment in New York." *Psychiatric Services* 61: 996–9.

Hiday, V.A., M.S. Swartz, J.W. Swanson, R. Borum, and H.R. Wagner. 2002. "Impact of Outpatient Commitment on Victimization of People with Severe Mental Illness." *American Journal of Psychiatry* 159: 1403–11.

Lamb, H.R. and L.E. Weinberger. 2005. "The Shift of Psychiatric Inpatient Care from Inpatient Hospitals to Jails and Prisons." *Journal of the American Academy of Psychiatry and the Law* 33: 529–34.

Lamberti S.I., R. Weisman, and D.I. Faden. 2005. "Forensic Assertive Community Treatment: Preventing Incarceration of Adults with Serious Mental Illness." *Psychiatric Services* 55: 1285–93.

Miller, H.A., A. Amenta, and M.A. Conroy. 2005. "Sexually Violent Predator Evaluations: Empirical Evidence, Strategies for Professionals, and Research Directions." *Law and Human Behavior* 29: 29–45.

Morrissey, J. 2014. "Forensic Assertive Community Treatment: Updating the Evidence." SAMHSA GAINS Center. Accessed January 31, 2015. http://gainscenter.samhsa.gov/cms-assets/documents/141801-618932.fact-fact-sheet---joe-morrissey.pdf.

Morrissey, J., P. Meyer, and G. Cuddeback. 2007. "Extending Assertive Community Treatment to Criminal Justice Settings: Origins, Current Evidence, and Future Directions." *Community Mental Health Journal* 43: 527–44.

New York State Office of Mental Health. 2005. *Kendra's Law: Final Report on the Status of Assisted Outpatient Treatment.*

Phelan, J.C., M. Sinkewicz, D. Castille, S. Huz, and B.G. Link. 2010. "Effectiveness and Outcome of Assisted Outpatient Treatment in New York State." *Psychiatric Services* 61: 137–43.

Rotter, M. and W.A. Carr. 2013. "Reducing Criminal Recidivism for Justice-Involved Persons with Mental Illness: Risk/Needs/Responsivity and Cognitive-Behavioral Interventions." *SAMHSA's GAINS Center for Behavioral Health and Justice Transformation* October 2013: 1–6. Accessed November 1, 2015. http://gainscenter.samhsa.gov.

Rotter, M. and E. Olson. 2010. "Targeting Criminal Recidivism in Mentally Ill Offenders: Cognitive Behavioral Approaches." Presented at the CMHS National Gains Center Conference. Orlando, Florida, May 2010.

Sarteschi, C.M., M.G. Vaughn, and K. Kim. 2011. "Assessing the Effectiveness of Mental Health Courts: A Quantitative Review." *Journal of Criminal Justice* 39 (1): 12–20. doi: 10.1016/j.jcrimjus.2010.11.003.

Skeem, J., S. Manchak, S. Vidal, and E. Hart. 2009. "Probationers with Mental Disorder: What (Really) Works?" Paper presented at the American Psychology and the Law Society Annual Conference, San Antonio, Texas, March 2009.

Swartz, M.S., J.W. Swanson, and V.A. Hiday. 2001. "A Randomized Controlled Trial of Outpatient Commitment in North Carolina." *Psychiatric Services* 52: 325.

Swartz, M.S., J.W. Swanson, H.J. Steadman, P.C. Robbins, and J. Monahan. 2009. *New York State Assisted Outpatient Treatment Program Evaluation*. Duke University School of Medicine.

Swartz, M.S., J.W. Swanson, R.H. Wagner, B.J. Burns, V.A. Hiday, and R. Borum. 1999. "Can Voluntary Outpatient Commitment Reduce Hospital Recidivism? Findings from a Randomized Trial with Severely Mentally Ill Individuals." *American Journal of Psychiatry* 156: 1968–75.

Tarasoff v. Regents of the University of California, 17 Cal. 3d 425 (1976).

Tighe, J., C. Henderson, and G. Thornicroft. 2002. "Mentally Disordered Offenders and Models of Community Care Provision." In *Care of the Mentally Disordered Offender in the Community*, edited by Alec Buchanan, pp. 89–110. Oxford: Oxford University Press.

U.S. Probation and Pretrial Services: Sex Offender Treatment. Accessed December 2, 2015. http://www.txnp.uscourts.gov/content/sex-offender-treatment.

Ward, T., R.E. Mann, and T.A. Gannon. 2007. "The Good Lives Model of Offender Rehabilitation: Clinical Implications." *Aggression and Violent Behavior* 12: 87–107.

Young, S.J. and R.R. Ross. 2007. "R&R2 for Youths and Adults with Mental Health Problems: A Prosocial Competence Training Program." *Ottawa: Cognitive Centre of Canada.* Accessed September 19, 2015. cogcen@canada.com.

Zonana, H. 2012. "Forensic Psychiatry." In *The American Board of Psychiatry and Neurology: Looking Back and Moving Ahead*, edited by Michael J. Aminoff and Larry R. Faulkner, pp. 151–9. Arlington VA: American Psychiatric Publishing.

CHAPTER 19

Change in Management of Persons with Problem Sexual Behaviors

Dominique Bourget

INTRODUCTION

Sexual offending is known to be a major problem with legal, social, public health, and public safety ramifications. The forensic evaluation, treatment, and overall management of patients with problem sexual behaviors have posed significant challenges to forensic mental health professionals over time. Patients carrying the stigma of having committed sexual offenses encounter significant barriers to community integration, even for the successfully treated patient. These matters are of great concern to many forensic mental health professionals, by the mere fact that problem sexual behaviors can often lead to criminal behavior. This being said, many individuals with deviant sexual interests will never engage in real-life deviant sexual behavior.

The publication of the 5th edition of the *Diagnostic and Statistical Manual of Mental Disorders* (DSM-5) (American Psychiatric Association 2013) has evoked numerous questions and debates about the definition and diagnostic classification of the paraphilic disorders. Furthermore, sexual deviance is often resistant to treatment; thus, risk management and protection of the public are enduring issues that require sophisticated attention from the forensic specialist. Such factors demand that the forensic specialist be aware of changes that might facilitate improved management of these difficulties. This chapter will examine the conceptual evolution and changes in the assessment, treatment, and at times complex risk management of patients, in both inpatient and outpatient settings, who present a history of problem sexual behaviors.

PARAPHILIA DEFINED

Evolution Over Time

At the end of the nineteenth century, Richard von Krafft-Ebing, a German psychiatrist, published his first treatise on human perversions. Using descriptive case studies, he analyzed and categorized "sexual perversion" as any form of sexual activity not intended to foster procreation. The 12th edition of *Psychopathia Sexualis* contained 238 case studies and introduced four categories of "cerebral neuroses": paradoxia, anaesthesia, hyperaesthesia, and paraesthesia (Krafft-Ebing 1903, 52–5). The latter category was concerned with perversion of the sexual instinct and discussed numerous types of sexual perversions, as they were perceived at the time. *Psychopathia Sexualis* became an authoritative reference on sexual pathology. Notwithstanding the tremendous work involved in this book, the analyses were tainted with considerable religious and moral overtones. These terms are no longer in use nowadays when we discuss sexual behaviors. The expression "sexual perversions" has been replaced by interchangeable expressions such as "sexual disorders," paraphilias, or paraphilic disorders.

A paradigm shift has truly occurred in the way we now approach paraphilic disorders. It was previously assumed that deviant sexual interests formed part of lifelong disorders and were unchangeable. Some clinicians and researchers now conceptualize paraphilic disorders as disorders in which consensual sexual interests have failed to develop (Marshall et al. 2006).

Despite the fact that the views on paraphilic disorders have evolved considerably after a century of debate on the adequacy of classifying human sexual behavior and its variants, including behavior considered dysfunctional or otherwise sanctioned by cultural, moral, or ideological norms, much controversy remains concerning the current diagnostic models (Giami 2015; Downing 2015).

While it is beyond the scope of this chapter to elaborate on the evolutionary and ideological perspectives outlining the diagnosing of paraphilic disorders or equivalent labels, it is nevertheless observable that social norms and policies have indeed greatly influenced the concept of normal versus abnormal sexual behavior, as discussed at greater length in recent papers (Giami 2015; Downing 2015). Giami commented on the fact that the current perspective has moved from pathologization/criminalization of non-reproductive sexual behavior to a model that considers sexual well-being and responsibility of the individual as well as the absence or limitation of consent, as will be shown in the next section (Giami 2015).

The DSM Definitions and Classification

The *Diagnostic and Statistical Manual of Mental Disorders* (DSM) was first introduced in 1952 by the American Psychiatric Association to provide clinicians with a classification framework and associated criteria for mental disorders. Sixty-five years after Krafft-Ebing's efforts to catalogue sexual perversions, the second edition of the DSM offered a disease classification for "sexual deviations" under the broader heading of "Personality disorders and certain other nonpsychotic mental disorders" (American Psychiatric Association 1968). The categorization provided a rather rudimentary definition, stating it applied to individuals with sexual interests directed primarily toward objects other than people of the opposite sex, sexual acts not usually associated with coitus, or coitus performed under bizarre circumstances. It listed eight specific disorders: homosexuality, fetishism, pedophilia, transvestitism, exhibitionism, voyeurism, sadism, and masochism. No specific criteria were defined.

The DSM-III, published in 1980, was more sophisticated and provided specific criteria for eight paraphilias in a subsection entitled "Paraphilias" under the general heading of "Psychosexual Disorders" (American Psychiatric Association 1980). Definitions of the paraphilias generally stated that the act or fantasy of engaging in the sexual activity in question was a repeatedly preferred or exclusive method of achieving sexual excitement, over and beyond sexual arousal to a consenting sexual partner. The DSM-III classification of the paraphilias included fetishism (use of nonliving objects or body parts), transvestism (recurrent and persistent cross-dressing), zoophilia (animals), pedophilia (prepubescent children), exhibitionism (exposure of genitals to an unsuspecting person), voyeurism (observing unsuspecting people, naked, disrobing or engaged in sex), sexual masochism (own suffering), and sexual sadism (suffering of another person). It excluded homosexuality as a deviant sexual interest. Another possible diagnosis was atypical paraphilia, a residual category for individuals with other paraphilias.

The DSM-IV edition renamed the paraphilias under "Sexual and Gender Identity Disorders," together with sexual dysfunctions, and essentially retained the same specific paraphilias with a minimum duration criterion of six months of "recurrent, intense sexually arousing fantasies, sexual urges, or behaviors," as well as an impairment criterion for the diagnosis to be met (American Psychiatric Association 1994).

The DSM-5 introduced a newly revised criteria set in 2013 (American Psychiatric Association 2013). Paraphilic disorders are now considered under their own separate heading. The most important change, however, is that paraphilia is no longer a diagnosis, in contrast to the language used in DSM-IV (American Psychiatric Association 1994). For the first time, a distinction is drawn between the presence of a paraphilia and paraphilic disorder. A paraphilia is defined as "any intense and persistent sexual interest, other than sexual interest in genital stimulation or preparatory fondling with phenotypically normal and physically mature consenting human partners." In some instances, the criteria "intense and persistent" are hardly applicable and paraphilias may then be defined as "any sexual interest greater than or equal to normophilic sexual interests" or "preferential" sexual interests. More simply, a paraphilia is a term used to define an anomalous sexual interest. It only translates to a paraphilic disorder when the presence of this anomalous sexual interest carries negative consequences such as distress or impairment to the individual, or harm to others. Paraphilias involve erotic activities or erotic targets and the same concept applies to paraphilic disorders. The first type, based on abnormal activity preferences, is divided into courtship disorders (voyeuristic disorder, exhibitionistic disorder, and frotteuristic disorder), while the second type is concerned with abnormal target preference (pedophilic disorder, fetishistic disorder, and transvestic disorder). In other words, for a diagnosis of paraphilic disorder to be made, both the presence of a paraphilia (Criterion A) and its adverse consequences (Criterion B) must be met. It is thus important to keep in mind that "individuals with paraphilia," "individuals with paraphilic disorders," and "sexual offenders" are not interchangeable expressions at this point in time.

Critics of the most recent DSM revisions have complained that the DSM retained the six-month duration criterion, noting that early treatment is more likely to be effective (Fedoroff 2011). They also pointed out the lack of evidence that individuals with paraphilias have higher sex drive or more intense fantasies than non-paraphilic individuals and that such language is potentially confusing (Fedoroff 2011; Berlin 2011). Berlin cautioned about the use of the word "preference," as it relates to the concept of paraphilia, owing to the fact that many individuals struggling with abnormal sexual urges might well prefer otherwise (Berlin 2011). Others have criticized the lack of clear boundaries between paraphilia and its associated disorder, as well as the lack of precision surrounding mental illness, deviant behavior, and criminality, as it pertains to some paraphilic disorders (Zonana 2011).

SCOPE OF THE PROBLEM

Precise prevalence rates on paraphilias and paraphilic disorders are not available and are, at best, estimated. There are likely several reasons to explain this: the lack of sound methodological studies, fear of disclosure and underreporting, and difficulties in applying the DSM criteria while surveying populations. The lack of specificity of DSM criteria, as aptly pointed out in a recent commentary, complicates comparisons and classification (Ranger and Fedoroff 2014).

Voyeurism is one of the most common paraphilias and may manifest in various fashions, including legally sanctioned activity. The highest possible prevalence of voyeuristic disorder in males is estimated at 12% and at 4% in females (American Psychiatric Association 2013). Exhibitionistic disorder is less common, estimated at 2–4% in males, and sexual masochism disorder is equally rare (American Psychiatric Association 2013). A review on the prevalence of frotteurism in adult populations identified four earlier studies that addressed this issue (Johnson et al. 2014). With the exception of one statistical outlier, three out of the four studies found prevalence rates below 10%.

With regards to pedophilic disorder, undoubtedly one of the most researched paraphilic disorders, the highest possible prevalence in the male population is estimated at 3–5%, and is believed to be much lower in the female population (American Psychiatric Association 2013). The prevalence for sexual sadism disorder varies widely, ranging from 2% to 30% in forensic samples (Krueger 2010). That variation is attributed in part to weaknesses in the reliability and validity of diagnostic criteria, as well as the variability of the samples under scrutiny (Briken, Bourget, and Dufour 2014). Sexual sadism disorder, in the extreme, is associated with rape and sexual homicide. In a study by Hill, the prevalence of sexual sadism in a large sample of sexual homicide offenders, using DSM-IV criteria (therefore consistent with modern criteria) was 37% (Hill et al. 2006). Although zoophilia is a rare paraphilia, categorized under Other Specified Paraphilic Disorder in the DSM-5, it is, however, said to be associated with the highest rate of crossover paraphilic behavior across paraphilic disorders (Abel 2008).

THE ROLE OF FORENSIC PSYCHIATRY

Forensic psychiatrists have traditionally been called upon to assess and treat individuals with potential paraphilic disorders. While it should be argued that any psychiatrist needs to be trained in the assessment of any mental disorder, training in the assessment of paraphilic disorders often occurs in the course of specialized forensic psychiatry training provided by sexual behaviors clinics. The reason for individuals with paraphilic disorders to be commonly seen in forensic psychiatry programs is the criminal behavior resulting from acting out abnormal sexual urges associated with common paraphilias such as pedophilia, exhibitionism, voyeurism (including accessing child pornographic material), sadism, or other less common paraphilias. Individuals who have engaged in criminal behavior due to a paraphilia are often referred for psychiatric and risk assessment by the courts. In turn, courts have often relied on such assessments to render the most appropriate sentence (O'Shaughnessy 2015).

The Problem of Informed Consent

Free informed consent is paramount in the evaluation of paraphilic disorders. There are risks inherent to the consent process in a forensic context. The courts increasingly rely on experts' opinions before rendering sentence. An individual referred by the court, where the forensic mental health professional will submit a report and/or possibly testify, can hardly decline his participation in an assessment, at the risk of appearing uncooperative and culpable. The risk of coercion, albeit not sanctioned by the medical community, is high and genuine, and merits further clinical consideration. Preventive measures need to be entertained at an early stage. Overtly expressed coercion is to be confronted differently from covert coercion. The individual who will clearly indicate that he feels obligated to submit to a psychiatric and sexual behaviors evaluation at the expense of his freedom of choice will be reminded of his right to refuse to submit to assessment procedures and encouraged to seek further advice from his lawyer. The forensic psychiatrist would do well to refrain from taking the advocate's role in this scenario. It would be appropriate, however, depending on circumstances, to discuss the proposed assessment, the pros and cons, which could also include legal consequences, and have the individual initiate further contact once a decision is made. Other individuals may state that they already have weighed pros and cons of moving forward with an assessment and even though they believe they have no other real choice, will nevertheless be able to provide a relatively free informed consent from a clinical perspective. Special populations, for instance those with an intellectual disability, may represent a greater challenge, and the ultimate question will be their capacity to consent. If deemed incapable of consenting to a medical procedure, further actions may be required on the part of the professional, based on enacting provisions in the applicable jurisdiction. All in all, the issue of coercion is complex, as multiple factors need to be considered. There may not be any clear-cut solution at this time, but recognition that it does indeed exist may lead to further reflection and solutions for the future.

Implications of Diagnosing Paraphilic Disorder in a Forensic Population

One must be careful to distinguish properly between clinical and forensic implications of a paraphilic disorder diagnosis, for the implications can be largely detrimental to certain groups of individuals. A good example of this is possession or viewing of child pornography, sometimes considered a paraphilia. Such diagnosis requires either acknowledgment of a predominant sexual interest in children or documented history of behavior confirming a primary pedophilic sexual interest (Nielssen et al. 2011). Between 47% and 65% of child pornography offenders meet the DSM criteria, based on Nielssen's study, which examined child pornography offenders detected by surveillance of the internet or by other methods (Nielssen et al. 2011). It has been shown that accessing child pornography is not, on its own, a predictor that the individual with no prior history of hands-on contact behavior will go on to commit a contact offense (Seto, Hanson, and Babchishin 2011).

Sexually Violent Predator Civil Commitment Legislation

Civil commitment of sexually violent predators (SVP) was rendered legal in the United States after two notorious cases tried in Kansas. In *Kansas v. Hendricks* (1997), the U.S. Supreme Court upheld the constitutionality of civil commitment legislation for sex offenders who, due to "mental abnormality" or "personality disorder," are likely to reengage in predatory violent sexual acts. Hendricks had a lengthy history of child molestation and had received a diagnosis of paraphilic disorders, including pedophilia and exhibitionism. He continued to experience uncontrollable sexual urges when under stress. *Kansas v. Crane* (2002) concerned a man who was found to have antisocial personality disorder and exhibitionism. The court stated that rather than "a total or complete lack of control," a "serious difficulty in controlling his sexual behavior" owing to the mental abnormality or personality disorder was sufficient to justify indefinite civil commitment of an individual. Legislation allowing for the involuntary civil commitment of mentally disordered sexual offenders is in effect in twenty states and federally (Frances and First 2011a).

The proceedings rely heavily on forensic mental health experts to guide them in establishing whether an offender presents with a mental abnormality or personality disorder (Fabian 2011). Since experts utilize the DSM classification system, issues of validity and reliability of diagnoses are most relevant and may need to be qualified. To date, the two most commonly used diagnoses have included pedophilia and paraphilia NOS (Frances and First, 2011a). Potential misuse of psychiatric diagnoses, such as paraphilia NOS—nonconsent, or hebephilia—has been cause for concern (Fabian 2011; Frances and First 2011a; Frances and First 2011b). Although the legislation is well intended and aims at protecting the society against violent sexual predators who might otherwise be released at the end of sentence, one wonders whether they indeed should be indefinitely civilly committed, under the pretense of an ambiguous mental condition rather than serve longer prison terms (Frances and First 2011a). This remains open to debate.

ASSESSMENT OF PARAPHILIA AND PARAPHILIC DISORDER

In contrast to the language used in DSM-IV (American Psychiatric Association 1994), sexual paraphilia is no longer a diagnosis in the DSM-5 (American Psychiatric Association 2013). Paraphilic disorders will be diagnosed based on the criteria set defined in the DSM. In admitters who self-report deviant sexual interests, their clinical history may at times suffice to establish an initial diagnosis. However, in order to gain a full understanding of the dynamics involved and enable effective individualized treatment, it will be necessary to obtain a comprehensive clinical evaluation (Bourget and Bradford 2008, Seto, Kingston and Bourget, 2014). Typically this evaluation will include a detailed psychiatric history with emphasis on psychosexual history and mental status examination that should permit identification of any existing co-morbid conditions. Not all sex offenders are paraphilic-disordered men. Sometimes other causes for deviant sexual behaviors will be identified; the more thorough the history, the easier it is to guide the diagnosis and eventual interventions.

A full sexual behaviors assessment will normally include a sexual hormone profile, sexual questionnaires and other objective measures of sexual arousal. The sexual hormone profile can prove useful to screen for any anomaly and to serve as a baseline before potential pharmacological treatment. Sexual questionnaires are used to elicit a structured sexual history and gather information on the type and intensity of sexual fantasies, sexual activities, sexual drive, and the eventual presence of cognitive distortions as they relate to the paraphilia. Physiological measures of sexual arousal can help to detect abnormal sexual arousal or sexual interests in individuals suspected of suffering from a paraphilic disorder. Common physiological measures are penile plethysmography (PPG) and the Abel Assessment of Sexual Interest (AASI).

Phallometry

Penile plethysmography (PPG) or Penile Tumescence Testing (PTT) is the measurement of changes in penile tumescence (volume or circumference) in response to external auditory or visual sexual and non-sexual stimuli. PPG is currently the gold standard for objectively evaluating deviant physiological sexual arousal in men, particularly for pedophilia or sadism. In recent years, images of human subjects have been increasingly replaced by avatars, out of concerns arising from the use of prohibited pornographic material. Research by Hanson suggests that male sexual arousal to pedophilic stimuli, as measured by plethysmography, is a risk factor robustly associated with sexual offending against children (Hanson and Bourgon 2008). PPG has utility in assessing age and gender preferences, risk, treatment needs, and effects of intervention. While its use as a clinical diagnostic tool is generally well accepted, its use in criminal proceedings is controversial, owing to the lack of standardized methods and variable data on sensitivity and specificity (O'Shaughnessy 2015; Purcell, Chandler, and Fedoroff 2015).

Abel Assessment of Sexual Interest

This procedure uses visual reaction time to assess sexual interest. The subject is exposed to a series of standardized slides that depict clothed models in several categories of age, gender, and deviant sexual behavior, while a computer records visual reaction time to each slide. The AASI is applicable to both males and females and is generally considered to be less intrusive than phallometry (Bourget and Bradford 2008). Studies have shown that the sensitivity of the AASI is comparable to that of PPG in adult and adolescent child molesters (Abel et al. 1998; Abel et al. 2004).

Other Types of Investigations

In recent years, a number of studies have used functional brain imaging in an attempt to find distinct patterns of brain activation in men with pedophilic interests. A meta-analytical review of six studies published up to 2012 revealed there were no significant differences between pedophiles and non-pedophiles (Polisois-Keeting and Joyal 2013). The number of significant foci was higher in the pedophilic group, either reflecting anomalies in response to sexual arousal or stronger response to sexual stimuli. Because of limited subjects and different methodologies used in the studies, it was not possible to draw any decisive conclusions, leading the authors to recommend further studies. Preliminary results suggesting the potential of noninvasive investigational procedures for the assessment and treatment of sex offenders, such as virtual reality and eye-tracking technologies, are encouraging (Renaud et al. 2002; Renaud et al. 2005).

Risk Assessment and Use of Actuarial Tools

In order to implement effective relapse prevention strategies, it is important to assess risk by reviewing risk factors associated with reoffending. Examining predictors of sexual recidivism, Hanson updated an earlier meta-analysis and reviewed eighty-two studies involving 29,450 sexual offenders, to conclude that the strongest predictors included sexual deviancy and antisocial orientation (antisocial personality, antisocial traits, history of rule violations) (Hanson and Morton-Bourgon 2005).

There exist several actuarial prediction tools to assess the risk of sexual recidivism. Among them, the Violence Risk Appraisal Guide (VRAG), Violence Risk Appraisal Guide—Revised (VRAG-R) and associated Sex Offender Risk Appraisal Guide (SORAG) are well-known instruments used in the prediction of violent and sexually motivated recidivism (Harris et al. 2015, 286–99). Interestingly both the VRAG and SORAG incorporate other scales such as the PCL-R psychopathy scale (Hare 1991), the Cormier–Lang Criminal History Score for Violent (and nonviolent) Offenses (Akman and Normandeau 1967), and diagnoses using DSM criteria. The Rapid Risk Assessment for Sexual Offense Recidivism or RRASOR (Hanson 1997) is a precursor to the Static-99 (Hanson and Thornton 2000), and Static-2002 (Hanson and Thornton 2003). The VRAG, SORAG, RRASOR, and Static-99 were compared in a study that showed they all reliably predicted violent and sexual recidivism (Harris et al. 2003). Other tools include the Minnesota Sex Offender Screening Tool—Revised or MnSOST–R (Epperson et al. 1998), and Sexual Violence Risk-20 or SVR-20 (Boer et al. 1997). This list is not inclusive, as new instruments are being developed to increase reliability and usefulness of actuarial measures. These various tools are normally used in conjunction with clinical examinations, with the goal of obtaining comprehensive assessments.

A recently published study examined familial aggregation and the contribution of genetic and environmental factors to sexual crime in men convicted of a sexual offense (Langstrom et al. 2015). Not unlike a previous pilot study published in 2012 (Labelle et al. 2012), this paper reports on evidence of clustering of sexual offending in families, a phenomenon primarily accounted for by genes rather than environmental factors. This finding raises the question of selective prevention strategies for male first-degree relatives of sexually aggressive individuals.

TREATMENT AND MANAGEMENT OF PARAPHILIC DISORDERS

Evidence-Based Treatment

A paraphilia, in the absence of a negative impact on oneself or others, is not considered a disorder, and clinical intervention may not be necessary (American Psychiatric Association 2013, 686). There is an open debate as to whether paraphilic interests can be changed, and consequently, treatment needs will be evaluated at an individual level to determine whether changes may be achieved in a particular individual (Briken, Bourget, and Dufour 2014). This being said, there is substantial evidence that sexual offenders who receive treatment have a lower rate of recidivism than those who do not. Treatment is available and is strongly recommended for all those who suffer from a paraphilic disorder.

Historically, surgical castration was the only treatment option available and was widely used in the treatment of sex offenders (Bourget and Bradford 2008). Nowadays, the use of reversible and less intrusive treatments is preferred in order to reduce sexual drive and deviant sexual urges. The pharmacological arsenal to treat paraphilic disorders includes selective serotonin reuptake inhibitors (SSRI), antiandrogens and hormonal agents such as medroxyprogesterone acetate (MPA), cyproterone acetate (CPA), or luteinizing hormone-releasing hormone (LHRH) agonists.

MPA, CPA, and LHRH influence the production of androgens by various mechanisms, and reduce plasma testosterone levels, a hormone associated with sexual behavior in males. MPA was first used in the early 1970s to treat paraphilic disorders. Results of numerous studies indicate that these pharmacological agents significantly reduce the frequency of sexually deviant fantasies, urges, and behavior in men with paraphilic disorders (Gagné 1981; Briken 2002; Krueger and Kaplan 2001; Bradford and Pawlak 1993; Cooper 1981).

SSRIs have been utilized to treat paraphilic disorders since about the mid-1990s. This class of antidepressant medication increases brain serotonin and can affect sexuality in several ways, including reducing sexual interest. They have been found to be effective in decreasing the intensity of deviant sexual fantasies, and this method of treatment is generally well accepted by patients (Bourget and Bradford 2008). A trend to use intra-muscular LHRH as a first-line option has appeared in the last few years (Fedoroff 2011). These medications act centrally on the pituitary–hypothalamic axis to affect negatively the production of gonadotrophic hormones, resulting in a dramatic reduction of testosterone blood levels and of sexual desire of all types.

An algorithm for the pharmacological treatment of paraphilias proposed by an international task force has become a helpful tool to guide treatment decisions based on the severity of the pathology (Thibaut et al. 2010). The three first levels are concerned with relatively mild risk. At level 1, cognitive behavioral therapy is the treatment of choice for the control of paraphilic fantasies, compulsions and behaviors without impact on conventional sexual activity and sexual desire. At Level 2, the use of SSRIs is recommended for mild cases or those cases where paraphilic fantasies, compulsions, or behaviors bear a minor impact on conventional sexual activity and sexual desire. Level 3 applies to paraphilic fantasies, compulsions, or behaviors impacting moderately on conventional sexual activity and sexual desire with the recommendation of adding a low dose antiandrogen (e.g. CPA) to SSRIs.

Levels 4 to 6 apply to cases where the risk of sexual violence ranges from moderate to high. Treatment recommendations at level 4, for cases where there is a substantial reduction of conventional sexual activity or desire, or severe paraphilias (except sadism) with more intrusive fondling but limited number of victims, include full dosage of antiandrogen medications. At level 5, the use of a long-acting LHRH agonist (triptorelin or leuprolide acetate) is recommended in the presence of a high risk of sexual violence, severe paraphilias, and/or sexual sadistic fantasies/behavior. Level 6 is for most severe paraphilias when no satisfactory response to level 5 interventions has occurred. Treatment recommendations include the use of antiandrogen medications (CPA or MPA) in addition to LHRH agonists.

Individual and group psychotherapies, as well as cognitive-behavior techniques (CBT) have also been found of utility in the treatment and management of paraphilic disorders (Association for the Treatment of Sexual Abusers 2001). Group therapies are usually preferred over individual therapy, although a one-to-one approach is often helpful to assist with specific needs. CBT in particular has long been used to challenge cognitive distortions that maintain deviant sexual interests and that justify the acting-out or minimize consequences (Bourget and Bradford 2008).

Risk Management

Relapse prevention will necessarily involve treatment. Psychopharmacological interventions, as well as individual and group therapy, have shown their utility in reducing the risk of re-offense in populations of sexual offenders. Two large meta-analysis studies produced evidence of effectiveness of treatment for sexual offenders, using CBT and/or relapse prevention strategies, with lower rates of sexual recidivism in treated versus untreated offenders (Hanson et al. 2002, Lösel and Schmucker 2005). Other studies, however, detected no significant effect of treatment in similar populations (Marques et al. 2005). Limitations to these studies were the lack of standardization of treatment methods and treatment targets such as non-sexual factors. More recent studies comfort us with the notion that individuals with paraphilic disorders need no longer be considered a chronic risk to society.

A retrospective chart review study by Müller et al. (2014) challenged the belief that pedophilic interests are chronic and lifelong, using PTT as a measure of dynamic change. Post-treatment changes in PTT measures of sexual interest were recorded in approximately half of the sample of men with diagnosed pedophilia, supporting the idea that pedophilic interests can change over time and differ from sexual orientation (Müller et al. 2014). This finding represented a significant breakthrough with regards to perceptions of pedophilia, emphasizing the need for treatment and repeat assessments of risk. A recent paper by Hanson also provided evidence that the risk for sexual recidivism declines substantially the longer a sex offender remains offense-free in the community, not unlike the risk for general violent recidivism in the forensic population (Hanson et al. 2014). Based on twenty-one samples with a total of nearly 7,800 sexual offenders, Static-99R scores were used to define categories of low, moderate, and high risk. While the recidivism rates were consistently low (1–5%) for the low risk category, the rate was 4.2% for high-risk offenders after ten years (Hanson et al. 2014).

Successful transition from prison to the community and rehabilitation can also be influenced by the provision of social support to sex offenders, as evidenced by better recidivism outcomes (Duwe and King 2012). An innovative community-based model of reintegration referred to as "Circles of Support and Accountability (CoSA)" began in 1994 in Canada (Bates et al. 2014). Based on restorative justice principles, the circles consist of groups of volunteers supported by professionals whose goal is to facilitate the community reintegration of high-risk convicted sexual offenders. Circles may now be found in many parts of the world, including Canada, the UK, several U.S. states and other countries. The effectiveness of the CoSA model implemented in Minnesota was evaluated in a study comparing recidivism among CoSA participants and controls. A cost–benefit analysis was favorable, showing that significant reductions in recidivism generated economies to the state (Duwe 2012). CoSA initiatives have proven useful in lowering rates of recidivism in convicted sexual offenders and provide a rationale to the need for increased supports in rehabilitative efforts (Wilson, Cortoni, and McWhinnie 2009).

However, effective community reintegration for sexual offenders is fraught with many barriers. Negative public perceptions and fears of a persistent risk, as well as legislation permitting long, when not indefinite, terms of civil commitment or supervision and mandatory registry of sexual offenders perpetuate the stigmatization of those individuals whose risk can be mitigated by many factors. While public protection is paramount, decisions need not be based on subjective factors but rather on objective critical assessment of risk factors at an individual level and adequate follow-up.

THE FUTURE

The last decades have brought significant changes in the understanding, diagnosing, assessment methods, evidence-based treatment, and risk evaluation of paraphilic disorders. The major change has to do with a shift of paradigm on how paraphilic disorders are now considered from a clinical perspective. One hundred years ago, all sexual disorders were seen as chronic perversions affecting the human mind. Today, paraphilic disorders are viewed as treatable conditions, so treatable in fact that the rate of re-offense is surprisingly low for outpatients entered in specialized treatment programs. The language by which we now refer to these disorders has changed and acknowledges the notion that the disorders, beyond the fact that they may present a risk to society, in many instances cause the affected individual distress or some impairment in function.

Clinical assessment of the paraphilias has also undergone change, from the traditional use of phallometry to more sophisticated and less invasive procedures. The development of new technology has led to research using virtual reality imaging and avatars. Interest has developed in functional brain imaging techniques, neurological correlates of abnormal sexual behaviors and genetics, in an attempt to understand better the etiology of such disorders and help predictions of risk. Actuarial risk assessment tools have changed as well to reflect the many factors known to influence the expression of deviant sexual interests.

Treatment approaches have evolved considerably, from irreversible physical castration to use of reversible pharmacological agents, with their effectiveness proven by scientific methods. The availability of pharmacological treatment has widely contributed to changes of practices within the forensic psychiatric community and more particularly treatments offered in specialized sexual behaviors clinics. Other approaches involving cognitive-behavioral therapy, psychotherapy, therapeutic support groups, and community support have also been shown to be beneficial, from both a clinical perspective and a social perspective, with lower recidivism and improved cost–benefit analysis. On the whole, these many changes have impacted forensic clinical practice in such a positive way as to lead clinicians to find inspiration and reward in treating these individuals (Fedoroff 2011).

There still remain numerous avenues in research that will likely improve our knowledge and competence in managing these conditions. Such avenues involve research into potential novel investigational tools or refinement of existing ones, the approach to diagnosis, focused and standardized effective treatment methods, and better comprehension of the etiology and expression of normal and deviant sexual behavior.

Ultimately, mental health professionals and policy makers need to be sensitized to the importance of reducing stigma and the means to achieve the safe and effective rehabilitation of those individuals struggling with paraphilic disorders. Planning into the future also means effecting further changes in terms of improving access to treatment. Individuals suffering from paraphilic disorder have limited options. Most of the care, as of now, is offered in a limited number of specialized clinics, most of which can only be found in major urban centers. Only a few physicians and therapists receive training to deal with this population and those who are trained will not necessarily orient their professional career in that particular direction. A welcome change would be to enhance access to formal training in the area of assessment and treatment of the paraphilic disorders during medical residency training. In addition to educating mental health professionals, another necessary change is to inform the public and the decision-makers on changes in the perspective of risk and rehabilitation of individuals found to suffer from paraphilic disorders. The ultimate message is that we now have well-supported evidence that the risk these individuals may pose can be mitigated in a much more effective manner with proper management.

REFERENCES

Abel, G.G. 2008. "What Can 44,000 Men and 12,000 Boys with Sexual Behavior Problems Teach Us About Preventing Sexual Abuse?" Paper presented at the annual training conference for the California Coalition on Sexual Offending, San Francisco, California, May 14–16.

Abel, G.G., J. Huffman, B. Warberg, and C.L. Holland. 1998. "Visual Reaction Time and Plethysmography as Measures of Sexual Interest in Child Molesters." *Sexual Abuse: A Journal of Research and Treatment* 10: 81–96.

Abel, G.G., A. Jordan, J.L. Rouleau, R. Emerick, S. Barboza-Whitehead, and C. Osborn. 2004. "Use of Visual Reaction Time to Assess Male Adolescents Who Molest Children." *Sexual Abuse: A Journal of Research and Treatment* 16: 255–65.

Akman, D.D. and A. Normandeau. 1967. "The Measurement of Crime and Delinquency in Canada: A Replication Study." *The British Journal of Criminology* 7: 129–49.

American Psychiatric Association. 1968. *Diagnostic and Statistical Manual of Mental Disorders*. 2nd ed. Washington, DC: American Psychiatric Publishing.

———. 1980. *Diagnostic and Statistical Manual of Mental Disorders*. 3rd ed. Washington, DC: American Psychiatric Publishing.

———. 1994. *Diagnostic and Statistical Manual of Mental Disorders* 4th ed. Washington, DC: American Psychiatric Publishing.

———. 2013. *Diagnostic and Statistical Manual of Mental Disorders* 5th ed. Arlington, VA: American Psychiatric Publishing.

Association for the Treatment of Sexual Abusers. 2001. *Practice Standards and Guidelines for Members of the Association for the Treatment of Sexual Abusers* (pp. 24–5). Beaverton, OR: Association for the Treatment of Sexual Abusers.

Bates, A., D. Williams, C. Wilson, and R.J. Wilson. 2014. "Circles South East: The First 10 Years 2002–2012." *International Journal of Offender Therapy and Comparative Criminology* 58 (7): 861–85.

Berlin, F.S. 2011. "Commentary on Pedophilia Diagnostic Criteria in DSM-5." *The Journal of the American Academy of Psychiatry and the Law* 39: 242–4.

Boer, D.P., S.D. Hart, P. Randall Kropp, and C.D. Webster. 1997. *Manual for the Sexual Violence Risk—20: Professional Guidelines for Assessing Risk of Sexual Violence*. Vancouver, BC: The British Columbia Institute Against Family Violence, co-published with the Mental Health, Law, and Policy Institute at Simon Fraser University.

Bourget, D. and J.M.W. Bradford. 2008. "Evidential Basis for the Assessment and Treatment of Sex Offenders." *Brief Treatment and Crisis Intervention* 8 (1): 130–46.

Bradford, J.M.W. and A. Pawlak. 1993. "Double-blind Placebo Crossover Study of Cyproterone Acetate in the Treatment of the Paraphilias." *Archives of Sexual Behavior* 22: 383–402.

Briken, P. 2002. "Pharmacotherapy of Paraphilia with Luteinizing Hormone-Releasing Hormone Agonists." *Archives of General Psychiatry* 59: 469–70.

Briken, P., D. Bourget, and M. Dufour. 2014. "Sexual Sadism in Sexual Offenders and Sexual Motivated Homicide." In *Psychiatric Clinics of North America*, edited by John M.W. Bradford and A.G. Ahmed, pp. 215–30. New York: Elsevier.

Cooper, A.J. 1981. "A Placebo Controlled Trial of the Antiandrogen Cyproterone Acetate in Deviant Hypersexuality." *Comprehensive Psychiatry* 22: 458–65.

Downing, L. 2015. "Heteronormativity and Repronormativity in Sexological 'Perversion Theory' and the DSM-5's 'Paraphilic Disorder' Diagnoses." *Archives of Sexual Behavior* 44: 1139–45. doi 10.1007/s10508-015-0536-y.

Duwe, G. 2012. *An Outcome Evaluation of Minnesota Circles of Support and Accountability (MnCoSA)*. Minnesota Department of Corrections: St. Paul, MN.

Duwe, G. and M. King. 2012. "Can Faith-Based Correctional Programs Work? An Outcome Evaluation of the InnerChange Freedom Initiative in Minnesota." *International Journal of Offender Therapy and Comparative Criminology* 57 (7): 813–41.

Epperson, D.L., J.D. Kaul, S.J. Huot, D. Hesselton, R. Goldman, and W. Alexander. 1998. *Minnesota Sex Offender Screening Tool-Revised (MnSOST-R)*. St. Paul, MN: Minnesota Department of Corrections.

Fabian, J.M. 2011. "Diagnosing and Litigating Hebephilia in Sexually Violent Predator Civil Commitment Proceedings." *Journal of the American Academy of Psychiatry and the Law* 39: 496–505.

Fedoroff, J.P. 2001. "Paraphilic Worlds." In *Handbook of Clinical Sexuality for Mental Health Professionals*, edited by Stephen B. Levine, Candace B. Risen, and Stanley E. Althof, pp. 401–24. New York: Routledge.

———. 2011. "Forensic and Diagnostic Concerns Arising from the Proposed DSM-5 Criteria for Sexual Paraphilic Disorder." *The Journal of the American Academy of Psychiatry and the Law* 39: 238–41.

Frances, A. and M.B. First. 2011a. "Paraphilia NOS, Nonconsent: Not Ready for the Courtroom." *Journal of the American Academy of Psychiatry and the Law* 39: 555–61.

———. 2011b. "Hebephilia is Not a Mental Disorder in DSM-IV-TR and Should Not Become One in DSM-5." *Journal of the American Academy of Psychiatry and the Law* 39: 78–85.

Gagné, P. 1981. "Treatment of Sex Offenders with Medroxyprogesterone Acetate." *American Journal of Psychiatry* 138: 644–6.

Giami, A. 2015. "Between DSM and ICD: Paraphilias and the Transformation of Sexual Norms." *Archives of Sexual Behavior* 44: 1127–38. doi 10.1007/s10508-015-0549-6.

Hanson, R.K. 1997. *The Development of a Brief Actuarial Scale for Sex Offender Recidivism (User Report No. 1997-04)*. Ottawa, ON: Department of the Solicitor General of Canada. http://www.defenseforsvp.com/Resources/Hanson_Static-99/RRASOR.pdf.

Hanson, R.K. and G. Bourgon. 2008. "A Psychologically Informed Meta-Analysis of Sex Offender Treatment Outcome Studies." In *The Proceedings of the 2007 North American Correctional and Criminal Justice Psychology Conference*, edited by Guy Bourgon, R. Karl Hanson, Joanna D. Pozzula, Kelly E. Morton-Bourgon, and Carry L. Tanasichuk. p. 5. Ottawa: Public Safety Canada.

Hanson, R.K., A. Gordon, A.J.R. Harris, J.K. Marques, W. Murphy, V.L. Quinsey, and M.C. Seto. 2002. "First Report of the Collaborative Outcome Data Project on the Effectiveness of Psychological Treatment for Sex Offenders." *Sexual Abuse: A Journal of Research and Treatment* 14: 169–94.

Hanson, RK., A.J.R. Harris, L. Helmus, and D. Thornton. 2014. "High Risk Sex Offenders May Not Be High Risk Forever." *Journal of Interpersonal Violence* 29 (15): 2792–813. doi:10.1177/0886260514526062.

Hanson, R.K. and K.E. Morton-Bourgon. 2005. "The Characteristics of Persistent Sexual Offenders: A Meta-Analysis of Recidivism Studies" *Journal of Consulting and Clinical Psychology* 73 (6): 1154–63. doi: 10.1037/0022-006X.73.6.1154.

Hanson, R.K. and D. Thornton. 2000. "Improving Risk Assessments for Sex Offenders: A Comparison of Three Actuarial Scales." *Law and Human Behavior* 24: 119–36.

———. 2003. *Notes on the Development of Static-2002*. (Corrections Research User Report No. 2003-01). Ottawa, ON: Department of the Solicitor General of Canada. http://www.publicsafety.gc.ca/cnt/rsrcs/pblctns/nts-dvlpmnt-sttc/index-eng.aspx.

Hare, R.D. 1991. *The Hare Psychopathy Checklist—Revised*. Toronto: Multi-Health Systems.

Harris, G.T., M.E. Rice, M.L. Lalumière, V.L. Quinsey, D. Boer, and C. Lang. 2003. "A Multisite Comparison of Actuarial Risk Instruments for Sex Offenders." *Psychological Assessment* 15 (3): 413–25. doi: 10.1037/1040-3590.15.3.413.

Harris, G.T., M. Rice, V.L. Quinsey, and C.A. Cormier. 2015. *Violent Offenders: Appraising and Managing Risk*. Washington, DC: American Psychological Association.

Hill, A., N.C. Habermann, W. Berner, and P. Briken. 2006. "Sexual Sadism and Sadistic Personality Disorder in Sexual Homicide." *Journal of Personality Disorder* 20: 671–84.

Johnson, R.S., B. Ostermeyer, K.A. Sikes, A.J. Nelson, and J.H. Coverdale. 2014. "Prevalence and Treatment of Frotteurism in the Community: A Systematic Review." *The Journal of the American Academy of Psychiatry and the Law* 42: 478–83.

Kansas v. Crane, 534 U.S. 407 (2002).

Kansas v. Hendricks, 521 U.S. 346 (1997).

Krafft-Ebing, R. von. 1903. *Psychopathia Sexualis with Especial Reference to the Antipathic Sexual Instinct: A Medico-forensic Study*. Only authorized English adaptation of the twelfth German edition, translated by F.J. Rebman. New York: Rebman Company. https://ia801408.us.archive.org/26/items/psychopathiasexu00krafuoft/psychopathiasexu00krafuoft.pdf.

Krueger, R.B. 2010. "The DSM Diagnostic Criteria for Sexual Sadism." *Archives of Sexual Behavior* 39 (2): 325–45. doi: 10.1007/s10508-009-9586-3.

Krueger, R.B. and M.S. Kaplan. 2001. "Depot Leuprolide Acetate for Treatment of Paraphilias: A Report of Twelve Cases." *Archives of Sexual Behavior* 30: 409–22.

Labelle, A., D. Bourget, J. Bradford, M. Alda, and P. Tessier. 2012. "Familial Paraphilia: A Pilot Study with the Construction of Genograms." *International Scholarly Research Network Psychiatry* 2012: 1–9. doi:10.5402/2012/692813.

Langstrom, N., K.M. Babchishin, S. Fazel, P. Lichtenstein, and T. Frisell. 2015. "Sexual Offending Runs in Families: A 37-Year Nationwide Study." *International Journal of Epidemiology* 0: 1–8. doi:10.1093/ije/dyv029.

Lösel, F. and M. Schmucker. 2005. "The Effectiveness of Treatment for Sexual Offenders: A Comprehensive Meta-Analysis." *Journal of Experimental Criminology* 1: 1–29.

Marques, J.K., M. Wiederanders, D.M. Day, C. Nelson, and A. van Ommeren. 2005. "Effects of a Relapse Prevention Program on Sexual Recidivism: Final Results from California's Sex Offender Treatment and Evaluation Project (SOTEP)." *Sexual Abuse: A Journal of Research and Treatment* 17: 79–107.

Marshall, W.L., L.E. Marshall, G.A. Serran, and Y.M. Fernandez. 2006. *Treating Sexual Offenders: An Integrated Approach*. New York: Routledge.

Müller, K., S. Curry, R. Ranger, P. Briken, J. Bradford, and J.P. Fedoroff. 2014. "Changes in Sexual Arousal as Measured by Penile Plethysmography in Men with Pedophilic Sexual Interest." *Journal of Sexual Medicine* 11: 1221–9.

Nielssen, O., J. O'Dea, D. Sullivan, M. Rodriguez, D. Bourget, and M. Large. 2011. "Child Pornography Offenders Detected by Surveillance of the Internet and by Other Methods." *Criminal Behaviour and Mental Health* 21: 215–24. doi: 10.1002/cbm.809.

O'Shaughnessy, R. 2015. "Commentary: Phallometry in Court—Problems Outweigh Benefits." *Journal of the American Academy of Psychiatry and the Law* 43 (2): 154–8.

Polisois-Keating, A. and C.C. Joyal. 2013. "Functional Neuroimaging of Sexual Arousal: A Preliminary Meta-Analysis Comparing Pedophilic to Non-Pedophilic Men." *Archives of Sexual Behavior* 42: 1111–13. doi 10.1007/s10508-013-0198-6.

Purcell, M.L., J.A. Chandler, and J.P. Fedoroff. 2015. "The Use of Phallometric Evidence in Canadian Criminal Law." *Journal of the American Academy of Psychiatry and the Law* 43 (2): 141–53.

Ranger, R. and P. Fedoroff. 2014. "Commentary: Zoophilia and the Law." *Journal of the American Academy of Psychiatry and the Law* 42: 421–6.

Renaud, P., J. Proulx, J.-L. Rouleau, S. Bouchard, G. Madrigrano, J. Bradford, and P. Fedoroff. 2005. "The Recording of Observational Behaviors in Virtual Immersion: A New Research and Clinical Tool to Address the Problem of Sexual Preferences with

Paraphiliacs." *Annual Review of CyberTherapy and Telemedicine: A Decade of VR* 3: 85–92.

Renaud, P., J.-L. Rouleau, L. Granger, I. Barsetti, and S. Bouchard. 2002. "Measuring Sexual Preferences in Virtual Reality: A Pilot Study." *Cyberpsychology and Behavior* 5: 1–10.

Seto, M.C., R.K. Hanson, and K.M. Babchishin. 2011. "Contact Sexual Offending by Men with Online Sexual Offenses." *Sex Abuse* 23: 124–45.

Seto, M., D. Kingston, and D. Bourget. 2014. "Assessment of the Paraphilias." *Psychiatric Clinics of North America* 37: 149–61.

Thibaut, F., F. De La Barra, H. Gordon, P. Cosyn, J. Bradford, and the WFSBP Task Force on Sexual Disorders. 2010. "The World Federation of Societies of biological Psychiatry (WFSBP) Guidelines for the Biological Treatment of Paraphilias." *World Journal of Biological Psychiatry* 11: 604–55.

Wilson, R.J., F. Cortoni, and A.J. McWhinnie. 2009. "Circles of Support and Accountability: A Canadian National Replication of Outcome Findings." *Sexual Abuse: A Journal of Research and Treatment* 21: 412–30.

Zonana, H. 2011. "Sexual Disorders: New and Expanded Proposals for the DSM-5—Do We Need Them?" *The Journal of the American Academy of Psychiatry and the Law* 39: 245–9.

CHAPTER 20

Correctional and Institutional Psychiatric Treatment: History and Litigation

Paul Amble

So act to treat humanity, whether in thine own person or in that of any other, in every case withal, never as a means only.

Critique of Practical Reason (1788), Immanuel Kant,
German philosopher (1724–1808)

Forensic psychiatrists are commonly sought to care for, consult on or provide administrative oversight in the provision of mental health care to inmates and those housed in state hospitals across the United States. In order to appreciate the role institutions currently play in the lives of the mentally ill it is imperative to understand the history of institutional care and how we arrived where we are today. As said by George Santayana, and later paraphrased by Winston Churchill, "Those who do not learn history are doomed to repeat it."

This chapter begins by summarizing the history of mental health care and how civilization has sought solutions to the challenges faced by the populations affected by such severe illness. As you will discover, and as anyone who finds themselves in a position to effect change on these systems must humbly acknowledge, mental health management in institutional care follows the law of Newtonian physics; namely, for every action there is an equal and opposite reaction.

In 1407 the first hospital in the world devoted to provide care to the mentally ill, Hospital de los Inocentes [Hospital of the Innocents], was established in Valencia, Spain. The organization and functioning of this institution so impressed the Catholic Church and regional governments during the fifteenth century that similar institutions spread throughout the Iberian Peninsula and subsequently Europe. This progress was generally sustained until the Concordat of 1851 established Catholicism as the state religion in Spain and, in concession, the church was required to disentail a substantial portion of its properties to the state resulting in hospital closures and a severe regression of services to the mentally ill (López-Ibor 2008).

In the meantime, in the New World, little attention was paid to the societal needs of the mentally ill. In the early eighteenth century a western British colony, later to be known as the United States of America, served, in part, as a repository for convicted criminals from Great Britain who were transported via "prisoner ships" and sold at auction or targeted for the settlement of a region (Christianson 1998). Historian A. Roger Ekirch estimates that as many as one-quarter of all British emigrants to colonial America up to 1776 were convicted criminals (Ekirch 1987). It remains unknown what portion of these individuals suffered from mental illness; but if they were debilitated by mental illness, unable to pull their own weight in their new surroundings, and without family to care for them, they had few choices and often ended up homeless.

Imprisonment as a form of criminal punishment only became widespread in the United States just before the American Revolution, despite a long-standing prison system in Europe. Homelessness among the paupers of colonial American society, which included the severely mentally ill, was a growing concern. Minor street crimes committed by paupers during early colonial times had frequently been addressed through public humiliation and corporal punishments (Friedman 1973). These short-term punishments did little to solve the problems confronted by the loitering of the homeless mentally ill, prompting communities to come up with methods to address this situation.

Into the nineteenth century three options for addressing these societal concerns became prominent in towns and cities where homelessness was prevalent (Wagner 2005). One was the appointment of an Overseer of the Poor, who was a government elected official with a small budget supported by the taxpayers to provide direct assistance for immediate needs such as clothing, shelter, and fuel. Another option was the auctioning off of the pauper to the *lowest* bidder. The lowest bidder was the individual who would ask the government for the least amount of money to house and feed an individual for a certain period of time, often a year, in exchange for which the winning bidder is given the services provided by the pauper. A third option was for an individual or organization in the town to contract with the local government to house a group of paupers, which became the forerunner to the establishment of poor houses, also termed alms (charity) houses, in the early nineteenth century. While in residence at the almshouse, the individual was required to work.

Rather than a place of refuge, almshouses struck fear in the hearts of many as a place of forced work and confinement (Wagner 2005). These almshouses started out on a small scale, often in private homes, but into the 1820s when America became a more industrialized nation and immigration was on the rise the number and size of these institutions grew (Wagner 2015). Those in colonial American society, up through the mid-nineteenth century, with debilitating mental illness who had family to care for them typically remained at the family home unless the illness caused violence that made that placement untenable. In such cases, with or without arrest, individuals were frequently jailed and their conditions of imprisonment depended on whether they had family to pay for their care.

In the late 1700s and into the early 1800s prisons were often little more than cages or closets, with jailers residing in an apartment attached to the jail. There were few standards, no separation of adults and children and there were few official efforts to maintain the inmates' health or see to their basic needs (Hirsch 1992). After the War of 1812, reformers from Boston and New York began to look closely at the fledgling prison facilities in America and therein began a crusade to move children out from jails and into juvenile detention centers. Society further asked the larger question as to whether prison was for punishment or penitence (ushistory.org 2015).

In the early nineteenth century, debate was heated as to whether the imprisonment of the mentally ill was just. This debate was advanced by the Boston Prison Discipline Society, which was founded in 1825 by Reverend Louis Dwight, a Congregationalist minister and Yale graduate. Rev. Dwight began his crusade for the mentally ill while taking bibles to the inmates in prison and noting the deplorable conditions for the mentally ill (Grob 2008).

The Massachusetts legislature in 1827, largely in response to Rev. Dwight's efforts, convened a committee to investigate the lamentable conditions for the mentally ill and found that "Less attention is paid to their cleanliness and comfort than to the wild beasts in their cages which are kept for show" (Grob 1966). Following the disclosure of this report the committee recommended that the mentally ill no longer be confined in prisons and jails and over the ensuing six years the Massachusetts legislature approved and built a free-standing psychiatric hospital in Worcester, the first of its kind in the United States. When the hospital opened in 1833, more than half of the admissions during the first year were transfers from jails, prisons and almshouses (Torrey 2014).

From Abraham Lincoln to Harriet Beecher Stowe the antebellum saw many social reformers on abolitionism, temperance, voting, and the plight of the deaf and blind. Pre-Civil War America was a time of enlightenment as the country wrestled over states' rights, slavery, and expansion to the West. The nation also saw its city populations growing rapidly, which brought new challenges for law enforcement. At the very beginning of the nineteenth century jails were becoming more densely populated and developing a criminal subculture. During the Jacksonian era, 1828–1850, the first major prison reformation movement in America began in an effort to combat problems with the present system and address the ever-expanding U.S. population. These reforms took different paths as two different prison styles emerged, the Auburn system and the Pennsylvania system, both having their roots in the Quaker tradition of reform.

The Pennsylvania system, also known as the "separate system," was a new prison concept adapted from the Quaker philosophy that penance could be paid by prisoners through silent reflection on their crimes and behavior. This system attempted to keep prisoners isolated in individual cells that prevented them from communicating. Prisoners were even kept in solitary confinement during exercise times. The first prison built according to this system was the Eastern State Penitentiary in 1829 in Philadelphia, Pennsylvania.

A second system, the Auburn system, modified this philosophy by sustaining solitary confinement at night behind cell bars, with silence enforced by flogging. Hard labor was assigned during the day under the justification that the jail administration was rehabilitating prisoners by teaching them personal discipline and respect for work. This system originated the black and white striped outfits, prisoners transported in lockstep and silence kept between prisoners during the entire workday.

Determining the percentage of mentally ill imprisoned in the early nineteenth century is difficult for many reasons, due not only to lack of documentation but also because criteria for making a diagnosis was a widely debated and emerging science. According to the American Psychiatric Association, what might be considered the first official attempt to gather information about mental health in the United States was an inquiry in the 1840 census asking whether the person met criteria for "idiocy/insanity" (DSM 2015). It was not until over 100 years later that the first edition of the DSM would be published.

DOROTHEA DIX

Standing prominently in the history of advancing the care for the mentally ill, Dorothea Dix was the offspring of alcoholic parents. Her father is described as a man prone to religious rants who made his living distributing religious tracts, while her mother suffered from debilitating bouts of depression (Tiffany 1890; history.com 2009). Dorothea Lynde Dix was born April 4, 1802 in Hampden, Maine. At age twelve, she left her parents to live with her wealthy grandmother in Boston, then later with an aunt in Worcester, MA. She began teaching at age fourteen and around age nineteen founded the Dix Mansion, a school for girls. Over the next fifteen years Dix ran schools and wrote books, primarily devoted to children, often interrupting her work due to poor health. In 1836 she closed her school and traveled to England to pursue medical treatment for herself. While there she met the Rathbone family, who were Quakers and prominent social reformers who advocated for the plight of the mentally ill in Great Britain.

In 1841, Dix had returned to America and began teaching Sunday school at the East Cambridge Jail, a women's prison, where she discovered appalling conditions for the prisoners, but especially for those with mental illness. Dix began a series of visits to public and private facilities and presented her findings to the legislature of Massachusetts. Her dramatic account began, "I proceed, Gentlemen, briefly to call your attention to the present state of Insane Persons confined within this Commonwealth, in cages, stalls, pens! Chained, naked, beaten with rods, and lashed into obedience" (Dix 1842). Through her efforts and the work of others advocating for the mentally ill, legislatures in many states established funding that led to the establishment or expansion of state hospital systems throughout the United States. Dix was later appointed to organize, outfit, and oversee the vast nursing staff on the Union Army during the Civil War.

From 1843, the year of Dorothea Dix's address to the Commonwealth, to the end of the nineteenth century, state-run mental health facilities were established throughout the country, thereby alleviating the population housed in prisons. In the 1880 census, which was the first census to record women but also contained categories for mental illness including mania (schizophrenia), melancholia (depression), monomania (bipolar), paresis, dementia, dipsomania (alcoholism), and epilepsy. The census found only 397 "insane persons" in prisons and jails out of a total of 59,006 prisoners, an astonishingly low rate of 0.7% (Wines 1888).

The advocacy that moved insane persons from jails and almshouses to institutions designed and organized to treat mental illness was hardly the end of woes experienced by the mentally ill. In 1887 Nellie Bly, a pen name for

American journalist Elizabeth Cochrane Seaman, who was notable for her record-breaking trip around the world in seventy-two days as a media spectacle modeled after the fictional character Phileas Fogg, devised an idea to act as a psychiatric patient and have herself psychiatrically committed for ten days. The conditions she found were deplorable: detestable food, undrinkable water, dangerous patients tied together, human feces in eating places, rats, and abusive conduct of the staff. This resulted in a media expose that ultimately caused a grand jury investigation and an $850,000 increase in the budget of the Department of Public Charities and Corrections.

Over the ensuing decades with precious little effective treatment and admissions far exceeding discharges, the population of mentally ill in institutional settings continued to expand, though largely in the state mental health institutions and not in jails. Methodically throughout the early 1900s a pattern of abuses in mental institutions would come to light, be presented in a public forum, a response would often follow only to be followed by the next revelation. Little seemed to ebb the flow of mentally ill into institutional care and the costs continued to expand.

A growing public unrest with these institutions was prompted by exposés such as the 1967 film, *Titicut Follies*. This film featured inmates and patients at the Bridgewater State Hospital for the criminally insane, a Massachusetts Correctional Institution in Bridgewater. The film was named for the talent show put on by the hospital's inmates, but was a raw portrayal of life in a psychiatric ward. The film won acclaim at a time when the move toward deinstitutionalization was being forwarded.

By the end of the 1960s a number of medicine and other treatment modalities had become available. Electroconvulsive therapy had been introduced to the psychiatric community in 1939 (Endler 1988). In 1948 lithium carbonate was discovered as a treatment for manic depression (Shorter 2009). In 1952 Laborit and colleagues published a study recognizing chlorpromazine as a "new vegetative (autonomic) stabilizer" (Laborit, Huguenard, and Alluaume 1952). Although somatic treatments had been introduced years before, the psychiatric community was occasionally wary of implementing new techniques so it wasn't until the 1960s when the use of somatic treatments was essentially universal across mental health systems. At this same time the rising costs of institutional care for the mentally ill along with the civil rights regarding the justification of long-term confinements came to a head.

DEINSTITUTIONALIZATION

With the pressures described above, state mental institutions saw a remarkable decline in population. From 1955 to 1980 the resident population in state run mental health facilities dropped from 559,000 to 154,000. During this same time period the U.S. population grew from 165 million to 227 million, a 36.9% increase. If the inpatient census had simply matched pace with the population growth, the 1980 state hospital census would have been over 765,000! Aiding in this decline was the courts limiting involuntary institutionalization and setting standards of care at those institutions. The national deinstitutionalization movement was in full force with the launching in 1965 of community mental health center programs that were envisioned to meet the needs of the mentally ill without the expense and the unsavory aspects of inpatient care.

Unfortunately, many patients who were either discharged from long-term hospital care or who would have otherwise been a candidate for those services often did not receive or refused to accept outpatient care, did not obtain stable housing, and ended up homeless or incarcerated. According to E. Fuller Torrey, the founder of the Treatment Advocacy Center, deinstitutionalization "was probably the most well-meaning but poorly planned medical-social policy of twentieth-century America" (Torrey 2002).

What had begun as an attempt to better the plight of those with mental illness, at least in part, caused a flood of admissions to the correctional centers across the country. Witmer, in writing about the experience of the state of California, noted that emptying the hospitals has "forced a large number of these deinstitutionalized patients into the criminal justice system" (Whitmer 1980).

Through the 1970s to the turn of the century, more and more mentally ill were being committed to correctional institutions. A 1998 federal Department of Justice survey noted that 16% of inmates in state and local jails reported either that they suffered from a mental condition or had an overnight stay in a mental hospital (Ditton 1999). Swanson and colleagues in 2013, reporting on the costs of criminal involvement among persons with serious mental illness in Connecticut, found that in a two-year period, 28% of individuals with schizophrenia or bipolar illness who were served by the Department of Mental Health and Addiction Services were also involved in the criminal justice system. The care for those individuals cost twice as much as those with the same disorders in the civil system (Swanson et al. 2013).

ESTABLISHING CARE STANDARDS THROUGH FUNDING

Ernest Amory Codman, MD (1869–1940) was born in Boston and became a surgeon who advocated outcome management in patient care (Berwick 1989). His work helped lead to the founding of the American College of Surgeons, under which was created the Hospital Standardization Program that eventually became the Joint Commission on Accreditation of Healthcare Organizations (JCAHO) that in 2007 changed its name to The Joint Commission (TJC).

In 1965, near the time Medicare and Medicaid were established, the federal government decided that in order for hospitals to receive Medicare funding they had to meet Joint Commission accreditation. This continued until the Medicare Improvements for Patients and Providers Act of 2008 when, effective July 15, 2010, TJC was subject to the Centers for Medicare and Medicaid Services (CMS) requirements for organizations seeking accrediting authority. Thus, if an organization such as a long-term state psychiatric hospital receives funding from Medicare or Medicaid that organization is subject to meeting the standards of CMS, which has the authority to terminate funding.

Funding for corrections health care follows a different path. Local county government funds health care provided in the jail, while prison health care is funded by the state. Medicaid billing for inmates comes into play in such circumstances as when an inmate receives overnight care in a community hospital.

The United States Supreme Court in 1976 released the landmark decision, *Estelle v. Gamble*, ruling that prisoners have a right to be free from "deliberate indifference to their serious health care needs." In 1982 in *Youngberg v. Romeo*, the United States Supreme Court further expanded the responsibility of state institutions to include "Reasonably safe conditions of confinement, freedom from unreasonable bodily restraint, and such minimally adequate training [treatment] as reasonably may be required by these interests." Over the past few decades hundreds of legal cases have been brought against correctional institutions and from these three basic rights have emerged: the right to access to care, the right to care that is ordered, and the right to a professional medical judgment (Rold 2008). Subsequent to this ruling various accreditation agencies were established to help correctional institutions objectively determine whether they were meeting these new standards. Unlike hospitals which are required to have been accredited by TJC in order to be reimbursed by federally based insurance, correctional facilities are not required to obtain this and most have not. Organizations who provide accreditation for treatment programs in corrections include the National Commission on Correctional Health Care (NCCHC), the American Correctional Association (ACA), and occasionally TJC.

RESHAPING MENTAL HEALTH THROUGH THE COURTS

Institutions such as prisons and state psychiatric hospitals are often slow to change. Despite problems being identified within the system, the task of effecting change on recalcitrant administrations and staff is an uphill battle. One avenue that has brought recent change to the mental health system is actions by the court. There are three main sources from which streams of lawsuits, including class-action suits, are being brought against mental health systems:

1. private and not for profit law firms such as the American Civil Liberties Union;
2. the Department of Justice Special Litigation Section;
3. the Office of Protection and Advocacy.

Following are case examples of each.

Example #1: California Prison Overcrowding

Ralph Coleman became a decorated Marine Sergeant while serving in the Vietnam War. A decade later, in 1978, while working as a janitor in Sacramento, he fatally shot his wife, son, and niece. Coleman attempted to use the insanity defense but was found legally responsible for his actions but diagnosed with a mental illness as he began a life sentence in the California penal system (*People v. Coleman* 1985). During his sentence, Coleman was sent to Pelican Bay State Prison, where the mental health staff for 3,500 prisoners consisted of a single person with a master's degree in psychology (Daly 2012).

Coleman sought the assistance of volunteer lawyers in the Prison Law Office in Berkeley, California and began a class-action suit against the State of California in 1990 under the Civil Rights Act of 1871, Eighth and Fourteenth Amendment to the United States Constitution, and the Rehabilitation Act of 1973, alleging unconstitutional mental health care by the California Department of Corrections and Rehabilitation (CDCR) (*Coleman v. Brown* 2011). Based on this suit a Special Magistrate was appointed to oversee mental health care in the California corrections system. Multiple suits followed, and in 2001 Marciano Plata joined Coleman, with the suit of *Plata v. Brown* furthering the complaint to include inadequate provision of general medical care to this series of suits (*Plata v. Brown* 2011). As time went by California maintained that the provision of the requested services would be too costly. In the ensuing litigation it was established that California prisons were overcrowded, some reports indicating 200% of capacity, and that if the state was not prepared to fund better care then a reduction of the prison population was in order (Yi and Egelko 2009). On August 4, 2009 a three-judge panel ordered that the State of California submit a plan within forty-five days detailing "a population reduction plan that will in no more than two years reduce the population of the CDCR's adult institutions to 137.5% of their combined design capacity," which at the time required California to reduce its inmate population by 40,000 (Moore 2009). In 2011 this case went on appeal to the United States Supreme Court in *Brown v. Plata*, with a finding that affirmed the ruling by the three-judge panel (*Brown v. Plata* 2011).

This series of cases illustrates the powerful impact that small not-for-profit legal foundations can have on large governmental mental health providers. In this case California said it could not afford to provide the care the courts demanded, so the courts forced the system to reduce the number of inmates, a highly politically charged solution, rather than continue to provide what they believed to be substandard care. Forensic psychiatrists had many roles to play in this process, from representing the administrations accused of providing substandard care to being involved as independent monitors in assuring the California correctional system abided by the court order.

Example #2: State Hospital in Crisis

A patient found Not Guilty by Reason of Insanity (NGRI) after committing an assault has been an inpatient at the state hospital for several years. He had been given grounds passes (the ability to self-escort on hospital grounds) for over a year even though staff had noticed the patient had been getting more symptomatic over the past two weeks. Within weeks of showing signs of a decompensation this patient escaped by walking off grounds during an unescorted grounds pass. He immediately went to a nearby town and killed a young child. Reacting to public outcry the Governor of the state requires all patients who were found NGRI to no longer have grounds passes, regardless of stability, and further requires all patients who were previously found NGRI and had been receiving treatment in the community (conditionally released from the hospital) to be returned to the hospital and reassessed to make sure they were sufficiently stable to have been released.

- What should be the response of the hospital director to the Governor's order?
- What is the liability of the institution and individuals on the treatment team?
- What treatment arrangements can possibly be made for this patient, who will inevitably be returned to the same hospital?

A forensic psychiatrist will face these questions and many more, including how to address the fears and anxieties of staff and patients in the aftermath of such a tragic situation. Although such a sensational case will play out differently depending on circumstances, there are central themes that will need to be addressed in most cases.

First, it is noteworthy that the response of the government was to swiftly, if not haphazardly, issue a recall of all such patients on conditional release for a review of their status. This review and conservative process for re-release took such a long time that another suit was filed claiming that these patients' rights were being violated. The forensic psychiatrist within the administration of the hospital must begin thinking through such a matter by recalling the history of institutional care and appreciating that a rapid change in the system without proper funding or structuring of the change does not typically lead to a successful outcome. Therefore, moving the system backwards in history by filling up hospital beds with patients who are better served in the community is not the best answer, despite the public outcry. However, at the same time, it is also unwise to immediately work against or defy the Governor's order, especially when arguably there was a fault by the treatment team allowing a patient on a grounds pass who was seen to be deteriorating.

When such a case occurred in Connecticut, and the stalemate between the hospital's desire to return patients' privileges and the government's determination to promote a protective stance toward the public seemed as if it would never end, no solution appeared obvious. Knowing change is slow in institutional care and that patients' rights were compromised daily, the hospital administration considered legal action from an unusual source, the American Civil Liberties Union (ACLU). The ACLU was founded in 1920 following World War I in which the Attorney General at the time, Mitchell Palmer, rounded up and deported "radicals" without warrants or regard to their constitutional rights (ACLU.org). The ACLU and other private, not-for-profit legal groups commonly act in court cases in the context of perceived civil rights violations.

Growing frustrated with pressures from the state to confine the NGRI population, hospital administration officials met with and encouraged the ACLU to bring suit against the department of mental health to restore patient privileges. Though this route took time, ultimately an agreement of settlement was put in place that offered a plan to restore patient privileges but also became an opportunity for the hospital and legal rights advocates to work together to develop an improved system of risk monitoring and overall care (*Roe, et al. v. Hogan, et al.* 2007). Some of the changes are as follows:

- Independent forensic psychiatrists were hired into permanent positions to oversee risk when patients were granted privileges that allowed for community access.
- Any restrictions in patient privileges were reviewed on a weekly basis by an independent forensic psychiatrist.
- A new group of legal advocates, paid for by the state, were hired to be readily available to the patients should they have concerns about their rights being violated.
- Rather than being spread throughout the hospital system, NGRI patients were kept on separate units, which eventually led to care that better addressed their individual needs.

One outcome that did not directly arise from this, but may occur in similar circumstances, is additional state funding for more community- and inpatient-based programs for the safe treatment of patients who are at a higher risk for violence.

Example #3: State Hospital Undergoes a Department of Justice Investigation

Although the DOJ was not officially established until 1870, the origins of the Department began with the signing of the Judicial Act on September 24, 1789. This Act, signed by President George Washington, created the position of Attorney General. According to the Department of Justice (DOJ) website, they receive hundreds of complaints weekly regarding a wide array of civil rights violations within public and private settings who serve minority and disabled populations. It is up to the discretion of DOJ to choose to act on any particular complaint, but if that complaint involves a jail, prison, juvenile detention facility, or health care facility for persons with disabilities, that case is handled by the Special Litigation Section, which is one of several sections within the Civil Rights Division of DOJ.

How Are Complaints Brought to the DOJ?

Anyone willing to identify him or herself can bring a complaint to the attention of DOJ alleging a civil rights violation. The DOJ website offers several avenues to file complaints including by phone, mail, e-mail, or a filing through a link on their website. Complaints can also be lodged by other government agencies, including from CMS in the course of their own separate investigation.

In this example, a state hospital has had a short series of suicide attempts and one completed suicide. A complaint was submitted to the DOJ by a person who remained anonymous to the hospital, but not to the DOJ who does not accept complaints from anonymous sources. After a period of examination, DOJ decided to refer this case to the Special Litigation Section.

Is the DOJ Investigation Restricted to the Complaint Filed?

No. On their website justice.gov: "The Special Litigation Section protects the rights of people in institutions run by state or local governments, and in private facilities receiving public money." An investigation conducted by the DOJ is not simply restricted to the complaint but rather has a sweeping mandate, including to "ensure that people are safe, receive adequate care, and have access to that care in the most integrated setting appropriate to their needs. [DOJ] can also act on behalf of people who are at serious risk of being institutionalized unnecessarily."

Under What Laws Does the DOJ Conduct Their Investigation?

The DOJ primarily uses two different Acts in the course of their investigations. One is the Civil Rights of Institutionalized Persons Act (CRIPA 42 U.S.C. § 1997), which allows the Attorney General to review conditions and practices within the state or local (not federal) institution. CRIPA allows the DOJ to act with criminal charges against an institution if they identify a systemic pattern or practices, not just an individual case, that the DOJ believes violates the civil rights for a class of persons and causes harm.

Another Act which may be used in litigation by the DOJ is the Americans with Disabilities Act (ADA, 42 U.S.C. § 12132). When conducting an investigation under the ADA, the Attorney General is inquiring whether the state is using institutions to house people who would most benefit from and prefer to receive similar services in the community. Using the landmark case of *Olmstead v. L.C.* (1999), which states that people with disabilities have a right to be served in the most integrated setting appropriate to their needs and wishes, the ADA-based investigation may well be determining if the state has done enough to support community-based treatment. This gives teeth to the historical concerns discussed earlier in this chapter where the deinstitutionalization movement did not properly plan or fund for individuals released from hospitals into the community.

What Are the Consequences of an Investigation?

After determining that there has been a CRIPA or ADA violation, the DOJ will typically initially attempt to reach an agreement with the state or local government involved. This will often take the form of a consent decree wherein the offending agency or department will agree to a series of remedies to the

DOJ allegations. If an agreement cannot be reached, the Attorney General may file a lawsuit in federal court. Should the federal court rule against the agency or facility in question, the court may impose a wide array of consequences, including closing the facility, monetary damages, and imposing their own agreement of settlement to correct the infractions.

How Active Is the DOJ Is Pursuing Cases?

Very active. As of August 2015 the DOJ had open cases in more than half the states. The DOJ website lists scores of active consent decrees, including agreements about the entire system serving people with developmental and intellectual disabilities in Virginia, the entire mental health system in Delaware, and all of the state-run mental health hospitals in Georgia.

What Was the Outcome of the Case Example, in Which a Complaint Was Lodged Against a Hospital After a Series of Suicide Attempts?

After years of investigation, a Settlement Agreement (SAMHSA 2011) was reached between the DOJ and state mental health institution in which the hospital agreed to the following:

- integrated treatment planning;
- mental health assessments that are thorough and done shortly after admission;
- enhanced psychiatric and psychological services;
- active discharge planning and community integration—the DOJ mandated the state fund a specific number of additional community beds;
- implementing standards of care to reduce the use of seclusion and restraint;
- enhanced documentation;
- physical plant changes to reduce suicide attempt potential, such as breakaway shower poles and handle-less faucets;
- suicide prevention including guidelines for suicide risk assessments.

An important part of reaching a settlement agreement for the institution being investigated is that they are allowed to deny the allegations and do not admit to liability. However, if the agency or facility is considered by the DOJ to have violated the settlement agreement then they are subject to this agreement going before the federal court (*U.S.A. v. State of Connecticut* 2009).

What Are the Roles for Forensic Psychiatrists in This Case?

- DOJ hires experts to investigate care provided at institutions.
- Hospital administration includes forensic psychiatrists who help to identify and resolve facility and agency shortfalls.
- Forensic psychiatrists are active in the treatment of patients in these facilities and are responsible for delivering an acceptable standard of care.
- The facility or agency being investigated often consults independent forensic psychiatrists to assist them in identifying and addressing concerns before they are discovered by the DOJ.
- Should such a case go to federal court, forensic psychiatrists would be consulted to testify regarding an appropriate standard of care the facility or agency should be employing.
- Ongoing independent monitoring of compliance with the settlement agreement.

Example #4: Action Taken Against a Prison

For years both patients in state hospitals and inmates with mental illness have complained about conditions in the institutions where they were housed. Congressional inquiry found widespread abuse, neglect, and exploitation of mentally ill individuals in institutional care such that in 1986 the federal Protection and Advocacy for Individuals with Mental Illness (PAIMI) Program was founded (SAMHSA 2011). This program established Protection and Advocacy agencies in all states, the District of Columbia, five territories and one to serve several Native American Tribes. Five states have Protection and Advocacy agencies housed within state government while the remaining exist as private, non-profit organizations. In Connecticut this is known as the Office of Protection and Advocacy (OPA) and operates under both state and federal legislative mandates to pursue investigations for legal and administrative remedies on behalf of people with disabilities who experience discrimination based on their disability (Office of Protection and Advocacy for Persons with Disabilities 2015). Because of their state and federal mandates, OPAs often have greater access to institutional records than cases being pursued by private attorneys.

In this example the Connecticut OPA was receiving ongoing complaints that appeared to center on two specific prisons in Connecticut, one that had been designated to house the mentally ill population and the other being the most restrictive prison, the state's only "super-max." What appeared to coalesce in the complaints was that the state prison was not providing sufficient treatment for the mentally ill, but also that minor infractions often resulted in extended periods of solitary confinement, which can have a particularly detrimental effect on the mentally ill (Grassian and Friedman 1986). Although it is possible for legal actions to be brought by multiple complainants, such as by both the DOJ and OPA, typically a matter is brought by only one agency due to the extensive commitment of resources to investigate such a case.

In the present example, attorneys from OPA filed complaints against two Connecticut correctional facilities. In the course of their investigation they hired independent forensic psychiatrists to inspect the facilities. Due to PAIMI legislation allowing open access (42 USC §§ 10801-10827) to records of patients unable to provide consent and ready access to institutions, the OPA attorneys were able to enter both correctional institutions and walk cell to cell inquiring about complaints from the inmates and inviting them to release their correctional records to be included in the suit. Forensic psychiatrists hired by the OPA were given access to all the released mental health records and the ability to interview all staff and inmates who signed releases. The forensic psychiatrists found numerous deficiencies including:

- deficient staffing of certain shifts;
- too few hours of psychiatric coverage to meet the demand of assessments and medication management;
- excessive punishments, such as extended loss of visiting privileges for minor infractions;
- lack of group and individual therapy;
- excessive use of seclusion for the severely mentally ill;
- excessive use of force to restrain out of control inmates; and
- excessive use or restraints (such as a Texas belt) during recreation.

What Are the Options for OPA at the Conclusion of Their Investigation?

OPA can drop their action, pursue their claims in court, or purse a settlement agreement. Similar to the DOJ settlement agreement, in a settlement agreement with OPA there is no admission of fault or liability by the institution under investigation. Further, the institution has their own legal representative, who participates in the structuring of the settlement agreement, creating an opportunity to have a greater say in their future.

What Were the Results from This Example?

OPA pursued a settlement agreement with the Connecticut Department of Corrections. The agreement specifically addressed each finding of the forensic psychiatrists who conducted the investigation. Recommendations in this case were specific, including such detail as the specific maximum amount of visitation that could be lost for an infraction and the specific amount of clinical treatment time to be offered to each inmate.

The settlement agreement also expressed specific staffing patterns that were required for each shift, penalties for not meeting the staffing patterns, and the allowance for ongoing inspections to assure compliance. Further, the agreement specifically outlined training that staff members should receive on such topics as suicide prevention, recognizing signs of mental illness, and alternate forms of discipline and intervention for the seriously mentally ill. The agreement included that it was in effect for a certain timeframe, three years in this case.

The settlement agreement concluded that seriously mentally ill inmates could not be housed at the "super-max" because that facility was not able to meet the needs of this population. In order to assure that no inmates remained at the "super-max" who had a serious mental illness, an independent team of clinicians, including a forensic psychiatrist on each team, from the state's department of mental health was assigned to evaluate each inmate with a history of mental illness to determine if they met the criteria for a serious mental illness, the definition of which was specifically outlined in the agreement of settlement.

Independent forensic psychiatrists remained involved in this case to monitor compliance throughout the settlement agreement. On occasion when experts on both sides were unable to agree on a certain issue, such as whether there was thorough charting of treatment plans, the two sides looked for options. One of which is to take the entire matter to state court, another is for one side to sue the other for breach of contract, and yet another is to attempt a resolution. In this case both the OPA and the Department of Corrections agreed to hire an independent forensic psychiatrist who had not been involved in the case to determine if the treatment plans were appropriate.

CONCLUSION

When problems arise in institutional settings regarding the care of individuals with mental illness, forensic psychiatrists are at the forefront of addressing the matter. First, forensic psychiatrists within the organization must look again at their own process and determine if changes need to be made by the organization. Second, forensic psychiatrists may be asked to consult for attorneys involved on either side of a lawsuit to assess whether there was an act of malpractice or deliberate indifference. Third, when there is a question about an agency's accreditation a forensic psychiatrist will be involved to render an opinion. Fourth, forensic psychiatrists may be retained to provide ongoing independent monitoring of institutions once settlements have been reached. Further, forensic psychiatrists have a role to advocate in the community and in government for quality mental health care in all institutions.

Understanding the present state of mental health care and predicting the future direction of care requires a strong grasp of the history of institutional care. Presently private, state and federal entities monitor and investigate potential incidents of civil rights violations of the disabled, including the mentally ill, and are available and active in pursuing cases of abuse. When investigations or lawsuits are taken against an institution it is understandable that administrations view these actions as troublesome and occasionally unfair. It is important, however, for the forensic psychiatrist who is involved in managing the institution to appreciate that this can be an opportunity that may ultimately lead to positive change to their system.

REFERENCES

"American Civil Liberties Union." Accessed December 1, 2015. https://www.aclu.org/.

Berwick, D.M. 1989. "E.A. Codman and the Rhetoric of Battle: A Commentary." *The Milbank Quarterly* 67 (2): 262.

Brown v. Plata, 563 U.S., 131 S.Ct. 1910, 179 L.Ed.2d 969 (2011).

Christianson, S. 1998. *With Liberty for Some: 500 Years of Imprisonment in America.* Boston: Northeastern University Press.

Coleman v. Brown, docket no. Civ S-90-0520-LKK-JFM (E.D. Cal.) [1] (E.D. Cal.) (2011).

Daly, M. 2012. "California Inmates Get Better Health Care Than Ordinary Citizens." *The Daily Beast*. April 10. http://www.thedailybeast.com/articles/2012/04/10/california-inmates-get-better-health-care-than-regular-citizens.html.

Ditton, P.M. 1999. *Mental Health and Treatment of Inmates and Probationers*. Washington, DC: Bureau of Justice Statistics Special Report, US Department of Justice.

Dix, D.L. 1842. *Memorial to the Legislature of Massachusetts*. University Park Press. 2.

"DSM: The History of the Manual." 2015. Accessed December 1, 2015. http://www.psychiatry.org/psychiatrists/practice/dsm/history.

Ekirch, A.R. 1987. *Bound for America: The Transportation of British Convicts to the Colonies, 1718–75*. Oxford: Clarendon Press.

Endler, N.S. 1988. "The Origins of Electroconvulsive Therapy." *Convulsive Therapy* 4: 5–23.

Friedman, L.M. 1973. *A History of American Law*. New York: Simon and Schuster.

Grassian, S. and N. Friedman. 1986. "Effects of Sensory Deprivation in Psychiatric Seclusion and Solitary Confinement." *International Journal of Law and Psychiatry* 49: 49–65.

Grob, G.N. 1966. *The State and the Mentally Ill*. Chapel Hill: University of North Carolina Press.

———. 2008. *Mental Institutions in America: Social Policy to 1875*. New York: Transactions.

Hirsch, A.J. 1992. *The Rise of the Penitentiary: Prisons and Punishments in Early America*. New Haven: Yale University Press.

History.com. 2009. "Dorothea Lynde Dix." Accessed September 20, 2015. http://www.history.com/topics/womens-history/dorothea-lynde-dix.

Laborit, H., P. Huguenard, and R. Alluaume. 1952. "A New Vegetative Stabilizer." *Presse Med* 60 (10): 206–8.

López-Ibor, J.J. 2008. "The Founding of the First Psychiatric Hospital in the World in Valencia." *Actas Esp Psiquiatr* 36 (1): 1–9.

Moore, S. 2009. "California Prisons Must Cut Inmate Population." *The New York Times*, August 4.

"Office of Protection and Advocacy for Persons with Disabilities." Connecticut's Official State website. Accessed December 1, 2015. http://www.ct.gov/.

Olmstead v. L.C. 527 U.S. 581 (1999).

People v. Coleman, 38 Cal. 3d 69 (1985), 211 Cal. Rptr. 102; 695 P.2d. 189.

Plata v. Brown, docket no. 3:01-cv-01351-TEH (N.D. Cal.), (2011).

Roe, et al v. Hogan, et al. 2007. Connecticut District Court, Case No. 2:89-cv-00570-PCD.

Rold, W.J. 2008. "Thirty Years After Estelle V. Gamble: A Legal Retrospective." *Journal of Correctional Health Care* 14 (1): 11–20.

Shorter, E. 2009. "The History of Lithium Therapy." *Bipolar Disorders* 11(0–2): 4–9. doi:10.1111/j.1399-5618.2009.00706.x.

Substance Abuse Mental Health Services Administration (SAMHSA). 2011. "Evaluation of the Protection and Advocacy for Individuals With Mental Illness (PAIMI) Program, Phase III: Evaluation Report." Accessed December 1, 2015. samhsa.gov.

Swanson, J.W., L.K. Frisman, A.G. Robertson, H.-J. Lin, R.L. Trestman, D.A. Shelton, K. Parr, E. Rodis, A. Buchanan, and M.S. Swartz. 2013. "Costs of Criminal Justice Involvement Among Persons With Serious Mental Illness in Connecticut." *Psychiatric Services* 64: 630–7.

Tiffany, F. 1890. *The Life of Dorothea Lynde Dix*. Boston & New York: Houghton & Mifflin.

Torrey, E.F. 2002. *The Insanity Offense*. New York: W.W. Norton.

———. 2014. *The Treatment of Persons with Mental Illness in Prisons and Jails: A State Survey*. Treatment Advocacy Center.

United States Code (42 U.S.C. § 10801-10827). 2006. "Chapter 114 Protection and Advocacy for individuals with Mental Illness. Subchapter 1 Protection and Advocacy Systems." *2006 Edition Supplement 4, Title 42 The Public Health and Welfare.*

United States Code (42 U.S.C. § 1997). 2006. "Chapter 21 Civil Rights. Subchapter 1a Civil Rights of Institutionalized Persons." *2006 Edition Supplement 4, Title 42 The Public Health and Welfare.*

United States Code (42 U.S.C. § 12132). 1994. "Chapter 126—Equal Opportunity for Individuals with Disabilities Subchapter II Public Services Part A Prohibition Against Discrimination, and Other Generally Applicable Provisions." *1994 US Code Title 42—The Public Health and Welfare.*

"U.S. Department of Justice." Accessed December 1, 2015. http://www.justice.gov/.

U.S.A. v. State of Connecticut, Joint Motion for Entry of Settlement Agreement, United States District Court for the District of Connecticut, January 20, 2009.

USHistory.org. 2015. "Prison and Asylum Reform." Accessed December 1, 2015. http://www.ushistory.org/us/26d.asp.

Wagner, D. 2015. "Poor Relief and the Almshouse." Disability History Museum. Accessed August 25, 2015. http://www.disabilitymuseum.org/dhm/edu/essay.html?id=60.

———. 2005. *The Poorhouse: America's Forgotten Institution*. Lanham, MD: Rowman & Littlefield Publishers.

Whitmer, G.E. 1980. "From Hospitals to Jails: The Fate of California's Deinstitutionalized Mentally Ill." *American Journal of Orthopsychiatry* 50: 65–75.

Wines, F.H. 1888. *Report on the Defective, Dependent, and Delinquent Classes of the Population of the United States*. Washington, DC: Government Printing Office.

Yi, M. and B. Egelko. 2009. "State Fails Federal Demand to Cut Prisoners." *San Francisco Chronicle*, September 19.

CONCLUSION

Summarizing Change in Forensic Psychiatry and Psychology Practice

Ezra E.H. Griffith

INTRODUCTION

It is my hope that this text has fulfilled its promise to bear witness to the decades-long process of progressive change in forensic psychiatry and psychology practice. I thought it would also be instructive to reflect on other indices that could bring into sharper relief this theme of change over time in the two disciplines.

PERSONAL PRAXIS

A review of a recent week of my own forensic activities highlights a picture of my practice in that short space of time. I wanted to take note of the forensic topics that occupied my attention and to see what could be gleaned from such a personalized, qualitative approach. There is of course no claim that my own work stands as a reference point for others. But I believe the review could still provide a useful cross-sectional slice of one academic's activity in forensic work.

I noted that during a recent week's time, I had participated in a discussion about involuntary outpatient commitment. This subject concerns seriously ill psychiatric patients, who on repeated occasions have refused to follow treatment recommendations from their care-givers. As a result, their clinical condition deteriorates, and they may end up needing to be coerced into care. The mechanism used to coerce this group of patients is a judge's order that mandates the patient into care on an outpatient basis. This subject of involuntary outpatient commitment continues to provoke heated discussion by forensic specialists for a number of reasons. On the one hand, some scholars see involuntary outpatient commitment as a legitimate tool for keeping the community safe from severely ill psychiatric patients who are in need of treatment. It is also claimed by some that the involuntary treatment protects the health of these patients. Others argue that the involuntary treatment in such a context is unnecessary and demeans the dignity of the patient. Still others point out that there are methods for engaging the patients and having them accept treatment voluntarily, such as with the use of peers (Rowe 2013).

A particularly interesting aspect of this debate is that many individuals from a variety of disciplines are participating in the discussion about involuntary outpatient commitment. They include forensic specialists who are conducting research on the topic, advising legislators, and articulating parameters of the debate that include ethics and theorizing about patients' rights. There are even dimensions of this argument that touch on human rights principles (see, for example, Morrissey, Domino, and Desmarais 2013; Dlugacz 2008–9; Szmukler 2016).

In another setting, the discussion turned to physician-assisted suicide. A number of forensic specialists, in addition to other non-forensic professionals, have been concerned about the possibility that this topic may gain more ground in the United States. The result may well be that patients will progressively increase their demand for physicians' help in terminating their lives. In this debate, attention is focused on the possibility that assisted dying might be extended from the terminally ill to individuals who are experiencing non-diagnosable mental suffering or even diagnosable psychological suffering. While it is true that some parts of Europe have made more concrete strides in this particular debate than has the U.S., some American psychiatrists seem to be apprehensive that the talk has now turned to assisting the death of psychiatric patients. Some participants in the debate are of course looking to the forensic specialist for guidance, presumably because of the latter's familiarity with ethics and the legal dimensions of the discussion. Everyone is acutely aware of the fact that the debate will eventually be of interest to policy makers and legislators (see, for example, Prokopetz and Lehmann 2012; Raus and Sterckx 2015).

Another discussion that occupied my time centered on the subject of solitary confinement in prisons. Some forensic colleagues are arguing that medical and other health care organizations should take a stronger stand against the practice of isolating prisoners for twenty-three hours a day (for a thorough discussion, see Appelbaum 2015). Forensic colleagues make the point that forensic psychiatrists and psychologists have a special relevant expertise because of their involvement with the care of these inmates. They see first-hand the psychological impact of such isolation. Thus, their professional disciplines should be concerned about the potential impact of such prolonged isolation on the mental health of prisoners. Such advocacy on behalf of prisoners is likely to be a direct result of the fact that mental health care practice carried out in correctional settings is now an established responsibility of forensic mental health professionals. Indeed, this form of practice, defined as correctional psychiatry, has recently merited its own academic consideration through a significant textbook edited by Trestman, Appelbaum, and Metzner (2015).

A treatment-oriented discussion focused on the problems of treating anger and aggression in patients residing in a forensic psychiatric hospital. Such discussions are of course frequent in the daily professional lives of forensic psychiatrists and psychologists. It is so because the troublesome forensic patient is commonly found in such specialized facilities these days (see the discussion in Chapters 13 and 15). The discussions bear testimony to the evolution of the care provided to these special patients. For one thing, in the past these patients may have been more readily found in the classic state hospital across the country. But they have been found over time to present special problems, already described in Chapters 13 and 15. These patients with complex legal problems have increasingly required forensic experience and technical knowledge. This is seen in the management of the sex offender (see Chapter 19), and those with intractable behavioral problems (see Chapter 15). The particular difficulty in treating aggressive and violent behavior has forced consideration of employing specialized pharmacotherapy (Felthous et al. 2013) and other behavioral treatments (Glancy and Saini 2005).

During the particular week I have been discussing so far, I taught a class on "oral performance." The objective of that class is to help forensic psychiatry and psychology trainees understand some of the finer points of making an oral presentation in a way that is persuasive to the audience. I draw from accumulated literature in the law, anthropology, sociology, communication arts, and literature. I illustrate how the construction and presentation of an oral argument requires practice and reconceptualization of relevant principles that have not been consistently embraced by our relatively new forensic disciplines. Some of this theorizing has already been treated in Chapter 7 of this text and explicated previously by Griffith and Baranoski (2011).

Langellier (1999) makes a natural and seemingly easy connection of performance to narrative while dividing narrative into a structural type and a more performance-based, pragmatic form. In this context, such developments lead to a clearer understanding of how the forensic expert can beneficially prepare for his work in court trials. The task facing forensic experts is to understand techniques that are available to them as they seek to frame the narrative that they wish to convey persuasively to the jury and judge. The point, of course, is not to exaggerate or distort parts of the story in order to persuade the audience. It is to appreciate how to utilize performative techniques effectively. Such effectiveness would include: use of the expert's own voice and body to deliver the narrative; appreciation of how to avoid unwittingly putting one's self into the narrative; and recognizing other potential roadblocks to an impressive presentation.

It is especially noteworthy that at the October 2015 Annual Meeting of the American Academy of Psychiatry and the Law, the Academy's president presented a lecture that highlighted the importance of the mock trial. This increasingly popular technique is a means of preparing forensic trainees for their activities in the courtroom. The president outlined the salience of practical experience in this sort of preparation; the need for the training to be melded to technically supportive and corrective feedback; and a recognition that improvement requires assiduous attention to the specialized form of work. It is now commonly appreciated that such training is essential in forming the future expert witness for this task. Ultimately, the most constructive and helpful preparation for oral performance in court will rest on a solid theoretical base and repeated practice sessions. Forensic psychiatry and psychology have advanced their fields by welcoming the contributions of scholars from other disciplines who are thinking about practical performance.

In this section that I have entitled "Personal Praxis," I have employed several examples from a single week of my own forensic activity. The examples represent forensic work in a present-day context. It is not just that these activities may have been unknown to the forensic practitioner in bygone years. I believe it is also possible to see in these examples the influence of factors that are tinged with modernity. The subject of involuntary outpatient commitment is an interesting example. Certainly, commitment of the psychiatric patient has been a subject preoccupying communities for years. But this form of involuntary care is being talked about by some as a solution to many problems, and on an outpatient basis; and there are constituencies lined up on all sides of the debate. Laws will ultimately define the contours of the debate, and the forensic specialist grounded in ethics and political argument will have more contributions to make to this heated discussion. Similarly, the conversation about the potential effects of solitary confinement in prisons highlights the role of the forensic specialist in the treatment and care of patients to a degree that was not present years ago. But it also demonstrates the renewed awareness of the forensic specialist in the civic task of effecting change through political action, activities that are highlighted in Chapters 5 and 11.

In considering the development of our forensic subspecialties, I reflected on my most unique activities in forensic psychiatry over several decades of practice. The first consultation worth mentioning occurred in the early 1980s. I was part of a team of mental health experts engaged to advise the Grenada government about the restructuring of their mental health services. The consultation was described fully by Fisher, Griffith, and Mahy (1988). It was requested because the principal psychiatric hospital had been destroyed by American military forces during their invasion of this Caribbean island. The consultation was unique as a result of the financial, sociopolitical, and diplomatic factors that complicated the work. But a central question that arose in the consultation was where to house the psychiatric patients who were seriously ill and presented major behavioral management problems. Some of these patients were facing significant legal charges. But even those without charges presented serious dilemmas. The community culture did not favor treatment of these problematic patients in their home communities. Space limitations do not permit further exposition of these difficulties. However, the case example highlights the use of forensic expertise in conditions complicated seriously by culturally defined systemic barriers and by a shortage of human and economic resources.

Another consultation deserving mention is my involvement in the investigation of the Miroslav Medvid Incident (1987). Several colleagues and I participated in a report to the Commission on Security and Cooperation in Europe, which was made up of several individuals from the United States Congress. Miroslav Medvid was a Russian sailor who attempted to jump ship in New Orleans, and questions were raised about his psychiatric status. Of course, his psychiatric condition was only one of myriad factors considered in the report that complicated the review of the complex interplay of legal and administrative elements that led to his being returned to his home nation.

Perhaps some of the most special work I have engaged in was centered on the interaction of culture, race/ethnicity, and the forensic psychiatry and psychology specialties. I first addressed the intersection of these matters in a co-authored piece (Griffith and Griffith 1986) that contemplated the interaction of racism, psychological injuries, and a potential claim for compensable damages. I was of course struck by the dearth of literature on this forensic topic, even though by the late 1980s, race was an important topic in other disciplines. Needless to say, it was a pleasure over two decades later to see the work by Carter and Forsyth (2009) addressing the forensic assessment of race-based traumatic stress reactions. An earlier piece by Butts (2002) had lamented the fact that some forensic specialists and non-forensic colleagues had excluded trauma generated by racial discrimination as meriting classification as post-traumatic stress disorder. In my view, it remains an area in the forensic arena that cries out for further scholarly attention. This inattention by forensic specialists was a major reason I addressed the major lack of attention to cultural factors that glaringly appeared in the debate about ethics in forensic psychiatry (Griffith 1998). A central part of my thesis then was that there can be no serious conversation about ethics principles in forensic practice if we ignore the concerns of minority members in the society.

FORENSIC PROFESSIONAL GROUPS

An important indicator of development and change in any academic or medical specialty can be discerned through examination of the activities pursued by professional groups associated with the particular specialty area. It is these groups that often act as their own change-agents within the professions and produce transformative results.

Forensic Psychology

The central organization in the United States that represents the discipline of psychology is called the American Psychological Association (APA). Within it, there are several sub-groups responsible for specialty areas within psychology. One of these subspecialty sub-groups is the American Psychology-Law Society Division 41 of the APA. This sub-group is interdisciplinary, while being both free-standing and a part of the umbrella APA organization. The AP-Law Society promotes scholarship, practice, and public service in psychology and the law (information available at www.ap-ls.org). It is also responsible for publication of two well-known forensic psychology journals, *Law and Human Behavior*, and the more specialized publication, *Psychology, Public Policy, and Law.*

The main journal, *Law and Human Behavior*, was first published in 1973 and had four issues that provided twenty-one articles (www.ap-ls.org). Examples of these original pieces were: "Consent of the Unfree: Medical Experimentation and Behavior Modification in the Closed Institution"; "Legal Approaches to Juror Stereotyping by Physical Characteristics"; "Imprisonment v. the Death Penalty as a Deterrent to Murder"; "The Parole Hearing: Decision or Justification? "; and "Strategies for an Empirical Analysis of the Prediction of Violence in Emergency Civil Commitment."

TABLE 21.1 Sample of Titles from *Law and Human Behavior*, Volume 39, Issues 1–5, 2015

Issue 1
Double-blind photo lineups using actual eyewitnesses: An experimental test of a sequential versus simultaneous lineup procedure.
Reporting guidance for violence risk assessment predictive validity studies: the RAGEE Statement.
Issue 2
Eyewitness identification: Bayesian information gain, base-rate effect equivalency curves and reasonable suspicion.
DSM-5 antisocial personality disorder: Predictive validity in a prison sample
Issue 3
Static-99R reporting practices in sexually violent predator cases: Does norm selection reflect adversarial allegiance?
Taking the blame for someone else's wrongdoing: The effects of age and reciprocity.
Issue 4
Rater differences in psychopathy measure scoring and predictive validity.
Lay understanding of forensic statistics: Evaluation of random match probabilities, likelihood ratios, and verbal equivalents.
Issue 5
Does evidence really matter? An exploratory analysis of the role of evidence in plea bargaining in felony drug cases.
Interviewing to elicit information: Using priming to promote disclosure.

From the outset, *Law and Human Behavior* seemed bent on identifying itself as a place for publishing empirical scholarship in this progressively emerging specialty discipline. Some would say this suited many psychology scholars well, and over the years it has become fully recognized that forensic psychologists have extended the reaches of the discipline through this brand of scholarly activity. By the first five issues of 2015 (a sixth issue is expected later), *Law and Human Behavior* has already published forty-six articles. Table 21.1 displays examples of the articles published in 2015, and confirms the continued emphasis on empirical work in the discipline.

The American Board of Professional Psychology (ABPP) (information available at www.abpp.org) was incorporated in 1947 and has long been charged with the task of certifying candidates seeking specialty qualifications in psychology through an examination process. The ABPP is in fact made up of a number of different specialty boards. One of these is the American Board of Forensic Psychology (ABFP) which was established in 1978 with the task of establishing standards and qualifications for those wishing to practice forensic psychology (information available at www.abfp.com).

There are general requirements demanded of all candidates for ABPP examinations, such as having obtained a doctoral degree from an APA-approved graduate program and being licensed by the appropriate state licensure board. Individuals seeking specialty certification in forensic psychology must then complete additional requirements specific to the forensic specialization. Examinations of both the ABPP and ABFP are written and oral. ABFP diplomates become members of the American Academy of Forensic Psychology, which is dedicated to promoting continuing education and early career development in forensic psychology. The Bylaws of the ABFP state the following in the Mission Statement: The purpose of the ABFP is to protect the consumer of forensic psychology services through two mechanisms: "Establishing, promoting, and revising, as necessary, standards and qualifications for those who practice forensic psychology; and certifying as ABFP specialists those voluntary applicants who qualify under the standards established by the Board" (see www.abfp.com).

The year 1978 establishes the point at which the ABFP was created and underlines the essential youth of the subspecialty. But its foresight in creating an arm (the American Academy of Forensic Psychology) charged with continuing education and early career development of its diplomates makes plain that the group intended to pursue the double mission of education and certification which undergirds the professionalism of the group and likely has enhanced the economic status and general prestige of the diplomates. In addition, it is probable that these efforts have been magnified by other activities of the APA's Division 41. No doubt, all of this has been further reinforced by the expansion of degree-granting university programs in forensic psychology.

Forensic Psychiatry

In 1969, the American Academy of Psychiatry and the Law (AAPL) was born, the brainchild of a number of colleagues who were doing the work in the penumbra of psychological medicine. They were unsung heroes, although it must be said that some of their antecedents in years gone by had earned a reputation for themselves. Men like Walter Channing and Isaac Ray were known for their testimony in court or their publications and presentations years earlier. Certainly Jonas Rappeport, Robert Sadoff, and Seymour Pollack, the first three presidents of AAPL, had reputations in forensic psychiatry before 1969. They obviously decided that the time was ripe for the establishment of the organization, and that giving structure to this budding discipline would be ultimately beneficial.

The new organization was dedicated to excellence in practice, teaching, and research in forensic psychiatry. We know that by 2001 the membership roll of the organization had doubled in size. It has remained close to 2000 for the last fifteen years (available from AAPL). Between 1969 and 1979, AAPL had elected five presidents who served two-year terms. From 1979 through the present term of 2015–2016, thirty-seven presidents will have served one-year terms. The group's governance is directed by seven officers and nine councilors. In addition, there are numerous committees, appointed by the president of the organization, who participate in leadership activities and provide advice in arenas such as: ethics, bylaws, peer review, geriatric psychiatry, private practice, research, addiction psychiatry, cross-cultural psychiatry, forensic neuropsychiatry, and sexual offenders. This list is not exhaustive, but certainly demonstrates how far the impact of forensic psychiatry has penetrated into general psychiatry practice (www.aapl.org).

AAPL currently lists on its website (available at www.aapl.org) forty-four training programs that have been accredited by the Accreditation Council on Graduate Medical Education. Graduates of these certified programs may apply to the American Board of Psychiatry and Neurology to take the examination that leads to Added Qualifications in Forensic Psychiatry. Recertification is required at ten-year intervals. Certification in general psychiatry is required for eligibility to sit for the subspecialty examination.

Each Annual Meeting offers an extensive program of continuing medical education. Table 21.2 provides a summary of topic areas presented at the 2015 Annual Meeting (AAPL 2015b). This information suggests a flourishing subspecialty organization participating vigorously in supporting the continuing medical education of its members. Furthermore, for the last several years, the Academy offers an intensive three-day course that covers an in-depth review of selected topics in forensic psychiatry and provides a summary of legal cases that are generally considered to be among the most influential in American forensic psychiatry.

In 2004, AAPL established the AAPL Institute for Education and Research with the mission of stimulating important and creative educational and research programs in forensic psychiatry. Between 2006 and the present, the Institute has funded fourteen grants to support investigators' scholarly work in the field (see www.aapl.org).

Over the last decade or so, AAPL has also undertaken to publish several Guidelines that provide standards for different areas of forensic psychiatry practice. Among them is the "AAPL Ethics Guidelines for the Practice of Forensic Psychiatry" (adopted May 2005) (see www.aapl.org), which sets out a framework to guide the forensic practitioner interested in maintaining an

TABLE 21.2 Summary of Topic Areas Presented: 2015 Annual Meeting Program, American Academy of Psychiatry and the Law

• Addiction Forensic Psychiatry	• Child and Adolescent Forensic Psychiatry
• Competency	• Correctional Psychiatry
• Cults	• Death Penalty
• Disability Claims	• Emergency Forensic Psychiatry
• Ethics	• Expert Testimony
• Forensic Evaluations	• Forensic Neuropsychiatry
• Gender Issues	• Forensic Publishing
• Human Rights	• Geriatric Forensic Psychiatry
• International and Military Courts	• Insanity Defense
• Malpractice	• Jail Diversion
• Oral Performance	• Mental Illness and Violence
• Private Practice	• Post-Traumatic Stress Disorder
• Psychological Testing	• Professional Organizations
• Psychopharmacology	• Psychopathy and Personality Disorders
• Topics in Forensic Legislation	• Sexual Offending
• Transgender Issues	• Training and Education Approaches

ethics-based practice of the subspecialty. Other Guidelines address the topics of competence to stand trial (Mossman et al. 2007), psychiatric disability (Gold et al. 2008), forensic psychiatric evaluation of defendants raising the insanity defense (AAPL 2014), and forensic assessment (AAPL 2015a).

The *Bulletin of the American Academy of Psychiatry and the Law* published its first volume of four numbers in 1973. The total number of regular articles was sixteen. Examples of the titles were: "Legal Problems Involved in Implementing the Right to Treatment"; "Teaching Materials in Forensic Psychiatry"; "Judicial Remedies and Institutional Standards"; "A View of Traumatic Neurosis"; and "The Psychiatrist and the Subpoena" (Available at www.jaapl.org/content/1/1.toc.).

In 1997, the *Bulletin* changed its name to the *Journal of the American Academy of Psychiatry and the Law.* It continued to publish four editions a year. In 2015, it will have published by the end of that year thirty-eight peer-reviewed articles (some of which were accompanied by commentaries), in addition to robust sections of Editorials, Legal Digest, and Books and Media. The following are examples of titles that appeared in the section of peer-reviewed articles: "John H. Wigmore on the Abolition of Partisan Experts"; "Approaches to Involuntary Admission of the Mentally Ill in the People's Republic of China"; "The Use of Phallometric Evidence in Canadian Criminal Law"; "Physician-Assisted Suicide: Considering the Evidence,

Existential Distress, and an Emerging Role for Psychiatry"; "Mental Health and Immigrant Detainees in the United States: Competency and Self-Representation"; and "Application and Utility of Psychodynamic Principles in Forensic Psychiatry Assessment" (available at www.jaapl.org/content/43/1.toc). Certainly the increase in numbers of the peer-reviewed articles, variability in their titles, and the mix of empirical and qualitative scholarship suggest a solidification of forensic psychiatry's identity as a discipline. This is further confirmed by the robust expansion of the different departments in the *Journal*, such as the Legal Digest section and the common use of editorials and commentaries. The *Journal* is also known to publish fairly regularly the work of scholars from outside the United States.

CONCLUSION

In this text, the editors and authors set out to bear witness to the changes that have attended forensic psychiatry and psychology during the last four decades or so. They structured this examination of the potential changes in a functional way, thinking about the origin of the factors likely to influence change. They utilized chapters within each arena to illustrate the mechanisms through which change actually occurred. First came the External Factors that produced change, and the illustrative examples used, such as: The Law; Consumer Movements such as Peer Support; Global Developments such as those giving rise to the increase in refugees and forced migration; and Politics. These elements have produced a greater need for forensic expertise connected to the mental health disciplines. Indeed, my personal experiences in the Grenada consultation and the Miroslav Medvid incident demonstrate how these external events, seemingly unrelated at first blush to the traditional arenas of psychiatry and psychology, suddenly demand contributions from these disciplines and lean on their connection to the law. Recent developments, for example in the War on Terror, have magnified an interest in questions such as why individuals are motivated to participate in these acts.

The second section of the framework is based on seeing forensic psychiatry and psychology as their own change-agents. In Chapters 6, 7, and 8, examples were provided of mechanisms employed in this way. I have added in this Conclusion another way of contemplating change developed by activities internal to the two professions. They were based on notions of continued professional development fostered by education and training, political activity, and a sharply honed understanding of what special strengths each profession might lean on. For example, given the forensic psychologists' focus on developing tests such as those that address matters of risk and violence, they have been particularly committed to this area of work and have clearly redefined the practice in this area. Similarly, their interest in empirical work has led them to the study of factors influencing jurors and other participants in the trial ritual. Psychiatrists have pursued medicalized areas of work in understanding the forensic dimensions of fronto-temporal dementia. We note the collaborative work between forensic psychiatrists and psychologists on subjects such as sexual offending, and contributions toward meeting the needs of ecclesiastical courts.

Changes in the traditional evaluative and consultative roles of forensic professionals (as seen in Section 3) have been produced by both professional groups. These forms of practice are likely to be limited in the future only by the availability of fiscal remuneration for the individuals carrying out the work. The same may be said about the forensic practice focused on the treatment and care of patients, as illustrated by the chapters in Section 4. It is evident that a number of different factors impact such practice. First, many communities are sensitive to the distinction between being housed in a correctional facility and in a hospital. Consequently, efforts are being constantly made to place the mentally ill in hospitals even if they are displaying disruptive and violent behaviors. In addition, many researchers are continuing to seek treatment solutions for those exhibiting personality disorders marked by a history of violence. Looking back, both forensic disciplines have made substantial strides and have established solid foundations. Thus the future is bright for both groups of professionals.

I suggest that there is still room for greater collaboration, especially in the educational preparation of their trainees. There should also be a greater openness of both groups to accessing the knowledge base provided by scholars in other disciplines such as anthropology, sociology, political science, and communication arts. Needless to say, there are still areas that beg for exploration and study. The influence of race and ethnicity on the praxis of forensic evaluation demands attention. The impact of language difference between evaluator and evaluee on the integrity of the evaluation is another void in the forensic knowledge base. And the debates about forensic ethics, as treated in Chapter 6, are far from completed. More forensic professionals must be trained to work with the hearing impaired. And further exploration is needed in teaching forensic trainees about fostering the dignity of their evaluees and carrying out the evaluations with compassion. So there is work to do, despite the fact that much ground has already been covered.

REFERENCES

American Academy of Psychiatry and the Law. 2014. "Practice Guideline: Forensic Psychiatric Evaluation of Defendants Raising the Insanity Defense." *Journal of the American Academy of Psychiatry and the Law* 42 (4 Supplement): S3–S76.

American Academy of Psychiatry and the Law. 2015a. "Practice Guideline: The Forensic Assessment." *Journal of the American Academy of Psychiatry and the Law* 43 (2 Supplement): S3–S53.

American Academy of Psychiatry and the Law. 2015b. "2015 Annual Meeting Program." Distributed at the 46th Annual Meeting, Ft. Lauderdale, FL.

Appelbaum, K. L. 2015. "American Psychiatry Should Join the Call to Abolish Solitary Confinement." *Journal of the American Academy of Psychiatry and the Law* 43: 406–15.

Butts, H.F. 2002. "The Black Mask of Humanity: Racial/Ethnic Discrimination and Post-Traumatic Stress Disorder." *Journal of the American Academy of Psychiatry and the Law* 27: 633–5.

Carter, R.T. and J. Forsyth. 2009. "A Guide to the Assessment of Race-Based Traumatic Stress Reactions." *Journal of the American Academy of Psychiatry and the Law* 37: 29–40.

Dlugacz, H.A. 2008–9. "Involuntary Outpatient Commitment: Some Thoughts on Promoting a Meaningful Dialogue between Mental Health Advocates and Lawmakers." *New York Law School Law Review* 53: 79–96.

Felthous, A.R., S.L. Lake, B.K. Rundle, and M.S. Stanford. 2013. "Pharmacotherapy of Impulsive Aggression: A Quality Comparison of Controlled Studies." *International Journal of Law and Psychiatry* 36: 258–63.

Fisher F.D., E.E.H. Griffith, and G.E. Mahy. 1988. "Recent Developments in the Grenada Mental Health Program." *Hospital and Community Psychiatry* 39: 980–5.

Glancy, G. and M. Saini. 2005. "An Evidence-Based Review of Psychological Treatments of Anger and Aggression." *Brief Treatment and Crisis Intervention* 5: 229–48.

Gold, L.H., S.A. Anfang, A.M. Drukteinis, J.L. Metzner, M. Price, B.W. Wall, L. Wylonis, and H.V. Zonana. 2008. "AAPL Practice Guideline for the Forensic Evaluation of Psychiatric Disability." *Journal of the American Academy of Psychiatry and the Law* 36 (4 Supplement): S3–S54.

Griffith, E.E.H. 1998. "Ethics in Forensic Psychiatry: A Cultural Response to Stone and Appelbaum." *Journal of the American Academy of Psychiatry and the Law* 26: 171–84.

Griffith, E.E.H. and M. Baranoski. 2011. "Oral Performance, Identity, and Representation in Forensic Psychiatry." *Journal of the American Academy of Psychiatry and the Law* 38: 32–42.

Griffith, E.E.H. and E.J. Griffith. 1986. "Racism, Psychological Injury and Compensable Damages." *Hospital and Community Psychiatry* 37: 71–5.

Langellier, K.M. 1999. "Personal Narrative, Performance, Performativity: Two or Three Things I Know for Sure." *Text and Performance Quarterly* 19: 125–44.

The Miroslav Medvid Incident. 1987. *Report Findings, Conclusions and Recommendations Submitted to the Commission on Security and Cooperation in Europe*. Washington, DC: U.S. Government Printing Office.

Morrissey, J.P., M.P. Domino, and S.L. Desmarais. 2013. "Involuntary Outpatient

Commitment; Current Evidence and Options." A Report Prepared for the Continuity of Care Panel. Maryland Department of Health and Mental Hygiene, Maryland, October 30.

Mossman, D., S.G. Noffsinger, P. Ash, R.L. Frierson, J. Gerbasi, M. Hackett, C.F. Lewis, D.A. Pinals, C.L. Scott, K.G. Sieg, B.W. Wall, and H.V. Zonana. 2007. "AAPL Practice Guideline for the Forensic Evaluation of Competence to Stand Trial." *Journal of the American Academy of Psychiatry and the Law* 35 (4 Supplement): S3–S72.

Prokopetz, J.J. and L.S. Lehmann. 2012. "Redefining Physicians' Role in Assisted Dying." *New England Journal of Medicine* 367: 97–9.

Raus, K. and S. Sterckx. 2015. "Euthanasia for Mental Suffering." In *New Directions in the Ethics of Assisted Suicide and Euthanasia*, edited by M. Cholbi and J. Varelius, pp. 79–96. Switzerland: Springer International Publishing.

Rowe, M. 2013. "Alternatives to Outpatient Commitment." *Journal of the American Academy of Psychiatry and the Law* 41: 332–6.

Szmukler, G. 2016. "Coercion in Psychiatric Treatment and its Justifications." In *Philosophy and Psychiatry: Problems, Intersections, and New Perspectives*, edited by D. Moseley and G. Gala, pp. 125–60. New York: Routledge.

Trestman, R., K. Appelbaum, and J. Metzner (eds). 2015. *Oxford Textbook of Correctional Psychiatry.* New York: Oxford University Press.

Index

Entries in **bold** denote tables; entries in *italics* denote figures.

For Product Safety Concerns and Information please contact our EU representative GPSR@taylorandfrancis.com
Taylor & Francis Verlag GmbH, Kaufingerstraße 24, 80331 München, Germany

www.ingramcontent.com/pod-product-compliance
Lightning Source LLC
LaVergne TN
LVHW011105300926
849160LV00008B/291

9781498754231